Just and Unjust Military I

MW00358398

Classical arguments about the legitimate use of force have profoundly shaped the norms and institutions of contemporary international society. But what specific lessons can we learn from the classical European philosophers and jurists when thinking about humanitarian intervention, preventive self-defense, or international trusteeship today? The contributors to this volume take seriously the admonition of contextualist scholars not to uproot classical thinkers' arguments from their social, political and intellectual environment. Nevertheless, this collection demonstrates that contemporary students, scholars, and policymakers can still learn a great deal from the questions raised by classical European thinkers, the problems they highlighted, and even the problematic character of some of the solutions they offered. The aim of this volume is to open up current assumptions about military intervention to critical reflection and to explore the possibility of reconceptualizing and reappraising contemporary approaches.

STEFANO RECCHIA is University Lecturer (assistant professor) in International Relations at the University of Cambridge.

JENNIFER M. WELSH is Professor of International Relations at the European University Institute, Florence, Italy, and Co-director of the Oxford Institute for Ethics, Law and Armed Conflict.

Just and Unjust Military Intervention

European Thinkers from Vitoria to Mill

Edited by

Stefano Recchia and Jennifer M. Welsh

CAMBRIDGE
UNIVERSITY PRESS

CAMBRIDGE
UNIVERSITY PRESS

University Printing House, Cambridge CB2 8BS, United Kingdom

Cambridge University Press is part of the University of Cambridge.

It furthers the University's mission by disseminating knowledge in the pursuit of education, learning and research at the highest international levels of excellence.

www.cambridge.org
Information on this title: www.cambridge.org/9781107665491

© Cambridge University Press 2013

This publication is in copyright. Subject to statutory exception and to the provisions of relevant collective licensing agreements, no reproduction of any part may take place without the written permission of Cambridge University Press.

First published 2013
First paperback edition 2015

A catalogue record for this publication is available from the British Library

Library of Congress Cataloguing in Publication data
Just and unjust military intervention: European thinkers from Vitoria to Mill / edited by Stefano Recchia and Jennifer Welsh.
    pages   cm
Includes bibliographical references and index.
ISBN 978-1-107-04202-5 (Hardback)
1. Peace-building – Europe.   2. Humanitarian assistance – Europe.
3. Intervention (International law).   I. Recchia, Stefano, 1978– contributing editor.   II. Welsh, Jennifer M. (Jennifer Mary), 1965– contributing editor.
JZ5584.E85J87 2013
341.5′84–dc23   2013014384

ISBN 978-1-107-04202-5 Hardback
ISBN 978-1-107-66549-1 Paperback

Cambridge University Press has no responsibility for the persistence or accuracy of URLs for external or third-party internet websites referred to in this publication, and does not guarantee that any content on such websites is, or will remain, accurate or appropriate.

Contents

Notes on contributors

WILLIAM BAIN is Associate Professor in the Department of Political Science, National University of Singapore. He is currently working on a project entitled *The Political Theology of International Society: God, Man, and the Ways of Order*, which explores the theological foundations of the modern states-system. He is the author of *Between Anarchy and Society: Trusteeship and the Obligations of Power* (2003), as well as several articles and book chapters that take up issues of international political theory, the English School, and the history of ideas.

ARIEL COLONOMOS is Senior Research Fellow at the National Center for Scientific Research (CNRS) in Paris. He is also a Research Professor at Sciences Po, where he teaches courses on international relations theory and the ethics of war. He is the author of *The Gamble of War: Is it Possible to Justify Preventive War?* (2013), *Moralizing International Relations: Called to Account* (2008), and *Eglises en réseaux: trajectoires politiques entre Europe et Amérique* (2000). He has published widely in the areas of international relations, the ethics of war, and political sociology.

MICHAEL W. DOYLE is the Harold Brown Professor of International Affairs, Law and Political Science at Columbia University. His major publications include *Ways of War and Peace* (1997), *Empires* (1986), *Making War and Building Peace* (2006), and *Striking First: Pre-emption and Prevention in International Conflict* (2008). From 2001 to 2003 he served as Assistant Secretary-General at the United Nations, where his responsibilities included strategic planning (the "Millennium Development Goals"), outreach to the international corporate sector (the "Global Compact") and relations with Washington. He currently chairs the UN Democracy Fund.

EDWIN VAN DE HAAR is an international relations scholar who has taught at Leiden University and Ateneo de Manila. He specializes in the liberal tradition in international political theory and is the author of *Classical Liberalism and International Relations Theory: Hume, Smith, Mises and Hayek* (2009), and *Beloved Yet Unknown: The Political Philosophy of Liberalism* (2011, in Dutch). He has contributed to the *Oxford Handbook of Adam Smith* (2013) and published a number of articles on Smith, Hume, and the wider liberal tradition in political thought.

PIERRE HASSNER has been a fellow at CERI-Sciences Po in Paris since 1959. Between 1964 and 2003 he taught International Relations at Sciences Po and the Johns Hopkins University, Bologna. A member of the editorial board of the journal *Survival* and a fellow of the American Academy of Arts and Sciences, he was awarded the Alexis de Tocqueville Prize in 2003 and was made Doctor Honoris Causa of Université du Québec à Montréal in 2008. His many publications include *Change and Security in Europe* (1968), *Violence and Peace: From the Atomic Bomb to Ethnic Cleansing* (1997), and, with Gilles Andréani, *Justifying War? From Humanitarian Intervention to Counterterrorism* (2008).

ANDREW HURRELL is Montague Burton Professor of International Relations at Oxford University and a fellow of Balliol College. His research interests cover theories of international relations, theories of global governance, the history of thought on international relations, comparative regionalism, and the international relations of the Americas, with particular reference to Brazil. His book, *On Global Order: Power, Values and the Constitution of International Society* won the International Studies Association Prize for Best Book in the field of International Relations in 2009. Other publications include (with Ngaire Woods), *Inequality, Globalization and World Politics* (1999), and (with Louise Fawcett), *Regionalism in World Politics* (1995).

SAMUEL MOYN is Professor of History at Columbia University, where he has taught since 2001. He is the author of three books, most recently *The Last Utopia: Human Rights in History* (2010). He has also edited, with Andrew Sartori, *Global Intellectual History* (2013).

JENNIFER PITTS is Associate Professor of Political Science at the University of Chicago. She is author of *A Turn to Empire: the Rise of Imperial Liberalism in Britain and France* (2005) and editor and translator of *Alexis de Tocqueville: Writings on Empire and Slavery* (2001).

Her research interests lie in the fields of modern political and international thought (particularly British and French thought of the eighteenth and nineteenth centuries), empire, the history of international law, and global justice. She is a co-editor of the Cambridge University Press series Ideas in Context.

STEFANO RECCHIA is a lecturer (assistant professor) in International Relations at Cambridge University. His research interests are in contemporary international security studies, international ethics, and classical international political thought. He obtained a PhD from Columbia University in 2011 (with distinction) and has held fellowships at Harvard, the Brookings Institution, and the European University Institute. He has published a number of journal articles on questions of international intervention and trusteeship and has edited (with Nadia Urbinati) *A Cosmopolitanism of Nations: Giuseppe Mazzini's Writings on Democracy, Nation Building, and International Relations* (2009).

DAVID TRIM is Director of the Archives of the General Conference of Seventh-day Adventists. A fellow of the Royal Historical Society, he has published over forty scholarly articles or book chapters, and edited or co-authored nine books including *The Huguenots: History and Memory in Transnational Context* (2011), *Humanitarian Intervention: a History* (Cambridge University Press, 2011), *European Warfare 1350–1750* (Cambridge University Press, 2010) and *Amphibious Warfare 1000–1700: Commerce, State Formation and European Expansion* (2006).

RICHARD TUCK is the Frank G. Thomson Professor of Government at Harvard University. His work addresses a variety of topics in political theory, including political authority, human rights, natural law, and toleration, and focuses on a number of thinkers, including Hobbes, Grotius, Selden, and Descartes. His publications include *Natural Rights Theories* (Cambridge University Press, 1979), *Hobbes* (1989), and *The Rights of War and Peace* (1999).

JENNIFER M. WELSH is Professor of International Relations at the European University Institute, Florence, Italy, and Co-director of the Oxford Institute for Ethics, Law and Armed Conflict. She is the author of *Edmund Burke and International Relations* (1995), and the editor/co-editor and author of several works on the ethics and politics of humanitarian intervention, including *Humanitarian Intervention and International Relations* (2004) and *The United Nations Security Council and War* (2008). She is currently leading a research project on the prevention of mass atrocity crimes.

Acknowledgements

In the course of this project we have acquired a number of debts to individuals and institutions. We would like to thank, first and foremost, the authors who have contributed chapters to this volume. Our contributors make up a truly international and inter-disciplinary group, including scholars from European, North American, and Asian institutions; and spanning the academic disciplines of international relations, history, and political theory. All of them have displayed remarkable patience, accepting several rounds of revisions and tolerating our sometimes intrusive editing aimed at ensuring an intellectually coherent final product. We have immensely enjoyed working with these extraordinary individuals and have learned a great deal from each of them in the process.

Furthermore, we would like to thank several scholars who contributed to our initial two-day conference held at Columbia University in 2009 by writing papers and serving formally or informally as commentators, but who did not write chapters for this volume. Their sharp comments and insights have improved many of the chapters and have had a positive impact on the volume as a whole. These scholars include Andrew Arato, Gary Bass, Jean Cohen, Alex Gourevitch, Stephen Holmes, Pablo Kalmanovitz, Benedict Kingsbury, Melissa Schwartzberg, and Tim Waligore. We are especially grateful to Nadia Urbinati, who strongly supported the idea of an edited volume about classical European thought on intervention from the beginning, and offered much welcome advice. Michael Doyle, in addition to being a chapter author, has also been a source of encouragement throughout and aided us in the crucial task of selecting a title for the book.

We also thank the institutions that provided financial support for our conference: the Center for European Studies at Columbia University; the Saltzman Institute for War and Peace Studies; the Political Science Department at Columbia; the Institute for Social and Economic Research and Policy (ISERP); and the Columbia-Sciences Po Alliance Program. We are particularly grateful to the leaders of those institutions, especially Richard Betts of the Saltzman Institute and Victoria de Grazia of the European Institute, who decided to support us from an early stage.

We appreciate the efforts of John Haslam, our remarkably efficient and supportive commissioning editor at Cambridge University Press. We further wish to thank Fleur Jones, the assistant editor, as well as Tom O'Reilly and Gaia Poggiogalli, our production editors, who cheerfully helped us steer the manuscript to publication. Finally, we are grateful to the two anonymous reviewers, whose constructive and generous feedback has helped us significantly strengthen the book.

As co-editors, this project has allowed us to further develop our mutual friendship and esteem. We have played roughly equal and complementary roles in defining the focus and scope of the volume, coaxing authors, editing draft chapters, crafting the introduction, and making final judgments on the quality of potential contributions. It has been much more enjoyable "steering the ship" with a collaborator, rather than trying to "sail solo." Jennifer Welsh would particularly like to thank Stefano Recchia for initially proposing the idea of the conference and an edited volume, and for patiently putting up with the competing demands on her time. Working on this project over the last three years has exposed us to new ideas and modes of thinking that have enriched our own individual research in numerous ways. We hope that our readers will also find these chapters illuminating and thought-provoking, and that they will be reminded of the great treasure that lies within classical thinking on war and intervention.

Introduction: the enduring relevance of classical thinkers

Stefano Recchia and Jennifer M. Welsh

Recent years have witnessed a notable resurgence of interest in the politics and ethics of military intervention among scholars, policymakers, and the informed public. While during the Cold War, the superpowers engaged in covert and sometimes overt intervention within their respective spheres of influence, since the early 1990s, intervention has become a more prominent feature of the international landscape. The perception of intervention in some corners of international society appears to have shifted from an act that was primarily viewed negatively – as "dictatorial interference," in the words of international legal scholar Lassa Oppenheim[1] – to a good deed, motivated by the desire to spread universal principles or to "right" a wrong committed within the boundaries of a particular state. As a consequence, for present-day supporters of the practice intervention is no longer an act that a target society "suffers,"[2] but rather something that it benefits from.[3]

Military intervention has increasingly been justified by reference to humanitarian purposes, reflecting a growth in both the potency of international human rights norms and the willingness of the United Nations Security Council to consider humanitarian crises as threats to international peace and security. As Martha Finnemore notes, while states often consciously avoided humanitarian justifications for intervention during the Cold War – even when they plausibly could have offered them (as, for example, in the cases of India's 1971 intervention in East Pakistan or Vietnam's 1979 intervention in Cambodia) – "humanitarian

[1] L. Oppenheim, *International Law: A Treatise* (London: Longmans, 1920), vol. I, p. 221.
[2] R. J. Vincent, *Nonintervention and International Order* (Princeton University Press, 1974), p. 3.
[3] See e.g. N. Wheeler, *Saving Strangers: Humanitarian Intervention in International Society* (Oxford University Press, 2000); T. Weiss, *Humanitarian Intervention*, 2nd edn (Cambridge: Polity, 2013); and the essays in J. L. Holzgrefe and R. O. Keohane (eds.), *Humanitarian Intervention: Ethical, Legal and Political Dilemmas* (Cambridge University Press, 2003); J. Welsh (ed.), *Humanitarian Intervention and International Relations* (Oxford University Press, 2004); and T. Nardin and M. Williams (eds.), *Humanitarian Intervention* (New York: NYU Press, 2005).

claims now frequently trump sovereignty claims," provided that interventions can be authorized and carried out multilaterally.[4] At the same time, powerful states have occasionally relied on a more contested rationale for intervention – the toppling of ostensibly hostile authoritarian regimes to instill or restore a democratic government. In those latter cases, where formal multilateral backing has been difficult to secure, interveners have sometimes been prepared to "go it alone," even in the years following the Cold War, thus challenging established international norms.[5]

Regardless of its ultimate purpose, military intervention always carries with it the potential for further death and destruction. It also stands in an uneasy relationship with fundamental principles of international society, notably self-determination, noninterference, and political independence. Military intervention (like the use of force more generally) is thus always morally problematic – or *evil* to some degree – although sometimes it might be the lesser of two evils, when compared with the costs of unhindered genocide and other mass atrocities, or the prospect of irreparable damage to one's own vital national interests. As a result, today's interventions have resulted in lively debate over a number of ethical questions.

The first set of questions – which has traditionally fallen under the rubric of *jus ad bellum* – relates to the circumstances under and purposes for which military intervention can be justified. Apart from the right of individual and collective self-defense in response to an armed attack, as enshrined in Article 51 of the UN Charter, *when (if ever) is it permissible to intervene militarily in a foreign country?* Does the existence of an undemocratic and oppressive regime alone generate a prima facie right of intervention on human protection grounds, as some cosmopolitan philosophers argue?[6] Or must there instead be evidence of ongoing genocidal violence, war crimes, or crimes against humanity – that is, of gross human rights violations that "shock the moral conscience of mankind," as Michael Walzer famously

---

[4] M. Finnemore, *The Purpose of Intervention: changing beliefs about the use of force* (Ithaca, NY: Cornell University Press, 2003), p. 79.

[5] See e.g. K. Von Hippel, *Democracy By Force* (Cambridge University Press, 2000); E. Luck, "The United States, International Organizations, and the Quest for Legitimacy," in S. Patrick and S. Forman (eds.), *Multilateralism and U.S. Foreign Policy* (Boulder, CO: Lynne Rienner, 2002); and A. Thompson, "Why Did Bush Bypass the UN in 2003?" *White House Studies* 11, no. 3 (2011), 1–20.

[6] See e.g. B. Barry, "International Society from a Cosmopolitan Perspective," in D. Mapel and T. Nardin (eds.), *International Society: Diverse Ethical Perspectives* (Princeton University Press, 1998); F. Tesón, "The Liberal Case for Humanitarian Intervention," in Holzgrefe and Keohane (eds.), *Humanitarian Intervention*; and A. I. Applbaum, "Forcing a People to Be Free," *Philosophy & Public Affairs* 35, no. 4 (2007), 359–400.

put it?[7] Between the two poles of "merely" undemocratic governance, on the one hand, and ongoing genocide, on the other, there is arguably a large gray zone. For instance, do outsiders have a right to *preventive* humanitarian intervention during the early stages of a popular uprising, with the goal of averting mass atrocities that are only anticipated – as in the case of Libya in 2011?[8] The legitimacy of preventive military intervention more generally, of course, remains heavily contested – even when contemplated for more traditional purposes of self-defense.[9]

The second set of questions relates to means, rather than ends – matters which have traditionally fallen under the rubric of *jus in bello*. If a case can be made that armed intervention is justified in principle, *what kind of military action and what level of force are acceptable?* Can human rights legitimately be protected by relying exclusively on high-altitude air strikes (as NATO did in the cases of Kosovo and Libya) – or does just intervention instead require the deployment of ground troops in combat, at greater risk to the intervener, in order to minimize civilian casualties among the local population? In spite of their increased precision, air strikes still often result in high "collateral damage," especially when used in forested or urban areas. More generally, what level of collateral damage – understood as the accidental destruction of civilian lives and property – is acceptable to achieve one's objectives?

Finally, a third set of questions concerns the source of normative judgment, or the question of *right authority*. Who should pass judgment on the legitimacy of intervention – the UN Security Council and regional multilateral bodies; the targeted population itself; or the leaders and citizens of powerful states that actually have the capabilities to intervene?[10] Even if one agrees that multilateral approval is normatively desirable and should always be sought as a matter of principle, to minimize the risk of

---

[7] M. Walzer, *Just and Unjust Wars* (New York: Basic Books, 1977), p. 107.

[8] According to Walzer, such cases do not meet the threshold for humanitarian intervention. See M. Walzer, "The Case Against Our Attack on Libya," *The New Republic*, March 20, 2011. For the opposite argument, see A. Bellamy, "Libya and the Responsibility to Protect," *Ethics and International Affairs* 25, no. 3 (2011), 263–9; and more cautiously, R. Pape, "When Duty Calls: A Pragmatic Standard of Humanitarian Intervention," *International Security* 37, no. 1 (2012), esp. 61–9.

[9] For insightful analyses that reach differing conclusions, see M. Doyle, *Striking First: Pre-emption and Prevention in International Conflict* (Princeton University Press, 2008), and R. Betts, "Striking First: A History of Thankfully Lost Opportunities," *Ethics & International Affairs* 17, no. 1 (2003), 17–24.

[10] See J. Welsh, "Authorizing humanitarian intervention," in R. Price and M. Zacher (eds.), *The United Nations and Global Security* (London: Palgrave, 2004); M. Doyle, "The Ethics of Multilateral Intervention," *Theoria* 53, no. 109 (2006), 28–48; and J. Pattison, *Humanitarian Intervention and The Responsibility to Protect: Who Should Intervene?* (Oxford University Press, 2010).

self-serving interventions by powerful states, what about those cases where it is either unavailable or might simply be too costly to achieve? Concluding that in such instances unilateralism should be generally admissible risks doing away with precious checks and balances, precisely at the moment when military intervention is likely to be most internationally controversial. At the same time, making formal multilateral approval a necessary requirement for intervention might undermine the credibility of coercive threats where such approval is unavailable, thus reducing outsiders' ability to effectively deal with hostile opponents and to address large-scale human rights violations short of actually using force.

Our answers to the aforementioned questions reflect to a significant degree the particular features of our current age. For example, instantaneous access to information from around the world has heightened our awareness of human suffering and domestic political crises abroad, and the proliferation of human rights organizations and other non-governmental advocacy groups has intensified the pressure brought to bear on states to "do something" in the face of large-scale atrocities. More traditional international actors – the world's most powerful states, together with institutions such as the United Nations and NATO – have also crucially shaped debates about the legitimate goals and means of intervention. Finally, public discourse about the merits of armed intervention at any given time is inevitably influenced by contingent political views and commitments, technological possibilities (which have greatly expanded in recent decades), and the existence of relevant precedents that function as focal points in the debate. In short, judgments about the "rightness" or "wrongness" of intervention are heavily influenced by our contemporary material and ideational context.

The classics in context

The above-noted influence of context would suggest that there is little to be gained from considering the writings of the classical European thinkers featured in this book, who operated within a different material and ideational environment. Trying to mobilize classical thinkers from the era of the principalities of Christendom, to find solutions to the challenges facing today's interveners, involves the risk of "presentism."[11] As Stanley Hoffmann points out, "all ethical judgments in politics, but particularly in [international relations] are historical judgments. They are, as the jargon would put it these days, contextual or situational;

---

[11] See B. Jahn, "Classical theory and international relations in context," in Jahn (ed.), *Classical Theory in International Relations* (Cambridge University Press, 2006), p. 3.

they are not separable from the concrete circumstances."[12] We therefore need to take seriously the "contextualist" challenge, articulated most fully by Quentin Skinner, about the need to move beyond the surface meaning of words and concepts to understand the specific, subjective *intentions* behind them. Those intentions, he asserts, can only be uncovered through a detailed examination of the political, social, intellectual, and linguistic universe within which a particular thinker participated.[13] According to Skinner, textual approaches to the study of a thinker too often engage in the "mythology of parochialism" by finding something apparently familiar in what remains an alien argument. Simply because a similar concept appears does not mean it conveys the same idea or is used with the same intention. As he writes: "There *is* no determinate idea to which various writers contributed, but only a variety of statements made with the same or approximately equivalent words by a variety of different agents with a variety of intentions."[14]

Skinner's injunction reminds us that the works we consider here are social acts, rather than abstract statements. As a result, our treatment endeavors to provide the context for each thinker's perspective on intervention, so as to illuminate whether he is accepting, rejecting, or revising the prevailing ideas and conventions of his time. Moreover, we acknowledge that terminology is historically contingent. Indeed, the very term "intervention," as we use it here, is a relatively recent one, and was not used by most of the authors discussed in this book.[15] As shown by David Trim in Chapter 1, while the word has existed in both English and French from at least the sixteenth century, it only came to refer to coercive interference in the affairs of another state involving the use of force in the middle of the nineteenth century – when Giuseppe Mazzini and John Stuart Mill (the last thinkers we address) penned their works on intervention.

Nevertheless, while aiming to provide historical context, we concede that we stop short of providing the kind of contextual picture to which Skinner aspires. But we also question whether his method can in fact deliver on its promise, given the inescapable obstacles to being an

[12] S. Hoffmann, *Duties Beyond Borders: On the Limits and Possibilities of Ethical International Politics* (Syracuse, NY: Syracuse University Press, 1981), p. 27.
[13] Q. Skinner, "Meaning and Understanding in the History of Ideas" in J. Tully (ed.), *Meaning and Context: Quentin Skinner and his Critics* (Cambridge University Press, 1988), pp. 29–67.
[14] *Ibid.*, p. 56.
[15] We define military intervention as the cross-border deployment of armed force, aimed at changing the domestic politics of a foreign country, without the explicit consent of local authorities. For a similar definition, see Vincent, *Nonintervention*, p. 8.

uninvolved observer or chronicler of ideas. We can only ever approxi-
mate a re-enactment of each author's intentions in writing a specific
tract, and there will always be a certain "fusion of horizons" between a
classical thinker and a contemporary interpreter.[16] More fundamentally,
we contest Skinner's view that we should not necessarily look to classic
texts for inspiration, given the contrast between their milieu and our
own, but rather should "learn to do our thinking for ourselves."[17] The
authors analyzed here, we contend, are not solely epiphenomena of the
issues and tensions in their own societies, but offer insights and modes of
argumentation that can assist contemporary scholars. And we have
chosen them, rather than some of their lesser-known contemporaries,
because of the quality and impact of their work. As Friedrich Meinecke
wrote, the "ideas which guide historical life, do certainly not indeed
spring solely from the intellectual workshop of the great thinkers ...
But it is in this workshop that they condensed and solidified; it is there,
in many cases, that they first assume the form which will have an effect on
the progress of events and the actions of men."[18]

Despite the contextualist challenge, then, there are at least three
reasons to think that a close reading of classic texts can enhance our
understanding of intervention, in terms of both its origins and its controversial status in international society. First, as Trim shows, even if etymologically the term "intervention" is relatively new, the practice of what
came to be called intervention – particularly humanitarian intervention –
has a much longer history. From the sixteenth century onward, princes
and states have sent their troops to fight in foreign lands against the will of
local rulers, and in many instances the justification for doing so has been
the appalling acts of those local rulers. Evidence of this longstanding
practice reinforces the revisionist interpretation of the Peace of
Westphalia (advanced by scholars such as Krasner, Osiander, and
Teschke), according to which absolute state sovereignty and the attendant
rule of nonintervention were not magically enshrined in 1648.[19] Not only
did the Westphalian treaties provide guarantees of freedom of conscience
for some religious minorities, which effectively *mandated* intervention if

[16] See e.g. the critique of Skinner by J. Femia, "An Historicist Critique of 'Revisionist' Methods for Studying the History of Ideas," in Tully (ed.), *Meaning and Context*, pp. 156–75.
[17] Skinner, "Meaning and Understanding," p. 66.
[18] F. Meinecke, *Machiavellism: The Doctrine of Raison d'Etat and its Place in Modern History*, transl. D. Scott (New Haven, CT: Yale University Press, 1957), p. 21.
[19] S. Krasner, *Sovereignty: Organized Hypocrisy* (Princeton University Press, 1999); A. Osiander, "Sovereignty, International Relations, and the Westphalian Myth," *International Organization* 55, no. 2 (2001), 251–87; and B. Teschke, *The Myth of 1648* (London: Verso, 2003).

that freedom was breached, but through the seventeenth and eighteenth centuries (the period when several of the authors discussed in this volume wrote), Europe's princes regularly considered the behavior of fellow sovereigns as having breached common standards of acceptability, triggering limited interventions aimed at stopping oppression and massacre. For instance, Cromwell's show of force in 1655 on behalf of the Vaudois of Savoy, while partly motivated by religious affinity to fellow Protestants, was primarily driven by outrage over their inhumane treatment by a tyrannical local ruler.

Second, the particular European thinkers showcased here all played an important part in constituting the kind of international society we have today – one that is now based on a universal ideal of sovereign equality, but which evolved from a European "core" and still has embedded within it notions of hierarchy and exclusion. As subsequent chapters illustrate, colonialism and imperialism were often bound up with attempts by the classical European thinkers to establish a basis for intervention, or to contest its legitimacy.

Authors from other cultural traditions have undoubtedly produced valuable and original contributions on the ethics of war and intervention.[20] However, for better or worse, classical European thought on these matters has had a unique impact on our contemporary conceptual categories and normative standards – and consequently it has fundamentally shaped the parameters of legitimate intervention, including intervention by non-Western states. As Brendan Simms and David Trim note in their comprehensive history of humanitarian intervention, recent "interventions by Asian and African states ... [have] to a great extent reflected the experience of the Western world and the 'Law of Nations,' which began to emerge in early modern Europe, drawing partly on concepts in late medieval European philosophy and theology."[21]

This gives rise to a final reason for consulting the works of the classical European thinkers: they themselves represent "interventions" into a

---

[20] See e.g. S. Hashmi, "Islamic Ethics in International Society," in Mapel and Nardin (eds.), *International Society*; K. Roy, "Just and Unjust War in Hindu Philosophy," *Journal of Military Ethics* 6, no. 3 (2007), 232–45; and the chapters on Buddhist, Hindu, Chinese, and Islamic just war traditions in P. Robinson (ed.), *Just War in Comparative Perspective* (Aldershot: Ashgate, 2003).

[21] D. J. B. Trim and B. Simms, "Towards a History of Humanitarian Intervention," in B. Simms and D. J. B. Trim (eds.), *Humanitarian Intervention: A History* (Cambridge University Press, 2011), pp. 18–19. On how classical European thought has shaped the norms and rules of modern international society, see also J. Donnelly, "Human Rights: A New Standard of Civilization?" *International Affairs* 74, no. 1 (1998), 1–23; and E. Keene, *Beyond the Anarchical Society: Grotius, Colonialism and Order in World Politics* (Cambridge University Press, 2002).

debate about the strength and meaning of core norms and ideas, such as
sovereignty, humanity, and self-determination. So, for example, William
Bain shows in Chapter 3 that Vitoria's argument about human beings
created equal "in the image of God," from which he derived a natural
right to self-rule, or *dominion*, for political communities everywhere, gave
him the normative leverage to challenge Spanish colonial interference
in the religious practices of American Indians. Similarly, as Jennifer
Pitts demonstrates in Chapter 6, Vattel's conception of sovereign
equality and independence led with to embrace a strong rule of non-
interference and condemn military intervention on religious or civilizational grounds – of the kind sanctioned by the Westphalian treaties and
regularly practiced by the European empires of his time in their empires
overseas. Of course, the nature of the political contestation over the
meaning of these norms is different from the one we are engaged in
today, and therefore we should endeavor to understand what Antje
Wiener calls their "meaning-in-use."[22] Nevertheless, participants in
current debates over the legitimacy of military intervention, whichever
side they endorse, can benefit from consulting the arguments of
the classical European philosophers and jurists. While the contextualists
would deny the very existence of any enduring issues or questions
in international politics, we contend that the debate over intervention,
both then and now, pivots around two central issues: first, what is a
legitimate basis for intervention? Second, what is the likely impact of
intervention and what are the associated risks? Both questions appear
in the writings analyzed here, although each thinker addressed them
differently and to a greater or lesser extent.

The first issue, regarding the basis or rationale for intervention, arises
out of the strength of the injunction to allow the affairs of princes and
states to remain largely their own "business." For much of the modern
era, three factors supported this tendency towards nonintervention.
First, particularly in the early modern period, princes had a conception
of sovereignty as affording a right of property, or *dominium*, over their
respective territories and populations; and that, combined with the belief
that rulers were divinely ordained, partially explains why they engaged in
forcible interference in each other's affairs only in extreme circumstances, and then only for limited periods of time.[23] The objective – as

[22] A. Wiener, *The Invisible Constitution of Politics: Contested Norms and International Encounters* (Cambridge University Press, 2008).
[23] F. Kratochwil, "Sovereignty as Dominium: Is there a Right of Humanitarian Intervention?" in G. M. Lyons and M. Mastanduno (eds.), *Beyond Westphalia: State Sovereignty and International Intervention* (Baltimore, MD: Johns Hopkins University Press, 1995). See also D. Trim, ch. 1 in this volume.

shown by Elizabeth's intervention in the Netherlands in the late sixteenth century, or Cromwell's coercive diplomacy in the seventeenth century – was not to change the political "regime," but simply to enforce conformity with common standards, and then withdraw. Second, the Just War framework that Vitoria developed further from Augustine and Aquinas, and which Grotius then sought to revive and legalize, took as its starting point the belief that killing is evil, and that therefore the employment of force through war can only be justified as a punitive measure in response to a specific, unjust act. Thus, in contrast with more contemporary conceptions of Just War, such as Walzer's, which revolve around the idea of individual and collective self-defense, the earlier conception pivots around the idea that wars are an exceptional instrument of retribution: their goal is to uphold justice by punishing either the external aggressor, or the tyrannical ruler who is killing his subjects.[24] Third, as we move into the nineteenth century, we encounter the perspective of thinkers such as Mazzini and Mill, who argue that armed interference to promote representative democracy abroad is both illegitimate (since it violates the principle of self-determination) and futile (since democracy established with the help of foreign armies can neither be genuine nor lasting). "Nonintervention," which by then had become a recognizable term, is viewed as a principle that facilitates the development of authentic and truly self-determining political communities.

It was against this backdrop, where political autonomy and nonintervention were accepted and advised as general rules of international society, that certain classical thinkers developed their counterarguments *in favor* of intervention. The bases for intervention which they advanced varied a great deal: they ranged from humanitarian rationales, which included the imperative to rescue fellow human beings abroad from egregious harm, such as cannibalism and human sacrifice (Vitoria); the punishment of vicious oppression by a tyrannical ruler (Grotius); or stopping large-scale massacres of religious or ethnic minorities (Mazzini) – to the need to "preventively" oppose and neutralize looming dangers – whether stemming from pirates hiding in foreign lands (Suarez); states threatening to disrupt the traditional

---

[24] N. Rengger, "On the Just War Tradition in the Twenty-first Century," *International Affairs* 78, no. 2 (2002), 353–63; J. T. Johnston, "The Idea of Defense in Historical and Contemporary Thinking About Just War," *Journal of Religious Ethics* 36, no. 4 (2008), 543–56. More recent ethical treatments of war, such as those of D. Rodin and J. McMahan, are attempting to revive the earlier conception of just war as "punishment." See J. McMahan, *Killing in War* (Oxford University Press, 2009); and D. Rodin, *War and Self-Defense* (Oxford University Press, 2002).

balance of power (Vattel); or revolutionary governments that more fundamentally challenge the European political order (Burke). Each of these rationales, though a product of a particular context, can usefully be probed by contemporary scholars concerned with the legitimate basis for intervention.

In terms of the likely impact of military intervention and associated risks, the views of most of the thinkers studied here travel in a cautious and sometimes skeptical direction. Whether we consider Vitoria's concerns about safeguarding the vitality of indigenous customs and practices; Hobbes's warnings about the risk that intervention might erode a ruler's scarce resources; Vattel's worry about the weakening of his ideal of sovereign equality; or Kant's discussion of the dangers of power and interest corrupting moral purpose – the classical thinkers are often scathing in their condemnation of military intervention, and especially of long-term occupation of fellow European states. Of course, this theme of caution is much less prominent in the classical thinkers' discussion of empire and colonial rule, where the desire to bring "civilized governance" to "barbarous" (non-European) peoples is frequently viewed as justifying a much longer-term and more intrusive presence. But even here, some thinkers – particularly Burke, Hume and Smith – worry about the deleterious effects of the exercise of arbitrary rule in the colonies on the health of the "mother country."

Therefore, as we seek to demonstrate, the classical European philosophers and jurists covered in this book – from central figures of international thought such as Grotius, Vattel, and Kant, to authors not especially known today for their arguments about international politics, such as Locke and Mazzini – all provided a perspective on the two aforementioned issues, although their material and ideational context means that their precise ethical concerns and judgments cannot be directly applied to the present. In some cases, we may find strong elements of continuity between the subjects of analysis, even if the precise terminology is different and the solutions offered are not always relevant or possible in the contemporary context. In others, we find strong elements of discontinuity between contemporary and early modern analyses – and then we come away from our reading of the classic texts with a keen sense of historical contingency, the possibilities for historical change, and the need to understand the particular underpinnings of contemporary values and norms. Either way, we hope that contemporary readers will find the discussions in this book to be both thought provoking and illuminating.

Outline of the book

Several edited volumes and anthologies have been published in recent years on classical international relations theory.[25] However, most of these previous works have discussed the classical thinkers' general arguments about international politics and society. To our knowledge, the present book is the first that specifically focuses on classical European thought about the law, ethics, and politics of *military intervention*. Our aim is not to provide an exhaustive or authoritative interpretation of each thinker's "international theory," but rather to examine – through close attention to political and intellectual context – the classics' views on the theory and practice of intervention in the period in which they wrote. The arguments about just war and intervention of several of the classical thinkers discussed in this volume are scattered among different and often hard-to-access primary sources. That has hitherto made a comprehensive understanding and sophisticated engagement with those arguments exceedingly difficult for contemporary audiences. Our book seeks to address this challenge, by providing a single-volume overview and discussion.

The book collects twelve essays authored by an international group of scholars. The specific time period we cover ranges from the sixteenth century (which witnessed the emergence of the first sovereign states in Europe, and thus the first instances of "intervention," understood as an exceptional practice that deviates from prevailing patterns of behavior) to the late nineteenth century (when the process of nation-building in Western Europe was largely completed, and European international society had come close to assuming its contemporary contours, which later spread to the rest of the world).[26]

In Chapter 1, David Trim discusses the origins and evolution of the term "intervention," before providing an overview of some of the key instances of military intervention in the period covered by the book, from Elizabethan interventions in Scotland and France in the mid-sixteenth

---

[25] See e.g. W. D. Clinton (ed.), *The Realist Tradition and Contemporary International Relations* (Baton Rouge, LA: Louisiana State University Press, 2007); D. Bell (ed.), *Political Thought and International Relations: Variations on a Realist Theme* (Oxford University Press, 2009); Jahn (ed.), *Classical Theory*; I. Clark and I. Neuman (eds.), *Classical Theories of International Relations* (London: Palgrave, 1999); C. Brown, T. Nardin, and N. Rengger (eds.), *International Relations in Political Thought* (Cambridge University Press, 2002); T. Nardin and D. R. Mapel (eds.), *Traditions of International Ethics* (Cambridge University Press, 1993).

[26] For the argument that "a complete analysis of intervention ... must begin ... in the late sixteenth century," see Trim and Simms, "Towards a History of Humanitarian Intervention," p. 24.

century, to the nineteenth-century interventions by Britain, France, and Russia in the Ottoman Empire. Trim focuses particularly on interventions motivated by humanitarian purposes, arguing that this practice is not peculiar to the nineteenth and twentieth centuries (as some have argued), but was instead already evident in previous efforts by princes and states to address tyrannical rule that transgressed commonly accepted standards of behavior. He concludes that while the terminology used to characterize the nature of ethical problems faced by the community of Christian princes was specific to that time, there are continuities in the nature of some of those problems, as well as some of the solutions devised to address them. In general, he notes, interveners during the early modern period were more likely to seek to change the target's policy or behaviour, rather than the "regime" itself. But this aversion to countenancing a change of political regime began to shift in the nineteenth century, as peoples in Asia, Africa and elsewhere were considered less sovereign, and less equal, than "civilized" European nations.

Following on from Trim's opening essay, each of the remaining chapters – roughly arranged in chronological order – discusses the contribution of either one classical European thinker or several closely related ones. The chapters situate the classical thinkers' arguments within their specific historical context. At the same time, several of our contributors have chosen to carefully extrapolate insights and judgments from those classical writings that might inform contemporary debates about military intervention.

In Chapter 2, Ariel Colonomos scrutinizes the arguments of four early modern thinkers – Francisco Suarez, Alberico Gentili, Hugo Grotius, and Emerich de Vattel – to illuminate the origins and some of the inherent ambiguities of Western ethical discourse on the preventive use of force. For Suarez and Grotius, anticipatory strikes are justified when they simultaneously aim at *punishing* enemies that have already harmed us, and at *preventing* future injustice. Based on this reasoning, both classical thinkers also justified anticipatory strikes against hostile non-state actors, such as pirates who have already committed a wrong and are hiding within the boundaries of an "imperfect," weak state. Grotius further emphasized that the traditional laws of war may legitimately be suspended in such cases. As Colonomos points out, these early modern arguments bear surprising resemblance to contemporary justifications for preventive strikes against alleged terrorists in "failed states," and to the recent US practice of declaring them "unlawful combatants."

Nevertheless, as Colonomos explains, the Just War tradition ultimately sought to constrain the legitimate use of force. The fundamental problem, as he sees it, is that classical thinkers like Suarez and Grotius for the most part failed to take into account the effect of epistemic uncertainty in this context and its normative significance. Re-reading the classics therefore alerts us to the importance of *moral luck* in any attempt to justify preventive war. States that wage preventive wars can be morally lucky or unlucky: as a war unfolds, new evidence usually becomes available, which may either further legitimize the use of force or seriously undermine its justification.

In Chapter 3, William Bain examines how another classical Just War thinker, Francisco de Vitoria, developed a very different rationale for intervention – the protection of "innocents" against oppression. As Bain demonstrates, Vitoria viewed independent political communities as necessary to a good human life; he insisted that non-Christian "infidels" also had a right to political independence; and he effectively used this reasoning to reject traditional theological arguments used to justify the Spanish conquest of South America. Vitoria embraced the Just War position of Augustine and Aquinas, according to which the only just cause for war is the receipt of injury that causes harm. Taking that argument further, he then famously justified armed intervention to prevent or stop harm from being inflicted on innocent foreigners.

However, as Bain explains, for Vitoria military action in defense of the innocent was decoupled from the notion of punishment that dominates Just War thinking in the early modern period. Instead, Vitoria justified such action from a broader, theological perspective that conceives of fellow human beings, no matter where they reside, as created equal in the image of God. In contrast to Vitoria's international theory, which presupposes a rationally ordered Christian universe, contemporary thinking about the principle of the "responsibility to protect" has for the most part attempted to ground states' rights and duties in positive international law – most notably the 1948 Universal Declaration of Human Rights and the 1951 Convention on the Prevention and Punishment of Genocide. Therefore, Bain concludes, to the extent that Vitoria's thought remains of enduring value, it is not so much because he gave an early blueprint for engaging in humanitarian intervention, but rather because of the fundamental questions he raised about political autonomy, the basis for our common humanity, and the sources of normative arguments about the legitimacy of intervention.

Richard Tuck moves firmly into the seventeenth century in Chapter 4, discussing the arguments for and against humanitarian intervention developed by Hugo Grotius, Thomas Hobbes, and Samuel Pufendorf. As Tuck notes, while Grotius rejected any domestic right of rebellion, thereby following other Protestant and humanist thinkers of the time, he famously justified war to punish foreign sovereigns who violated the laws of nature by abusing their subjects. Grotius still viewed international society as governed by a universal moral framework, although – Tuck argues – for Grotius that framework had narrowed significantly; and, unlike previous scholastic thinkers, Grotius grounded the right of punishment in a *secular* theory of natural law.[27] Even such limited universalism was unambiguously rejected by Hobbes only a few decades later: for Hobbes, notions of right and wrong do not apply in the state of nature among sovereign commonwealths. Nevertheless, Tuck successfully demonstrates that Hobbes advocated an ethics of prudence in states' dealings with one another, which led him to be skeptical of military intervention. Prudent rulers understand that interventions in the absence of a vital threat are like gambling – unlikely to achieve one's objectives, and in most instances merely squandering limited resources. One might thus view Hobbes as a theorist of nonintervention.[28] Finally, Pufendorf – the last of the three classical thinkers discussed by Tuck – shared Grotius's universalism but rejected the latter's paternalism, and was thus reluctant to countenance military intervention on behalf of strangers, unless it was requested by an oppressed population itself. Taken together, Grotius's moral universalism, Hobbes's skepticism, and Pufendorf's anti-paternalism help us identify some of the tensions and dilemmas inherent in most current debates about humanitarian intervention.

In Chapter 5, Samuel Moyn draws our attention to John Locke's portrayal in the *Second Treatise of Government* of a dispute between the biblical figure of Jephtha and the Ammonite king about whether there is a legitimate *casus belli* between them. In Moyn's interpretation, Locke uses the Jephtha story, where war ultimately ensues, as a parable illustrating the difficulties of moral judgment about war under conditions of uncertainty: even when both parties to a dispute are *subjectively* convinced that justice is on their side, only an impartial and authoritative judge – God, in this case – will be able to determine who is *objectively* in the right. At the domestic level, the problem of adjudication had largely been resolved for Locke when people left the state of nature and instituted via the social contract a supreme political authority to whom they could appeal. One might infer from this that Locke could also have conceived of authoritative international institutions, based on a contract among nations, capable of impartially adjudicating disputes about justice – but Moyn is

---

[27] See also S. Chesterman, *Just War or Just Peace? Humanitarian Intervention and International Law* (Oxford University Press, 2001), pp. 12–13.

[28] On Hobbes as a theorist of nonintervention, see also J. Havercroft, "Was Westphalia 'All That'? Hobbes, Bellarmine, and the Norm of Non-intervention," *Global Constitutionalism* 1, no. 1 (2012), 120–40.

reluctant to pursue this line of reasoning.[29] Nevertheless, while Locke's solutions to the ethical dilemmas he encountered were rooted in his own contemporary ideas of what was "right" and possible, the questions he asks are relevant in the context of current efforts to achieve an authoritative consensus on the circumstances that might warrant intervention. Towards the end of his essay, Moyn also shows that Locke posited a right to insurgency against (what the local population perceives as) unjust intervention. This argument cannot only be seen as a justification for anti-colonial struggles (though Locke, paradoxically, regarded colonialism as legitimate) – it also throws a very interesting light on recent local responses to Western interventions in places such as Afghanistan and Iraq.

Following on from that, in Chapter 6, Jennifer Pitts relies on Emerich de Vattel's *Droit des Gens* – and, to a lesser degree, the writings of Christian Wolff – to develop a powerful critique of the currently existing international sovereignty regime. Vattel famously theorized an international system of legally equal and politically independent sovereign states (as distinct from princes or rulers) with a strong attendant rule of nonintervention. But according to Pitts, Vattel always understood this to be an ideal-type rather than an accurate depiction of post-Westphalian international society, and we should therefore read Vattel's theory as normative rather than descriptive. Pitts then goes on to note that the modern international system continues to be marked by significant legal as well as political inequalities, thus falling short of Vattel's normative objective. Even after the demise of colonial empires, intervention by powerful states in peripheral regions of the globe has continued to be far from exceptional. Indeed, Pitts claims that foreign interference, military and otherwise, has quite literally been *the norm* – in the sense of having been institutionalized in the form of various unequal treaties and legal regimes. In short, Pitts concludes that although the present international order is ostensibly based on Vattel's ideals of sovereign equality and nonintervention, we continue to see too much harmful intervention by powerful states, which helps to prop up despotic and corrupt rulers in many parts of the world.

Chapter 7, by Edwin van de Haar, takes us into the Scottish Enlightenment, with a detailed discussion of David Hume's and Adam Smith's views on international ethics and intervention. Although the two eighteenth-century thinkers at times displayed a markedly "realist" concern with international power politics, and developed no explicit doctrine

---

[29] On Locke's political thought as pointing towards international institutionalism, see M. Doyle, *Ways of War and Peace* (New York: Norton, 1997), p. 221.

of intervention, Van de Haar insists that their overall moral and political theory is compatible with a limited right of humanitarian intervention. First, as part of their acceptance of the Just War paradigm, the two thinkers appear to have embraced Grotius's justification of intervention to punish foreign oppressors. Furthermore, they could certainly have conceived of, and would probably have justified, humanitarian intervention on those rare occasions where the enlightened self-interest of a powerful state overlaps with the requirements of universal justice. At the same time, Van de Haar points out that Hume and Smith were critical of colonial rule and repeatedly emphasized the likely negative effects of prolonged foreign occupation. Ultimately, therefore, the principal lesson to be derived from the two Scotsmen is one of caution: foreign interventions are always driven by mixed motives; partially for that reason, they are inevitably selective; and beware of interventions that aim at radically transforming foreign societies – they are exceedingly costly and may end up doing more harm than good.

On the European continent, meanwhile, the years between the late eighteenth and early nineteenth centuries were marked by popular uprisings driven by a combination of universal democratic ideals and the emerging principle of nationality. In Chapter 8, Pierre Hassner discusses how the tension between universal or cosmopolitan ideals and particular or national interests is reflected in the writings of Jean-Jacques Rousseau, Immanuel Kant, and G. W. F. Hegel. As Hassner points out, those three thinkers all touched upon the problem of intervention and raised several questions worthy of consideration by contemporary scholars. Rousseau's political philosophy displays a tension between, on the one hand, his advocacy of positive liberty and of compassion towards strangers, and on the other hand, his at least equally strong emphasis on national self-sufficiency and his suspicion of self-appointed liberators and their motives. For Hassner, it is impossible to predict for certain on which side Rousseau would have come down in the contemporary debate about humanitarian intervention, although it appears that his philosophy would have precluded armed interference aimed at saving foreigners or making the world "safe for democracy." Kant's thought, Hassner argues, is marked by similar contradictions: Kant first expresses strong opposition to military intervention and to violent revolution in principle; but he then justifies intervention to change the domestic constitution of an "unjust enemy," and his attitude towards the French Revolution in particular was ambivalent and, at times, outright sympathetic.[30] Finally, of the three

[30] For a helpful discussion of Kant's complex views on revolution, see R. Maliks, "Kant, the State, and Revolution," *Kantian Review* 18, no. 1 (2013), 29–47.

classical philosophers that Hassner discusses, Hegel was the most unambiguously bellicose and interventionist. For Hegel, military intervention
and conquest are welcome instruments of historical progress, which
foster the development of the "World Spirit" and bring the rule of law
and civilization to "barbarian peoples." Hassner concludes by discussing
the influence of these three classical thinkers on war and intervention
since their time. Hegel, he suggests, arguably had a decisive impact on
world history in the twentieth century, with the rise of statist and expansionist totalitarian ideologies; but since the end of the Cold War, the
clock appears to have turned back to the earlier dialogue between Rousseau and Kant.

Kant's thinking on military intervention, and contemporary interpretations of the Kantian argument, are discussed in more detail by
Andrew Hurrell in Chapter 9. A close textual reading of Kant's
writings, Hurrell notes, leaves little room for intervention on human-
rights grounds: the "unjust enemy" argument refers to states that are
first and foremost internationally aggressive (rather than internally
oppressive), and in *Perpetual Peace*, Kant explicitly writes that "no
state shall forcibly interfere in the constitution and government of
another state." Nevertheless, modern scholars have interpreted Kant's
writings as compatible with various forms of interventionism. Hurrell
groups them into "transnational cosmopolitans" (mainly German) and
"liberal interventionists" (mainly American). According to Hurrell,
the former, led by Jürgen Habermas, overestimate contemporary
changes in the character of international law and society towards a more
cosmopolitan order. Liberal interventionists like Fernando Téson,
meanwhile, who argue that democracies ought to take the lead in promoting republican government abroad – including through the use
of force – risk stretching the Kantian argument beyond recognition.
Contrary to most contemporary authors of self-proclaimed Kantian
lineage, Hurrell argues that the Prussian philosopher himself never
assumed that all people share a fundamental understanding about justice; and instead, he started from the strikingly modern assumption of
deep conflict over values. Therefore, on Hurrell's reading, Kant was a
"pluralist" who thought that sovereignty and national independence
ought to be protected by means of a strong rule of nonintervention.

In England, at about the same time when Kant was developing his ideas
on nonintervention, Edmund Burke set forth a very different conception
of international society. As Jennifer Welsh notes in Chapter 10, Burke
insisted that pluralist rules of sovereign equality and nonintervention
could only work in "ordinary" times. In Burke's mind, the French
Revolution, with its attack on religion and dynastic rule, represented

an assault on the very foundations of European civilization, which necessitated extraordinary measures. Crucial to Burke's justification of
counter-revolutionary intervention was his argument that Europe constituted one united Commonwealth, buttressed by a common culture and
tradition (which in turn generated extensive rights and responsibilities),
as opposed to a region of independent and self-contained states. Welsh
further notes that Burke developed important reflections on the relationship between the Commonwealth of Europe and the non-European
world: Burke's critique of the excesses of Warren Hastings, the Governor
of Bengal, and the British East India Company continue to have relevance
for contemporary debates about international state-building and trusteeship. But above all, Welsh concludes, Burke's writings prompt us to
analyze the role of common culture and values in building and sustaining
international order, and to regard the aspirations to universality of twenty-
first century liberalism with some skepticism.

The thinking of conservative intellectuals like Edmund Burke was
turned on its head by the nineteenth-century revolutionary democrat
Giuseppe Mazzini, whose solidarist internationalism is discussed by
Stefano Recchia in Chapter 11. Critics have sometimes portrayed Mazzini as the prototypical *liberal interventionist* – someone who justified and
indeed called for military crusades by powerful liberal states to spread
freedom and democracy abroad. But Recchia shows that this interpretation is largely unfounded. Mazzini was certainly no pacifist: he believed
that popular insurrections are legitimate and perhaps even necessary in
the face of despotic rule; he called for a "Holy Alliance of the peoples,"
aiming to unite Europe's revolutionary democrats; and he justified
humanitarian intervention under exceptional circumstances, to stop
massacres of ethnic or religious minorities. However, Mazzini opposed
regime change through direct military intervention, pointing out that
democracy achieved with the help of foreign regular armies would not
be genuine and could not be lasting. His democratic republicanism
requires that each people develop its own *ethos* of liberty, by fighting for
it if necessary and actively participating in its sustenance and progress,
day after day. As Recchia points out in conclusion, Mazzini's efforts to
square his strong belief in national sovereignty with an equally deep
commitment to democratic universalism and human equality probably
explain why many of his arguments appear so familiar and relevant today.

Mazzini's conception of international society resembles that of his
contemporary John Stuart Mill, whose arguments on intervention and
nonintervention Michael Doyle discusses in Chapter 12. Mill emphasized the importance of nonintervention, which he thought would allow
each people the necessary space to develop their own free institutions

over time. (Like Mazzini, he opposed the forcible "export" of democracy abroad.) Nevertheless, as Doyle explains, Mill justified military intervention in a number of circumstances, including struggles for national liberation and cases of protracted civil war. It is especially interesting to note that according to Mill, following a successful war of self-defense against a foreign despot, the liberal victor may legitimately change the vanquished state's domestic constitution, in view of removing a standing "menace to the peace." Therefore, Mill (like Kant in his argument on the "unjust enemy") did after all justify externally imposed regime change – although only following a just war, when the continued existence in power of a despotic regime would constitute a threat to international order (Mill obviously had Napoleon in mind). This scenario, however, leaves the door potentially wide open to regime change in the aftermath of just wars and humanitarian interventions in genocidal states. It also shows once again how contemporary debates on the politics and ethics of military intervention are deeply rooted in and reflect several of the tensions and contradictions of classical European thought.

Conclusion

As this brief introduction to our volume suggests, the arguments on just and unjust military intervention developed by the classical European thinkers are of enduring relevance, although evidently not all of the answers they offered will seem persuasive to contemporary audiences. The perspectives of late eighteenth and nineteenth-century thinkers like Kant, Mazzini, and Mill, who lived in an age of democratic revolution and emerging nation-states, and who attempted to balance a deep commitment to human dignity and equality with an equally strong attachment to state sovereignty and nonintervention, will probably appear more familiar to present-day readers than those of earlier generations of thinkers. Previous thinkers in the sixteenth and seventeenth centuries lacked a strong conception of national sovereignty, and their understanding of international society was still indebted to medieval notions of a universalist Christian commonwealth, or *Res publica Christiana*.

Regardless of which specific subset of the period covered in this book we focus upon, reading or re-reading the classics today will hardly provide a blueprint for determining when and how to intervene. Nevertheless, our central claim is that contemporary students, scholars, and policymakers, though divided in both time and space from these earlier philosophers and jurists, can still learn a great deal from the questions raised by the classical European thinkers, the problems they highlighted, and even the problematic character of some of the solutions they offered. The key challenge these thinkers faced in balancing the "pluralist" values of communal autonomy and independence, on the one hand, with a more universalist, or "solidarist" belief in human dignity and personal freedom, on the other, is still very much with us today. Similarly, the classical thinkers' concern with the difficulties involved in "objectively" ascertaining the existence of a just cause for military action, their warnings about its potential downsides and costs, and their emphasis on the importance of endogenous democratization and liberalization, continue to be relevant and might assist those who wish to partake in current ethical and legal debates about intervention.

We acknowledge and take seriously the admonition of contextualist scholars not to uproot the classical thinkers' arguments from their social, political, and intellectual environment. But our guiding assumption as editors of this volume is that re-reading the classics can assist us in developing *our own approaches* to the particular dilemmas surrounding intervention in our time. Put differently: our goal is not to confirm or legitimize current assumptions about intervention, but rather to open them up to critical reflection, and with the help of the classical thinkers, to explore the possibility of reconceptualizing and reappraising contemporary problems.

1 Intervention in European history, c.1520–1850

David Trim

This book is concerned with military interventions motivated at least in part by humanitarian purposes, or ethical concerns, in the "classical period" (from the early sixteenth century until around the middle of the nineteenth century). Skeptical readers may demand, before proceeding, whether, in any meaningful sense, there were any such interventions in that period. Contemporary discussion among scholars and media pundits tends to assume that "humanitarian intervention" is a recent invention. However, a close reading of history confirms that, in fact, humanitarian intervention "has a long-term history, developing from a variety of sources, over several centuries, in ways that were complex and historically contingent." Any analysis of intervention must therefore "incorporate the long-term history and must begin, not in 1990, nor in 1945, nor even the 1820s, but in the late sixteenth century."[1]

Because the essays that follow examine texts, and language and concepts, it is important to consider what key terms such as "intervention" meant in the period that is subject to scrutiny. Linguistic and literary scholars have shown that the words we use to *describe* what we witness and experience influence the ways we *think* about what has been seen and experienced; and the particular "power of language" in international relations has been demonstrated in recent scholarship.[2] Given that, as we will see, "intervention" has had different meanings over the three centuries that form the heart of this book, it is proper to ask: can events or concepts from the sixteenth century reasonably be compared, or analyzed as though comparable, to events and concepts from subsequent centuries that were described with different terminology? Is not there a grave danger of comparing like and unlike?

---

[1] D. J. B. Trim and B. Simms, "Towards a History of Humanitarian Intervention," in B. Simms and D. J. B. Trim (eds.), *Humanitarian Intervention – a History* (Cambridge University Press, 2011), pp. 24, *cf.* 8–10.
[2] S. Beaulac, *The Power of Language in the Making of International Law*, Developments in International Law (Leiden: Martinus Nijhoff, 2004), p. 46.

This chapter briefly traces the meanings of "intervention" and shows that modern usages are relatively recent. It also argues that, although etymologically the term "intervention" is of recent vintage, intellectually the concept of what is today embodied in intervention is much older. The reason why, as the editors suggest, "classical thinkers" grappled with some of the same ethical dilemmas that confront scholars and policy-makers today,[3] is because, from the sixteenth century onwards, princes (and their counselors) faced moral quandaries in their relations with other princes to a previously unprecedented extent. The terms used to characterize the nature of these ethical problems are by no means unim-portant; nonetheless, essential continuities can be identified not only in the nature of the problems facing the community of Christian princes (the *communitas Christiana* or *res publica Christiana*), but also in the solutions that were devised. Even when not called by the name "inter-vention," from the sixteenth century onward, princes and states deployed armed force against foreign princes or states, in actions that were carried out without the consent of local authorities. These actions were intended to change the domestic policies pursued by other princes or states, and were justified not by traditional *casus belli*, but on the grounds of appal-ling acts on the part of the foreign regimes in question.[4]

However, simply because actions approximating modern "interven-tions" were carried out *avant la lettre*, does not mean they necessarily were qualitatively similar. What look, on the face of it, like interventions, must be investigated more thoroughly to see whether superficial similar-ities mask deep-seated differences. While this chapter argues that there *are* crucial continuities and commonalities, both in problems and in responses, this conclusion only carries weight if one first analyses the circumstances in which princes and states "intervened." These circum-stances include the conceptual or theoretical basis for intervention, as well as *how* states intervened in practice. As we shall see, there were shifts in both the concepts and practice associated with ethically generated coercive interference in foreign countries. In particular, the grounds for intervention shifted: in the sixteenth century, it was "tyranny," i.e., egregiously tyrannical rule; by the nineteenth century, it was "mas-sacres," but often as part of a wider concept of "uncivilized" governance.

This chapter therefore provides a history of the *idea* and the *practice* of intervention, more than of the word itself. This is a necessary foundation for the chapters that follow, allowing readers to have a sense of the framework into which "classical" writings about the state, politics and

---

[3] See above, Introduction, pp. 8–10.
[4] This definition draws on but amplifies that in the Introduction, above, p. 5, fn. 15.

international relations, fit; but it also helps to illustrate why it is worth examining these classic texts. Early-modern discussions of just war (especially with regard to what constituted legitimate *casus belli*), of tyranny, and of religious toleration were all discourses from which nine-teenth- and twentieth-century discourse of ethical international politics and humanitarianism evolved.

The meaning of "intervention" in European history

In both English and French, "intervene" and cognate words are of ancient origins. In English, "intervention" dates at least to the early fifteenth century, and while the first usage of "intervene" recorded in the *Oxford English Dictionary* is from the 1580s, it is likely to have been in use earlier, given not only the earlier usage of intervention but also the currency of cognate terms in French. The origins of the terms *intervenir*, *intervenue*, *entrevenue* and *intervention* have all been ascribed by French lexicographers to the fourteenth century, and the terms were certainly in use in the sixteenth and seventeenth centuries. In both languages, the various terms were used in a variety of ways, but most were not akin to the modern sense of a coercive state act.[5] There were two exceptions.

First, in the sixteenth century, the French notion of *intervention* began to have specifically military usages. At first it was used to describe combat situations in general, but it soon began to acquire a usage at the state level, describing the act of joining a military coalition. This French usage of "intervention" was mirrored in English. When James I of England discussed the possibility of joining a European Protestant alliance in the early stages of the Thirty Years' War, for example, in letters written in French (which was starting to replace Latin as the language of diplomacy), James uses "intervention" in this sense.[6] Yet probably more often in this period (and, again, both in French and English), "intervention" refers to

[5] *Oxford English Dictionary*, online edn (hereafter *OED*), *s.v.* "intervention" and "intervene", 5; *Le grand Robert de la langue française: dictionnaire alphabétique et analogique de la langue française*, 2nd edn (1985), *s.v.* "Intervenir," "Intervention"; Frédéric Godefroy, *Dictionnaire de l'ancienne langue française, et de tous ses dialectes du IXe au XVe siècle*, 10 vols. [1880–1902] (New York: Kraus, 1961), vol. III, p. 305 ("entrevenue"), vol. IV, p. 602 ("intervenue").
[6] *Grand Robert*, s.v. "Intervenir," 2. James I to States General, 4 July 1619, in S. Rawson Gardiner (ed.), *Letters and Other Documents Illustrating the Relations Between England and Germany at the Commencement of the Thirty Years' War*, Camden Soc., XC, XCVIII (London: 1865, 1868), vol. I, p. 151; *OED*, *s.v.* "intervene," 3.a (citing a similar diplomatic usage from 1669). French only finally trumped Latin as the international language of diplomacy in the eighteenth century (*cf.* Beaulac, *Power of Language*, p. 180), but was increasingly used for diplomatic correspondence, if not for international instruments, in the early seventeenth century.

what, in the correspondence between James and his potential allies, is alternatively called an "interposition": a purely diplomatic involvement, aimed at making a general peace – i.e., mediation, rather than military intervention. Indeed, it is explicitly described, at one point in that correspondence, as intended partly to avoid the ill effects of war.[7]

The second exception foreshadows the modern concept of humanitarian intervention. It was not until the nineteenth century that "intervention," "intervene" and associated terms began to be used, at first occasionally, then regularly, to refer to coercive interference by a state in the affairs of another state, carried out, at least nominally, for ethical purposes. The shift occurred in English first, where during the 1830s "intervention" and "interventionist" began to be used this way. They were used increasingly in the 1840s and the 1850s (when John Stuart Mill wrote about intervention), and in the second half of the nineteenth century, it was commonplace for these terms to be used for coercive interference, for which the verb "intervene" also began to be used.[8] It is striking that "humanitarian" and cognate terms (words which are not recorded before the eighteenth century) likewise began to acquire their most common present-day senses in the 1840s.[9] The usage of "intervention" just described was adopted slightly later in French than in English, but French international lawyers contributed to the evolution of the specific language of "humanitarian intervention" from the 1860s onwards. This eventually gave rise, around the turn of the twentieth century, to the use, in French, of *interventionnisme* and *interventionniste* for political–military interventions. In the second half of the twentieth century, *ingérence* began to be suggested, in some French political and humanitarian circles, as an alternative to *intervention* (giving rise to the "droit d'ingérence humanitaire," proposed by Bernard Kouchner, as a French alternative to a "right of humanitarian intervention").[10] In the second half of the nineteenth century, however, "humanitarian intervention" or cognate terms existed

---

[7] Viscount Doncaster to Robert Naunton, 9 July and 7 Aug. 1619, Gardiner, *Letters and Documents*, vol. I, pp. 160–1, 163, 189, 193, 201 (the latter cited in *OED*, *s.v.* "intervention," 1.a).

[8] *OED*, *s.v.* "intervention," 1.a (citing usages from 1831, 1866) and, *infra*, "interventionist;" "intervene," 3.a (citing usages from 1874, 1880); for Mill's views, see John Bew, "'From an Umpire to a Competitor': Castlereagh, Canning and the Issue of International Intervention in the Wake of the Napoleonic Wars," in Simms and Trim (eds.), *Humanitarian Intervention*, ch. 5; and ch. 12, by Michael Doyle, below.

[9] *OED*, *s.v.* "humanitarian," A.3 and B.2.a; "humanitarianism," 2.

[10] *Grand Robert*, *s.v.* "Intervention," 2.b; "Interventionisme," 1; "Interventionniste," 1–2; and "Ingérence" (this usage of which is characterised as "spécialité"); D. J. B. Trim, "Humanitarian Intervention in Historical Perspective," in Simms and Trim, *Humanitarian Intervention – a History*, p. 398.

in English, French, and German and were used by practitioners of the relatively new discipline of international law, by scholars, and by statesmen and leaders of the various networks that lobbied for international humanitarian action by the Great Powers.[11] Meanwhile, by the 1860s, "the principles of humanity" were recognized as grounds for intervention by the Great Powers in Ottoman-ruled Crete (according to the French government).[12]

Nevertheless, as already indicated, "intervention" *was* a recognized term in the language of war and diplomacy in early-modern Christendom. And there is at least one usage which hints at something foreshadowing a concept of humanitarian intervention.

In 1619 the States General of the Netherlands wrote to James I of England concerning the "violence" and "oppression" of Protestant princes in the Holy Roman Empire by "the house of Austria" (i.e., the Habsburgs), and urging "that without the intervention and powerful help of your Majesty it is impossible" for the affairs of the Evangelical Union (of Protestant princes) to "be maintained in the Empire ... with safety."[13]

Thus, to write, as the contributors to this volume do, about intervention in the centuries *up to* John Stuart Mill, is by no means a simple anachronism. Intervention existed as a concept, albeit not the concept most often today identified with "intervention." And while the word "humanitarian" did not even exist, two relevant concepts had, as we shall see, emerged: the first was that there were actions and practices inimical to the state of being human (an idea explicitly referenced by statesmen by the middle of the seventeenth century); while the second was that, where those actions and practices were the work of princes and were appalling enough, foreign princes could intervene, in both the early-modern diplomatic *and* military senses, to correct them. It is with the history of this idea and its implementation in practice that we shall now be concerned.

---

[11] E.g., see J. A. Joyce, *The New Politics of Human Rights* (London: Macmillan, 1978), pp. 20–3; F. Rigaux, "'Humanitarian' Intervention: the Near East from Gladstone to Rambouillet," paper presented at the International School on Disarmament and Research on Conflicts, Andalo, 2002 (available at http://www.isodarco.it/courses/andalo02/paper/andalo02-rigaux1.html); and, more substantially, see D. Rodogno, *Against Massacre: Humanitarian Interventions in the Ottoman Empire, 1815–1914. The emergence of a European concept and international practice* (Princeton University Press, 2011).

[12] Quoted in Rodogno, *Against Massacre*, p. 130: "principes d'humanité."

[13] States General to James I, 21 Sept. 1619, in Gardiner, *Letters and Other Documents*, vol. II, p. 20 ("la maison d'Autriche"), p. 21 ("que sans l'intervention et puissante ayde de vostre Majeste il est impossible que les affaires de l'Union se puissent maintenir dans l'empire n'y ... avec seureté").

The practice of intervention in European history

Early-modern princes believed that the domestic affairs of other states were their legitimate business, in certain circumstances – especially when a neighboring prince was guilty of governing "tyrannically." This meant more than ordinary maladministration, malfeasance or incompetence. A tyrant, according to sixteenth-century writers, was a prince who was guilty of shedding his subjects' blood carelessly and with uncommon cruelty; and whose misrule was motivated by partisan or factional interest – in other words, one who was *not* governing for the "common good" (the *bien publique*, in French, or "common weal" in English, both loose translations of the Latin *res publica*). A tyrant was a prince whose misgovernment along these lines – his "afflicting his own people" – was so great that it resulted in the "general subversion of the political order and of the fundamental law of a realm," or the "throwing downe [of] the props and stayes of his common wealth."[14] Tyrannical actions could be those both of commission and omission. They included the perpetration of massacres or atrocities, or the widespread subversion of subjects' established liberties and privileges, in both cases whether by a prince or by his officials, with his effective consent. But tyranny was also present where the prince allowed chaos and misery to proliferate, endangering the *bien publique*, not only of the ill-governed polity, but also of its neighbors. In other words, there was a concept that tyrannical misrule could arise either from a prince's direct choice to oppress his people, or from his inability, or lack of capacity, to maintain order. Furthermore, the common weal could be either within a country, or the common good of Christians across borders, since Christendom was conceptualized as the *res publica Christiana*.

These concepts of tyranny drew on those of classical antiquity and of scholastic thinkers, such as St Thomas Aquinas, but to a great extent in earlier times they had been the subject chiefly of academic debate. From the sixteenth century onwards, however, "tyranny" became an intensely practical, rather than theoretical, matter, and this was why, as already noted, statesmen of the sixteenth and seventeenth centuries were faced with ethical issues in their foreign relations to a previously unprecedented extent.

The Protestant Reformation (starting in the late 1510s but having political effects from the 1520s) is a large part of the reason why these debates about tyranny became important in relations between princes.

---

[14] Quoted, as part of detailed analysis, in D. J. B. Trim, "'If a prince use tyrannie towards his people': Interventions on behalf of foreign populations in early-modern Europe," in Simms and Trim, *Humanitarian Intervention – a History*, pp. 34, 35.

The unity of the "commonwealth of Christendom," the *res publica Christiana*, was fractured by the Reformation. This resulted in the creation in many European polities of significant minorities, whose faith both excited the hostility of their own princes and appealed to the faith of rival princes, who felt bonds of obligation to aid suffering fellow believers. Religious persecution became far more extensive, and its effects felt far more widely across Christendom, than ever before. Where once burnings of dozens would have sufficed, the death toll needed to restore confessional unity in some countries numbered in the thousands or tens of thousands: imprisonments and formal executions increased, but massacres and outright wars also became common in some countries, and religious wars frequently involved foreign princes, as Catholic and Protestant alike intervened on behalf of communities of co-religionists in foreign countries.

The hundred-odd years from 1550 to 1650 were, without doubt, *the* era of religious war in European history and constitute "one of the most brutal and bigoted [periods] in the history of modern Europe," an era of "iron and blood."[15] Atrocities were committed on truly horrendous scales – there were 3,000 Protestant victims of the St Bartholomew's Massacre in Paris on August 24, 1572, yet this was only the worst of many massacres during the French Wars of Religion (if admittedly the worst by a considerable margin). Other notorious massacres of the Huguenots (as France's Protestants were known) included that at Vassy in 1562, which triggered the decades-long French Wars of Religion by the terror it engendered; and the copycat massacres in the provinces in the weeks after St Bartholomew's which resulted in around another 7,000 deaths.[16] France was not unique. The Spanish committed appalling atrocities in the Netherlands, with perhaps the most infamous being those at Naarden in 1572 and Antwerp in 1576. Naarden had not resisted the Spanish army, but was nevertheless the victim of "the third massacre of civilians by Spanish troops in seven months"; and the "Spanish Fury" at Antwerp was, as even scholars sympathetic to the Spanish concede, "one of the worst atrocities of the age."[17] While these

---

[15] R. B. Wernham, "Introduction" to *New Cambridge Modern History*, vol. III, *ibid.* (ed.), *The Counter-Reformation and Price Revolution 1559–1610* (Cambridge University Press, 1968), p. 1; H. Heller, *Iron and Blood: Civil Wars in Sixteenth-Century France* (Montreal and Kingston: McGill-Queen's University Press, 1991), esp. p. 5.

[16] Trim, "'If a prince use tyrannie'," p. 44.

[17] J. D. Tracy, *The Founding of the Dutch Republic: War, finance, and politics in Holland, 1572–1588* (Oxford University Press, 2008), p. 92; F. González de León, *The Road to Rocroi: Class, culture and command in the Spanish Army of Flanders, 1567–1659* (Leiden: Brill, 2009), p. 111.

were not everyday occurrences, neither were they uncommon events. They "were merely the more spectacular barbarities of an age unsurpassed for cruelty until our own day."[18]

Elizabethan intervention in Scotland and France

Massacres and widespread brutality were by no means limited to France and the Netherlands in this period, but in the late sixteenth century they were among the chief sites of violence; and, as we shall see, they were also the chief sites of intervention against "tyrannical" misrule. In France the crown veered between instituting violence against the Calvinist Huguenots, and simply allowing Catholic zealots to carry out massacres.[19] In the Netherlands, the Spanish authorities were clearly responsible for violence by commission, rather than omission, and their actions, while particularly targeted against Protestants, encompassed the population as a whole. Dutch Roman Catholics were periodically the victims of massacres by royal troops, as well as of more sustained and systematic oppression exercised through judicial proceedings, which entailed the suppression of local laws and customs.[20]

During the reign of Elizabeth I (1558–1603), England intervened in Scotland, France, and the Netherlands, on multiple occasions in each country. In Scotland, intervention was against the French Catholic regency ruling for the absent Queen Mary, later against Mary herself, and finally against the regency ruling for the then infant King James VI. Elsewhere, England acted at times unilaterally and at times in partnership with German Protestant princes: in France, against its Valois monarchs on behalf of their Protestant subjects; and in the Netherlands against its Spanish Habsburg rulers, on behalf not only of local Protestants but also of the significant portion of the Catholic population which rejected Spanish rule as tyrannical.

[18] I. M. Green, "'England's Wars of Religion'? Religious Conflict and the English Civil Wars," in J. van den Berg and P. G. Hoftijzer (eds.), *Church, Change and Revolution: Transactions of the Fourth Anglo-Dutch Church History Colloquium* (Leiden: E. J. Brill/Leiden University Press, 1991), pp. 109–17 at p. 109.
[19] There is a complex historiography: see esp. N. Zemon Davis, "The Rites of Violence: Religious Riot in Sixteenth-Century France," *P&P*, no. 59 (1973): 51–91; D. Crouzet, *Les guerriers de Dieu. La violence au temps des troubles de religion, vers 1525–vers 1610* (2 vols, Seyssel: Champ Vallon, 1990); D. Crouzet, *La Nuit de la Saint-Barthélemy. Un rêve perdu de la Renaissance* (Paris: Fayard, 1994); M. Greengrass, "Hidden Transcripts: Secret histories and personal testimonies of religious violence in the French Wars of Religion," in M. Levene and P. Roberts (eds.), *The Massacre in History* (New York & Oxford: Berghahn, 1999), pp. 69–88.
[20] Trim, "'If a prince use tyrannie'," p. 48.

   Interventions in Scotland all took the shape of armed incursions by
English armies or expeditionary forces: one in 1560, two in the spring of
1570, one in the summer of 1570 and one in 1573. They are better
described as *interventions* than as *invasions*, because no attempts were
made at (neither was there interest in) conquest – only in changing the
existing regime's policy. The grounds for intervention were partly religious. In all these years, the overtly Protestant regime of Elizabeth
consistently sought a confessionally friendly regime on its northern
border. However, in 1560, in particular, the plight of persecuted Protestants prompted anger, while the existence of an organization of
Calvinist nobles, the "Lords of the Congregation," which was defying
the French regents, made successful intervention a realistic possibility.
Elizabeth and her counselors were also concerned about the consequences of anarchy in Scotland. Disorder there endangered England –
and indeed in 1569–70, the civil war between Protestant and Catholic
in Scotland spilled over into violence in northern England, and the
English feared a recurrence when civil strife broke out in Scotland
again in 1573. The English government's fear of chaos and disorder on
the northern border was realistic, but was parochial, inasmuch as, from
their (Protestant) point of view, its root cause was (mis)government that
was partisan, factional, and thus tyrannical, whereas Catholics would
have seen things differently. It is significant, however, that what was
seen at stake was the "common wealth" both of Scotland and of
England.
   The influence of "common good" arguments about tyranny are evident from the speech of one of Elizabeth's leading ministers made to the
Privy Council in late 1559, in which he claimed that it was "necessarie . . .
for the common Wealth of o[u]r countrie, to assist openly and presently"
the Lords of Congregation "and their adherentes to expell the ffrench."
Their influence can also be seen in the widely read and very influential
Holinshed's Chronicles, in which, as Steven Gunn shows, "English interventions in the 'great warres betweene the nobilitie of Scotland divided
into factions'" were explained as the actions of "a carefull neighbour."[21]
   English interventions in France were of three types: actual armed
incursions; provision, through covert operations, of deniable military
assistance in the shape of "volunteers" and privateers who fought against
Catholic armies; and the provision of financial and material assistance to

---

[21] Nicholas Bacon, speech of 15 Dec. 1559, Huntington Library, MS EL 2573, art. 9,
   [p. 2]; S. Gunn, "The International Context," in P. Kewes, I. Archer and F. Heal (eds.),
   The Oxford Handbook to Holinshed's Chronicle (Oxford University Press, 2012), citing
   Holinshed, 1587 edn, vol. V, pp. 399, 423.

Huguenot forces. In 1562, 1576 and 1587, Elizabeth sent or arranged for armies to invade France – these were direct military interventions. In 1562, it was a royal English army, aided by squadrons of the Royal Navy, all dispatched by the queen, and directed to aid the Huguenots. In 1576 and 1587, the armies were largely of Calvinist Germans, allies both of England and of the Huguenots but paid for largely by English money and with a token presence of English soldiers; they fought to aid coalitions of both Calvinists and sympathetic Catholics. In 1568–9, 1573–4 and 1577, units of soldiers and squadrons of warships, recruited with the English government's consent and connivance, served in the Huguenot forces; and in the same conflicts, the English government dispatched arms, equipment, munitions and money, including for non-military purposes, to help repair the damage done by Catholic forces. From 1589 onwards there was more sustained military action by English armies, but by this time they were acting in alliance with the French crown, against rebellious Catholic princes, and so these cannot realistically be defined as interventions.

The English government's public statements, that it intervened in France to end banishments, deprivation of property, illegal executions and massacres, were not just propaganda. Its declarations that it was opposed, not to Catholic rule, but rather to tyrannical rule and abuse of a large minority of the population by the crown and the Catholic majority, were largely sincere, for the deeds of the English state bear out its words. Official English actions clearly had the relatively limited aim of creating a society in which Protestants could live peacefully.[22]

In 1562, Elizabeth sought territorial compensation for the army she sent to northern France to aid the Huguenots. With this exception, none of the interventionist actions of the 1560–70s aimed at conquest, annexation or the overthrow of reigning kings. Instead, England's consistent aim was to change the policies of the French kings (and their counselors): to persuade successive kings to uphold the rights and privileges which they, themselves, had granted the Huguenots in a series of royal edicts aimed at creating peace, but which the kings then either repudiated, or connived to undermine. The grounds for interventions were the persecution, imprisonment and mass murder of French Protestants. Massacres, such as those in 1572, were indeed, as one English noble described them, "horryble and tyrannical dealinges."[23]

---

[22] For this and the next two paragraphs generally, see Trim, "'If a prince use tyrannie'," pp. 42–7. It should be noted that the aim would not have seemed limited to most contemporaries.

[23] Lord Grey de Wilton to Lord Burghley, 19 Sept. 1572, British Library, Lansdowne MS 14, fo. 183r.

When French kings enforced the edicts of toleration, upheld the laws and protected all their citizens, so that "Justice [was] equallie administred," as Elizabeth herself put it, then her government was willing to engage in alliance with them; indeed, English policy was to prop up the Valois monarchs whenever possible, since they were (rightly) regarded as more likely to govern impartially, as the English saw it (i.e., to protect Protestants) than were many of their zealously Catholic subjects. However, the Elizabethan regime feared, not only for the fate of Protestants in France, but also that internal disputes, between Catholic and Protestant, would tear France apart, resulting in something like anarchy. It believed that, as well as governing in a bloody fashion, for narrow confessional interests (in other words, tyrannically), the French crown was thereby endangering the country's *bien publique* more generally, and indeed of its neighbors, including England. Elizabeth believed that the good governance (or otherwise) of France was her legitimate concern, for if France "languisshed in civill troubles" it was not to "the common benefit of . . . all christendome."[24]

Elizabethan intervention in the Netherlands

Elizabethan intervention in the Netherlands was undertaken over a prolonged period. Its grounds were general Spanish tyranny, atrocity and oppression, and the fact that these not only were so extreme that neighboring princes were obliged to step in, on behalf of the Netherlanders themselves, but also that the resultant chaos endangered the stability of neighboring polities.

As in France, English intervention in the Netherlands took various forms. In 1578 and 1585, armies were openly sent: in 1578, an army of Germans, with English funding; in 1585 a large English army that was then maintained in the Netherlands for another eighteen years. Earlier, however, from 1572, the English government had covertly helped to recruit, equip and transport to the Netherlands significant bodies of English troops, who fought nominally as volunteers in the army of the rebellious Dutch provinces. England also provided very substantial loans and grants of money to those resisting Spanish tyranny, as they consistently dubbed it.

In 1567–8, there was a revolt against Habsburg plans to extend central authority and diminish traditional liberties and privileges – a program many Netherlanders believed to be illegal and incipiently tyrannical. Calvinist violence during early protests led Philip II, the King of Spain

[24] Instructions to Lord North for embassy to Henri III, Oct. 1574, Folger Shakespeare Library, MS X.d.90, [p. 2].

and a member of the House of Habsburg, to identify the rebels as radical
Protestants, when in fact these were a minority. As a result, Philip sent a
Spanish army under the Duke of Alba, an intolerant and fervent Catholic,
who used force to destroy not only active armed resistance but also moderate protest carried out by means that were traditionally legitimate. Alba
established what became nicknamed the "Council of Troubles" or "Council
of Blood" to impose, as both he and Philip saw it, law and order on a
turbulent and disorderly region. However, the Council, with Alba's bless-
ing, went to extremes. Its actions were greatly exaggerated, both at the time
and since, but there was substance beneath Dutch denunciations.[25]

Over a thousand formal executions can be documented between 1567
and 1574, while in addition, especially as the Spanish regained control,
in 1567–8, there were many killings by soldiers that are not included in
the Council of Troubles' tally. The southern cities, "which had taken
unto them the free exercise of the religion," suffered the most. In
Valenciennes, which "had been one of the first and most zealous to
religion," the local commander immediately hanged not only those
rebels taken in arms but also "the ministers, and the richest Protestant
merchants," without trial. Later, after the establishment of the Council,
the city averaged an execution for religious or political dissidence every
other week; in the nearby city of Tournai, over four years there was on
average an execution nearly every week.[26]

In 1572, a new, more purposeful insurrection was able to drive the
Spanish and their local allies out of most of the provinces of Zeeland and
Friesland, and significant parts of the province of Holland. England
began supplying covert military and financial assistance, which helped
sustain the Dutch cause. The revolt was stalemated until late 1576, when
the "Spanish fury" in Antwerp, which was a city loyal to the Spanish
crown, inspired a more broadly based revolt across the whole of the
Netherlands, which briefly expelled all Spanish troops. But they returned
in late 1577 and hence, in 1578, Elizabeth agreed to help the "United
Provinces," as they called themselves, openly. Nearly five thousand English
troops were sent across the North Sea, under trusted commanders (albeit
still under the pretense that they were in Dutch employ). They were joined
by a large German army, raised in the Palatinate, the Calvinist state in
the Rhineland that was England's firmest ally in the Holy Roman Empire

---

[25] Trim, "'If a prince use tyrannie'," p. 48.
[26] W. Monter, "Heresy Executions in Reformation Europe, 1520–1565," in O. P. Grell
and B. Scribner (eds.), *Tolerance and intolerance in the European Reformation* (Cambridge
University Press, 1996), pp. 59–60. E. Grimeston, *A Generall History of the Netherlands*
(London: 1609), pp. 416, 417.

and had raised an army to help intervene on behalf of France's Calvinists only two years earlier. These helped to turn the tide.[27]

As Philip II pumped resources into the Netherlands, however, gradually the Dutch were driven back. Continued English military, logistical and financial aid was supplied, but on a lesser scale than in 1578, and could not match the investment by the Spanish monarchy until eventually, in 1585, Elizabeth felt obliged to go to war. From then until after the queen's death (1603), there was an English army in the Netherlands. Possibly, this period should be defined not as an intervention but as a war. However, it is hard to argue against the repeated injections of men, money and munitions up to that point as interventions. However, there was still no desire on England's part to overthrow Philip II. Indeed, Elizabeth clung to the fantasy that the United Provinces might be reconciled with the Habsburgs long after the Dutch were determined on independence. The English objective, at least up to the early 1580s, was to stop Spanish commanders and their troops wreaking havoc in the Netherlands, to force Philip to concede freedom of religion to Dutch Protestants, and then to achieve a negotiated peace, with Philip still the sovereign, but of a confessionally plural Netherlands.

Initially, the English believed that it was only Philip II's Spanish officials, far removed from the king's personal oversight, who were guilty of excesses, of which he was unaware and would have disavowed were he fully cognizant of them. For example, an anonymous tract, translated into English and printed in London in 1573, complained about the suppression of the inhabitants of the Netherlands by "the tyranny of the Duke of Alba and Spaniards."[28] Soon enough, though, English observers were sharing in the Dutch identification of Spanish rule in general as tyrannical – and of Philip II himself, rather than his viceroy, as a tyrant. This, indeed, ultimately became the source of Dutch determination to achieve independence. Another anonymous tract, published in Antwerp around 1575 and then in English translation, avowed that the king was not the father of his country, but rather a tyrant, so that his subjects were "no more bound to him."[29]

[27] See D. J. B. Trim, "Fighting 'Jacob's Warres': The employment of English and Welsh mercenaries in the European Wars of Religion: France and the Netherlands, 1562–1610" (Ph.D. thesis, University of London, 2002), ch. 4. On how the experience of intervention in the Dutch Revolt motivated thinkers like Gentili and Grotius to theorize a right of humanitarian intervention, see ch. 4 by R. Tuck in this volume, esp. pp. 104, 106.

[28] *A supplication to the Kinges Maiestie of Spayne, made by the Prince of Orange, the states of Holland and Zeland, with all other his faithfull subiectes of the low Countreys, presently suppressed by the tyranny of the Duke of Alba and Spaniards* (London: 1573).

[29] J. M. B. C. Kervyn de Lettenhove (ed.), *Relations politiques des Pays-Bas et de l'Angleterre sous le regne de Philippe II*, 11 vols. (Brussels: Académie Royale, 1882–1900), vol. VIII, p. 55, no. 3021.

In his celebrated (albeit ghostwritten) "Apology" for rebellion, published in 1581, William of Orange urged other subjects of the Habsburgs, in Spain and Italy, to follow the Dutch "example, that this tyraunt ought not to be suffered on the earth."[30]

While the personal views of Elizabeth remain opaque, there is no doubt that her chief ministers eventually agreed that Philip personally, and the Spanish generally, were guilty of tyrannical rule – and that this underpinned their policy vis-à-vis Spain over the Netherlands. The Elizabethan government's reasons for its actions were made explicit in public pronouncements, justifying the war with Spain to the rest of Europe, which will be examined below; but they were also the views expressed in private by Elizabeth's ministers and counselors. In the first half of the 1570s, they seem sincerely to have believed that they could persuade Philip II to change his policy. In the summer of 1575 an ambassador from Elizabeth encouraged William of Orange with the news that an embassy was about to be sent to Philip II "to perswade him to growe to some such composition with his subjects of the lowe Countreyes as they may be assured of their safetie and to enjoy freedome of Conscience."[31] These hopes were dashed by the "Spanish fury" at Antwerp in November 1576, when untold numbers of citizens of one of the greatest cities of Europe were killed during a three-day rampage by the Spanish army, confirming the perceptions formed by Alba's rule. Elizabeth's counselors concluded that Spanish government had become systemically tyrannical. One of her Secretaries of State declared in a memorandum in the spring of 1577 that Philip II was "violent, wilful, faithlesse, and not contented that right showlde everywhere take place."[32] The following year, the Earl of Sussex, who generally advocated a conciliatory policy to the Catholic monarchies of France and Spain, nevertheless specifically urged the queen to oppose "the suppressyen of the lowe contryes by the spanyshe tyrannye."[33]

The perception of the Spanish government's tyranny was widely held in England. The 1587 edition of the popular *Holinshed's Chronicles* was at pains to explain the long history of Anglo-Dutch friendship, trade, and

[30] *The Apologie of Prince William of Orange* (Delft, 1581), ed. H. Wansink (Leiden: 1969), p. 50, quoted in H. Dunthorne, "Resisting Monarchy: the Netherlands as Britain's school of revolution in the late sixteenth and seventeenth centuries," in R. Oresko, G. C. Gibbs and H. M. Scott (eds.), *Royal and Republican Sovereignty in Early Modern Europe: essays in memory of Ragnhild Hatton* (Cambridge University Press, 1997), p. 125n.

[31] Elizabeth, instructions to Daniel Rogers, sent as envoy to William, 7 June 1575, Cambridge University Library, MS Gg.5.36, fo. 17.

[32] Thomas Wilson to Earl of Leicester, 18 May 1577, Historical Manuscripts Commission, *Salisbury MSS*, vol. II, p. 151, no. 458.

[33] Sussex to Elizabeth, 28 Aug. 1578, Hatfield House, Cecil Papers, MS 10, fo. 33r.

alliance, Elizabeth's repeated requests that Philip "restreine the tyrannie of his governours and crueltie of his men of warre" in the Netherlands, and "disclaimed any ambition for conquest or profit, wishing only for England's neighbors to regain their 'ancient lawfull liberties'."[34] Writing in the 1610s, another English writer celebrated Elizabeth's deeds as queen, praising her policy in the Netherlands, not because she had aided fellow Protestants, but because she had aided the Dutch against the "violent tyranny" of the Spanish.[35]

The English accused the Spanish of attributing the conflict to religion, when its real cause was tyrannical misgovernment. The Elizabethan regime protested at Spanish treatment of the population of the Netherlands in general, not just of the various types of Protestants. In 1585, a justificatory proclamation, published across Europe, emphasized that, "howso ever in the beginning of these cruell persecutions, the pretence thereof was for maintenance of the Romish religion, yet they spared not to deprive very many Catholiques and Ecclesiasticall persons of their franchises and priviledges."[36] Furthermore, just as with France, there was the perception that Elizabeth had a particular obligation to the Netherlanders, because of England's "natural" position as neighbor of the Low Countries, and the long history of "much commerce and entercourse" and "speciall mutuall amitie ... betwixt the people and inhabitants" on either side of the North Sea. Elizabeth asserted a right to offer "continuall frendly advices to the king of Spaine for restraining of the tyrannie of his governours." This having been ignored, she had a right to do something about Spanish oppression.[37]

Thus, it is clear that there was self-interest, but an enlightened self-interest, in English concerns not to allow what was effectively a neighbor to fall into chaos and disorder. But underlying it all was a clear concept that Philip and his lieutenants, by their extreme misrule and abuse, had forfeited the Habsburgs' sovereign rights. Elizabeth hoped that, once corrected in their conduct, the forfeiture would be only a temporary suspension; the Dutch themselves (and some of Elizabeth's ministers, earlier than the queen), recognized that it was permanent. But regardless of the consequences of intervention, they seemed to have had no doubt that intervention was a legitimate response to tyranny.

---

[34] Gunn, "International Context," citing Holinshed, 1587 edn, vol. VI, pp. 1414–18.
[35] H[enry] H[olland], *Heroologia Anglica* (Arnhem: 1620), p. 39.
[36] Proclamation, 1 Oct. 1585, printed as *A declaration of the causes moving the queene to give aide to the oppressed in the lowe Countries* (London, 1585), p. 6.
[37] *Ibid.*, pp. 2–3, 8.

Among the many significant points about Elizabeth's interventions are their limited nature and the reluctance with which the English contemplated what might today be called "regime change."

Cromwell's "humanitarian" intervention in Savoy

The next significant intervention on ethical grounds was not until 1656, when Oliver Cromwell, Lord Protector of the British republic, mobilized commercial, diplomatic and naval power to bludgeon Savoy into halting persecution of the Vaudois (or Waldenses). Cromwell had earlier, in 1649, been guilty of initiating one of the first forced migrations, attempting with some success to drive large portions of the Catholic population of Ireland from the best agricultural land in order to make way for Protestant settlers. However, this did not mean that he was oblivious to the sufferings of other religious minorities, either at home or abroad.[38]

In the spring of 1655 the Catholic government in Turin, which had undertaken periodic persecutions of Savory's Protestant minority, initiated a series of massacres (the "bloody Easter"), in which several hundred Vaudois were killed and thousands other driven from their homes. In the end, the actual killings, hunger and freezing weather together produced a death toll that probably approached 2,000 – around 8 percent of the Vaudois population at the time. It was not genocide, as sometimes has been claimed.[39] However, "ethnic cleansing" is appropriate, especially given that, in the conflict that gave rise to the term, in the former Yugoslavia, "one of the chief markers distinguishing Croatians, Bosnians, and Serbs ... was religion," rather than language. Furthermore, the distinctive religio-cultural practices of the Vaudois separated them from their neighbors, defining them clearly as "other," despite sharing a common language and skin color. Thus, the massacre is best conceptualized as confessional-ethnic cleansing by the state.[40]

Cromwell was horrified and deeply moved. When diplomatic action by the Protestant Swiss cantons and the Dutch republic was without impact, Cromwell took action. Two embassies were dispatched to Savoy, via Paris, and naval forces were mobilized and ordered to the Ligurian Sea.

---

[38] On the Cromwellian intervention, see Trim, "'If a prince use tyrannie'," pp. 54–64.

[39] *Pace*, Giorgio Tourn, *The Waldensians: the first 800 years* (trans. C. P. Merlino, ed. C. W. W. Arbuthnot) (Turin: Claudiana, 1980), p. 124.

[40] See Trim, "'If a prince use tyrannie'," p. 57, quotation from fn. 98; and, for "religio-cultural practices" as fault lines within communities, Richard Bonney and D. J. B. Trim "Introduction," in Bonney and Trim (eds.), *The Development of Pluralism in Modern Britain and France* (Oxford and Bern: Peter Lang, 2007), pp. 36, 64–5.

In this case, the threat of force sufficed, especially when combined with massive diplomatic pressure, exerted through Savoy's giant neighbor, France, which was told that the British alliance it hoped for, in war against Spain, would not be forthcoming unless Paris reined in Turin.

It is worth stressing, however, that, aiding the Vaudois did little or nothing to aid the British republic's national security, its geopolitical position, or its strategic interests, even given that Cromwell's policy was war against the Spanish monarchy because he believed the latter's Catholicism made it, together with the Papacy, Antichrist. The Vaudois were too weak to be useful future allies in any renewed war of religion, whereas Savoy, as English and British rulers throughout the seventeenth century knew well, was a rare potential Catholic ally against the Habsburgs. British commerce with Savoy was of minimal importance and the intervention was a distraction from Cromwell's strategy of military operations in Flanders and the Caribbean. There was little to be gained, by Cromwell, his government or by Britain, and much to be lost, by intervening on behalf of the Vaudois. Cromwell's "laying aside [of] all other Reasons of State" to aid the Vaudois (as one of his diplomats described it), is an example of acting for ethical reasons rather than *raison d'état*.[41] Intervention often reflects a degree of self-interest on the part of the intervening power, whether roughly balanced by altruistic considerations, or outweighing them – though as I have argued elsewhere, to distinguish between them is often a false dichotomy.[42] However, some interventions are undertaken out of concerns that can rightly be termed, if not humanitarian, at least "humane."

In fact, the British intervention in Savoy is perhaps the first to which the term "humanitarian" could reasonably be applied. Cromwell had a sense of solidarity with the Vaudois that transcended the physical and figurative distance that separated England and Savoy. Samuel Morland, one of the two ambassadors sent to Turin, writing of Cromwell's concern for the plight of the Vaudois noted that he "was often heard to say, *That it lay as near or rather nearer his heart than if it had concerned his nearest and dearest Relations*." Cromwell expressed similar sentiments to the French ambassador in London, declaring that he felt for the Vaudois as if they were his near kin.[43]

---

[41] Samuel Morland, *The History of The Evangelical Churches Of the Valleys of Piedmont* (1658), sig. A2v.

[42] Trim, "Humanitarian Intervention in Historical Perspective," pp. 398–401, esp. 401.

[43] *Ibid.*, p. 552; C. H. Firth, *Oliver Cromwell and the Rule of the Puritans in England* ([1900]; London: Oxford University Press, 1953), p. 371.

There is no question that this solidarism was largely confessional in nature. Indeed, Morland praised the Lord Protector precisely because he had shaped policy to the one end, "that Your own Interest may appear one and the same with the Universal Interest of the Evangelical Churches in their respective Nations"; and Cromwell himself urged members of the British Parliament to "have a brotherly fellow-feeling of the interest of all the Protestant Christians in the world."[44] Nevertheless, it is clear from Cromwell's emotive language that he conceived of the Vaudois as fellow suffering human beings, rather than simply types of Protestant martyr-heroes. Both Morland and the Dutch ambassador to the British republic record the Lord Protector's heartfelt language about the Vaudois, referring to "the poor people of Piedmont" and "the poor people's calamities."[45] The Dutch ambassador in London reported being told by English officials that plans for a treaty of alliance with France and war with Spain were well advanced, but all were put to one side, because, for Cromwell, putting a halt to "the inhuman murther of the Vaudois" was the first priority.[46] Morland praised his master by contrasting Cromwell with "those other Princes … who had little regard … to the honest Maximes of Humane Policy."[47] This language comes at second hand, but the fact that both an English and a foreign source use the language of humanity (and inhumanity) about Cromwell's thinking suggest it was used, if not by Cromwell himself, then in his government circles. In sum, Britain intervened in Savoy in 1655 because the actions of the Duke of Savoy were perceived as inhumane. Religious fellow feeling played a large part in what actions were and were not seen in terms of humanity, but the very concept that some kinds of state behavior were incompatible with humane policy is notable.

Westphalia and "intervention": the Imperial Council and guarantor powers

The Cromwellian intervention ended with Britain and the Swiss Confederation guaranteeing those provisions of the Treaty of Pinerolo (1655), concluded between the Duke of Savoy and the Vaudois, by

---

[44] Quoted in J. W. Thompson and S. K. Padover, *Secret Diplomacy. A Record of Espionage and Double-Dealing: 1500–1815* (London: Jarrolds, 1937), p. 83; Morland, *History of The Evangelical Churches*, sig. A2v.

[45] Morland, *History of The Evangelical Churches*, p. 552; Nieupoort to Ruysch, 28 Jan. 1656, in Thomas Birch (ed.), *A collection of the State Papers of John Thurloe*, 7 vols. (London: n.p., 1742), vol. IV, p. 433.

[46] Despatch, 17 Sept. 1655, in Birch, *State Papers of John Thurloe*, vol. IV, p. 18.

[47] Morland, *History of The Evangelical Churches*, sig. A3r.

which the former granted the latter religious toleration. Sadly, this was by no means the last persecution of the Vaudois by their duke, and in 1704 both Great Britain and the Dutch republic used diplomatic, rather than military, pressure to oblige Savoy to concede to the Vaudois the "entire and inviolable observance" of their religion, which they guaranteed by treaty.[48] In 1704, as in 1655, the British, Swiss and Dutch governments, in becoming guarantor powers, were following a precedent set in "the peace treaties of Westphalia [which] specifically included guarantees of freedom of conscience for some religious minorities within the Empire – and made some states from outside the Empire guarantors of the rights of religious minorities in other states."[49] This is at odds with some of the prevalent ideas about the nature of the Westphalian settlement and it reinforces the point, argued by scholars such as Stephen Krasner, Andreas Osiander, Brendan Simms, and others, that a new concept of absolute state sovereignty was not really inaugurated by the treaties of Westphalia; and as I have stressed elsewhere, it certainly did not create a norm of nonintervention as part of the concept of sovereignty. Indeed, in the case of treaty guarantees of minorities, "not only was sovereignty not absolute, but interventions actually were legally mandated."[50]

The Westphalian guarantor powers of the rights of minorities within the Holy Roman Empire were Sweden for Protestants, and France for Catholics. In 1660 this model was followed again when, by the terms of the Treaty of Oliva, Brandenburg-Prussia and Sweden guaranteed the rights of Protestants in Polish Prussia. Meanwhile, within the Holy Roman Empire, the treaties of Westphalia established new mechanisms to check tyrannical power. First established in 1498 as an instrument of imperial power, the Imperial Aulic Council (*Reichshofrat*) had its composition altered at Westphalia, making it both a more representative and a far more consensual body. In consequence, in the late seventeenth century and throughout the eighteenth century it was more active and

---

[48] Quoted in Randolph Vigne, "Richard Hill and the Saving of Liberty of Conscience for the Vaudois," in Bonney and Trim, *Development of Pluralism*, p. 163. See Trim, "'If a prince use tyrannie'," p. 61.

[49] Trim, "Humanitarian Intervention in Historical Perspective," pp. 381–2.

[50] *Ibid.* See, e.g., S. Krasner, "Rethinking the Sovereign State Model," *Review of International Studies* 27 (2001), 17–42; A. Osiander, "Sovereignty, International Relations, and the Westphalian Myth," *International Organization* 55 (2001), 251–87; B. Teschke, *The Myth of 1648: Class, Geopolitics, and the Making of Modern International Relations* (London & New York: Verso, 2003); Beaulac, *Power of Language*; B. Simms, "'A false Principle in the Law of Nations': Burke, state sovereignty, [German] liberty, and intervention in the Age of Westphalia," in Simms and Trim, *Humanitarian Intervention – a History*, pp. 89–110.

assertive, intervening in the affairs of individual sovereign territories to defuse confessional tension and constrain tyrannical rulers.[51]

On numerous occasions over the century following Westphalia, ruling princes were deposed, or suspended from power, by the Council, "for bankruptcy, imbecility, disturbing the peace, treasonable correspondence with outside powers – and abuse of power." They included Ferdinand-Karl-Franz of Hohenems-Vaduz, "deposed in 1683 for excessively cruel persecution of witches"; his "indictment specifically mentioned his use of torture." William-Hyacinth of Nassau-Siegen "was sanctioned in 1709 for mistreating his Protestant subjects." The "tyrannical Duke Karl Leopold of Mecklenburg" was sanctioned in 1719 and "eventually deposed in 1728" on the grounds of his repeated attempts, using harsh measures, to deprive his subjects "of their age-old privileges, freedoms and rights."[52] Most of these interventionist actions did not involve military force, and so do not fall under the umbrella of the military interventions with which this volume deals; though it has to be observed that behind the legal mechanisms of the Empire was the implicit threat of force. In any event, these interventions are important in this context because they show that the notion, clearly evident in the late sixteenth century and in Cromwell's actions, that some types of princely behavior were simply too extreme to be countenanced by other princes, was widely accepted. Despite the Westphalian "myth," this remained true in the century after Westphalia – the century in which many of the classical texts, examined in the chapters that follow, were written.

There was at least one military intervention in the eighteenth century, carried out under the actual Westphalian paradigm. As noted earlier, the Elector of Brandenburg had guaranteed the rights of Protestants in Polish Prussia. In 1724, the kingdom of Prussia, as it had now become, mobilized troops to force the Polish government to protect Protestants in Thorn from Catholic violence. There had been an outbreak of communal violence, which resulted in the seizure of Protestant property (including the last Lutheran church) and judicial murder of over a dozen of the leaders of the town's Lutheran population. But the rights of minorities, guaranteed by treaty, were regarded as a solemn matter. When Prussian troops took up positions along his border, King Augustus of Poland agreed to restore the Protestant church, and in 1725 agreed to the

[51] Trim, "Humanitarian Intervention in Historical Perspective," pp. 382–3; Simms, "Burke, State Sovereignty, and Intervention," pp. 92–3.
[52] Simms, "Burke, State Sovereignty, Liberty, and Intervention," pp. 93–5.

negotiation of a new treaty regulating the position of Protestants in Poland, with Britain, as well as Prussia, as a guarantor power.[53]

Nineteenth-century interventions

There had been two nineteenth-century military interventions before John Stuart Mill wrote: in Greece and Belgium. In Greece, a ten-year-long revolt resulted, in 1830, in Greek independence from the Ottoman Empire, but only after Britain, France and Russia sent an allied fleet that destroyed the Ottoman fleet, and after France and Russia then intervened with land forces. In the Low Countries, the independence of Belgium was imposed on the Netherlands by more limited military and naval action by France and Britain.

Recent scholarship highlights that, though the Greek population had suffered harsh repression by Ottoman military forces since the 1770s, Ottoman atrocities were exaggerated by European journalists, poets and artists, particularly in Britain and France. The sympathies of these "philhellenes" for the Greeks of classical antiquity helped to blind many of them to the realities of modern Greece.[54] However, by the early 1820s massacres were undoubtedly taking place, as the Ottomans, increasingly frustrated, took a harsher line against rebellious Hellas. As Gary Bass argues, places such as Scio (an island whose population was put to the sword in 1822) "became as notorious," in their time, "as Guernica or Srebrenica" in the 1930s and 1990s: "no longer just the name of a place, but a synonym for massacre of the worst kind."[55]

The situation worsened, from a humanitarian perspective, in the mid-1820s with the involvement of Mohammed Ali, pasha of Egypt – theoretically a vassal of the Ottoman Sultan (and not himself a Turk), but creator of a dynamic political regime and nascent new nation state in Egypt. For political reasons, Mohammed Ali deployed Egypt's considerable military and naval resources to help Constantinople subdue the Greeks. In 1825 his son Ibrahim occupied the Morea with a largely Egyptian army. As well as changing the Russians' geopolitical view of the situation (making them pro-Greek independence, having previously been against), this also resulted in a ratcheting up of violence and an increase in atrocities, as Ibrahim was determined to crush the revolt.

---

[53] A. C. Thompson, "The Protestant Interest and Humanitarian Intervention," in Simms and Trim, *Humanitarian Intervention – a History*, pp. 81–3.

[54] Rodogno, *Against Massacre*, pp. 63, 65, 72, 76. *Cf.* G. Bass, *Freedom's Battle: The Origins of Humanitarian Intervention* (New York: Alfred A. Knopf, 2008), pp. 78 *et passim*.

[55] Bass, *Freedom's Battle*, pp. 67–72 at 67.

As Davide Rodogno notes, if Ottoman oppression was still exaggerated, it was undoubtedly "pitiless": "There were wholesale massacres …, extreme cruelty in the treatment of prisoners, and the enslavement of women and children."[56] In Western Europe the perception was now widespread "that the Turks had resorted to … 'inhuman butchery' in the Morea."[57]

In January 1826 the British Foreign Secretary, Canning, wrote to the British ambassador at Constantinople that Britain now saw "a new ground" for what he termed "interference" (rather than intervention). These grounds for action were:

much higher than any that we have yet had open to us – I mean the manner in which the war is now carried on in the Morea – the character of barbarism and barbarization which it has assumed. Butchering of captives we have long witnessed on both sides of the contest …. But the selling into slavery – the forced conversions – the dispeopling [*sic*] of Christendom … these are … facts new in themselves, new in their principle, new and strange and hitherto inconceivable in their consequences, which I do think may be made the foundation of a new mode of speaking if not acting.[58]

In a sense, Canning was right that they led to a new mode of speaking, for Britain's new willingness to countenance action by the Great Powers on behalf of Greece gave rise to the new nineteenth-century terminology of intervention, replacing "interference."[59] The 1820s also marked a renewal of the language of common humanity as a basis for intervention (even while religious solidarism continued to be significant); thus, for example, in Britain *The Times* justified the dispatch of the allied fleet to Greece in 1827 partly on the grounds of "humane and Christian feeling."[60]

The fleet was sent by the terms of the Treaty of London of July 1827, by which Britain, France and Russia agreed to aid the Greeks, but only to become a semi-independent province, with the Sultan retaining some rights. As with the early-modern interventions, there was a pronounced preference for changing policies, not regimes. The Greeks accepted the terms, but the Ottomans rejected them. By the autumn of 1827, the allied fleet was in Greek waters, and when Ibrahim's forces continued hostilities, the Egypto-Turkish fleet was attacked and almost entirely

[56] Rodogno, *Against Massacre*, p. 80.
[57] Bew, "Intervention in the Wake of the Napoleonic Wars," p. 132.   [58] Quoted *ibid*.
[59] This was also the term used in 1831, when the jurist James Mackintosh opposed intervention, even to stop "acts of flagrant injustice and cruelty," on the grounds that even if "such interference were justified, there would be no end of them": quoted in Bew, "Intervention in the wake of the Napoleonic Wars," p. 124.
[60] Quoted in Bew, "Intervention in the wake of the Napoleonic Wars," p. 133.

destroyed by the allied fleet at the Battle of Navarino. This cut off Ottoman and Egyptian land forces from relief or reinforcement by sea. The following year, a Russian army invaded Ottoman-ruled Bulgaria, while a French expeditionary corps landed in Greece. Recognizing that he could not resist the Great Powers, the Sultan conceded Greek independence, in the hope of preserving the rest of the Ottoman Empire.

In 1830 there was a nationalist revolt in the southern half of the Kingdom of the Netherlands, which had been retained by Spain after the Dutch Revolt. It had remained under Habsburg rule until 1815 when the Congress of Vienna rewarded the new King of the Netherlands for his support of the allied cause against France by giving him the southern Netherlands. While half the south spoke the same language as the northern Netherlands (Dutch), the other half spoke French, and Catholicism was the majority, rather than minority religion in the south, unlike in the north. There were no significant massacres or atrocities in the southern Low Countries, but draconian Dutch religious and linguistic policies evoked considerable opposition, to which northern officials responded with repressive measures.[61] The fact that the Belgians (as they were soon to style themselves) were able to portray the Dutch regime as illiberal and repressive was to be to their advantage in garnering support in Britain and France. However, it is also striking that part of their complaint was that the King of the Netherlands was not ruling in the interest of all, but only of his northern, Dutch-speaking and Protestant, subjects. In other words, his rule was portrayed as illegitimate partly on the same grounds as the Spanish regime in the Low Countries 250 years earlier.

The so-called Belgian revolution of August 1830 developed after "Riots in Brussels triggered additional unrest as the situation in the Belgian province developed its own dynamic." William I's initial response was indecisive, but he eventually ordered troops "to march on Brussels." Fighting in the streets ensued and the resultant bloodshed both "stiffened Belgian resistance" and discredited the Dutch abroad. A provisional government was established in September and independence declared on October 4, 1830.[62] William I now turned to his cousin Frederick William of Prussia for assistance, but the latter referred him to the other Great Powers: Austria, Great Britain, France, and Russia.[63]

---

[61] J. Rogiers and N. C. F. van Sas, "Revolution in the North and South, 1780–1830," in J. C. H. Blom and E. Lamberts (eds.), *History of the Low Countries*, trans. J. C. Kennedy (Oxford: Berghahn, 1999), p. 307.

[62] *Ibid.*, p. 309. *Cf.* display on the Belgian revolt at the *Legermuseum* (army museum), Delft.

[63] C. B. Wels, "The Foreign Relations of the Netherlands between 1813 and 1945," in H. F. van Panhuys et al. (eds.), *International Law in the Netherlands* (Alphen aan den Rijn:

In November, the Conference of London convened, with representatives from all five Great Powers and the Netherlands present. On the face of it, there was little reason to think they would do other than maintain the status quo. Yet in the end, partly because of the perception that the Dutch had governed in a brutal, partisan and illiberal fashion, and partly because, as a result of the Greek intervention, the British government was now more willing to act on behalf of oppressed nationalities than it had been up to the mid-1820s, on December 20, 1830, the conference recognized the independence of Belgium.[64]

Despite the Great-Power consensus, the following year William I dispatched his army into what had been his southernmost provinces, in the so-called "ten days campaign." France responded by sending an expeditionary force into Belgium, while Britain used the Royal Navy to impose a blockade of the Scheldt, a vital waterway for the whole of the Low Countries. Before the end of 1831, the Dutch king recognized the reality of the situation and ceased military action in Belgium. Belgian independence had been secured by Anglo-French military intervention. That intervention was a response, not to large-scale massacres or atrocities, but to what was seen as uncivilized government – something that might be grudgingly stomached in other parts of the world but was no longer acceptable in Western Europe.[65]

Conclusion

On the whole, in the period up to *c*.1850 (the effective end point of this volume), intervening states were more likely to seek a change in a regime's policy, or practice, rather than to change the regime itself. The results of interventions were sometimes codified in treaties that guaranteed the rights of groups which had been subject to gross oppression or atrocities, and provided a basis for future interventions, if need be. There were exceptions: English acquiescence in the assertion of independence by the Netherlands; the Great Powers' imposition of Greek independence in 1830; and Anglo-French enforcement of Belgian independence in 1831. They *were* exceptions, however, which were motivated by extreme Spanish intransigence in the late sixteenth century; by Ottoman refusal to accept Great-Power mediation, and renewal of

Sijthoff & Noordhoff, for T. M. C. Asser Institute, 1978), pp. 51–52. Rogiers and Van Sas, "Revolution in the North and South," p. 309.

[64] Wels, "Foreign Relations of the Netherlands," pp. 53–4; Rogiers and Van Sas, "Revolution in the North and South," pp. 309–10.

[65] Rogiers and Van Sas, "Revolution in the North and South," p. 310; Wels, "Foreign Relations of the Netherlands," pp. 55–6, 58.

hostilities against the Greek rebels at a key point in the 1820s; and by a partly fortuitous conjunction of events in the 1830s, that included, however, distaste at Dutch misrule, which, though moderate compared to that in Eastern Europe, was seen as unacceptable by the elites in London and Paris.

As we have seen, interventions generally aimed at enforcing conformity to common standards of reasonable conduct. This was not just true of the early-modern period, but also extended into the nineteenth century. None of the five interventions in the Ottoman Empire in the eighty years after the Greek war of independence had as their objectives either annexing territories to the European powers or creating them as independent states.

In the early-modern era, reverence for divinely ordained princes meant that their removal could only be contemplated by fellow sovereigns with the utmost reluctance. In the nineteenth century, Europeans believed that the Ottomans, albeit not yet completely civilized, were nevertheless certainly not savages and so could be shepherded, or nursed, into a fully civilized state, whereas some of their subject people were perceived as barbaric or savage, needing the supervision of a more civilized regime. The Ottomans were regarded as "at best, half civilised" and therefore legitimately subject to interventions to halt massacres. In a worst-case scenario, the effort to enforce civilized governance would be too much, and so, as a "last-resort measure," at times it would be necessary to enforce the concession of independence to subject peoples who were themselves close to civilized (as in Greece).[66] But there was also a recognition that Ottoman history and culture meant they were close to being able to govern "in accordance with the so-called 'standard of civilization'," and in consequence, on several occasions, as in Macedonia in the first decade of the twentieth century, the European powers instead made (as they thought) efforts to tutor the Ottomans in more humane and civilized governance – especially of peoples who themselves were regarded as being close to savage.[67]

Nevertheless, from the second half of the nineteenth century onwards, there was increasing willingness to contemplate real regime change. This probably was in part because of a growing number of interventions in Africa and Southeast Asia – whether to stop slavery, or simply to impose

[66] Rodogno, *Against Massacre*, pp. 22–3.
[67] Mark Mazower, *Hitler's Empire: How the Nazis ruled Europe* (New York: Penguin Press, 2008), p. 586. See D. Rodogno, "The European Powers' Intervention in Macedonia, 1903–1908: an instance of humanitarian intervention?," in Simms and Trim (eds.), *Humanitarian Intervention*, pp. 205–25.

"civilized" government. Yet there was also an increased willingness to defend ideals, initially of liberty and civilization, but eventually the ideal of humane treatment – of what by the end of the century not only were, but also were called, humanitarian ideals. However, African and most (though not all) Asian rulers were regarded as manifestly savage, and therefore needing to be subjugated. This attitude towards intervention was underpinned by developments in international law which created a two-tier system of "civilized" and "uncivilized" states.[68] It is striking that, at the very end of the century, Americans, in effect, defined the Spanish Empire (which they perceived as corrupt and moribund) as being like the Ottomans – they had no doubt that making Cuba independent, and colonizing Puerto Rico and the Philippines, was the right way to proceed, rather than trying to enforce "civilized" governance on Spanish colonial authorities. Undoubtedly, at times, such attitudes underpinned imperialism, yet they also held out the possibility of relief for oppressed peoples.

In the last forty-odd years, brutal regimes have been overthrown and replaced in Uganda, Cambodia, Haiti, Sierra Leone and Iraq, and independent states created and maintained in Bangladesh, East Timor, and (in effect) Kurdistan and Kosovo, all in response, to a greater or lesser extent, to humanitarian abuses and "mass atrocities" – in response, in fact, to "tyranny," in the political language of early-modern Europeans, and "massacres," as nineteenth-century Europeans would have put it.

It could be argued that the scale of atrocity in East Pakistan, Uganda and Kampuchea in the 1970s was on a greater scale than anything witnessed during the sixteenth to nineteenth centuries, so that unprecedented measures were called for; and that the responses in these latter cases should not be seen as normative precedents for future action. It might also then be argued that, in modern interventions, there has too often been insufficient regard for complex political and social circumstances, and too great a willingness to impose settlements which, though they satisfy a public that both consumes and constructs humanitarian tragedies, are unlikely to last – and that the early-modern approach, which rarely aimed at full-fledged regime change, could profitably be followed. To be sure, one might also argue that early-modern reverence for sovereignty (albeit of individuals who were, as it was supposed, divinely mandated, rather than of humanly constructed states) meant there was too great a willingness to perpetuate in power regimes that had shown themselves all too ready to "breake the bonds of pietie

---

[68] Trim, "Humanitarian Intervention in Historical Perspective," pp. 395–6; Rodogno, *Against Massacre*, pp. 22, 48; *cf.* Mazower, *Hitler's Empire*, p. 586.

and justice."[69] Nevertheless, the early-modern approach did not simply reflect concepts of sovereignty with which few today would sympathize. With hindsight there is a good case that they also were motivated by a mindset fundamentally different to that underlying many recent interventions: those who acted to stop "inhuman murther" regarded intervention as a temporary measure that would (to use terminology that would never have been used in the sixteenth century) help states to exercise their sovereignty responsibly and appropriately – without fundamentally changing the target state's domestic political structure.

Regardless of how they are interpreted, there is no doubt that interventions, in the three centuries or so in which the authors examined in this book wrote, were in some ways more limited in their objectives than interventions in the century and a half or so since John Stuart Mill wrote. Yet interventions of the period were regularly intended to arrest appalling oppression or atrocities and to prevent their recurrence. These were not modest aims. In sum, in the era of the "classic" texts, governments – whether of the polities of the *Res publica Christiana* or of the "Great Powers" of the "Concert of Europe" – had to come to grips with the same problem that continues to challenge the twenty-first-century "international community." In the face of appalling actions, which are conducted by, connived at, or passively permitted by other governments, and which shock the conscience of mankind, *what can be done?* Although presuppositions about the nature of government have changed and concepts of both "conscience" and "mankind" have likewise evolved since the sixteenth century, nevertheless, there are numerous continuities. This is true not only in the sorts of actions that have been regarded as unacceptable, but also in how governments have responded (and, indeed, in the problems they face in responding) to egregious religious persecution, widespread massacres, ethnic cleansing, or outright genocide. It is precisely for this reason that, despite the difficulties in comparing texts of different ages, produced in very different cultural contexts, scholars will be rewarded by careful readings of "classic" authors, whether Vitoria and Suarez, Gentili and Grotius, Pufendorf and Vattel, or Burke, Mazzini and Mill. Their texts continue to be relevant to debates about intervention in the twenty-first century.

---

[69] Anon., *Vindiciae, contra tyrannos* (London: 1588), sig. B6v.

2   War in the face of doubt: early modern classics and the preventive use of force

Ariel Colonomos

Classical thinkers in the just war tradition, from Augustine to the present day, aim to limit war's scope and moderate its effects. More particularly, authors in this tradition – including those of the early modern period that are the focus of this chapter – have elaborated specific guidelines for restricting the resort to force, and constraining tactics during war. They assign normative significance to criteria like just cause, legitimate authority, and proportionality. They call for distinguishing combatants from civilians. Crucially, their arguments have laid some of the foundations for the development of modern international law.

For example, consider the rule of just cause, which is often invoked in discussions of self-defense. Befitting the just war tradition's origins in Christian culture, this criterion echoes Christian principles about the necessity of preserving one's life. Thomas Aquinas concluded that defending oneself against the immediate attack of a potential murderer is justified even if it results in the killing of the assailant.[1] Early modern authors either implicitly or explicitly use this analogy in contemplating whether self-defense is a just cause for war. The relation between just cause and self-defense is also reflected in contemporary international law: where a state has been invaded or targeted, it may retaliate as part of the principle of self-defense.

Of course, not all defensive wars are just, given the multitude of other criteria on which this assessment is ultimately based. Moreover, the principle that self-defense constitutes a just cause admits of possible extensions, which raise further questions. One such extension is the question of "preventive" war. Are wars that anticipate, rather than immediately respond to, an armed attack on a state's territory unjust? Not necessarily. Under certain conditions, striking first as an attempt to prevent a future attack might be justified – but precisely identifying those conditions poses numerous challenges.

---

[1] Thomas Aquinas, *Summa Theologiae*, vol. IX (ed. Marcus Lefébure) (Cambridge University Press, 2006), Question 64: "Homicide."

In this chapter, I examine the arguments on preventive war developed by four early modern thinkers: Gentili (1552–1608), Suarez (1548–1617), Grotius (1583–1645), and Vattel (1714–68). By any measure, these authors are among the most important of the just war tradition – and they are probably *the* most important ones in the period covered by this book. Each of them has crucially shaped the development of modern international legal and political thought. Their framing of legal and ethical discussions about war continues to be highly relevant for present-day international relations, and especially for the external behavior of liberal democracies. However, none of them fully resolves the enigma of preventive war, which points to a limitation in their accounts of what constitutes a *just cause*. That, in turn, draws our attention to a larger failing of the just war tradition: namely, its inability to adequately address certain epistemic and justificatory problems inherent in war. Uncertainty and ambiguity not only threaten to overwhelm the distinction between pre-emptive and preventive war, but also to undermine the very project of justifying war. Studying these classical authors therefore also helps us understand some pitfalls in current debates about just war, by drawing our attention to the normative significance of uncertainty.[2]

Preventive war and the just war tradition

The focus of this chapter is on preventive war. A preventive war is a war of anticipation, fought by a state in order to prevent future attacks on the state itself. *Prevention* differs from *pre-emption*. Preventive war is waged against remote threats. One example of a preventive use of force is an attack against another state's facilities (e.g., today, its chemical or nuclear laboratories) which produce weaponry that could be used in future attacks. The logic of pre-emption is different: war is pre-emptive when the danger is imminent, for example when a state attacks a foreign army with hostile intentions that is massed at its borders. Preventive and pre-emptive uses of force can both result in either full-scale war, or in more limited military operations, such as aerial incursions.

The terms "preventive war" and "pre-emptive war" were coined in the twentieth century. However, both terms involve justification based on anticipation. Suarez, Gentili, Grotius and Vattel all wrote extensively on this topic. There are important similarities in their thought. For instance, they all raise questions about the distinction between immediate and

---

[2] This chapter draws on a broader project by the author on the same topic. See A. Colonomos, *The Gamble of War: Is it Possible to Justify Preventive War?* (New York/London: Palgrave Macmillan, 2013).

remote threats. Nevertheless, each envisaged different justifications for anticipation and saw the legitimacy of anticipatory interventions somewhat differently. Hence these thinkers would not agree on a common standard for justifying anticipatory war. Their differences are instructive, since they foreshadow and, to a certain extent, explain contemporary debates about the definition and status of anticipatory force.

The classics of the just war tradition, and especially the four seminal thinkers discussed in this chapter, raise at least three important questions for contemporary discussions of preventive war. First, are wars of anticipation offensive or defensive? Second, can wars of anticipation be justified based on self-defense? Resolving these questions, I shall argue, requires criteria for distinguishing between preventive and pre-emptive wars. Third, can past wrongdoing by the target state justify an anticipatory attack on that state, if such an attack would not otherwise be justified as self-defense? This last question essentially asks whether several insufficient justifications for war (e.g., punishment and remote self-defense) can be combined to provide a sufficient justification. As we shall see, Suarez, Gentili, Grotius, and Vattel each offer distinct answers to these questions; and although none of them satisfactorily resolves all three, each of them advances our understanding of the normative dilemmas involved.

Francisco Suarez: combining prevention and punishment

For the sixteenth-century Spanish philosopher and theologian Francisco Suarez, when a state is attacked, it has the right to go to war. Acting in self-defense justifies military action, because "all laws allow the repelling of force by force."[3] When writing about the anticipatory use of force, Suarez distinguishes between two types of military action: first, anticipatory wars of an offensive character, or anticipatory "wars of aggression" (his arguments in this regard are relevant to the current debate about *prevention*); and second, anticipatory wars in self-defense (his arguments on this matter foreshadow present-day arguments about *pre-emption*).

Suarez claims that "wars of aggression," where a state strikes first without being attacked, are sometimes acceptable. In his view, "such wars [are] often necessary to a state in order to ward off acts of injustice and to hold enemies in check."[4] The essence of this argument resembles subsequent justifications of preventive war: enemies are a threat to the

[3] F. Suarez, *A Work on the Theological Virtues Faith, Hope and Charity* (Oxford: Clarendon Press, 1944). See esp. "Disputatio XIII," in chapter *On Charity*, I, 1, 4, p. 803.
[4] *Ibid.*, I, 5, p. 804.

sovereign and the injustice they will inflict upon his state must be anticipated and prevented. In such cases, recourse to arms is justified by
natural law. But Suarez construes the considerations that endow war
with permissibility quite broadly, to include any "molestation" of the
state.[5] This broad construction, in turn, informs Suarez's conclusions
about what is an acceptable "aggressive war."[6] If a state feels threatened
by an enemy who has already committed a wrong, the state is authorized
to intervene militarily against this enemy. Such a war is both preventive
and punitive. For Suarez, specific injuries that can justify such preventive
and punitive war include the seizure of the Prince's assets, the denial of
rights normally accorded to states, or even grave assaults on the state's
reputation and honor.[7]

Where crimes have already been committed or precedents set, the
thinking goes, the state has an imperative to prevent the commission of
future crimes. In such a case, the use of punishment prevents a danger
from being realized. This thinking involves backward-looking reasons
(e.g., punishment for a past wrongful action) and forward-looking
reasons (e.g., the deterrence of future wrongdoing). Yet, in punishment
theory as well as just war theory, these two types of reasons can become
intertwined. The question is whether this intertwining magnifies the
force of each type of reason. Suarez gives the example of the case of
"overt enemies of a sovereign" (e.g. pirates) who have previously committed wrongs and are currently located within the boundaries of a
foreign territory, "some imperfect state."[8] In such circumstances, war
is "not only" a matter of self-defense, Suarez says, but also an instance of
permissible "aggression, vengeance, and punishment."[9] Suarez's argument also implies that an enemy's location on a foreign territory where
no legitimate authority prevails – today, we would speak of "failed
states" – augments the threat posed to others, therefore strengthening
the justification for preventive war.

In recent years, arguments similar to those developed by Suarez have
been used to justify the 2001 US intervention in Afghanistan, the 2006
Israeli intervention in Lebanon, and the Israeli policy of targeted killings
of Palestinian militants. The United States and Israel both considered
the entities targeted by intervention – Afghanistan under Taliban rule,
contemporary Lebanon, and the Palestinian territories – to lack fully
legitimate and effective authority structures, which arguably made it
easier for alleged terrorists to take shelter there and plot future attacks.
In the case of Afghanistan, evidence shows that Al-Qaeda had in fact

[5] *Ibid.*, IV, 1, p. 816.   [6] *Ibid.*, I, 6, p. 804.   [7] *Ibid.*, p. 817.
[8] *Ibid.*, II, 3, p. 807.   [9] *Ibid.*, II, 3, p. 807.

planned further attacks on the United States.[10] In the case of Lebanon, Israeli officials considered Hezbollah's growing power too threatening to be left unchallenged. The individuals targeted in precision, or targeted, air strikes usually belong to organizations with a prior history of terrorism; furthermore, it is assumed they are preparing future attacks and thus to constitute "ticking time bombs."[11] Paralleling Suarez's thinking, all of those interventions are usually justified through a combination of backward-looking considerations (i.e., those targeted by intervention had previously committed wrongs) and forward-looking considerations, like the importance of preventing future attacks.

When no wrongs have yet been committed, Suarez claims, the case for war in anticipation is somewhat different. Such wars may look like unjustified wars of aggression, but if the danger is imminent, they can in fact be considered legitimate wars of self-defense.[12] Anticipatory self-defense is the most common contemporary justification for pre-emptive war. Contemporary justifications broadly follow what has become known as the "*Caroline* doctrine." In 1842, following a British attack against the rebel steamboat *Caroline* on US territory along the Niagara river, American and British officials reached an agreement that the pre-emptive use of force is acceptable only when the "necessity of that self-defense is instant, overwhelming, and leaving no choice of means, and no moment for deliberation."[13] Suarez is less restrictive: he considers pre-emptive war to be justifiable when an injustice is "about to take place." Suarez's argument therefore provides a greater margin for the sovereign who wants to strike first. Nevertheless, his argument seems to be that anticipatory self-defense is justified only to *pre-empt* an imminent danger; meanwhile, in order for *preventive* war against a more distant danger to be justified, the target already has to have committed some wrong.

Suarez's standard raises pressing questions. Who is to decide what constitutes an important injury that could justify a preventive "war of aggression," or when the appropriate moment has arrived for acting in self-defense to forestall an injustice that is about to be committed? Suarez acknowledges that there are often uncertainties about which side has a right to go to war.[14] Indeed, Suarez's discussion of the deliberation

---

[10] M. E. O'Connell, "The Myth of Preemptive Self-Defense," *American Society of International Law Task Force on Terrorism*, August 2002, p. 10.

[11] A. Kasher and A. Yadlin, "Assassination and Preventive Killing," *SAIS Review* XXV, no. 1 (Winter-Spring 2005), 41–57.

[12] Suarez, *A Work on the Theological Virtues*, I, 6, p. 804.

[13] J. B. Moore, *Digest of International Law*, 1906, p. 412.

[14] Suarez, *A Work on the Theological Virtues*, VI: "What Certitude as to the Just Cause of War is Required in Order that War May be Just?," pp. 828 and ff.

process leading up to an intervention between the Prince and his advisors foreshadows many deliberative problems faced by contemporary states. For Suarez, policymaking on intervention is led by the Prince, but with crucial advice and support from his generals and officers (who take an active role both in combat and in its planning). Suarez also mentions other senior officials, so-called "good men," who could play a role of counterbalancing possible errors of the Prince.[15] This model of deliberation is compatible with contemporary theories of politics that assign an important role to knowledge in the justification of political decisions. In contemporary states, some see the role of Suarez's "good men" as played by experts, whose advice has both moral and political significance. Expertise should be impartial. It should contribute to the political process without being influenced by it. This task is even more complicated in debates about striking first, which often draw on different modes of expertise (e.g., military, scientific, and medical).

However, Suarez's argument also points out the limits of experts' contributions. Although experts advise the prince, they do not ultimately make his decisions.[16] Furthermore, there is no authoritative basis for establishing the impartial merit of expert advice. For Suarez, the Prince will never follow the opinion of learned men he has not himself chosen, let alone of "foreign arbitrators."[17] In our times, these difficulties were highlighted in debates about the existence of weapons of mass destruction that preceded the 2003 Iraq War. Suarez also rules out the possibility of a supranational authority intervening in such debates.[18] Such a supranational institution (in Suarez's day, for example, the Pope) might in principle charge experts with ascertaining the existence of a just cause for war; but it could be fully effective, he claims, only if it also had broad powers and notably the capacity to use force. Suarez, in other words, identifies fundamental epistemic problems concerning the justification of war, although he does not offer convincing solutions.

Suarez points to another important issue in discussions of the ethics of war: the likelihood of success. He acknowledges that whether a war is just also depends on the likelihood of its success: a Prince who declares war "is bound to attain the maximum certitude regarding victory."[19] This criterion is particularly important in wars of choice, which include all aggressive wars.[20] Since, under Suarez's classification, preventive wars would be "aggressive" (unlike pre-emptive wars, which would be classified as defensive), the likelihood-of-success criterion applies to the justification of preventive force. A similar criterion is, implicitly or explicitly,

---

[15] *Ibid.*, VI, 5, p. 830. [16] *Ibid.*, VI, 6, p. 831. [17] *Ibid.*, VI, 6, p. 831.
[18] *Ibid.*, VI, 5, p. 830. [19] *Ibid.*, IV, 10, p. 822. [20] *Ibid.*, p. 823.

frequently used today in debates about the admissibility of preventive war. However, retrospective justifications of preventive war based on their success are always tenuous: if such wars are actually successful, the reasons for which a preventive war is ostensibly conducted never become manifest. Furthermore, the Prince who strikes preventively usually does not have full knowledge about the power and intentions of his enemy. Rather, he strikes because he *feels* threatened. But a war fought against an enemy whose power is not fully known is especially difficult to justify on the likelihood-of-success criterion.

These epistemic problems do not similarly apply to justifying defensive wars, which (in Suarez's terms) are wars of necessity.[21] Using Suarez's categories, pre-emptive wars are defensive wars that have the appearance of aggressive wars, at least in cases where "injustice is about to take place." However, although Suarez is not entirely clear on this point, his logic suggests that the likelihood-of-success criterion should also apply, to some extent, to justifying pre-emptive war. The only wars that are justified regardless of their likelihood of success are traditional wars of self-defense.

In sum, Suarez's criteria illuminate important questions about preventive war, but he does not fully resolve them, and his answers are sometimes problematic. That makes it difficult to apply Suarez's categories to contemporary action. For instance, if likelihood of success needs to be taken into account for justifying preventive and pre-emptive wars, then only dominant powers would ever be permitted to strike preventively. By implication, a threatened, weaker state could never strike first, even if military intervention could be tied to a concrete injustice. Inequalities in strength are prevalent in international politics. Utilizing Suarez's justificatory criteria would write these *de facto* inequalities into the norms of international conduct, therefore reinforcing the hegemonic position of the Great Powers.

Gentili's subjectivism

The Italian jurist and philosopher Alberico Gentili is a central figure in any discussion of preventive war. Gentili held one of the first chairs of law at Oxford, to which he was appointed in 1587, after escaping political persecution in Italy. Gentili's classic treatise *De Jure Belli Libri Tres* offers an extensive discussion of both *jus ad bellum* (the rules that justify recourse to war) and *jus in bello* (the rules of just behavior in war). His

---

[21] *Ibid.*

justification for the use of force is less restrictive than that of many others in the just war tradition, including his follower Grotius.

One chapter of *De Jure Belli Libri Tres* in particular highlights certain epistemic difficulties related to justifying preventive and pre-emptive war.[22] Gentili considers the necessity, when faced with a threatening challenger, for the Prince to strike at the "root of the growing plant."[23] (Incidentally, a similarly biological metaphor is employed in the current Israeli "lawnmower" doctrine concerning the prevention of terrorist attacks.[24]) Gentili argues that the Prince ought not to wait to be struck, if he has reason to believe that his adversary is "meditating evil."[25] Fear plays a crucial role in Gentili's justification for wars of anticipation, as does his broader subjectivism (which allows a war to be just on both sides).[26] Because Gentili assigns justificatory force to subjective assessments, his view allows that fear may appropriately color the Prince's perception of what constitutes a danger. This subjective standard supports Gentili's conclusion that "defense dictated by expediency" may justify war based on the "fear that we may ourselves be attacked."[27]

Gentili is aware that this subjective standard for justification raises potential difficulties, and he does not posit that fear and other subjective assessments should be the sole criterion for justifying wars. Indeed, Gentili argues, there are restrictions on what constitutes a "just cause for fear."[28] "Legitimate" causes for fearing others are those that provide reasons to believe that one will suffer a great evil if one does not act to anticipate the other's attack.[29] For example, states have reason to be wary of "powerful and ambitious chiefs."[30] If such an ambitious chief also threatens to shift the international balance of power to the Prince's disfavor, that provides a sufficient reason for the Prince to strike first.[31]

Even in recent decades, anticipatory uses of force have typically been motivated by fear, or perceptions of rising threat. The 1967 war fought by Israel against Egypt is a particularly interesting case in point. The Egyptian nationalist leader Nasser had clearly expressed his hostile intentions vis-à-vis Israel. Egypt had closed the straits of Tiran, and Egyptian troops were massed at the Israeli border. These facts provided

[22] A. Gentili, *De Iure Belli Libri Tres* (Oxford: Clarendon Press, 1933), vol. II, Book I, ch. XIV, "Of Defense on Ground of Expediency," pp. 61–6.
[23] *Ibid.*, p. 61.
[24] S. Cohen, *Israel's Asymmetric Wars* (New York: Palgrave, 2010), p. 118.
[25] Gentili, *De Iure Belli Libri Tres*, Book I, ch. XIV, "Of Defense on Ground of Expediency," p. 61.
[26] *Ibid.*, Book I, ch. VI, "That War May Be Judged Justly By Both Sides," pp. 31–3.
[27] *Ibid*, Book I, ch. XIV, "Of Defense on Ground of Expediency," p. 61.
[28] *Ibid.*, p. 62.   [29] *Ibid.*, p. 64.   [30] *Ibid.*
[31] *Ibid.*, p. 65. See below on the parallel with Vattel's thinking.

compelling reasons for Israelis to fear an Egyptian attack. Was the war justified, and if so, on what basis? Using Gentili's framework, the Israeli attack could have been justified based on fear, because Nasser appeared to be "an ambitious chief," one bent on changing the balance of power in the region.

Contemporary authors also sometimes refer to Gentili's subjectivist framework of justification. For example, Michael Walzer uses the example of Israel and Egypt to illustrate the principle of "anticipation."[32] On Walzer's argument, while *"fear by itself* establishes no right of antici-pation,"[33] Nasser's ambitions provided a quintessential "example of *just fear.*"[34] Walzer is less inclined to authorize anticipatory strikes than Gentili; yet both of their analyses integrate, albeit to different degrees, subjective considerations like fear into the criteria for justifying anticipa-tory warfare.

Needless to say, this standard of justification is highly problematic. Might fear arising from a remote threat justify striking first? Or, on the contrary, is imminence a necessary element of "just fears"? When Israel attacked Egypt in 1967, its leaders argued that they were anticipating an imminent Egyptian attack, and the war was considered to be pre-emptive.[35] Yet, on other interpretations, the danger of an Egyptian attack was, at best, remote. Egypt could simply have wished to force Israel to maintain a state of alert, and intended to strike Israel only in the future, after its forces had been diminished.[36] Assuming that Israeli leaders had been aware of such a plan by Egypt, that would convert a pre-emptive war into a preventive one. (Taking the argument further, if such a plan had been in place but Israeli leaders had been unaware of it, then Israel might have waged a war that was subjectively pre-emptive but objectively preventive).

Gentili, of course, does not distinguish between preventive and pre-emptive wars, since these categories did not exist in his time. Nevertheless, his framework can be applied to contemporary discussions. Gentili considers that "it is better to provide that men should not acquire too great power, than to be obliged to seek a remedy later, when they have already become too powerful."[37] This statement might imply that

[32] Michael Walzer, *Just and Unjust Wars: A Moral Argument with Historical Illustrations* (New York: Basic Books, 1977), pp. 74–85.
[33] *Ibid.*, p. 84. My emphasis.
[34] *Ibid.*
[35] D. Rodman, "Israel's National Security Doctrine: an Introductory Overview," *Middle East Review of International Affairs* 5, no. 3 (2001), 71–86. Some political scientists also consider this intervention as a classic case of pre-emption. See e.g. D. Copeland, *The Origins of Major Wars* (Ithaca, NY: Cornell University Press, 2000), p. 45.
[36] Walzer explicitly envisages this possibility. *Cf.* Walzer, *Just and Unjust Wars*, pp. 83–4.
[37] Gentili, *De Jure Belli Libri Tres*, Book I, ch. XIV, p. 65.

war – preventive war – is an appropriate response to even remote threats. However, Gentili's conclusion is more nuanced:

A defence is just when it anticipates dangers that are already *meditated* and *prepared*, and also those which are not meditated but are probable and possible. This last word, however, is *not to be taken literally, for in that case my statement would be that it is just to resort to a war of this kind as soon as any one becomes too powerful.*[38]

The distinction between what is "meditated" and what is "prepared" is important – indeed, it resembles debates in contemporary international relations between "intentions" and "capabilities." For Gentili, both hostile intent and the necessary capabilities to inflict harm need to be present for anticipatory warfare to be justified. Given that longer-term predictions about an opponent's intentions are notoriously difficult, and shifts in the balance of power alone are not sufficient to justify anticipatory strikes, one might conclude that Gentili was in fact reluctant to justify *preventive* (as opposed to *pre-emptive*) war. Unless, of course, the acquisition of certain capabilities (in Gentili's terms, the preparation) supports an inference about their intended use ("meditation").

The problem manifests itself in current debates. After the surprise terrorist attacks of September 11, 2001, authors like Ruth Wedgwood claimed that technology has radically changed the notion of self-defense. The behavior of states and non-state actors, the argument goes, becomes unpredictable once they acquire weapons of mass destruction (WMD).[39] Such non-state actors have different cognitive frameworks from states, and they cannot be deterred by threats of massive retaliation. This difference is taken to support a distinct argument for preventive war: intervention is justified against non-state actors who are on the verge of acquiring WMD, because their desire to acquire such weapons is *ipso facto* taken to indicate hostile intent. The implications of this argument are troubling. Contemporary international law recognizes a distinction between prevention and pre-emption: pre-emption is tolerated by a great number of international lawyers, while prevention is not. Wedgwood's argument infers intentions from limited, or potential, evidence about capabilities. This inference is, in turn, taken to justify a war of anticipation. Yet, on this logic, the distinction between pre-emption and prevention collapses. Gentili's categories of "preparation" and "meditation" are

---

[38] *Ibid.*, p. 66, emphasis added.
[39] R. Wedgwood, "The Fall of Saddam Hussein: Security Council Mandates and Pre-emptive Self-Defense," *American Journal of International Law* 97, no. 3 (2003), p. 584.

too weak to rule out arguments like Wedgwood's, and thus to serve as a framework for international law on this question.

Grotius: broad exceptions to a general rule against preventive war

The Dutch natural-law theorist Hugo Grotius is well-known in the field of international relations for touting the merits of caution. In his main work, *De Jure Belli ac Pacis* (1625), he argues that "in case of doubt we must refrain from war."[40] Under conditions of uncertainty (e.g., about the threat posed by the prospective target of military action), Grotius advises against using force: "fears of an uncertainty cannot confer the right to resort to force."[41] In this passage, Grotius directly targets Gentili's views on "necessary defense."[42] According to Grotius, Gentili stands among "those who hold that defence is justifiable on the part of those who have deserved that war be made upon them."[43] Grotius insists that Gentili's approach is misleading: "those who accept fear of any sort as *justifying anticipatory slaying* are themselves greatly deceived, and deceive others."[44] War must be a last recourse. There is usually room for diplomacy, and means other than war should be exhausted before engaging in armed conflict.

Evoking Suarez, Grotius considers that war is authorized under the principle of self-defense when danger is "immediate" and "certain."[45] Therefore, on Grotius's view, a *pre-emptive* war would be considered just in response to an imminent threat. But what does Grotius have to say on the subject of *preventive* war? He specifically discusses "how to forestall an act of violence which is not immediate."[46] In such cases, he argues, again following Suarez, self-defense cannot provide a general justification for war. A threat – "an act of violence which is not immediate" – ought not to be dealt with by declaring war, because doing so "would work

---

[40] H. Grotius, *De Jure Belli ac Pacis – The Law of War and Peace* (Oxford: Clarendon Press, 1925), Vol. 2, Book II, ch. XXIII, VI, p. 560.

[41] *Ibid.*, Book II, ch. I, XVIII, p. 185.

[42] Gentili, "Chapter XIII – Of Necessary Defense," in *ibid.*, *De Iure Belli*, Book I, ch. XIII, pp. 58–60.

[43] Grotius, *De Jure Belli*, Book II, ch. I, XVIII, p. 185.

[44] *Ibid.*, Book II, ch. I, V, 1, p. 173. My emphasis. Grotius's target, again, is Gentili. Both Gentili and Grotius refer to the same passage from Cicero and interpret it in two opposite directions. On this point, see also Hugo Castignani, *Guerres Justes et Guerres Préventives*, PhD Dissertation, Université de Paris IV Sorbonne, Département de philosophie, 2009, p. 204; and C. G. Roeloofsen, "Some Remarks on the 'Sources' of the Grotian System of International Law," *Netherlands International Law Review* 30 (1983), 73–80.

[45] Grotius, *De Jure Belli*, Book II, ch. I, V, p. 173.   [46] *Ibid.*, Book II, ch. I, XVI, p. 184.

injustice."[47] "For a wrong action commenced but not yet carried through," the threat should be dealt with *"indirectly"* through generally non-violent punishment.[48]

What are the implications of Grotius's view for contemporary thinking about the ethics of war? Grotius's praise of caution suggests that non-imminent threats should, as a rule, be handled through measures short of war. One such non-violent measure might be the infliction of punishment through economic sanctions. Such measures are, of course, widely used in contemporary international relations.[49] Economic sanctions are a form of punishment and are sometimes criticized as such, especially when those who suffer are civilians.[50]

That said, Grotius clearly does not rule out preventive military action entirely. He rules out preventive war on the basis of self-defense, at least as a general principle. But that does not apply to the use of preventive force as a matter of inflicting punishment. Under certain circumstances, punishment may be inflicted by recourse to arms:

[C]rimes that have only been begun are therefore not to be punished by force *unless the matter is serious* and has reached a point where a certain damage has already followed from such action, even if it is not yet which was aimed at ... so that the *punishment* is joined either with *a precaution against future harm* or protects injured dignity or checks a dangerous example.[51]

In the wake of a prior crime by the target state, preventive war is justified, even when the state using anticipatory force aims at a goal other than the infliction of punishment. Grotius refers to "crimes that have only been begun" – indicating a future intention to inflict more severe damage. A similar scenario arises in contemporary discussions about the preventive destruction of nuclear facilities. For example, many observers suspect not only that Iran's nuclear program is aimed at developing nuclear weapons, but also that this development will be realized in the near future. Such a development would involve wrongdoing, inasmuch as it would violate the Non-Proliferation Treaty, to which Iran is a party. In all likelihood,

---

[47] *Ibid.*   [48] *Ibid.* My emphasis.

[49] G. C. Hufbauer et al., *Economic Sanctions Reconsidered*, 3rd edn. (Washington DC: Institute for International Economics, 2008).

[50] T. G. Weiss et al. (eds.), *Political Gain and Civilian Pain – Humanitarian Impact of Economic Sanctions* (Lanham, MD: Rowman and Littlefield, 1997). One example is the multilateral and comprehensive sanctions regime against Iraq from 1991 to 1996. This regime was alleviated when the oil for food program was put in place in December 1996. For a critique of economic sanctions as collective punishment in the case of Iraq, see D. Cortright and G. Lopez, "Are Sanctions Just? The Problematic Case of Iraq," *Journal of International Affairs* 52, no. 2 (Spring 1999), 735–55.

[51] Grotius, *De Jure Belli*, Book II, ch. XX, XXXIX, 4, p. 504. My emphasis.

it would also encourage the nuclearization of neighboring states and shift the balance of power in the Middle East.[52] Moreover, there are obvious concerns about Iran actually using its nuclear weapons in the future. Given sufficient information about the future goals of Iranian policy, preventive war against Iran would be justified on the framework laid out by Grotius, as it would be for Suarez. In this case, the prevention of future harm inflicted by Iran and the punishment of Iran for breaking the Non-Proliferation Treaty would combine to justify military intervention.

But Grotius goes even further in his acceptance of the preventive use of force, identifying a few specific, or exceptional, cases where preventive war can be justified as defensive war. For Grotius, these cases include interventions against those who imperil women, because "the defense of chastity is in the highest degree justifiable."[53] Grotius more generally supports interventions that seek to defend innocents from attack – what today we call humanitarian interventions. He also specifically envisages that a state's responsibilities for protecting innocents can ground a "defensive" war in anticipation. When a state is responsible for the lives of innocents – either within its own borders or abroad – any attack against (or even threat to) the state would, by implication, expose to danger those whom the state is responsible for protecting.[54] In these circumstances, an intervention that responds to such attacks or threats would be "defensive" (and therefore legitimate) because of the danger to which innocents are exposed. By implication, if the state did not have any responsibility for innocents, then interventions in response to the same attacks or threats would not be defensive. In the current context, the principal body responsible for the security of innocents is the United Nations. Therefore, extrapolating from Grotius's logic, any preventive intervention authorized by the United Nations would by definition be defensive and, as such, legitimate. (The UN Security Council does, in principle, have the authority to approve preventive strikes.)

Finally, Grotius offers another justification for using force in an anticipatory mode that clearly foreshadows one of the most controversial issues in contemporary debates about preventive war. Are states bound to respect international law when they confront enemies that do not? In his discussion of piracy in *De Jure Belli ac Pacis*, Grotius allows that "some things which are not permissible according to the purpose of war, may follow therefrom without wrong."[55] Destroying a ship full of

---

[52] As Grotius would phrase it, this could serve as "a dangerous example." Grotius, *De Jure Belli*, Book II, ch. XX, XXXIX, 4, p. 504.

[53] *Ibid.*, Book II, ch. I, VII, p. 175.   [54] *Ibid.*, Book II, ch. I, VIII, p. 176.

[55] *Ibid.*, Book II, ch. I, IV, 1, p. 600.

pirates would be authorized even if "infants, women or other innocent persons" might get killed in the process.[56] In contemporary terms, a parallel question about the asymmetric application of international law concerns a sovereign who may strike first against those who present a danger and do not themselves conform to international law.

Grotius discusses these latter issues more in-depth in an earlier work, *De Jure Praedae*, dated 1604 and rediscovered in 1864. While *De Jure Praedae* focuses primarily on prize law and booty, it also discusses maritime law and raises the issue of piracy. In chapter VIII, Grotius recounts how Caesar punished the pirates who had captured and kidnapped him. Grotius also addresses the issue of extra-legal warfare more generally, explicitly recognizing the need for exceptional measures to confront and coerce public enemies.[57] When fighting against those who refuse to abide by the laws of war, sovereigns should not have their hands tied. Those who violate the laws of war might gain important tactical and strategic advantages when in conflict with legitimate powers that are bound by legal rules. Since "ordinary remedies do not serve in an extraordinary situation," there should be exceptions to legal procedures.[58] This leads Grotius to accept preventive action against these enemies, even if such action does not conform to the ordinary rule of self-defense.[59] The Prince has the right to repel without announcement those whom Grotius refers to as "*hostes*" ("public enemies").[60] In public wars fought by a legitimate authority, there is no obligation to respect the law vis-à-vis those who transgress it, "whenever matters *do not admit of delay*."[61] The same logic also applies to private wars, fought by actors that do not represent a legitimate authority: "in case of necessity and for the *purpose of preventing the loss of our rights* many things are permitted which otherwise would not be permitted."[62]

The latter argument on extra-legal warfare has special resonance in the contemporary world. Should terrorists be granted the same rights as soldiers of a state, who wear uniform and carry arms openly? Identifying the former as "unlawful combatants," as the George W. Bush administration did in the aftermath of 9/11, has important legal and military implications. Ordinarily, the killings of Al-Qaeda members in Yemen in 2002 and, more recently, in Pakistan, would be problematic. The US was not at war with either country, and the legal basis for US action remains unclear. Critics of these policies argue that they undermine a core

---

[56] *Ibid.*, p. 601.
[57] H. Grotius, *De Jure Praede Commentarius – Commentary on the Law of Prize and Booty* (Oxford: Clarendon Press, 1950), Book VIII, § 42, p. 95.
[58] *Ibid.*, § 42, p. 95.   [59] *Ibid.*, § 44, pp. 95–6.   [60] *Ibid.*, § 46, p. 101.
[61] *Ibid.*, § 44, p. 96, emphasis added.   [62] *Ibid.*, § 42, p. 95, emphasis added.

democratic value, namely the rule of law, and jeopardize the social contract between its members.[63] Furthermore, accepting the principle of extra-legal warfare introduces precedents that could undermine the international legal system. However, the Bush administration (and the Obama administration more recently) merely followed a longstanding argument that was first fully developed by Grotius: rules that ordinarily restrain the use of force among regular soldiers and rights that are ordinarily granted to combatants do not apply to conflicts with "public enemies," or "unlawful combatants."

Summing up, then, Grotius is generally known for praising caution and restraint in international conduct and pointing to remedies other than war for resolving international disputes. Nevertheless, he suggests that under conditions of uncertainty, concerns about intentions can justify the preventive use of force against opponents who commit serious crimes, threaten the lives of innocents, or fail to respect international law and actually manifest hostile intentions. These broad categories of exceptions come close to swallowing up Grotius's general rule against preventive war. By validating preventive strikes for a wide range of purposes, they might also paradoxically contribute to an international climate of suspicion and fear, which might undermine the stability of the international legal and political order that Grotius sought to preserve.

Vattel's peculiar realism

Emer de Vattel's analysis of war differs from that of his predecessors for his political realism, and notably for his interest in the international balance of power. This interest is also evident in his discussion of anticipatory warfare. Unlike Gentili, Vattel does not allow that a war can be just on both sides.[64] However, he concedes, war can be *seen* as legitimate on both sides, at least when both act in good faith and lack sufficient information for an objective judgment.[65]

Vattel explicitly considers whether a state is entitled to respond militarily to a build-up in the capabilities of a potential rival who expresses hostile intentions.[66] Vattel's underlying assumption is that a Prince will always try to advance his political and strategic interests. From this perspective, it is unrealistic to expect the Prince to wait until an invasion actually occurs before undertaking preventive measures. Rather, if the Prince has the capabilities to prevent an invasion by using force, he usually will – and in many cases he may legitimately do so.

---

[63] See R. Goodin, *What's Wrong with Terrorism* (London: Polity, 2006).
[64] E. de Vattel, *Le Droit des gens ou Principes de la loi naturelle* (Buffalo, NY: William Hein, 1995), Book III, ch. III, § 39, p. 30.
[65] Vattel, *Droit des gens*, § 40, p. 30.   [66] *Ibid.*, § 42, p. 32.

Combining this political realism with legal reasoning, Vattel asserts the *necessity* to protect oneself from certain types of future threats. This prerogative is constrained only by the political virtue of caution. In developing his justification of anticipatory warfare, Vattel distinguishes between military action against immediate and more remote threats, foreshadowing the contemporary distinction between pre-emption and prevention. According to Vattel, the case for pre-emption is straight-forward: immediate threats must be opposed, for the same reason that an individual who is targeted by another may respond, even if he cannot be certain that the other is actually going to attack. Just as it is not permissible to restrain a person who is imminently threatened from stopping his potential murderer, so it is not permissible to hold back a state intent on averting its impending destruction.[67]

But what if the threat is remote? Vattel mentions the case of a state confronted by a rival that is increasing its military power. Inaction will, at the very least, result in a shift of the balance of power favoring the rival. Vattel suggests that whether military intervention is justified or not depends on the rival's reputation. Vattel's logic thus supports the following standard: the worse the rival's record or reputation, the more likely it is that the rival's military build-up in fact reflects an intention of belligerence, which might in principle justify the preventive use of force.

However, for Vattel, political and institutional mechanisms ultimately govern responses to potential threats and may even allow for their non-violent resolution. The balance of power, in particular, is a regulatory mechanism that preserves stability and provides a major impediment to war.[68] Vattel's twofold argument is revealed in his discussion of the international politics of Europe. First, Vattel considers Europe to form a political body within which a certain balance of power is realized and maintained.[69] Second, anticipating an idea that has more recently been developed further by realist scholars of international relations, he argues that appraisals of the balance of power must account for the reality of alliances. The targeted state will, in all likelihood, be backed by others concerned about the stability of the existing international order (in his case, the European order). Such alliances aim at preserving an equilibrium that reduces the threat of external attacks.[70]

Vattel's analysis also anticipates the current dialectic between institutionalist and realist approaches to international politics.[71] In

---

[67] *Ibid.,* § 44, p. 36.   [68] *Ibid.,* § 47, p. 39.
[69] *Ibid.,* § 47, p. 40.   [70] *Ibid.,* § 48, p. 42.
[71] See e.g. R. O. Keohane, "Institutional Theory and the Realist Challenge after the Cold War," in D. A. Baldwin (ed.), *Neorealism and Neoliberalism* (New York: Columbia

particular, Vattel illustrates the deep affinities between, on the one side, institutionalist approaches that aim at creating and enforcing norms for the stabilization of international relations and, on the other, a soft, defensive realism that aims to preserve an extant balance of power. Vattel's logic suggests that defensive realism is a complement to and constraint against the excesses of offensive, "hard" realism. Vattel's own realism thus reflects a form of institutionalism, as manifested in his support for the development of supranational norms. Thus, Vattel might even be read as supporting a functionalist view, akin to David Mitrany's, where international integration is a strong disincentive to war and allows for the peaceful resolution of disputes.[72] In short, if the balance of power became enshrined in international rules and institutions, states would have less reason to be concerned about each other's intentions – and with international uncertainty reduced, there would be less need (and justification) for preventive war.

Searching for compromise: politics, morality, and law

Despite their different approaches to conceptualizing the preventive use of force, Suarez, Gentili, Grotius, and Vattel all shared the overarching goal of formulating some general principles that could demarcate justified from unjustified responses to potential threats. Each of these thinkers also recognized that the proliferation of phenomena like preventive war would have detrimental effects on international politics. Preventive war, if generalized, would lead to a state of permanent insecurity that would run counter to the goal of international regulation that has always been favored by the just war tradition. Hence the classical thinkers discussed in this chapter sought to restrict the anticipatory use of force, by elaborating specific criteria for the admissibility of preventive strikes.

These efforts at demarcation highlight important distinctions between politics, morality, and law. In *political* terms, prevention is usually justified as a matter of necessity. *Morally*, prevention is usually justified on the basis of saving one's political community or the lives of innocents who depend on the protection granted by a sovereign. Justifying preventive war in *legal* terms is particularly challenging, since the acceptance of a general norm authorizing preventive strikes jeopardizes a

University Press, 1993); and R. Jervis, "Realism, Neoliberalism, and Cooperation: Understanding the Debate," *International Security* 24, no. 1 (1999), 42–63.

[72] D. Mitrany, *A Working Peace System* (London: Royal Institute of International Affairs, 1943).

broader system of norms that ostensibly limits the occurrence of violence, and it opens the door to abuses.

The arguments and examples offered by Gentili, Grotius, and Vattel, in particular, remind us that there can ultimately be no military strategy without anticipation of future threats. But can prevention be politically and morally justified, even when it is not legal? Grotius and others suggest that suspending the law is sometimes acceptable, e.g., when a legitimate state's enemies are outlaws – i.e., they themselves do not abide by the rules in question. The Grotian project more generally points toward the building of an international society whose members follow a set of international rules based on reciprocity, so that free riding does not afford unfair advantage. This logic is dictated not only by principles of equity, but also by political pragmatism: expecting a state to follow rules that its opponents violate with impunity is not only unjust; it would also be politically and militarily self-defeating.

Grotius and Vattel both counsel leaving law outside the realm of politics, and they focus instead on the political and moral legitimacy of prevention. A state that expresses hostile intentions towards its neighbors and engages in an arms build-up exposes itself to a just anticipatory strike. Such action would be an exception to the usual standards of political and moral justification in foreign policy. It would derive its political legitimacy out of its putative *necessity* and its moral justification out of the *responsibility* to protect one's own community or foreign innocents. Very few such decisions could be legally justified – with pre-emptive action against imminent threats providing one possible exception. However, in the face of a strong political and legal justification, this lack of legal justification might not be especially troubling.

International law on the use of force is unlikely to change in the near future, especially with regard to preventive military action. A 2004 report by the UN Secretary-General notes the threat posed by the acquisition of nuclear weapons capability on the part of political entities with hostile intent.[73] But the report counsels against reforming article 51 of the UN Charter, which limits the inherent right of individual and collective self-defense to measures taken *in response* to an armed attack. While not outlawing preventive military strikes in principle, the report insists that any such measures must be authorized by the UN Security Council.[74]

---

[73] *A More Secure World, Our Shared Responsibility, Report of the Secretary-General's High Level Panel on Threats Challenge and Change* (New York: United Nations), § 188.

[74] *Ibid.*, § 190.

The inherent subjectivism of threat perception

Some historians see preventive war as inherently associated with authoritarian regimes. They argue that preventive wars were traditionally fought by totalitarian and authoritarian states and, more recently, by states with strong presidential systems.[75] This association of prevention with authoritarian regimes also finds some support among political scientists.[76] Conversely, others deny that the nature of political regimes helps explain decisions to fight preventively. In support, they note Washington's frequent resort to preventive military strikes since 1945.[77] The early modern classics discussed in this chapter can provide some insight into this authoritarianism-democracy divide, or the question of whether a state's political regime might explain the resort to preventive war. At the very least, the classics can contribute to the debate about justifying preventive war in modern liberal democracies.

It might seem surprising that the early modern classics can illuminate this debate, for at least two reasons. First, these authors were primarily concerned with providing normative analysis. Second, when they wrote, there were no democracies in the modern sense of the term. However, Suarez, Gentili, Grotius, and Vattel all analyze the *politics* of justifying preventive wars. Each stresses the importance of fear, or perceived threat, and evidence (usually about an opponent's past behavior, or his current intentions and capabilities) as justifications for the preventive use of force.

Contemporary efforts to justify preventive force routinely invoke two important epistemic notions that the early modern classics considered: that ideas are subjective, and that knowledge is a form of evidence. Fear is also an essential component of justification in contemporary democracies, where citizens are particularly risk adverse and the precautionary principle has been elevated to a meta-norm that strongly influences policy. When the members of a democratic society feel concerned for their security – whether this fear is objectively warranted or not – there is a strong social demand for protection. The politics of fear are crucial to preventive war decisions. For example, the US war against Iraq in 2003 was initially quite popular among American citizens (although this consensus eroded as the conflict became prolonged and evidence of the war's necessity

[75] A. Vagts, "Preventive War," in *Defense and Diplomacy: The Soldier and the Conduct of Foreign Relations* (New York: King Crows Press, 1956), pp. 264–350.
[76] R. Schweller, "Domestic Structure and Preventive War: Are Democracies More Pacific?" *World Politics* 44, no. 2 (1992), 235–69.
[77] M. Trachtenberg, "Preventive War and U.S. Foreign Policy," *Security Studies* 16, no. 1 (2007), 1–31.

evaporated). Similarly, Israeli military interventions in Lebanon in 2006 and Gaza in 2010, as well as targeted killings justified on preventive grounds, have all enjoyed strong support from Israeli public opinion.

The early modern classics provide a useful framework for understanding this phenomenon: political decisions to fight preventively arise out of social expressions of fear, where (ostensibly objective) evidence serves as a justification. Those factors are particularly important to the justification of preventive war in democratic regimes, where decisions about war can never entirely disregard the question of popular support.

However, the early modern classics leave out a significant explanatory and normative issue: namely, the problem of linking remoteness and just fear. How remote a threat may ground a just fear? Providing a general answer to this question is exceedingly difficult, and perhaps altogether impossible. But absent such an answer, the notion of a "threat" that undergirds justifications of preventive war invites charges of relativism, or worse. The classics see discretion and subjectivity as integral to the justification of preventive war. Yet these factors invite the prospect of arbitrary and unprincipled decisions to use force. To some extent, the early modern classics recognized the difficulties of assessing threats, by conceding that the preventive use of force implies a legitimate suspension of international law, rather than a straightforward application thereof. Nevertheless, the framework provided by the early modern classics discussed in this chapter does not provide any safeguards against deliberate threat inflation in liberal democracies, based on the political manipulation of evidence, to build up domestic political support for preventive war.

Conclusion

The early modern classics discussed in this chapter have left an indelible imprint on the laws and ethics of war. Their ideas are the default grammar of justice in warfare – a grammar regularly deployed by political leaders, lawyers, and pundits. Liberal democratic societies and current multilateral institutions have internalized many related norms and ideas, which have contributed to the regulation and limitation of warfare. We can, of course, better understand the criteria that limit the anticipatory use of force by tracking their origins. However, in this chapter, I have sought to highlight another aspect of this legacy: re-reading the classics also allows us to better understand the origins of some inherent limitations and contradictions of current ethical discourse on the preventive use of force.

When exactly is the preventive use of force legitimate, and when is it legal? These remain among the most difficult unanswered questions for just war theorists. The early modern classics do not provide convincing answers to these questions. They never fully debate the effect of uncertainty on the limits of knowledge. (Although some, like Gentili, are surprisingly modern in their conclusion that there may be no objective "truth" in matters of morality and that the existence of a just cause is often in the eye of the beholder.) The "good men" who, according to Suarez, should advise the Prince do not suffice, even if their advice is actually heeded. Expertise has its limits and human judgment is always fallible. Errors and misjudgments abound, even in contemporary liberal societies where there is a strong culture of dialogue and competition among experts.

Changing the procedures for justifying and authorizing preventive military action might result in improvements over our current situation. In principle, the strengthening of multilateral accountability procedures could reduce the strong biases of unilateral decisions. It could also reduce the risk that people's threat perceptions are manipulated by decision-makers for partisan political gain. However, as testified by current disagreements at the UN and elsewhere, such reforms are exceedingly difficult to implement. Furthermore, even if they were to be implemented, they could never fully resolve the epistemic problem inherent in decisions about the preventive use of force.

There can be no absolute certainty about the wisdom of acting preventively. The classical just war theorists – especially those steeped in the Christian natural-law tradition, like Suarez and Grotius – never fully confront this problem, although it is certainly implicit in their work. War, as Clausewitz noted, is the "realm of chance,"[78] and preventive wars are among the most hazardous, or chance-ridden, of all wars. As I have suggested elsewhere, therefore, the classics illustrate the necessity of addressing the issue of moral luck in any attempt to justify preventive war. States that wage preventive war may be morally lucky or unlucky.[79] Unforeseen and sometimes unforeseeable circumstances can alter the normative valence of any initial decision to wage such a war. As a war unfolds, new evidence becomes available and some uncertainties are resolved. That may further legitimize a preventive war. Or it might

---

[78] C. von Clausewitz, *On War* (London: Everyman, 1993), p. 117.
[79] Colonomos, *The Gamble of War*. I borrow the notion of "moral luck" from Bernard Williams' work and the resulting debate in moral philosophy. *Cf.* B. Williams, *Moral Luck* (Cambridge University Press, 1982), pp. 20–39. See also D. Statman (ed.), *Moral Luck* (Albany, NY: State University of New York Press, 1993).

undermine the war's legitimacy, by showing that the fears on which the war was based were largely unjustified. The early modern classics discussed in this chapter recognized the fact of uncertainty, but their normative frameworks do not adequately appreciate the ultimate significance of moral luck to the justification of preventive war.

3   Vitoria: the law of war, saving the innocent, and the image of God

William Bain

Francisco de Vitoria (1483–1546) is widely recognized as perhaps the greatest and most influential thinker of the late scholastic or early modern period. He was a Catholic theologian who made an enormous contribution to sixteenth-century thinking about the nature of civil power and the power of the papacy, and this at a time when the Lutheran reform movement convulsed the political and religious concord of Europe. However, to the modern reader Vitoria is perhaps best remembered for developing the just war tradition and contributing to the origin of international law, both in connection with the expansion of Europe and the conquest of the Americas. James Brown Scott described the profundity of this contribution as "a perpetual possession to the international lawyer," an achievement he compared favorably to the aspiration that Thucydides expressed for the longevity of his celebrated *History of the Peloponnesian War*.[1] Indeed, it is on the back of this reputation that Brown, writing in the early twentieth century, championed Vitoria as the father of modern international law.[2] In more recent years Vitoria has attracted the attention of international relations scholars, especially those interested in the legitimacy of humanitarian intervention, often in conjunction with the development of international law.[3] His suggestion that Spanish dominion in America might be justified on grounds that it is right to save the innocent from egregious harm, cannibalism and human sacrifice in particular, has obvious appeal in this regard. It should come as no

---

[1] See Brown's preface to Franciscus de Victoria, *De Indis et de Ivre Belli Relectiones* (ed. E. Nys, trans. J. Pawley) (Washington, DC: Carnegie Institution of Washington, 1917).

[2] For the historiography of this view see J. Muldoon, "The Contribution of the Medieval Canon Lawyers to the Formation of International Law," *Traditio*, 28 (1972), 483–97.

[3] For a range of views that make reference to Vitoria, see A. Anghie, *Imperialism, Sovereignty and the Making of International Law* (Cambridge University Press, 2004); A. Bellamy, "Ethics and Intervention: The 'Humanitarian Exception' and the Problem of Abuse in the Case of Iraq," *Journal of Peace Research*, 41, no. 2 (2004), 131–47; T. Nardin, "The Moral Basis of Humanitarian Intervention," *Ethics and International Affairs*, 16, no. 1 (2002), 57–70; and A. Orford, *Reading Humanitarian Intervention: Human Rights and the Use of Force in International Law* (Cambridge University Press, 2003).

surprise, then, that Vitoria is regularly included in the genealogy of humanitarian intervention, especially since his right to defend the innocent evokes parallel arguments concerning the prevention and punishment of genocide, war crimes, and crimes against humanity.

Vitoria formulates this right to defend the innocent with reference to God's command: "Love thy neighbor as thyself."[4] The Indians, he says, "are all our neighbors, and therefore anyone, and especially princes, may defend them from such tyranny and oppression."[5] That it is right to save the innocent is normally taken for granted. The immediate reason why is clear enough: practices such as cannibalism and human sacrifice involve the commission of injustice. Less clear, however, is the authority from which "injustice" derives its substantive meaning. It is this question that I want to explore. But an answer is not found in a closer reading of what Vitoria actually said about the defense of the innocent. As a matter of fact, Vitoria's elaboration of this right is accommodated on a single printed page, with room to spare. Instead, it is the presuppositions of Vitoria's argument that are of interest; for it is in respect of these considerations that it is possible to state the reasons why it is right to save the innocent. Answering this question also creates space for intelligent reflection on the didactic character of Vitoria's thought – that is, the extent to which his thought provides prescriptive guidance in the present.

This chapter will explore these questions in three parts: (1) the nexus of just war, legitimate (pagan) political power, and the idea of dominion understood as self-mastery; (2) the bearing this conception of dominion has on Vitoria's thinking about the right ordering of relations between the Spanish and the Indians; and (3) a conception of world order that enjoins the defense of the innocent while preserving the authenticity of independent political communities. The chapter will conclude by arguing that Vitoria's argument concerning the defense of the innocent is premised on the belief that man is created in the image of God, which, in turn, grounds his conception of dominion and his theory of world order. It is the inescapably theological character of Vitoria's thought that casts doubt on any attempt to harness it to the problems of contemporary international relations; and yet, having discarded the didactic project, it seems that Vitoria's writings remain instructive insofar as they are suggestive of the kinds of questions that we too must pose and answer as we confront the problems of our world.

---

[4] Leviticus 19:18; Romans 13:8.
[5] F. de Vitoria, "On the American Indians," in *Political Writings* (eds. A. Pagden and J. Lawrence) (Cambridge University Press, 1991), p. 288.

War and dominion

A general outline of Vitoria's thoughts on war is found in "On the Law of War," a *relectio* that followed his discussion of the right by which the king of Spain came to possess lands in the New World. Vitoria contends that it is war fought with a just cause that best accounts for Spanish possession and occupation of these lands. He begins the *relectio* by asking if it is permissible for Christians to wage war at all. He answers in the affirmative, citing a succession of authorities, as is characteristic of the scholastic method of argument. He points to Augustine's observation that the Gospel does not condemn war altogether by demanding that Christians throw down their arms; and to Thomas Aquinas's invocation of scripture, which affirms that temporal authorities are to wield the sword so as to punish those who do evil. Vitoria takes the second of these proofs as the basis of a conclusion which, today, would be seen as resting on the domestic analogy: "It is lawful to draw the sword and use weapons against malefactors and seditious subjects within the commonwealth; therefore it must be lawful to use the sword and take up arms against foreign enemies too."[6] To these proofs Vitoria adds that war is permitted by natural law and in Mosaic law. But most important of all is the authority and example of saints and good men, who are testimony to numerous instances of defensive and offensive war. They protected their homes and property, as well as punished enemies that planned against them. Indeed, Vitoria says that the authority and example of these men is "always the strongest argument in any moral question."[7]

The underlying purpose of war is to ensure the peace and security of the commonwealth, for the enjoyment of these goods depends on the deterrence of injustice through the fear of war. But these goods do not pertain to individual commonwealths, each isolated from the other. On the contrary, there is a close connection between war and the good of the whole world. It would be the worst of all possible worlds, Vitoria asserts, if tyrants and robbers could injure the innocent without fear of punishment. That said, he is equally adamant that princes "should strive above all to avoid all provocations and causes of war."[8] War is a course to be pursued with great reluctance, and only when necessary. His reasons for saying so turn on the fact that other men are neighbors, men who would otherwise suffer the destruction of war; they are fellows, also created by God, who are to be loved as ourselves. For "It is a mark of utter

---

[6] F. de Vitoria, "On the Law of War," *Political Writings*, p. 297.
[7] Vitoria, "Law of War," pp. 297–8.   [8] *Ibid.*, p. 326.

monstrousness," he says, "to seek out and rejoice in causes which lead to nothing but death and persecution of our fellow-men."[9] That the purpose of war is the peace and security of the commonwealth, and yet war is also the cause of great destruction, prompts Vitoria to offer additional advice to those who would wield the sword. War, he reminds the prince, is for the sake of justice; hence the restoration of peace and security is the legitimate aim of war, not the utter destruction of the enemy. And, in victory, the prince is to take the part of judge rather than prosecutor, which is to say that redress must be made to the injured, albeit short of reducing the guilty to ruin.[10] All told, this advice presupposes the underlying assumption of Vitoria's reflections on the law of war and the idea of just war generally: war is both a necessary activity and a limited activity.

Vitoria specifies limits in respect of the authorities that are entitled to wage war, the reasons that justify the resort to war, and what may be done in the prosecution of war. When it comes to the question of authority, he makes allowance for both private and public war. A private person is entitled to wage war, on his own authority, in defense of person and property. This authority does not, however, extend to exacting retributive punishment; nor does it extend to the recovery of property that has been seized in the past. Private war is justified in response to immediate danger; and once this danger has passed "there is no longer any license for war."[11] In contrast, public war encompasses both self-defense and inflicting punishment. Vitoria looks to Aristotle to make this argument, specifically to the idea that a true commonwealth is a perfect community – that is, self-sufficient. In this context, war is regarded as being necessary to the proper administration of human affairs: "the commonwealth cannot sufficiently guard the public good and its own stability unless it is able to avenge injuries and teach its enemies a lesson, since wrongdoers become bolder and readier to attack when they can do so without fear of punishment."[12] The immediate bearer of this authority is the prince, who is custodian of the common good. So a commonwealth is a public order concerned with peace, among other goods enjoyed by its members; and as a perfect community, complete in itself, the authority to wage war is vested in the prince as agent or representative. But when there is evidence of negligence on the part of the prince, necessity may confer on others the authority to wage punitive war. In such cases, Vitoria

---

[9] *Ibid.*, p. 327.   [10] *Ibid.*, p. 327.   [11] *Ibid.*, p. 300.

[12] *Ibid.*, p. 300. The relevant point of reference is found in Aristotle's *Politics*: "the state is the union of families and villages in a perfect and self-sufficing life, by which we mean a happy and honourable life." See also Aristotle, "Politics," in *The Complete Works of Aristotle*, vol. II (ed. J. Barnes, trans. B. Jowett) (Princeton University Press, 1984), $1280^b35-1281^a1$.

contends, it is permissible for persons other than the (negligent) prince to carry the war to the attacker, otherwise "enemies would not abstain from harming others, if their victims were content only to defend themselves."[13]

The resort to war is also limited by the range of permissible reasons that justify the use of force. Here Vitoria directly addresses Spain's affairs in America. He rejects difference of religion as a just cause of war, because acceptance of faith is a voluntary matter. He regards enlargement of empire as illegitimate because it confuses the distinction between the innocent and the guilty: the targeted population would be innocent, which would make all killing unlawful. And he rejects the pursuit of personal glory as a just cause of war for being contrary to the purpose for which political power is established. The powers of public office, he observes, including those pertaining to the right of war, are not given for the sake of personal aggrandizement. He then invokes Aristotle's distinction between a lawful king and a tyrant: "The tyrant orders the government for his own profit and convenience, whereas the king orders it for the common good."[14] What does justify the recourse to war is the receipt of injury that causes harm. Again, Vitoria makes use of the domestic analogy to illustrate the point: since a prince cannot draw the sword against his own subjects unless they have done some wrong, he cannot draw the sword against foreigners unless they too have done wrong. It follows, he continues, that the sword cannot be wielded against those who have not given injury; or, to formulate the point in more familiar terms, it is impermissible to kill the innocent. It is on these grounds that Vitoria concludes: "*the sole and only just cause for waging war is when harm has been inflicted.*"[15]

This emphasis on harm has other implications for limiting the lawful use of force. Vitoria makes reference to degrees of harm in arguing that the resort to war is not justified in response to any and all injuries. The seriousness of war is such that it results in all sorts of cruelty and devastation. It is necessary, then, to subject contemplation of war to a test of proportionality: "it is not lawful to persecute those responsible for trivial offences by waging war on them."[16] The idea of harm also has an important bearing on what may be done in the prosecution of war. Vitoria does not deny that it is lawful to reclaim all losses incurred as a

---

[13] The clarity of the distinction between private and public war is qualified by the political reality of late-medieval/early-modern Europe, where a prince might rule a part of a commonwealth while being subject to a political superior. In such cases, Vitoria admits that an inferior political authority may enjoy a right of war when it is grounded in custom. See Vitoria, "Law of War," p. 302.
[14] *Ibid.*, pp. 302–3.   [15] *Ibid.*, p. 303 (emphasis in original).   [16] *Ibid.*, p. 304.

result of the illegitimate use of force, including seizure of an enemy's property. Inflicting punishment is also permitted, for it is lawful to avenge injuries received by teaching the guilty a lesson and punishing these injuries. Indeed, Vitoria says that a prince *"may do everything in a just war which is necessary to secure peace and security from attack."*[17] But everything does not mean anything, which brings the cardinal importance of harm in to full view. Vitoria reminds his listeners that the foundation of the just war is the receipt of injury that causes harm, from which follows a prohibition on killing those who have not given injury. In other words, a person who has inflicted no harm is innocent and, for Vitoria, it is "utterly wrong" to kill the innocent for injuries committed by the wicked among them, even to avoid greater evil. It is forbidden to kill travelers and visitors in the enemy's territory, as well as peaceful civilians, who are all presumed to be innocent. And it is also forbidden to kill persons, otherwise innocent, who may pose a threat at some point in the future – that is, for transgressions not yet committed. Taken together, these prohibitions are grounded in the principle that *"it is never lawful in itself intentionally to kill innocent persons."*[18]

It is in the context of harm and innocence that Vitoria advances an argument that is of special interest to scholars of contemporary international relations, especially those interested in questions of humanitarian intervention. While elaborating on the right of punishment, he says that the prince has authority over foreigners, in addition to his own subjects, to prevent them from harming others. This right, he says, is grounded in the law of nations and natural law and, indeed, in the "authority of the whole world."[19] For the world could not exist, he continues, unless there is some power authorized to deter the wicked and to punish them for harm inflicted on the good and the innocent. So it is clear, Vitoria suggests, that "If the commonwealth has these powers against its own members, there can be no doubt that the whole world has the same powers against any harmful and evil men."[20] Less clear, however, is the extent to which this authority pertains to injuries inflicted within a commonwealth, other than one's own, and which inflicts no obvious harm on neighboring commonwealths. This issue is especially important because, elsewhere, Vitoria suggests that Christian princes lack jurisdiction to punish the Indians of America for sins against the law of nature committed by the Indians or to compel them to desist in these practices. And yet, elsewhere again, while addressing the crimes of cannibalism and human sacrifice, he says that it is lawful for Christian

---

[17] *Ibid.*, p. 305 (emphasis in original).   [18] *Ibid.*, pp. 314–16 (emphasis in original).
[19] *Ibid.*, p. 305.   [20] *Ibid.*, p. 306.

princes to prohibit the Indians from practicing such nefarious customs.[21] It is lawful because these customs inflict harm on the innocent. Vitoria gives as proof the opinion of Pope Innocent IV (1195–1254), who annexed the power to punish violations of natural law to papal authority; hence Christian princes might punish such violations on the pope's authority. I will return to Vitoria's argument about defending the innocent toward the end of this chapter. But to better understand his general views on intervention and international order, it is necessary to explore in some detail his arguments concerning political authority and legitimate rule beyond the Christian world.

In attempting to grapple with this apparent conundrum, there is a danger of attributing too much novelty to Vitoria's thought on the law of war. This danger is especially acute when modern scholars are anxious to demonstrate the "newness" of the states system and international law. In this context, Vitoria is made to cast a steady gaze toward the future, while leaving behind aspects of his thought that do not fit the modern narrative – his theological credentials and outlook in particular. In fact, Vitoria engaged questions raised by the discovery of the New World by cultivating a much older tradition of thought. The reference to Innocent IV is instructive in this regard. This older tradition of thought took as its point of departure Muslim occupation of the Holy Land, the common view attributing rightful possession to Christians because it had been unlawfully seized in an unjust war. Seen in this light, Muslims possessed the Holy Land in fact but not in law, which justified war in order to remedy an injury received. Innocent IV extended the scope of the traditional argument by asking if it is permissible for Christians to dispossess Muslims (and other infidels) of lands other than the Holy Land. He replies by linking the use of force with the legal disposition of the Holy Land as unjustly seized territory, a move that shifts the governing assumption of relations between Christians and infidels from one of war to one of peaceful coexistence, if not positive cooperation.[22] In doing so, Innocent lays the groundwork of an argument that would prove to be enormously influential in Vitoria's treatment of right relations between Christians and the Indians of America, as well as his seemingly contradictory views on saving the innocent from harm.

---

[21] Vitoria, "American Indians," pp. 273–5, 287–8.

[22] See Innocent IV, "*Commentaria Doctissima in Quinque Libros Decetalium*," *The Expansion of Europe: The First Phase* (ed. J. Muldoon) (Philadelphia: University of Pennsylvania Press, 1977), pp. 191–2; Muldoon, *Popes, Infidels, and Lawyers*, p. 9; and J. Muldoon, "The Conquest of the Americas: The Spanish Search for Global Order," in R. Robertson and W. Garrett (eds.), *Religion and Global Order* (New York: Paragon House, 1991), pp. 65–7.

At the centre of this argument is consideration of the phrase *extra ecclesiam non est imperium* (there is no legitimate power outside the church), which originally referred to questions of ecclesiastical jurisdiction within Christian society, such as the pope's role in conferring legitimacy on royal and imperial power. Eventually the language of *extra ecclesiam* acquired more explicitly political significance, especially as it relates to a general analysis of the legitimacy of all secular power.[23] This transformation parallels changing self-perceptions of Latin Christendom and the world of which it was a part, for it "reflected increasing awareness of the non-Christian world, not simply in terms of the Moslem threat to Christian Europe but in terms of peoples who posed no direct military threat and who could be dealt with diplomatically."[24] It is in view of this reality that Innocent poses the question: "Is it licit to invade a land that infidels possess or which belongs to them?"[25] The word "possess" should not in this context be taken to mean mere possession, as in occupation without title. As James Muldoon, a noted historian of canon law, argues, Innocent did not need to justify a crusade to recapture the Holy Land; his belief that Muslims possessed land unlawfully was enough to invoke the traditional language of a just war waged in order to rectify injustice. Instead, the question initiates what Muldoon describes as an interrogation of a general right to dispossess infidels of property and political power everywhere.[26] In other words, Innocent set out to consider whether or not it was licit for Christians to seize the lands of infidels and to depose their rulers, not because they have inflicted an injury on the Christian world, or pose a threat that Christians deem intolerable, but because they are not counted among the faithful.

Innocent's reply is twofold. First, he addresses the origin of property, taking as his starting point scriptural proof that God gave the earth to all men in common. However, the circumstances of the world brought about by the Fall necessitated a division of property, lest there be perpetual cause for dispute. By God's original grant man is entitled to use the things of the earth, including the beasts and the fish he captures; and he is entitled to use lands that are empty in order to till the soil and to graze his herds. But the strife caused by contradictory claims required that use of these things be transformed into possession. Hence Abraham said to Lot:

---

[23] See "*Summa Et Est Sciendum*, Commentary on *Dist.* 22 c.1," in B. Tierney (ed.) *The Crisis of Church and State, 1050–1300* (University of Toronto Press, 1989), p. 120; and J. Muldoon, "*Extra ecclesiam non est imperium*: The Canonists and the Legitimacy of Secular Power," *Studia Grotiana*, 9 (1966), 556–66.

[24] Muldoon, "*Extra ecclesiam*," p. 570.

[25] Innocent IV, "*Commentaria Doctissima*," p. 191.

[26] Muldoon, *Popes, Infidels, and Lawyers*, pp. 7–8.

"Separate yourself from me."[27] So in the institution of private property –
that is, distinguishing between mine and thine – a principal cause of
conflict is diminished, it being unlawful to seize the property of
another.[28] Second, Innocent addresses the origin of government. Here
again, the point of departure is the commonly accepted view, expressed,
for example, in Romans 13, that all political power is from God, the
purpose of which is to wield the sword of vengeance for the sake of good
and to punish the wicked who do evil.[29] Together, these arguments
concerning the origin of property and government inform Innocent's
conclusion that lordship, possession, and jurisdiction all belong to infidels lawfully. In other words, infidels are true masters, a status that is
neither corrupted nor impaired by unbelief.[30]

What is most interesting, however, is the underlying reason for
accepting the legitimacy of political power *extra ecclesiam*. To support
this argument, Innocent invokes the Gospel of Matthew: "He makes his
sun rise on the just and the wicked."[31] In appealing to this passage,
Innocent rejects the distinction between Christian and infidel as being
relevant in answering questions pertaining to dominion. In contrast, the
distinction that does matter is that between rational and irrational. For
Innocent is clear in saying that Christians do not possess property and
political power in virtue of faith; he is equally clear that infidels cannot be
despoiled of these things on account of unbelief. Dominion belongs to all
men, Christian and infidel alike, by virtue of being rational creatures. It is
in respect of this proposition that Innocent answers his initial question in
the negative: "It is not licit for the pope or the faithful to take away from
infidels their belongings or their lordships or jurisdictions."[32] This
narrowing of papal jurisdiction in (temporal) matters of property and
political power holds out the possibility that infidels could be entreated
on a basis other than war. Indeed, infidels are drawn into Christian
ecclesiology in so far as they are seen as rational creatures, all of which
are made for the worship of God; and, instead of being treated as

[27] Genesis 13:8.   [28] Muldoon, *Popes, Infidels, and Lawyers*, p. 8.
[29] This account of the origin of political power does not exclude the people from the
constitution of government. The king receives his power (*potestas*) directly from God;
however, the king's authority (*auctoritas*) to rule comes from the people. See R. W. Carlyle
and A. J. Carlyle, *A History of Medieval Political Theory in the West*, vol. V (Edinburgh:
William Blackwood, 1971), pp. 449–51, 468–72.
[30] Muldoon, *Popes, Infidels, and Lawyers*, p. 8; Innocent IV, "On *Decretales*, 3.34.8, *Quod
super*, *Commentaria* (c. 1250)" and "On *Decretales*, 2.2.10, *Licit* (c. 1250), *Commentaria*,"
in Tierney (ed.) *The Crisis of Church and State*, pp. 154–5.
[31] Innocent IV, "*Quod super*," p. 155; and Matthew 5:45.
[32] Innocent IV, "*Quod super*," p. 155; and Muldoon, "*Extra ecclesiam*," p. 573.

permanent enemies, they are to be loved as neighbors, capable of knowing God and receiving the faith.

The great achievement of Innocent's theory of dominion is affirmation of legitimate political power beyond the boundaries of Christian Europe, which "provided a basis for determining how these societies could live together in some kind of harmony."[33] It implied that peaceful intercourse is found in stability of possession and recognition of political power, both of which augur wide latitude in determining internal arrangements. But as Muldoon argues, coexistence was not the highest goal to be achieved, although it represented a tolerable second-best basis of relations. The real reward lay in the pastoral mission of the Church, a mission that justified an expanded notion of papal jurisdiction in spiritual matters.[34] Here Innocent interprets Christ's command to Peter, "Feed my sheep," to mean that "all men, faithful and infidels, are Christ's sheep by creation even though they are not of the fold of the church and ... that the pope has jurisdiction and power over all *de iure* though not *de facto*."[35] Thus, the pope has the power to judge and to punish infidel violations of natural law and, since all men are made for the worship of God, he can order infidels to admit missionaries into their lands. Of course, infidels cannot be forced to convert, acceptance of the faith being strictly a voluntary act; but infidels who refuse to admit missionaries can and should be punished.[36] It is this responsibility, a charge that transcends life in political community, which transforms a second-best arrangement of coexistence into a genuine world order directed to the well-being of all mankind.

Reason, dominion and the Indian

In the end, Innocent did not resolve all that was necessary to grow the seeds of a nascent world order into a plentiful field capable of sustaining all of Christ's flock. Muldoon attributes this failure to the pursuit of conflicting goals, the most important being the fulfillment of the Church's pastoral mission. However, Innocent also wanted to protect Christendom from infidel invasion as well as restore the Holy Land to Christian rule. But perhaps most difficult of all, and prescient in so

---

[33] Muldoon, "Conquest of the Americas," p. 67.

[34] Muldoon, *Popes, Infidels, and Lawyers*, p. 36.

[35] John 21:17; and Innocent IV, "*Quod super*," pp. 155–6.

[36] Innocent IV, "*Commentaria Doctissima*," p. 192. This argument is premised on the idea that the material sword, while not received from the pope, is employed to protect the Church and its mission. Thus, the pope can declare war against infidels in matters pertaining to spiritual well-being and the secular power can compel them to desist in those things. See Muldoon, *Popes, Infidels, and Lawyers*, pp. 9–15.

far as the conquest of the New World is concerned, Innocent could not guarantee the safety of infidel converts from Christian depredations.[37] Vitoria would confront this very same problem. In the introduction to his *relectio* on the American Indians he states that Spanish rule in America is neither so evidently unjust in itself nor so evidently just in itself as to exclude all doubt in conscience. But he then goes on to say that reports of "bloody massacres and of innocent individuals pillaged of their possessions and dominions" may well provide grounds for doubting the justice of Spain's business in America.[38] Unfortunately, the pervasive focus in recent debates on Vitoria's elucidation of the rights of war and peace tends to obscure what resides at the heart of his reply, namely an argument that issues from the freedom and equality of all men, Christians and infidels alike. What is more, the character of this argument is generally lost on scholars of international relations who tend to be tone deaf to the theological grounding of Vitoria's thought.

The crux of this argument is discerned in respect of the Church's pastoral mission and how it should be carried out. It is often forgotten that Vitoria begins his *relectio* on the Indians by stating the text to be re-read: "Go ye therefore, and teach all nations, baptizing them in the name of the Father, and of the Son, and of the Holy Ghost."[39] He then proceeds by demolishing many of the traditional arguments commonly used to justify Spanish rule in America. For example, he parries the argument of papal donation, saying that the pope has no power in temporal affairs except in relation to spiritual matters; hence the pope is unable to constitute the king of Spain as lord of the Indians, because no one can give more power than he possesses. Thus, the papal bulls, such as *Inter Caetera*, confer nothing more than jurisdiction for the purpose of bringing to the inhabitants of the New World "the worship of our Redeemer and the profession of the Catholic faith."[40] This view of papal power pushes the issue on to ground seeded by Innocent IV, namely that of determining the legitimacy of infidel dominion. Here

---

[37] Muldoon, *Popes, Infidels, and Lawyers*, p. 48.

[38] Vitoria, "American Indians," pp. 237–8.

[39] Matthew 28:19. This command raises the concomitant problem of whether or not it is lawful to baptise the Indian children against the wishes of their parents. See Vitoria, "American Indians," p. 233.

[40] Vitoria, "American Indians," pp. 258–64, 3.2 284; Francisco de Vitoria, "I On the Power of the Church," *Political Writings*, p. 85; Muldoon, *Popes, Infidels, and Lawyers*, pp. 136–7; Alexander VI, "The Papal Bull *Inter Caetera* (Alexander VI)," in H. Steele Commager (ed.), *Documents of American History*, vol. I, 4th edn. (New York: Appleton-Century-Crofts, 1948), p. 3; and L. Hanke, *The Spanish Struggle for Justice in the Conquest of America* (Philadelphia: University of Pennsylvania Press, 1949), p. 174.

the key distinction is not between Christian and infidels, to stress again a crucial point: it is between those creatures that are rational and those that are not.

The fundamental importance of this distinction can be traced to the story of creation as told in the book of Genesis, specifically that man was created in the image of God. Roger Ruston explains this idea as consisting in a description of the way men act, although human rationality both resembles and differs from God's.[41] Thus, Thomas Aquinas says: "God's knowledge is the cause of things. For God's knowledge stands to all created things as the knowledge of artists stands to what they produce."[42] In this sense, God is analogous to a carpenter in whom exists a rational pattern of things that is realized in the activity of carpentry, so that a chair reflects the intellect of its maker. God's reason is similarly reflected in his creation, whereby "the rational pattern of the Divine wisdom bears the character of art or exemplar or idea in relation to all the things which are created by it."[43] The same is true of God and man. Like all creatures, man reflects God's creative intellect or reason; but man is fundamentally unlike other creatures in so far as knowledge and understanding are concerned. In these capacities, Ruston argues, only man is like God. Man alone among creatures is rational in the sense of being a moral agent. Man can know justice. Man can act within the law. Man can understand what is good. Indeed, man can do all of these things, or not; which is to say that man is also fundamentally free, capable of self-direction, and liable to be held responsible for his actions.[44]

It is this status that informs Vitoria's account of dominion. Again, Thomas Aquinas provides the basis of argument: "Man has a natural dominion over external things because, by means of his reason and will, he is able to make use of external things to his own advantage, as if they were made for this purpose."[45] Of course, support for this contention is found in the scriptural account of creation: "And God said, Let us make man in our image, after our likeness: and let them have dominion over the fish of the sea, and over the fowl of the air, and over the cattle, and over all the earth, and over every creeping thing that creepeth upon the earth."[46] More interesting, however, is the connection Aquinas makes between reason and will, and the use of external things, which Brian

---

[41] R. Ruston, *Human Rights in the Image of God* (London: SCM Press, 2004), pp. 55–6.

[42] T. Aquinas, *Summa Theologiae, Questions on God* (ed. B. Davies and B. Leftow) (Cambridge University Press, 2006), 14.8.

[43] Aquinas, "Summa Theologiae," IaIIae 93.1.   [44] Ruston, *Human Rights*, 55–6.

[45] Aquinas, "Summa Theologiae," IIaIIae 66.1.   [46] Genesis 1:26.

Tierney explains as man's mastery over his own acts and his freedom to use things to achieve his end. For it is in virtue of reason and will that man imitates God in dominating the rest of creation; and, since God ordained the use of these things to support man's body, thereby making the imperfect subject to the perfect, use of external things is natural to man.[47] At base, then, the dominion that God grants to man is established in natural law, which presupposes the irreducible equality of all men. Moreover, it presupposes man's relationship with God, natural law being nothing but the way in which rational creatures participate in the eternal law – the Divine reason that governs the rational pattern of the universe.[48] Vitoria refines this conception of dominion, based on the use of things, to convey the sense of a "personal and self-referential authority conceded by a particular law," so that it is possible to say that man is capable of discerning what is right and what is evil and, consequently, he is free "to do *or not to do* a good act."[49]

With this conception of dominion annexed to man understood as a rational creature created in the image of God, Vitoria brings an important part of the Innocentian tradition to bear on the legitimacy of infidel dominion in the New World. Vitoria explicitly considers whether irrationals can be true masters (*domini*) of their public and private possessions (including political power), when he asks if dominion requires the use of reason. He answers in the affirmative, saying that dominion does require the use of reason.[50] Thus, man, being master of himself in a way that makes him a moral agent, is capable of doing good and suffering injury. In contrast, irrational creatures do not possess reason and therefore cannot be the subject of rights or the victim of injustice (*iniuria*). Vitoria gives as proof the fact that "to deprive a wolf or lion of its prey is no injustice against the beast in question, any more than to shut out the sun's light is an injustice against the sun."[51] So where rational creatures act in accordance with reason and will, in imitation of God, irrational creatures act in accordance with instinct and necessity.[52] In this way, Vitoria evades a broader conception of dominion, whereby mere control or *de facto* power over a thing is

---

[47] B. Tierney, *The Idea of Natural Rights: Studies on Natural Rights, Natural Law, and Church Law, 1150–1625* (Grand Rapids, MI: William Eerdmans Publishing, 1997), p. 268; and Aquinas, "Summa Theologiae," IIaIIae 91.1.

[48] Aquinas, "Summa Theologiae," IIaIIae 91.1–2; Ruston, *Human Rights*, 80–7; and Vitoria, "On Law," 168.

[49] A. Brett, *Liberty, Right and Nature: Individual Rights in Later Scholastic Thought* (Cambridge University Press, 1997), pp. 132–7 (emphasis in original).

[50] Vitoria, "American Indians," p. 247.   [51] *Ibid.*, p. 248.

[52] Vitoria, "On Law," pp. 168–9.

sufficient to establish dominion; otherwise, there would be no bar to theft apart from the absence of power required to bring the object of theft under a thief's control.[53] The narrower conception, according to which reason and law mediate power and control, serves permanently to exclude irrational creatures from dominion.

As Vitoria proceeds he makes it clear that neither immaturity nor lunacy undermine the centrality of reason in defining dominion. In the case of children, Vitoria denies that immaturity consequent to being before the age of reason is analogous to the state of irrational creatures. Since children can be victims of injustice they can have legal rights. Using a passage from Galatians (4:1) as a foil ("the heir, as long as he is a child, differeth nothing from a slave, though he be lord of all"), Vitoria defends this proposition in the context of guardianship. A child in guardianship is like a slave in so far as another wills his actions, and yet this same child remains a lord in so far as he has a legal right to his possessions. But the analogy of child and slave should not be equated with the analogy of child and irrational because, unlike irrational creatures, which exist for the sake of man's advantage, a child exists for the sake of itself. Thus, Vitoria justifies the dominion of children, arguing: "the foundation of dominion is the fact that we are formed in the image of God; and the child is already formed in the image of God."[54] When Vitoria turns to the case of madmen, "those who neither have nor ever expect to have the use of reason," he holds out the order disclosed by the complexity of Indian social life as exculpatory evidence. Moreover, he asserts the impossibility of an entire race of madmen, which would impute failure to God for making a creature in vain. Indeed, as Tierney puts it, for the late scholastics "the Indians cannot be a race whose rationality is potential rather than actual, because the existence of such a race would imply a failure of God and nature."[55]

The weight attached to man's reason also figures prominently in Vitoria's rejection of a view that links dominion and grace, a view that invokes the image of God in order to deny the legitimacy of Indian dominion. This account of dominion is rooted in the Donatist heresy, which held that authority to administer the sacraments depends on a priest being in a state of grace. So as God did not work through sinful priests, he did not work through sinful lords. Thus, the thirteenth-century English canonist Alanus Anglicus argues that before the coming of Christ there were only *de facto* emperors, for "none except those who believed in the true God had

---

[53] Vitoria, "American Indians," p. 248.   [54] *Ibid.*, p. 249.
[55] B. Tierney, "Aristotle and the American Indians – Again: Two Critical Discussions," *Cristianesimo nella storia*, 12 (1990), 312; and Vitoria, "American Indians," pp. 249–50.

a right to the sword."[56] Hostiensis, Innocent IV's student, extends this argument to the case of infidels: "It seems to me that with the coming of Christ every public office and every government and all sovereignty and jurisdiction, both by law and from just cause, was taken from infidels and given over to the faithful through Him who has the highest power and cannot err."[57] Vitoria was concerned to refute the same heresy, albeit as it was articulated by the fourteenth-century scholastic philosophers John Wycliff and Richard Fitzralph. Their account accepts that man is made in the likeness of God; however, they also argue that this likeness and the dominion consequent to it are corrupted by sin, the conclusion being: "the image of God is not in the sinner, hence the sinner cannot have such dominion."[58] Vitoria replies, arguing that since self-mastery reflects man's inborn nature – rational powers formed in the image of God – dominion cannot be destroyed by sin.[59] In other words, sin may cloud the operation of reason, and to that extent man is radically unlike God; but sin does not obliterate man's nature that provides the link to God.

Finally, Vitoria defends against the contention that unbelief vacates the enjoyment of dominion. To address this claim he looks again to the writings of Thomas Aquinas, who discusses the matter in the context of infidel dominion over Christians. The crucial distinction to bear in mind is that between the ordered jurisdictions of human and natural law, and the separate jurisdiction of divine law. Thomas says dominion and authority exist by human law, which in turn derives from natural law. In contrast, the distinction between believer and unbeliever is a function of divine law. The integrity of this distinction is maintained by the assertion that divine law, which comes from grace, does not abolish human and natural law, which are grounded in reason.[60] Vitoria rehearses this line of argument, observing that "all forms of dominion (dominia) derive from natural or human law; therefore they cannot be annulled by lack of faith."[61] Indeed, so important is man's rational essence that it also informs a discussion of natural slavery, a category which for Vitoria describes "men who are insufficiently rational to govern themselves, but are rational enough to take orders."[62] In this rather benign reading of Aristotle, as Tierney describes it, the natural slave is

---

[56] A. Anglicus, "Commentary on *Dist.* 96 c.6 (c.1202)," in Tierney (ed.), *The Crisis of Church and State*, p. 123.

[57] Hostiensis, "*Lectura quinque decretalium*," *The Expansion of Europe: The First Phase* (ed. J. Muldoon) (Philadelphia: University of Pennsylvania Press, 1977), p. 193; and Muldoon, *Popes, Infidels, and Lawyers*, pp. 15–19.

[58] Vitoria, "American Indians," p. 241.   [59] *Ibid.*, p. 242.

[60] Aquinas, "Summa Theologiae," IIaIIae 10.10.

[61] Vitoria, "American Indians," p. 244.   [62] *Ibid.*, p. 239.

the simple person who is better fitted to serve than to rule, which is something quite different from the person who is naturally in the power of another. Consequently, the person who is slow-witted or foolish is not severed entirely from relationship with God, the fundamental requirement of which consists in possession of reason; hence the natural slave cannot lose dominion over himself on account of being stronger in body than in mind.[63]

The principal significance of Vitoria's discussion of dominion, beyond the obvious fact that he comes down on the side of the Indians, is the significance attached to the freedom and equality of all men. Dominion consists in man's mastery over himself – that is, his actions – and external things. Through the use of reason, man is able to use these things, as is appropriate, in order to achieve his end. He is able to discern precepts of justice and he is able to act consequent to intelligent reflection. And through the use of reason man is related to God, by way of natural law, and to all other men, which founds the unity of all mankind. At this point the centrality of the Church's mission comes back into view. For the problem confronted by Vitoria turns on the ways Christians should "teach all nations." Stories of massacre and theft only underscored the need (if not urgency) to furnish a definitive answer. Of course, there should be no doubt that Vitoria and others held the ways of the Indians in a measure of contempt. But as men created in the image of God, free and equal like all others, the Indians had to be treated in a particular manner. They could not, without cause, be coerced; to do so would destroy the self-mastery in terms of which they are created in the image of God. Coercion is justified only so far as they give their consent, or give just cause that elicits the use of force. However, there is in Vitoria's argument a more fundamental basis on which to pursue the Church's pastoral mission: the Indian had to be persuaded to the truth of the Gospel.

World order

From Vitoria's conception of dominion it is possible to work out a theory of world order that enjoins the defense of the innocent while preserving the authenticity of independent political communities. Fundamental to this theory is the coordination of temporal and ecclesiastical power so as to form an interconnected whole. Vitoria accounts for the origin of the

---

[63] Tierney, "Aristotle," pp. 311–15. Tierney's position is part of a larger critique of A. Pagden, *The Fall of Natural Man: The American Indian and the Origins of Comparative Ethnology* (Cambridge University Press, 1982), esp. ch. 4.

commonwealth by making a distinction between man and the rest of creation. Man is, in a sense, inferior to other creatures. Animals have coats to protect against the elements and defenses to repel attack: "so some animals have wings to fly, or hooves to run, or horns, others have teeth or claws for fighting, and none lacks defenses for its own protection."[64] In comparison, man is born naked and helpless; he possesses no natural defense, leaving him vulnerable to attack. These deficiencies compel man to seek partnerships, with each helping the other bear all and sundry burdens. Of course, marriages, households, and villages are all examples of partnership that help ease the burdens of life, each in its own way; but civil partnership best fulfills man's needs, for it alone is self-sufficient and therefore "most conformable to nature."[65] At this point, Vitoria combines the language of Aristotelian natural sociability with the characteristics of man created in the image of God. For the constituent parts of the rational soul, understanding and will, are no less dependent on human partnership than is the physical body. Following Aristotle, Vitoria maintains that the faculty of understanding is perfected by training and experience, something that is impossible in a state of isolation. The will is similarly frustrated when isolated from the traffic of human relations, for there is little point in developing habits of right conduct when there is no possibility of giving or receiving injury. So it is true that man is a moral agent capable of discerning precepts of justice and acting in accordance with what they demand; however, it is equally true that self-mastery, the basis of man's freedom and equality, is effective only in partnership with others.

The same chain of reasoning informs Vitoria's account of civil power. In a sense, self-mastery poses its own peculiar problem: "If all members of society were equal and subject to no higher power, each man would pull in his own direction as opinion or whim directed, and the commonwealth would necessarily be torn apart."[66] A society divided against itself, with every man pursuing his own advantage without care for the common good, cannot attend to the safety and survival of its members. To address this problem, Vitoria invokes the analogy of the human body, according to which the good of the whole is realized in the coordination of the parts. So just as the movements of arms and legs must be coordinated for the good of the entire body, so too must the actions of citizens be coordinated in order to avoid inflicting harm on the whole. Civil power is that coordinating force. Thus, Vitoria argues that the purpose of civil

[64] F. de Vitoria, "On Civil Power," *Political Writings*, p. 7.
[65] Vitoria, "Civil Power," pp. 7–9.   [66] *Ibid.*, p. 9.

power is identical to that of the commonwealth itself: to ensure man's safety and survival by superintending the common good.[67] And like the commonwealth, civil power is said to be natural in so far as it is directed to the realization of man's end. This line of argument successfully draws infidel communities within the field of legitimate commonwealths, thereby removing faith from the definition of political life. It would be a mistake, however, to argue that this naturalist foundation severs political life from the realization of spiritual ends. Vitoria understands the commonwealth as merely a part of a larger whole that reflects an ordered universe that is "structured like a unified body or building, with its interconnected limbs or parts giving the whole a beauty worthy of its creator."[68] He notes in this regard that neither the commonwealth nor civil power is sufficient to ensure spiritual salvation, their purpose being the realization of natural ends – safety and survival. In contrast, spiritual power extends beyond the whole of nature to embrace man's supreme end: eternal happiness or beatitude.[69] Therefore, civil power and spiritual power are distinct in respect of purpose, but this distinctness should not be confused with equality of excellence. They are complementary powers, not independent but interdependent; and yet "the purpose of spiritual power far excels that of temporal power, in the measure that perfect bliss and ultimate felicity excel all human or earthly happiness."[70]

The whole that is of consequent interest – that is, the whole to be explained – is implicit in this relation between temporal and spiritual power understood as a coordinated and interconnected world composed of individual men, each being master of himself, and autonomous (though not independent) political communities, each also being master of itself. Both man and commonwealth have their respective ends, but these ends cannot be realized apart from the to and fro of social life. In such a world, the notion of exchange assumes special importance. Man has a right to use the things of the earth, thereby furthering his interests and satisfying his desires, so long as no harm is inflicted on others. In other words, trade is the way of reconciling God's gift of creation to man in common and the biblical commandment

---

[67] *Ibid.*, pp. 9–10.   [68] Vitoria, "I On the Power of the Church," p. 55.

[69] *Ibid.*, p. 73; and "Civil Power," p. 26.

[70] The proof of this proposition is found in a hierarchy of goods, whereby (imperfect) temporal goods are ordered to the realisation of (perfect) spiritual goods, just as the parts of the body are interconnected and subordinated for the sake of the whole. Vitoria gives as an example the pope's power to restrict trade, something that is licit according to natural law and the law of nations, if it is convenient for spreading the Christian religion. By the same token, the pope can exclude other Christian powers from participating in the Church's pastoral work if it is conducive to spreading the faith and preserving the peace. See Vitoria, "I On the Power of the Church," pp. 56, 82, 90.

"thou shalt not steal."[71] Just as important is communication, which is a manifestation of man's rationality and natural sociability. It is through the communication of knowledge that human partnerships, such as marriages and cities, are qualitatively different from a pride of lions or a colony of ants. However, the communication of knowledge is concerned not only with addressing physical necessity – safety and survival; it is also concerned with the well-being of man's soul. Thus, included within the scope of communication is the Church's pastoral mission, which is founded on the principle that Christians "must be able to teach [the Indians] the truth if they are willing to listen, especially about matters to do with salvation and beatitude, much more so than about anything to do with any other human subject."[72]

It is at this point that the law of war comes into view. To refuse the work of missionaries or not to permit conversions is to give injury in so far as it obstructs the propagation of truth, with the effect of denying the Indians a chance of salvation. Vitoria is clear in saying that if Christians are prevented from fulfilling their duty to preach the Gospel, and if the Indians are harmed in being prevented from hearing it, then it may be necessary to take up arms to re-establish a just state of affairs. But in keeping with notions of proportionality and last resort, which qualify the right use of force, Vitoria also says that the use of force must follow – rather than precede – an attempt at explaining the injustice committed. This commonsensical counsel is grounded in the character of a creature created in the image of God: a rational person, capable of knowing justice and obeying the law, is also the person that can be persuaded to the faith. For the same reason, forcible conversion is prohibited by natural law, because "to apply coercion to anyone is evil; therefore unbelievers cannot lawfully be compelled to believe."[73] This conclusion raises the related question: does the prohibition against coercion found in natural law also prohibit coercion to punish violations of natural law? It would seem that it does. Vitoria argues that Christian princes possess no jurisdiction to punish the Indians for sins against the law of nature; nor can they compel the Indians to give up practices that result in these sins. The same is true of the pope: the power to punish can be exercised only over those who have subjected themselves to the faith.[74]

---

[71] Exodus 20:15; and Ruston, *Human Rights*, p. 44.
[72] Vitoria, "American Indians," 3.2 284.
[73] F. de Vitoria, "Lecture on the Evangelization of Unbelievers," *Political Writings*, pp. 341–2; and "American Indians," p. 285.
[74] Vitoria, "American Indians," p. 274; and F. de Vitoria, "On Dietary Laws, or Self-Restraint," *Political Writings*, p. 218. This conclusion marks an important break with canonistic and papal thought on the extent of papal jurisdiction, including that of

Vitoria's refusal to countenance this kind of interference informs the familiar wish to avoid the destruction that accompanies continual war: "since every country is full of sinners, kingdoms could be exchanged every day."[75] Non-interference is the sentinel of peace. But if non-interference provides a serviceable foundation for a theory of world order, it would seem to throw other aspects of Vitoria's thought into disarray. Most important in this regard is his argument regarding the defense of the innocent. Indeed, his claim that Christians may wage war to suppress "nefarious custom or rite" might appear to some as precisely the kind of self-serving pretext Vitoria warned against: "a fraudulent calumny concocted to justify persecuting non-Christians."[76] But the air of confusion is cleared in view of the condition upon which punishment depends. To inflict punishment one must be a superior, which entails the further proposition that "no one can coerce or punish another unless he has power over him."[77] Vitoria demonstrates the truth of this principle with reference to Thomas Aquinas's injunction against forcible conversion. Aquinas says it is impermissible for a Christian prince to coerce non-subjects to accept the faith because his authority to exercise power is given by the commonwealth for the sake of the commonwealth. The same is true of the pope, for he too lacks jurisdiction. Vitoria says it would be strange to grant papal power to punish, while withholding power to impose laws on those he punishes. In the end, the authority to punish follows from a determination of jurisdiction: "the Church either has dominion (*dominium*) over non-Christians, or it does not. If it does not, then it cannot punish them for their crimes, however unnatural they may be."[78]

The crucial point to be made is that for Vitoria, inflicting punishment and defending the innocent are fundamentally different activities, although to the modern reader they might appear as different versions of the same activity. On this point Vitoria leaves little to interpretation: "the reason why the barbarians can be conquered is not that their anthropophagy and human sacrifices are against natural law, but because they

---

Innocent IV. See J. Muldoon, "Francisco de Vitoria and Humanitarian Intervention," *Journal of Military Ethics*, 5, no. 2 (2006), 138.

[75] Vitoria, "American Indians," p. 274. Vitoria illustrates the nature of this danger by saying it would give the king of France "a perfect right" to conquer Italy. See "Dietary Laws," p. 225.

[76] Vitoria, "Dietary Laws," p. 230.   [77] *Ibid.*, p. 218.

[78] *Ibid.*, pp. 224, 228. Elsewhere, Vitoria says that "authority can only be exercised through law." See "On Law," p. 167. See also D. Schwartz, "The Principle of the Defence of the Innocent and the Conquest of America: 'Save Those Dragged Towards Death'," *Journal of the History of International Law*, 9 (2007), 281.

involve injustice (*iniuria*) to other men."[79] Whereas the infliction of punishment is tied to law, the defense of the innocent is not. The reason why Vitoria adopts this position is somewhat less clear. He defends extra-jurisdictional intervention to suppress "nefarious" crimes against nature, cannibalism and human sacrifice, but he denies the legitimacy of intervention to suppress other sins against the law of nature. The answer to this puzzle is not found in a hierarchy of crimes, with more serious crimes justifying intervention and lesser crimes staying within the principle of non-interference. Vitoria says that fornication and theft are as much against natural law as sodomy and other unnatural acts, hence the Indians are prohibited – as are all men – from doing any of these things. Moreover, he says that some crimes, such as murder, are more serious than the unnatural acts that are said to justify the use of force. Indeed, Vitoria rejects the notion of a hierarchy of crimes in asking: "Why should it be right to wage war against unbelievers for sins against nature, but not for other sins?"[80] The most immediate reason for answering "it is not right" is the decidedly unwelcome consequence of grounding such a right in a universal (natural) law that is indifferent to belief: non-Christian princes would be entitled to wage war to suppress these same sins amongst Christians. There is, then, at a minimum, a prudential reason for restricting the use of force and for respecting the autonomy of all commonwealths, which is to say that world order depends on limitations that restrict the use of force, even when there are good reasons for going to war.[81]

The puzzle of Vitoria's argument concerning the defense of the innocent is made no clearer by taking refuge in the idea of necessity, whereby the circumstances of the situation force a choice between the lesser of two evils: transgressing law that limits jurisdiction and the use of force, or law that enjoins man to "love thy neighbor as thyself." Instead, the puzzle is resolved in respect of what it means to have dominion over oneself and what follows in train. Dominion consists in man's self-mastery that reflects the image of God. But Vitoria denies that man is master of his own life or the lives of others in the same way he is master of irrational creatures, which are made for his purpose and given (by God) for his use. Indeed, the dominion that man has over other men, either as master over slave or as master over free individuals, does not include unfettered power over life and death. Only God possesses that power, for he is "the Lord of life and death."[82] Therefore, man has no power to renounce his right of self-conservation; nor can this right be transferred so that he may be killed.

---

79 Vitoria, "Dietary Laws," p. 225.   80 *Ibid.*, pp. 224–5.
81 See Vitoria, "Civil Power," pp. 21–2; and "Dietary Laws," p. 225.
82 Vitoria, "Dietary Laws," p. 215.

To relinquish this right is to relinquish mastery over oneself. As a result, cannibalism and human sacrifice inflict injustice not only on the victim who is consumed or made an oblation; these practices also constitute an injustice to God because they illicitly destroy a part of his creation. Vitoria's use of the word "neighbor" in this context takes on special significance. He uses the Latin *proximus*, rather than *vicinus*, to render "neighbor," the former being a common biblical usage that denotes duties to fellow human beings. In contrast, *vicinus* derives from the Roman law of vicinage and evokes a geographical sense that refers to those who live nearby.[83] Thus, the Indians should be defended from such tyranny and oppression because they are fellow human beings, created in the image of God. Indeed, that is why it is right to defend the innocent from harm, even if they "consent to these kinds of rites and sacrifices, or ... they refuse to accept the Spaniards as their liberators."[84]

Scribe for the future?

Vitoria's conception of world order is certainly different from the international anarchy that is the stuff of much contemporary international relations theory. His lectures on the American Indians and the law of war portray a world of autonomous communities that are necessary for the enjoyment of a properly human life. But at no point is the good of the individual subsumed entirely to the needs and interests of the political community. His is a world in which the political community imparts permanent value, which makes it something worth preserving; but the good of the entire world is superior to the good of any constituent community. In this sense, individuals and political communities conjointly constitute an interconnected and coordinated world order that is justified for the sake of safety, survival, and peace – the common good; and yet the good of individuals, the principal parts of this whole, is greater in dignity and therefore superior to the good of the whole.[85] Vitoria's point was that neither the individual good nor the common good could be achieved without the other; in other words, individuals are individuals in the intrinsic moral sense but their intrinsic value cannot be vindicated without the assistance and cooperation of others.

---

[83] See Schwartz, "Principle of the Defence," p. 273.

[84] Vitoria, "American Indians," p. 288; "Dietary Laws," p. 225; "Civil Power," p. 18; "On Law," pp. 170–1; "Evangelization of Unbelievers," p. 346; and Pagden, "Introduction," p. xxvii.

[85] See M. S. Kempshall, *The Common Good in Late Medieval Political Thought* (Oxford: Clarendon Press, 1999), pp. 348–9.

There should be little doubt that large parts of Vitoria's conception of world order will appeal to modern sensibilities. For example, his account of the political community, understood as a human partnership justified for the sake of the safety and survival of its members, will appeal to proponents of the "responsibility to protect." The notion of civil power as the custodian of the common good, acting on behalf of the community's members, is likely to win approval as well. Both of these ideas fit squarely with the belief that sovereignty is evolving to embrace both internal and external duties. Thus, as the report of the International Commission on Intervention and State Sovereignty (ICISS) puts it, sovereignty implies responsibility for "protecting the safety and lives of citizens and promotion of their welfare"; and there is a residual responsibility in the "broader community of states" when one of its number is unable or unwilling to act in preventing or suppressing certain crimes and atrocities.[86] Moreover, the manner of carrying out the Church's pastoral mission, if adapted to the circumstances of the present, provides a reliable guide for the way in which human rights, democracy, and free market economy should be propagated. So, whereas there is normally a presumption against force in propagating these ideas, there is nothing preventing states as well as civil society groups from engaging in vigorous promotion and voicing criticism of others when necessary. And most obvious of all is Vitoria's argument regarding the defense of the innocent, which might appear to the modern reader as anticipating a theory of humanitarian intervention that is directed toward redressing genocide and other mass atrocity crimes.

But it is rather difficult to push these parallels, as well as the analogies they elicit, very far. In short, Vitoria's argument concerning the defense of the innocent presupposes a rationally ordered Christian universe and it depends fundamentally on the idea that man is created in the image of God; and the intelligibility and the authority of this argument are lost once it is abstracted from this context. We are left then to confront a Janus-faced problem. Muldoon picks up on the inescapably Christian character of neo-scholastic thought, Vitoria's included, in professing a feeling of pessimism about the contribution of Catholic thought to theorizing world order. The problem to be addressed, he argues, is one of difference and the extent to which it should be tolerated; however, his answer is clearly weighted in favor of difference: "Any modern liberal theory of global order must be based on an acceptance of the pluralistic nature of the modern world and an acceptance of differing views of the moral basis

---

[86] ICISS, *The Responsibility to Protect* (Ottawa: IDRC, 2001), pp. 12–17.

of society."[87] Vitoria and his successors took the first steps in theorizing such an order but they did not travel nearly far enough, for it was left to Protestant thinkers like Grotius and Vattel to complete the journey.[88]

In a curious way, however, Muldoon has it all backwards, for the issue is not simply one of Catholic and other Christian thinkers adjusting themselves to the reality of a pluralistic world. At this point the other face of the problem comes to light. The problem is equally intelligible in terms of a world that wants to avail itself of a particular discourse while ignoring its Christian character, which is to say that the contemporary world order may not be as pluralistic and, indeed, secular as many like to think. Indeed, Article 1 of the Universal Declaration is nothing but a classic statement of the Christian natural law tradition: "All human beings are born free and equal in dignity and rights. They are endowed with reason and conscience and should act towards one another in a spirit of brotherhood."[89] And what of this common dignity? If it is not in essence expressed as common possession of reason and will, consequent to our creation in the image of God, then perhaps it is something more like an onion: "peel away layer after layer and you are left, not with the 'essential' or 'natural' onion, but with nothing at all."[90] The point is not that these issues pose insurmountable obstacles. There are other ways of articulating intelligible accounts of human dignity, and other related ideas, without having to fall back on a natural law steeped in Christian theology. However, these other ways must be argued rather than asserted, which is to say that it is not enough to simply argue "for" some things: it is equally important to argue "about" them. In other words, questions concerning *what* we should do are inseparable, at least in the order of knowledge, from questions concerning *why* we should do these things and not something else.

It is commonplace in contemporary international relations scholarship to neglect the latter of these two kinds of question. An exploration of the presuppositions of *this* concept or the underlying justification of *that* value labors under the inherent disadvantage of not being obviously relevant to

---

[87] Consequently, Muldoon argues that it will be necessary for Catholic thinkers to move beyond natural law theories of order, based on Thomist teachings, if they are to make a contribution in the future. They will need to accommodate themselves to an international law that is more a record of what people actually do than an abstract and metaphysical law of nature that prescribes and prohibits what they ought and ought not to do. *Cf.* Muldoon, "Conquest of the Americas," pp. 82–3.

[88] Muldoon, "Conquest of the Americas," p. 82.

[89] "Universal Declaration of Human Rights," in I. Brownlie (ed.), *Basic Documents on Human Rights*, 3rd edn. (Oxford University Press, 1992), p. 22.

[90] R. W. Dyson, "Natural Law as a Problem in Moral Philosophy," Unpublished Paper, 2005.

the formulation of policy. To demand an account of the underlying justification of human freedom or private property is to muddy the water by hindering the speedy formulation and execution of policy. So it is not merely a matter of avoiding what is difficult or even impossible to answer with any certainty; these queries are to be bypassed altogether because they are also seen as being troublesome. In this sort of world, one that places a premium on useful knowledge, action will inevitably displace philosophical reflection. But this rather blinkered attitude obscures a point that is of considerable import to the person who is interested in questions of ethical conduct: the fact that someone believes something is not nearly as significant or illuminating as the reasons he or she has for holding that belief. Of course, philosophical reflection cannot be relied upon to solve practical problems, but answers elicited by philosophical reflection, though provisional and conditional, stand behind every prescriptive recommendation. Indeed, these answers are inseparable from any attempt at a solution because they are what transform utility into right; and it is this transformation that saves talk of ethics from being just that: talk.

So in a sense Vitoria does speak to the present, albeit not in the way that might be commonly imagined. It is in many regards anachronistic to apply Vitoria's thought to the problems of our day. He is no more the father of modern humanitarian intervention than he is the father of modern international law, which is to say that his thought provides no prescriptive guidance in the present. But if we refuse Vitoria a seat at the table of applied ethics, we are not forever cut off from the insights conveyed by his thought. The reason why is indicated by Janet Coleman, who observes:

there are important reasons why certain issues keep cropping up over the centuries in philosophical, theological and scientific circles, and one of these is that as a literate civilization, we have constructed our pasts from inherited texts, taken what we see as relevant to our own situation while discarding the rest until the next generation picks up the threads dropped by its fathers. Certain kinds of questions ... do not seem to have received definitive answers at any time, and we repeat the analyses, moving backwards and forwards, in every generation.[91]

It is in this context that Vitoria's thought is of enduring value. His engagement with questions that have yet to receive definitive answers is suggestive of the kinds of questions that we too must address. But we must not answer these questions with a lazy rehearsal of his arguments. Thus, Vitoria might provide a starting point for thinking about saving the innocent in contemporary international relations, but his notion of a

---

[91] J. Coleman, *Ancient and Medieval Memories* (Cambridge University Press, 1992), p. xvii.

rationally ordered Christian universe in which man is created in the image of God is largely unintelligible today, at least on a global scale. So in an attempt to move forward, to address these questions anew, we are reminded that moving backwards, to engage the past, issues an invitation to answer in ways that are sensitive and responsive to the peculiar circumstances of our own times.

4   Grotius, Hobbes, and Pufendorf on humanitarian intervention

Richard Tuck

The seventeenth century saw an extensive and pointed debate about the right of states to intervene in one another's affairs on behalf of oppressed or endangered citizens – what we now regard as "humanitarian" intervention – that is, intervention not governed by (for example) the interests of one's own nationals in the foreign country, but by the interests of the foreign citizens. The seventeenth-century debate was arguably the most extensive discussion of the subject before the twentieth century changed the terms of international relations for ever, and all the major writers on international law contributed to it. The debate was provoked both by a new way of thinking about global politics which had emerged in the Renaissance, and by a number of critical and intensely thought-provoking acts of intervention in the course of the sixteenth and seventeenth centuries, above all the intervention by the English and the French in the Dutch revolt against the King of Spain, but also the interventions by European powers in the (to their eyes) savage politics of Asia and the New World.

To modern eyes, the debate had a number of surprising features. We tend to assume today that advocates of humanitarian intervention in the affairs of other countries believe in something like an "international community" in which there is a duty upon nations to intervene in one another's internal affairs if clear moral boundaries have been crossed by the government in question – if the population (or a sizable proportion of it) is suffering grievous and unnecessary harm at the hands of its rulers. In addition, it is generally assumed by supporters of intervention (and indeed by almost all modern theorists of any kind) that the indigenous inhabitants of a state are entitled to resist oppression and violence unjustly exercised against them by their government, and that this resistance can include armed opposition, if peaceful means have failed. Armed intervention by another state on behalf of the oppressed is then understood as simply the extension of this internal right of resistance, in which the "international community" or some appropriate (usually neighboring) state acts primarily as the representative or agent of the native population.

It would seem very strange to modern theorists that there could be a right of intervention without a corresponding – and prior – right of resistance from within the state. It would also seem very strange that the decision to intervene could be taken by an individual state, with little attention being paid either to the international community or to the moral structures within which international affairs are supposed to operate, such as respect for a specifiable set of human rights. But none of these modern assumptions are to be found, at least straightforwardly, in these early-modern debates. Early-modern advocates of intervention tended to be both somewhat skeptical about international moral frameworks, and dismissive of the rights of citizens to resist their governments, while the theorists who stressed the moral character of international relations, and the reciprocal duties of rulers and ruled, tended to be wary of international intervention on humanitarian grounds. The modern way of thinking about international politics is not easily back-projected into earlier periods, and we have to be sensitive to the differences in order to understand where our modern ideas have come from, and how far they are historically contingent.

But before analyzing the thinking of Grotius, Hobbes, and Pufendorf on humanitarian intervention, I want to discuss in some detail how we should understand the historical genealogy of their arguments. I will show in particular how the arguments developed by Protestant thinkers like Grotius, Hobbes, and Pufendorf differ from those of scholastic philosophers such as Vitoria and Suarez (who emphasized the autonomy of states, rather than their freedom to intervene in each other's affairs) and build instead on ancient Roman views about war and peace that leave the door wide open to international (humanitarian) intervention.

Two traditions of early-modern thinking about war and intervention

As I suggested some years ago in *The Rights of War and Peace*,[1] one can understand medieval and early-modern thinking about war between states as formed by two parallel but opposed traditions, each deriving from the Roman world. On the one hand there was the ancient Roman view of war, according to which any degree of violence was justified against enemies who constituted, in the judgment of the Roman state, a threat to its existence. As Cato may have said about the most famous and important of Rome's many wars, "the Carthaginians are our enemies

[1] R. Tuck, *The Rights of War and Peace: Political Theory and the International Order from Grotius to Kant* (Oxford University Press, 1999).

already; for whoever is directing all his preparations against me, so that he may make war on me at the time of his own choice, is already my enemy, even if he is not yet taking armed action."[2] Pre-emptive strikes, based on suspicion of this kind, were part of the normal conduct of war, which could not be governed by any international bodies or even by consideration of wider interests than the advantage of the Roman state.

It did not follow, however, that Rome did not often see its own interests as aligned with those of oppressed citizens elsewhere in the world. Rome's mission, in the famous words of Vergil, could be thought of as "parcere subjectis and debellare superbos" ("to spare the oppressed and bring down the proud," *Aeneid* VI.852). Rome's status during its expansion into the Eastern Mediterranean as the only republic left in a world of military despotisms undoubtedly contributed to its self-image as a liberator, freeing the subject peoples of Greece and Asia from the despotic descendants of Alexander's generals (though, as the ruthless destruction of Corinth in 146 BC testifies, Rome could in practice be even more tyrannical to the Greeks than the Kings of Macedon or Pontus had ever been). Rome certainly felt free to respond to appeals for help from populations engaged in struggles against their rulers or in war with their neighbors, and to some extent its entire imperial expansion was driven by a succession of such responses. The Jugurthine War of 112 is a good example: Rome's initial involvement in the affairs of Numidia was as an international arbitrator to resolve a civil war there and to enforce the settlement, but – in an entirely familiar way – the war escalated, Rome was drawn in and eventually a Roman protectorate was established, which in turn became a Roman province.

The Roman view was that a state could make its own judgment about what kind of war was necessary or desirable and then act on it, drawing on a pretty open-ended set of considerations, of which aid to the oppressed was one. The alternative view, which supplanted the Roman ideas for most of the middle ages, developed from the Christian theology of late antiquity. Initially of course Christians were hostile to any form of violence or military action whatsoever, but as their participation in the Roman state increased, particularly after the conversion of Constantine, they began to reconsider their hostility. What became the classic position, at least in the Latin-speaking world, was the one put forward by Augustine at the end of the fourth century. He made clear that self-defense understood in the old Roman way was unacceptable, as being

[2] *Oratorum Romanorum Fragmenta* (ed. H. Malcovati) (Turin, 1967–79) I p. 78 (fr.195); trans. in P. A. Brunt, "Laus Imperii," in P. D. A. Garnsey and C. R. Whittaker (eds.) *Imperialism in the Ancient World* (Cambridge University Press, 1978) p. 177.

morally dangerous, but violence on behalf of someone else in a well-founded legal order could be justified:

A soldier who kills the enemy is acting as an agent of the law, so he can easily perform his duty without inordinate desire (*libido*). Furthermore, the law itself, which was established with a view to protecting the people, cannot be accused of any inordinate desire ... [But as for someone who defends his own life, for example against a highway robber], I do not see how they can be excused, even if the law itself is just. For the law does not force them to kill; it merely leaves that in their power. They are free not to kill anyone for those things which can be lost against their will, and which they should therefore not love [i.e. their earthly life].[3]

International warfare had to be seen strictly as a judicial act, comparable in all respects to the act of a judge in civil society ordering a punishment. Thus pre-emptive strikes, the basic technique of Roman warfare, were morally wrong, for no crime had yet been committed by the enemy; and ideally the state making war upon international criminals would possess some sort of authority comparable to the authority possessed over its citizens by a state. For many of Augustine's successors in medieval Western Europe, this ideal condition was rather easily fulfilled, as (depending on their political tastes) either the Christian Empire or the Papacy could count for them as a body possessing for good world-historical reasons the kind of authority needed to embark on a punitive war. The world was not a sphere of independent sovereign states, but in effect a single sovereign state with many provinces, and with no distinctive puzzle about international intervention.

But this idea was very far from being universally accepted even by Christians, and as skepticism about these supranational bodies increased, so many Christians became strikingly uneasy about wars of international punishment. If the world was not notionally a unified juridical entity, then there might be no, or very few, plausible grounds for intervening in another country's affairs, as the "judge" in the case would lack any legal standing. This was particularly true of the theologians who were influenced by the late thirteenth-century philosopher Thomas Aquinas: one of the key features of Thomism in this context was its recognition of the rights of the independent rulers of Europe (in particular the King of France) against Pope or Emperor in civil matters, and its corresponding hesitation over a right to inflict international punishment, especially where societies outside the Christian world were concerned.

This hesitation led a number of Thomists in the early sixteenth century to criticize the most striking case of such intervention, that by Spain in

---

[3] *On Free Choice of the Will* (ed. and trans. T. Williams) (Indianapolis: Hackett Publishing Company, 1993) p. 9 (I.5).

the affairs of the native peoples of the New World, which had been justified largely on humanitarian grounds (that is, rescuing the native peoples from oppressive and savage rulers such as the Aztec emperors, wiping out inhumane practices such as cannibalism, and introducing the benefits of Christianity). As the most extreme critic of the Empire, Domingo de Soto, said,

By what right do we maintain the overseas empire which has recently been discovered? To speak truly, I do not know. In the Gospel we find: "Go ye into all the world, and preach the Gospel to every creature" (Mark 16[:15]); this gives us a right to preach everywhere in the world, and, as a consequence, we have been given a right to defend ourselves against anyone who prevents us from preaching. Therefore if we were in danger, we could defend ourselves from them at their expence; but I do not see that we have any right beyond this to take their goods or subject them to our rule ...[4]

This was an extreme version of the Thomist respect for other sovereignties, and many Thomists did not go so far. The most influential Hispanic theorist of the early sixteenth century, Francisco de Vitoria, defended part of the Spanish imperial mission on the grounds that some degree of intervention was justified by general moral principles, even if there was no global authority. He used the examples of cannibalism and human sacrifice, which became the staple instances for the early-modern debate on intervention in the New World. If infidels (or anyone else) injured the innocent by these practices, then any ruler could intervene to stop them, even if the victims "neither seek nor wish this help; it is lawful to defend an innocent man even if he does not ask us to, or even if he refuses our help ..." But

the belligerent does not thereby have the power to eject the enemy from their dominions and despoil them of their property at whim; he can act only as far as is necessary to ward off injustices and secure safety for the future.[5]

This was not entirely what the Spanish government wished to hear, though it accepted Vitoria's authority. At the most, Vitoria's arguments implied a kind of "mandate" system for the government of the native peoples, and it is no coincidence that his writings became popular again, and were treated as newly authoritative, at the beginning of the twentieth century.[6] Of all the early-modern writers, Vitoria does indeed accord most with modern sensibilities.

---

[4] D. de Soto, *Relección "De Dominio"* (ed. J. Brufau Prats) (Granada, 1964).

[5] *Political Writings* (ed. A. Pagden and J. Lawrance) (Cambridge University Press, 1991), pp. 225–6; see the same points in *De Indis, ibid.* p. 288. For further discussion see also William Bain's chapter in this volume.

[6] See in particular the Carnegie Institution edition of *De Indies et De Iure Belli Relectiones* (Oxford University Press, 1917), e.g. James Brown Scott's Preface.

But that was far from being true for Vitoria's contemporaries, even among the Thomists of his time. For example, Vitoria's principal scholastic successor, the early seventeenth-century theologian Francisco Suarez, repeatedly insisted that

coercion or punishment without jurisdiction is unjust ... Therefore, just as one private individual may not punish or coerce another private individual, and just as one Christian king may not be accorded such treatment by another Christian [king], nor an infidel ruler by another infidel [ruler], so neither may an infidel state, supreme in its own order, be punished by the Church on account of its crimes, even if those crimes are contrary to natural reason.[7]

His one concession, which again corresponds to our modern assumptions more than (as we shall see presently) the ideas of his Protestant contemporaries, was that external intervention might be justified if there was an internal, "constitutional," right to resist on the part of the citizens. The right however had not merely to exist but actually to be exercised and (a substantial limitation) the citizens had to be allies or "friends" of the intervening state.

The cause is sufficient if the wrong be inflicted upon any one who has placed himself under the protection of a prince, or even if it be inflicted upon allies or friends, as may be seen in the case of Abraham (*Genesis*, Chap. xiv) and in that of David (I *Kings*, Chap. xxviii) ... But it must be understood that such a circumstance justifies war only on condition that the friend himself would be justified in waging the war, and consents thereto, either expressly or by implication. The reason for this limitation is that a wrong done to another does not give me the right to avenge him, unless he would be justified in avenging himself and actually proposes to do so. Assuming, however, that these conditions exist, my aid to him is an act of cooperation in a good and just deed; but if [the injured party] does not entertain such a wish, no one else may intervene, since he who committed the wrong has made himself subject not to every one indiscriminately, but only to the person who has been wronged. Wherefore, the assertion made by some writers, that sovereign kings have the power of avenging injuries done in any part of the world, is entirely false, and throws into confusion all the orderly distinctions of jurisdiction; for such power was not [expressly] granted by God and its existence is not to be inferred by any process of reasoning.[8]

"Friend" was not for Suarez a universal category – as his Scriptural citations illustrate, he had in mind some prior relationship between the peoples that could be called upon to elicit intervention (most obviously,

---

[7] F. Suarez, *Selections from Three Works* (ed. J. Brown Scott) (Carnegie Institution: Oxford University Press 1944), II p. 769 (*De Triplici Virtute Theologica* (1621) *Fides* Disp. XVIII).
[8] *Ibid.* p. 817 (*Caritas*, Disp. XIII).

the peoples might be co-religionists).[9] The thrust of his argument was consistently against a wide-ranging right of intervention in the affairs of other states, even where the rulers of those states were committing extensive crimes against their citizens, and in favor of the separateness and autonomy of states. The scholastic and Hispanic tradition of think-ing about war and intervention by the early seventeenth century had come to emphasize the moral constraints upon states, rather than their freedom to act against one another. The tradition did not at all rule out international violence, but it repeatedly stressed the moral danger impli-cit in it, and the need to respect legal authorities, even those of "infidel" nations. It accepted the general thrust of the Augustinian view, that war should be like a judicial act; but since it had come to believe that there was no international sovereign judge, the number of actual conflicts which could be justified along these lines were extremely few in number.

However, a very different approach had begun to appear by Suarez's time among writers who both admired the Roman world-view and had reasons of their own for hostility to Spain and what it represented. The most striking example of this combination of qualities is Alberico Gentili, an Italian humanist who converted to Protestantism and who fled from Spanish power in his native country to the post of Professor of Civil Law in Elizabethan Oxford. But to understand the pecularities of his position, and the way it was used later by Grotius, we must first understand the significance of the fact that he was a Protestant.

As is well known, the first generation of Protestants had been extremely wary of conceding any right of active resistance to subjects in a civil society; even Calvin went only so far as to allow such a right to lesser magistrates who might count (on some interpretations) as partici-pants in the sovereignty of the society. In this, as is also well known, they differed markedly from their Catholic contemporaries, and from the scholastic theologians of the late middle ages, among whom some right of resistance on the part of subjects was usually recognized. Suarez, for example, in the same disputatio *On Charity* from which the above quota-tion comes, also argued that an armed uprising by a population against a tyrannical ruler was perfectly justifiable. But the reluctance on the part of Protestant theorists to concede a right of armed resistance to citizens had the paradoxical effect that they put much more stress on the right of intervention by a foreign ruler than did the scholastics. A foreign ruler was

[9] The first Scriptural example was Abraham's war on behalf of Sodom to rescue Lot while Lot was a resident of Sodom, the second David's war on behalf of his friend Achish of Gath, who had acted as David's host while he was in exile (Suarez's reference to I Kings xviii is a reference to I Samuel xviii, using the Vulgate designation).

not guilty of taking up arms against a superior, and he might well be justified in intervening on behalf (say) of his oppressed co-religionists when they would not be justified in taking up arms themselves, and might not even have requested the intervention. The external power was not the *agent* of the internal dissidents. One disconcerting implication of this is that one might say that the Wars of Religion which devastated the Continent were the only way in which Protestants could feel morally comfortable in securing themselves against the Counter-Reformation – an ever-expanding war among states was the only way in which Catholic rulers could legitimately be overthrown.

So the first point Gentili made was that private individuals have no right to take up arms against a tyrannical sovereign – "the authority is not given to private individuals of being permitted to arouse the multitude. 'If any one in his private capacity, without the authority of the government, makes peace or war, let him be punished with death' is a law of Plato" (I.3).[10] But "unless we wish to make sovereigns exempt from the law and bound by no statutes and no precedents, there must also of necessity be some one to remind them of their duty and hold them in restraint," and this "some one" was a foreign ruler.

But, extraordinarily, he went on to argue that intervention on their behalf might be justified even if there was no clear evidence that the population was indeed oppressed – all depended on the judgment of the state contemplating intervention, just as it had for the Romans. In the critical chapter I.16 of *De Iure Belli* "On Defending the Subjects of Another Against Their Sovereign," Gentili argued, first, that if an oppressed population took up arms in sufficient numbers, the question of the legitimacy of its action became irrelevant as far as outsiders were concerned.

When a dispute arises regarding the commonwealth, there are no competent judges in the state, nor can there be any.

I say that a dispute concerns the commonwealth, when the number of subjects who are aroused to war is so great and of such a character, that since they defend themselves by arms, it is necessary to make war against them. For those who have so much power share as it were in the sovereignty, they are public characters and on an equality with the sovereign, just as one sovereign is said to be on an equality

[10] *De Iure Belli Libri Tres* (ed. J. C. Rolfe) (Carnegie Endowment: Oxford University Press 1933), vol. II (translation of 1612 edition). See also his remarks at I.11 about resistance for religious reasons: "I do not think it just that in this matter a subordinate should coerce a supreme magistrate. Only God, who is transcendent, can exert compulsion" (though he gave Calvin's qualification, that there might be lesser magistrates who could do so).

with another when he is able to resist the other in an offer of violence, no matter how much greater and more powerful the latter may be.

And, second, in such circumstances it was open to neighboring sovereigns to intervene even if it might be plausible to argue that the popular uprising was unjust.

What then if the cause of the subjects is an unjust one? In that case also the above-mentioned authorities say that one ought not to aid the subjects of another who are unjust, lest any one, by thus rendering aid, provoke the same action against his own country ... [But] even those who are unjust may be defended by us in war. For if a war is just when its purpose is to ward off injury, even though those who ward off injury themselves gave cause for the war, it would seem that the same thing may be established for the same reason with regard to the defence of others, even though they be subjects ... And so it seems to me that aid may be given to the subjects of another even when they are unjust, but only with the purpose of saving them from immoderate cruelty and unmerciful punishment; for it is the part of humanity to do good even to those who have sinned.

The particular case with which he was concerned was above all the English intervention in the Dutch Revolt against the King of Spain, the crucial military action of Elizabeth's reign which precipitated, *inter alia*, the retaliation of the Spanish Armada: "the English did right in aiding the Dutch against the Spaniards, even if the cause of the Dutch was unjust and although the Dutch are even now subjects of Spain."

Gentili thus represents a striking confluence of Protestant political theory and the Roman attitude to war. Conventional moral principles of the scholastic kind should not, he argued, govern international relations; the most remarkable and famous example of this is his entirely Roman attitude to pre-emptive strikes, such as when he asserted that

it is better to provide that men should not acquire too great power, than to be obliged to seek a remedy later, when they have already become too powerful ... This it is which was the constant care of Lorenzo de' Medici, that wise man, friend of peace, and father of peace, namely, that the balance of power should be maintained among the princes of Italy ... But both the peace and the balance of power ended with him, great scion of the Medici and mighty bulwark of his native city and the rest of Italy. Is not this even today our problem, that one man may not have supreme power and that all Europe may not submit to the domination of a single man? Unless there is something which can resist Spain, Europe will surely fall (I.14).

The other nations of Europe, notably the English, could resist Spain by helping the Dutch, even if the Dutch Revolt was illegitimate. But far-reaching war of this kind was reserved for sovereigns, whose rights were still those of the Roman state; oppressed populations, on this view, *had* to turn to outside help, for in the last analysis only outside sovereigns possessed the full right to take up arms on their behalf.

It is worth remarking that the same conjunction of Roman war theory and non-resistance appears, albeit in a somewhat less extremist fashion, in the most famous advocate of non-resistance in the sixteenth century, Jean Bodin. In the *Six Books* he argued that if "a wise prince"

finds that the outragious proceeding of a Tyrant against his [the tyrant's] subiects be irreconcileable, then ought he to take upon him the protection of the afflicted with a generous resolution: as that great *Hercules* did, who purchased to himselfe immortall praise and reputation, for that he tooke upon him the protection of afflicted people against the violence and crueltie of tyrants (which the fables call monsters) whom he went through the world to conquer: wherein the antient Romans did also exceed all other nations.[11]

Though he warned that such intervention should be very cautiously undertaken and not used to destabilize neighboring regimes: "he which persuadeth another Princes subiects to rebell under colour of protection (which should be as a holie anchor for people uniustly tyranized) ... doth open the gate of rebellion to his owne subiects, and brings his owne estate into danger, with an everlasting shame and dishonor."[12] Bodin's remarks on this subject constitute one of the principal qualifications to his general theory of sovereign power, for they offered dissident subjects an alternative to the submission to legally-constituted authority which in the main he advocated – and of course a particularly potent alternative in the context of the European religious wars of the late sixteenth century. This late sixteenth-century Protestant humanist theory about intervention has not, I think, been fully understood in its complexity by later historians, but it was clearly the dominant theory among writers in Protestant countries about the issue down to the late seventeenth century.

Grotius: humanitarian intervention to punish grievous violations of the laws of nature

Hugo Grotius's remarks on the subject of internal dissent and external intervention in Book II, chapter 25 of his *De Iure Belli ac Pacis* broadly correspond to the views of Bodin and Gentili. When he turned at II.25.8 to the question "Whether we have a just Cause for War with another Prince, in order to relieve his Subjects from their Oppression

---

[11] Bodin, *The Six Bookes of a Commonweale* (trans. R. Knolles) (London, 1606) p. 632.
[12] *Ibid.*, p. 632.

under him," he answered with the same combination of non-resistance theory and the right of intervention.

And indeed tho' it were granted that Subjects ought not, even in the most pressing Necessity, to take up Arms against their Prince (which is what those very Gentlemen who are such Advocates for the Power and Prerogatives of the Crown, are, as we shewed you, in suspence about) we should not yet be able to conclude from thence, that others might not do it for them. For whenever the Obstacle to any Action arises from the Person, and not from the Thing, then what one is not allowed to do himself, another may do for him ... Now what prohibits the Subject to resist, does not at all proceed from a Cause, which is the same in a Subject, as in him who is not so; but from the Quality and Circumstance of the Person, which Quality does not pass to others.

And therefore, according to *Seneca*, I may make War upon a Man, tho' he and I are of different Nations, if he disturbs and molests his own Country, as we told you in our Discourse about Punishments, which is an Affair often attended with the Defence of innocent Subjects. Antient and modern History indeed informs us, that Avarice and Ambition do frequently lay hold on such Excuses; but the Use that wicked Men make of a Thing, does not always hinder it from being just in itself. *Pirates sail on the Seas, and Thieves wear Swords, as well as others.*[13]

The principal example which Grotius had in mind was presumably once again the Dutch Revolt, though in his "Discourse about Punishments" referred to above (i.e. Book II chapter 20) he dealt at length with the question of intervention in the non-European world against the practices of native peoples which went against the laws of nature.

We must also know, that Kings, and those who are invested with a Power equal to that of Kings, have a Right to exact Punishments, not only for Injuries committed against themselves, or their Subjects, but likewise, for those which do not peculiarly concern them, but which are, in any Persons whatsoever, grievous Violations of the Law of Nature or Nations... And upon this Account it is, that *Hercules* is so highly extolled by the Antients, for having freed the Earth of *Antæus*, *Busiris*, *Diomedes*, and such like Tyrants, *Whose Countries, says Seneca of him, he passed over, not with an ambitious Design of gaining them for himself, but for the Sake of vindicating the Cause of the Oppressed...*

And so far we follow the Opinion of *Innocentius*, and others, who hold that War is lawful against those who offend against Nature; which is contrary to the Opinion of *Victoria, Vasquez, Azorius, Molina*, and others, who seem to require, towards making a War just, that he who undertakes it be injured in himself, or in his State, or that he has some Jurisdiction over the Person against whom the War is made. For they assert, that the Power of Punishing is properly an Effect of Civil Jurisdiction; whereas our Opinion is, that it proceeds from the Law of Nature (II.20.40).

The principal difference between Grotius and Gentili in this area was that Grotius was more troubled than Gentili had been about the strength

---

[13] *The Rights of War and Peace* (ed. J. Barbeyrac) (London, 1738).

of the moral framework in which sovereign agents acted. As far as Gentili was concerned, it was self-evident that the moral status of war was often obscure, and that both sides could reasonably suppose themselves to be in the right. This was true even if the choice facing a belligerent was between its self-interest and the morally right course of action – *neque parva est obscuritas, si utile cum honesto pugnet, quid nos sequi oporteat* he wrote in I.6.[14] And this was particularly the case, he said at the same place, when "one renders aid to allies, friends, kindred, neighbors and others whom one is under obligation to assist, and yet in so doing justly rouses against oneself the arms of the adversary whom one is attacking." Grotius's remarks on this issue in II.23 show his anxiety about taking up this insouciant position. On the one hand, "in the particular Acceptation of the Word, and as it regards the Action itself, War cannot be just on both Sides, nor can any Law Suit be so, because the very Nature of the Thing does not permit one to have a moral Power, or true Right, to two contrary Things, as suppose *to do a Thing, and to hinder the doing of it*." But on the other hand

it may happen that neither of the Parties in War acts unjustly. For no Man acts unjustly, but he who is conscious that what he does is unjust; and this is what many are ignorant of. So People may justly, that is, may honestly and fairly go to War. Because Men are very frequently unacquainted with several Things, both as to Matter of Right, and as to the Fact, from whence Right proceeds... An Instance of this we have in those who do not conform themselves to a Law, which without any Fault of theirs they are Strangers to, tho' that Law has been published, and so long too that they had Time enough to have been acquainted with it (II.23.2–3).

In other words, the test of whether one is acting justly may be whether one reasonably believes oneself to be doing so, even if there is infor- mation available which would, if known to one, undermine the belief. This fissure which Grotius had left open was of course to be widened into a devastating breach by Thomas Hobbes.

Hobbes – theorist of nonintervention?

Central to Hobbes's mature philosophy was the conviction that everyone was entitled to act defensively on their suspicion of a threat, and that no suspicion could be thought of as ill-founded, as the criteria for deciding

---

[14] "There is no little obscurity as to what course we ought to follow, when what is ethical conflicts with what is advantageous." *Honestum* is misleadingly translated as "honour" at this point in the Carnegie translation; Gentili was referring to the discussion in Cicero's *De Officiis* about the choice between what is *honestum*, i.e. morally correct, and what is *utile*, in our interest. Cicero believed that there was ultimately no real dilemma, as whatever is *utile* for the *respublica* of which we are part is *ipso facto honestum*; Gentili was prepared to countenance a more skeptical view.

this were in principle never available. (In the 1630s he even applied this
to the example of a legal action, when he wrote a brief for his employer
the young Earl of Devonshire to sue his mother for alleged peculation of
his inheritance during his minority; the brief asserts that everyone is
entitled to act on their suspicions.)[15] Accordingly, Hobbes's theory often
sounds in practice rather like Gentili's (whose lectures he could conceiv-
ably have attended as an undergraduate at Oxford), though the underlying philosophy was far more carefully worked out; one could say that
Gentili's defense of pre-emptive strikes became in Hobbes's hands an
entire political philosophy.

I do not need to go into detail here about the way in which Hobbes
developed this idea about the absence of secure epistemic criteria and its
relationship in his thought to the central principle of self-preservation.[16]
But I do want to emphasize that the implications for Hobbes's account of
international relations are not entirely what one might have expected.
While the Hobbesian commonwealth is undeniably in a state of nature at
the international level, and therefore (like Gentili's or Grotius's) it can
intervene in the internal affairs of other states if it judges such intervention necessary or appropriate (whereas the citizens of that other state
cannot resist their sovereign), Hobbes presumed that such intervention,
and international war in general, would be imprudent and much less
common than one might have supposed on a naive reading of his work.
In *Leviathan*, Hobbes's only observation on international war was the
well-known remark in that

> though there had never been any time, wherein particular men were in a
> condition of warre one against another; yet in all times, Kings, and Persons of
> Soveraigne authority, because of their Independency, are in continuall jealousies,
> and in the state and posture of Gladiators ... But because they uphold thereby,
> the Industry of their Subjects; there does not follow from it, that misery, which
> accompanies the Liberty of particular men.[17]

But even this passage hints that a state will not behave straightforwardly
like an individual in the state of nature, and in his earlier works Hobbes
had said as much directly. In the *Elements of Law* (II.9.9) he said that the
defense of a state

---

[15] See A. A. Rogow, *Thomas Hobbes: Radical in the Service of Reaction* (New York: Norton,
1986).

[16] For a full discussion, see for example my *Hobbes* (Oxford University Press, 1989).

[17] Ch. 13 (p. 63 original edn.). This is from my edition for Cambridge University Press
(1991). The pagination of the original (1651) edition is nowadays used in most citations
of *Leviathan* as a method of locating passages irrespective of which modern edition is
being cited.

consisteth partly in the obedience and unity of the subjects, of which hath been already spoken, and in which consisteth the means of levying soldiers, and of having money, arms, ships, and fortified places in readiness for defence; and partly, in the avoiding of unnecessary wars. For such commonwealths, or such monarchs, as affect war for itself, that is to say, out of ambition, or of vain-glory, or that make account to revenge every little injury, or disgrace done by their neighbors, if they ruin not themselves, their fortune must be better than they have reason to expect.[18]

Similarly in *De Cive*, outlining the methods by which a state might promote its citizens' prosperity, he observed that

great commonwealths, particularly *Rome* and *Athens*, at certain times so enlarged their country from the spoils of war, foreign tribute and the acquisition of territory by arms, that they did not impose taxes on the poorer citizens; in fact they actually distributed money and land to individuals. But we should not take enrichment by these means into our calculations. For as a means of gain, military activity is like gambling; in most cases it reduces a person's property; very few succeed. As there are only three things then which enable the citizens to increase their prosperity – *products of earth and water, hard work* and *thrift* – they are the only objects of a sovereign's duty (XIII.14).[19]

The power and industry which a state possesses give it a kind of security which no natural individual can possess, and as a result free it from ambition or vainglory. Hobbes had always argued that high among the laws of nature was a willingness to accommodate oneself to others and to eschew glory; a commonwealth could be free to live consistently in accordance with this law, and not be driven by the need to exercise power over its neighbors, and to experience this power as glorifying. There is a somewhat utopian tinge to this vision, which came out clearly in *Leviathan* when he described the "kingdom of darkness" in which all our commonwealths have hitherto been embedded.

Whence comes it, that in Christendome there has been, almost from the time of the Apostles, such justling of one another out of their places, both by forraign, and Civill war? such stumbling at every little asperity of their own fortune, and every little eminence of that of other men? and such diversity of ways of running to the same mark, *Felicity*, if it be not Night amongst us, or at least a Mist? [W]ee are therefore yet in the Dark. (Chapter 44, p.334 of the original.)

Here we see, surprisingly, that foreign war is as much a sign of darkness as civil war, and that the well-founded commonwealths which Hobbes envisaged would not constantly be at war with one another. Indeed, one

---

[18] *Elements of Law* (ed. F. Toennies) (London, 1889).
[19] This is from the Cambridge edition, *The Citizen* (ed. R. Tuck, trans. M. Silverthorne) (Cambridge University Press, 1998).

could argue that Hobbes's general philosophy was driven by a fear of war at the international level as much as at the domestic one: whereas Gentili and (in many ways) Grotius legitimized and even gloried in the internecine warfare of modern Europe and the piratical interventions by Europeans in Asia and America, Hobbes in fact took their premises and then argued that pacific, or noninterventionist, rather than belligerent conduct might be the correct conclusion to draw from them, even without a world state to police the international realm. The prudent ruler understands that "wars of choice" are like gambling, unlikely to ever fully achieve one's objectives and in most instances merely squandering limited resources.

But of course on anything other than the most sensitive reading, Hobbes's basic theory of the rights of war did resemble those of Gentili and Grotius, and it is clear that some other way of limiting the alarming consequences of their ideas, and the far-reaching character of the intervention they countenanced, was felt to be necessary by men caught up in the ever-expanding turmoil of European war.

Pufendorf: humanitarian intervention only if the oppressed specifically request it

Reading both Grotius and Hobbes in the 1650s and 1660s, the German philosopher Samuel Pufendorf realized that a theory was needed which would preserve the essential insights of what (he understood) was a new kind of ethics while avoiding its distasteful implications. Essentially (and simplifying wildly), what Pufendorf did was to transpose the Hobbesian picture of men making their own morality from civil society to the state of nature: even without a political sovereign, men were capable of "the polishing and the methodizing of a common Life" in areas which answered to their needs – including language, which to Pufendorf seemed one of the most obvious counter-examples to Hobbes's pessimism about the possibility of joint enterprises outside politics. Morality was in many respects a human creation (though God, understood as an agent like a human being, could also play a part in creating it), and to that extent Hobbes was correct; but it could still be seen as universal in character, and to that extent Grotius was correct.

When it came to the specificities of international relations, Pufendorf was particularly critical of the more extreme ideas of both Grotius and Hobbes. As I showed in *The Rights of War and Peace*, his theory of private property was largely designed to deny European powers the right to seize the uncultivated lands of the New World, while famously he denied that European powers could plead native practices like cannibalism as justification for war against them. Already in his first work, the *Elementa Jurisprudentiae Universalis* of 1660, he proclaimed on this subject that

When a man unjustly hurts a second person, unless he hurt me indirectly at the same time, or unless I myself am under obligation to defend that other person against unjust violence, there does not come to me the right of bringing force to bear upon the first person, as long, indeed, as he shows no evidences of a hostile mind towards me.[20]

And in his great work of 1672, *De Iure Naturae et Gentium*, he attacked as an example of the kind of view found in Gentili or Grotius a passage in Francis Bacon's *An Advertisement Touching an Holy War*.

My Lord *Bacon* ... gives this a sufficient Reason for making War upon the *Americans*, which I must confess I cannot agree with him in: "That they were to be look'd upon as People proscribed by the Law of Nature, inasmuch as they had a barbarous Custom of sacrificing Men, and feeding upon Man's Flesh." For it ought to be distinctly considered, whether Christian Princes have sufficient Licence given them to invade those *Indians*, as People proscribed by Nature, only because they made Man's Flesh their common Food? Or because they eat the Bodies of Persons of their own Religion? Or, because they devoured Strangers and Foreigners? And then again it must be ask'd, whether those Strangers they are said to kill and eat, come as Enemies and Robbers, or as innocent Guests and Travellers, or as forc'd by Stress of Weather? For this last Case only, not any of the others, can give any Prince a *Right of War* against them; and this to those Princes only, whose Subjects have been used with that Inhumanity by them.[21]

He said the same in his general discussion of the question "whether it be lawful to take Arms in Defence of the Subjects of a *foreign* Common-wealth, against the *Invasions* and *Oppressions* of their *Sovereign*."

We are not to imagine that every Man, even they who live in the *Liberty of Nature*, hath a Right to correct and punish with War any Person who hath done another an Injury, barely upon Pretence that common Good requires, that such as oppress the Innocent ought not to escape Punishment, and that what touches one ought to affect all. For otherwise, since the Party we suppose to be unjustly invaded, is not deprived of the Liberty of using *equal* Force to repel his Enemy, whom he never injured; the Consequence *then* would be, that, instead of one *War*, the World must suffer the Miseries of two. Besides, it is, also, contrary to the natural *Equality* of Mankind, for a Man to force himself upon the World for a *Judge*, and *Decider* of *Controversies*. Not to say what dangerous Abuses this Liberty

---

[20] *Elementorum Jurisprudentiae Universalis Libri Duo* (ed. H. Wehberg, trans. W. A. Oldfather and E. H. Zeydel) (Carnegie Endowment for International Peace, Oxford University Press, 1931) II p. 252.

[21] *The Law of Nature and Nations* (trans. B. Kennet), 5th edn. (London, 1749) p. 840 (VIII.6.5).

might be perverted to, and that any Man might make War upon any Man upon such a Pretence (VIII.6.14).

He conceded that one might be entitled to intervene if an oppressed subject specifically requested it, but "we cannot lawfully undertake to defend the Subjects of a foreign Commonwealth in any other Case, than when they themselves may lawfully take Armes to suppress the insupportable Tyranny and Cruelties of their own Governors" (which Pufendorf accepted might be legitimate – see his remarks at VII.8.6).

There was little in Pufendorf with which Suarez would have disagreed. The new ideas about intervention developed by Gentili and Grotius had been abandoned, and a highly moralized and noninterventionary attitude to international affairs had taken their place. Scared by what their continent had done to itself in the name of humanitarian intervention – for we must remember that this was how the Wars of Religion and the Thirty Years War appeared to their participants – Pufendorf and his successors, especially in Germany, turned to a kind of isolationism. This was appropriate to their age: religious turmoil had ended and the great wars of the early and mid-eighteenth century did not as a rule involve the sort of intervention in the internal affairs of another country or support for revolutionaries which had been at the heart of the religious wars of the earlier period. Not until the so-called "age of revolutions" began in the 1780s, with the American, Batavian and French revolutions, did the issues faced by the early-modern writers reappear. And importantly, the writers of this revolutionary period, and their immediate predecessors such as Rousseau, turned in many ways back to Hobbes as a theorist of modern states, and away from the pieties of Pufendorf: a world in which citizens could appeal for their liberation to neighboring states was one in which it could not be the case that states had above all to respect one another's integrity.

5   John Locke on intervention, uncertainty, and insurgency*

Samuel Moyn

In his chapter "Of Conquest" in the *Second Treatise of Government,* John Locke takes it as obvious that there are just and unjust wars. He examines the case of *"lawful War,"* and invasions in which "Victory favors the right side." Conversely, he considers it self-evident that the wrong side can win out: "That the *Aggressor,* who puts himself in a state of War with another, and *unjustly invades* another Man's right, *can,* by such an unjust War, *never* come to *have a right over the Conquered,* will be easily agreed by all Men."[1] Yet Locke never – either in this text or anywhere else to my knowledge – spells out what criteria make such straightforward classification of conflicts possible. Why not? Focusing on Locke's crucial but hitherto little-noticed obsession with the biblical character of Jephtha, this chapter argues that the *Second Treatise* contains some very modern premises about the ubiquity, or at least frequency, of epistemic uncertainty in the determination of the justice of intervention – especially when otherwise valid norms are in contention. Indeed, even though he conceptualized this difficulty around a biblical exemplum, Locke can be seen as a pivotal figure between a premodern and modern way of imagining the morality of conflict – between a universe of sacred meaning and one in which secular morality sets the standard.

Above all, Locke highlighted that the core difficulty in international affairs as in political life generally may not be the absence of norms but the gap between the subjective conviction of actors about the norms they invoke and objective confirmation of their applicability – especially when

* I am grateful to Stefano Recchia, Melissa Schwartzberg, and Jennifer Welsh for suggestions that were extremely useful in restructuring and finalizing my original conference paper, as well as to James Q. Whitman for some late-breaking remarks.
[1] J. Locke, *Two Treatises of Government* (student edn. P. Laslett) (Cambridge University Press, 1988), §§ 176–7. Hereinafter cited in the text by paragraph number (per convention). For a useful survey of sources outside this classic and circumstantial text, see D. Armitage, "John Locke's International Thought," in I. Hall and L. Hill (eds.), *British International Thinkers from Hobbes to Namier* (Basingstoke: Palgrave Macmillan, 2009), pp. 33–48.

parties in dispute claim different norms to their cause. As Hedley Bull recognized, a portrait of the international order as "the anarchical society" is actually Lockean, given his view that norms, while contested, do obtain there in spite of the self-interest of its constituent states. Hence the difficulty is not *non-existence* of such norms, but their refractory interpretation (and toothless enforcement). "In modern international society, as in Locke's state of nature," Bull writes, "there is no central authority able to interpret and enforce the law, and thus individual members of the society must themselves interpret and enforce it ... But there is nevertheless a great difference between this rudimentary form of social life and none at all."[2] States and other actors appeal to norms all the time in international affairs; insofar as it is still easy to invoke but difficult to validate such claims, Locke's remains perhaps the most persuasive picture of international affairs.

Locke's interest, put differently, is in the formalities of decision-making: bridging the gap between mere invocation of a norm and its validation. In spite of his affirmation of the existence of natural law norms, however, it is a very different matter to suppose he was the founder of internationalist "liberalism," as concerns the substantive matters he did not address. It remains tempting to avoid the fact that Locke never spells out the rules and regulations of international society – except in the unique case of justice *after* intervention – by assuming symmetry between Locke's commitment to rights at home and his beliefs about what laws of nature govern transactions among states. Michael Doyle adopts this strategy of interpretation in his classic account, presenting Locke as the forebear of contemporary liberal internationalism. For Doyle, the fact that Locke announced natural rights must mean that he extended them beyond the domestic purposes of state foundation into the international zone; and it is true that Locke's analogy between the state of nature and the international realm lends this assumption credence. At the same time, as Doyle himself points out, the assumption of symmetry runs up against Locke's surprisingly "realist" conception of the federative power in the *Second Treatise*, in which authority over foreign affairs is not as rule bound as executive power over domestic concerns. "[W]hat is to be done to *Foreigners*," Locke expressly says, "depending much upon their actions, and the variation of designs and interests, must be *left* in great part *to* the *Prudence* of those who have this [federative] Power committed to

[2] H. Bull, *The Anarchical Society: A Study of Order in World Politics*, 3rd edn. (New York: Columbia University Press, 2002), pp. 46–7.
[3] M. Doyle, *Ways of War and Peace: Realism, Liberalism, and Socialism* (New York: W.W. Norton, 1997), ch. 6.

them." (§ 147, cf. §§ 45, 146, 148). Given the difficulties of distilling from Locke's writing any specific substantive norms of international relations, therefore, it seems much more interesting to dwell on his own interest in a *formal* account of just and unjust war.

Unlike some of his colleagues amongst natural and early international law theorists, Locke never addressed humanitarian intervention. He worried more about the very real threat of unjust conquest: "the noise of War," as he called it, "makes so great a part of the History of Mankind" and it "is as far from setting up any government, as demolishing an House is from building a new one in the place" (§ 175). The fact that Locke forebore from outlining any moral rules for intervention, and instead ratified the possible moral credentials of insurgency against immoral incursion, makes him a rather different figure from most contemporary theorists of international relations – and once again difficult to enlist as a precursor of contemporary liberalism.[4] But it is precisely here that his work seems of obvious theoretical significance today, especially in the aftermath of recent years, in which theorizing and moralizing intervention would seem not without its own drawbacks. In the absence of a secure way to adjudicate disputes over the norms governing conflict, Locke's case suggests, the epistemic uncertainty of warfare makes a theoretical rationale for insurgency an essential complement to any theory of intervention.

*

Locke, famously, broke with Thomas Hobbes's fully normless picture of the international sphere. Instead, he imported norms into the state of nature which, as Richard Tuck has so penetratingly argued, both thinkers explicitly modeled on the international realm by a kind of analogy.[5] Where Hobbes found it impossible to discern any general norms of conduct beyond that of self-preservation in either realm, Locke identified a "law of nature" ostensibly "plain and intelligible to all rational Creatures" (§ 124). To be sure, the norms Locke insisted were there – however much the lenses of self-interest could distort them – remained tenuous in their purchase, even to him. Jephtha, the biblical character frequently referred to in Locke's *Second Treatise*, explained why. Jephtha also illuminated how the originally fractious situation of the state of nature, in which valid norms obtained but not

---

[4] There are, however, some interesting affinities with Giuseppe Mazzini's arguments on insurgency and insurrection against foreign despotism. See ch. 11 by S. Recchia in this volume, esp. pp. 245–8.

[5] R. Tuck, *The Rights of War and Peace: Political Thought and the International Order from Grotius to Kant* (Oxford University Press, 1999).

everyone agreed on what they were or how to proceed when they conflicted, could recur within organized political society.

It is easy to forget the generally religious and specifically biblical terms in which Western political – including international – thought has often taken place, down into the twentieth century.[6] But lest my approach still seem idiosyncratic, it is worthwhile to dwell upon the fact that Jephtha is indeed crucial to the *Second Treatise*, in spite of his strange neglect in scholarship, even in what is a golden age of taking Locke's religiosity seriously. Jephtha is the signature exemplum of the *Second Treatise*, for his use in thinking about conflict, whether prepolitical or intrapolitical, and the morality governing it, as the model of Locke's famous "appeal to heaven." Jephtha is discussed in detail in the text three times at critical points, and referenced half a dozen times more, more than Abraham, Isaac, Jacob, Moses, Joshua, Saul, and David, not to mention Jesus (or any other New Testament character) (see §§ 21, 176, 221). Only Adam, the central figure in the biblically saturated *First Treatise*, is discussed as much as Jephtha in its sequel explicitly – and far less, if the implicit references are counted, since Locke frequently uses variations of the idea of appealing to heaven, often apart from when (in fact, even before) Jephtha is cited by name (see §§ 19–20, 87, 91, 94, 168, and 242). Finally, these references are theoretically central, surfacing as part of the discussions that have made the *Second Treatise* famous: the state of nature, the right of revolution, and – as the last part of this chapter will address – the prerogatives of insurgency. If Locke's obsession with Jephtha provides striking proof for Tuck's general thesis about the template that "international affairs" provided for the state of nature and the state of war, one may add that the international affairs *of the Bible* were the ones he presented most often in this text as the truly relevant model.

Yet Jephtha's omnipresence has been considered only glancingly in commentary. In his epoch-making edition of the 1960s, Peter Laslett commented at two points in passing footnotes that Jephtha was "critical to Locke's use of Scripture to sanction his political theory" and "crucial to the scriptural foundations of his case about civil society and justice." That Locke plucked Jephtha from obscurity to make him *the* guide to conflict and war in the *Second Treatise* would seemingly have then been set for attention. Inaugurating the age of acknowledging Locke's religiosity, John Dunn insisted that "Locke continues to use [the Hebrew Bible's] exemplary resources as the accredited vocabulary for discussing political issues." And he footnoted as his first proof the Jephtha story –

---

[6] *Cf.* E. Nelson, *The Hebrew Republic: Jewish Sources and the Transformation of European Political Thought* (Cambridge, MA: The Belknap Press of Harvard University Press, 2010).

but did not otherwise discuss it in his classic book. Further, in the most imposing monument left (so far) by the Cambridge School on Locke, John Marshall's study, Jephtha doesn't merit a mention, contextual matters submerging a point of apparent textual importance. Meanwhile, in his recent *God, Locke, and Equality*, Jeremy Waldron – dissenting from Cambridge methods but certainly vindicating its intended stress on religion and scripture – kicks around for a chapter the problem of why Locke referenced the Old Testament more than the New Testament in the *Two Treatises*, but is interested in Locke's argument for basic equality rather than his social contract theory, and so references Jephtha only once in passing.[7]

So: what did Locke find of use in the Jephtha story? I want to argue that he uses it in effect as a parable about moral judgment under conditions of uncertainty about the legitimacy of warfare (and by analogy all social conflict). According to his story as told in the Book of Judges, Jephtha was the son of a harlot sought by the Israelites as a military leader in the era before the rise of kingship. It was a moment when the Israelites were menaced by the Ammonites, a group that had been displaced in the era when God's promise of occupation of the land had been fulfilled. Later, Jephtha wins the war but loses his daughter, whom he apparently sacrifices after he promises God to offer up the first person he sees if he returns victorious. Locke's interest in Jephtha's dialogue with his enemy prior to the fight is eccentric in the history of interpretation of the story, both in Jewish traditions and modern ones. Jephtha's "vow" and apparent sacrifice of his daughter have garnered far more attention.

Ignoring the rest of the biblical pericope, Locke focuses in a quite unusual way in the history of its interpretation on Jephtha's brief colloquy with the Ammonites when he heads out to meet them.[8] Jephtha sends a query to the Ammonite king, according to Judges 11, asking why he is preparing to invade. "And Jephthah sent messengers unto the king of the children of Ammon, saying, What hast thou to do with me, that thou art come against me to fight in my land?" (11: 12). In the verses that follow, Jephtha and his interlocutor engage in a very striking discussion of whether there is a legitimate *casus belli*. The Ammonite's answer is that the Israelites took the land, "from Ammon even unto the Jabbok, and unto Jordan," and now the Ammonites want it back (11: 13). Though the

---

[7] J. Dunn, *The Political Thought of John Locke: An Historical Account of the Argument of the "Two Treatises of Government"* (Cambridge University Press, 1969), p. 99, *cf.* p. 180; J. Marshall, *John Locke: Resistance, Religion, and Responsibility* (Cambridge University Press, 1994); J. Waldron, *God, Locke, and Equality: Christian Foundations in Locke's Political Thought* (Cambridge University Press, 2002), ch. 7.

[8] For further details, see my "Appealing to Heaven: Jephtha, John Locke, and Just War," *Hebraic Political Studies* 4, no. 3 (Summer 2009), 286–303.

prior history is, as is usual in these cases, not entirely clear, Jephtha responds by pointing out that the Ammonites had been displaced by a former king, Sihon, who lost the land when he attacked the Israelites, who were trying to pass through at a later date (*cf.* Numbers 20–1). But Jephtha soon turns to a different argument. Whatever their specific catalysts, it fulfilled a divine purpose for the Israelites to win these campaigns: Yahweh gave the Israelites the land and the Israelites took it, just, Jephtha says, as the Ammonites would keep with a clear conscience what their deity gave them. Anyway, Jephtha concludes, the Israelites have now been there three hundred years; if the Ammonites wanted to make some claim to the land, why wait all this time to assert it? In the crucial verse, Jephtha concludes: "Wherefore I have not sinned against thee, but thou doest me wrong to war against me: the Lord the Judge be judge this day between the children of Israel and the children of Ammon" (11: 27). To this message, the Ammonites "hearkened not," whereupon Jephtha brings the battle to the enemy amidst "very great slaughter" and wins out; not long after, he leaves the stage of history.

Of course, one of the three independent possible reasons Jephtha offers in this remarkable passage for the Israelite possession is simply God's promise; in Judges 11: 24, Jephtha says that you would take (and keep) what your god gave you, so he is right in doing the same. But Locke was correct to see two other elements; first, the argument that the occupation of the land had been just according to applicable rules of warfare; and second, even if the Ammonites had enjoyed a right of return of sorts after their expulsion, they lost it by not exercising it in time. As a result, Jephtha's military cause is *not* like elsewhere in the Bible a kind of pure holy or "divine" or "Yahweh" war, where God is supposed simply to favor his people. Rather, Jephtha appeals to God as a judge to determine whether he is in fact correct in his estimate of the justice of the dispute, according to specific applicable norms. (Indeed, though they may not know they are in effect following Locke, some contemporary scholars highlight this moment as a striking *divergence* from the Yahweh war tradition that otherwise dominates biblically. Susan Niditch, perhaps a little hyperbolically, given how spare the text is after all, calls Jephtha's "concern with political ethics stunning . . . [W]ars require just causes and to fight without just cause is to do evil.")[9]

[9] S. Niditch, *War in the Hebrew Bible: A Study in the Ethics of Violence* (Oxford University Press, 1993), p. 126. See also G. von Rad, *Holy War in Ancient Israel* (trans. M. J. Dawn) (Grand Rapids, MI: W.B. Eerdmans, 1991) and Sa-Moon Kang, *Divine War in the Old Testament and in the Ancient Near East* (Berlin: W. de Gruyter, 1989).

Now, in focusing rather interestingly on the story, and on this specific moment in it, Locke might have drawn on a couple of clear precedents, in spite of the general inattention to the dimensions of the story he favored. After all, the contest of norms and the basic difficulty of uncertainty long pre-existed Locke's thought, in Roman and Christian traditions that provided materials for subsequent just war approaches.[10] And in both Hugo Grotius and John Milton, albeit in passing, the stress falls not simply on Jephtha's colloquy with the Ammonites, but on the rationale for war that Jephtha offered. In *Samson Agonistes*, Milton writes of "Jephtha, who by argument, /Defended Israel from the Ammonite." It is first of all by appeals to norms, not by immediate force of arms, that Jephtha led the Israelites to victory. And though that conclusion is somewhat more implicit in Grotius, an illuminating passage from *The Rights of War and Peace* suggests the same drift. "GOD himself prescribed to his People certain general and established rules for making War, *Deut.* xx. 10, 15. thereby plainly shewing, that War might sometimes be just, even without a special command," Grotius maintained. Since in the Bible God ⸢did not declare the just Reasons of making War, he thereby supposes that they may be easily discovered by the Light of Nature. Such was the Cause of the War made by *Jephtha* against the *Ammonites*, in defense of their Borders, *Judges* xi."[11] ⸢It was the norms of natural law to which Grotius, too, thought Jephtha appealed in his colloquy on which Locke builds.⸥

Thus, in the *Second Treatise* Locke was not alone in seeking not simply in the Bible but in this specific story a theory of *jus ad bellum* norms (rather than the *jus in bello* ones that are typically seen as the Hebrew Bible's sole contribution – including by Jewish interpreters up to and including Michael Walzer lately).[12] ⸢But Locke went far further than Grotius, who simply saw the story illustrating the availability of non-revealed norms of conduct, where Locke deploys the story as part of an elaborate theory in which these norms control (though they may not obviate) conflict.⸥ It would not be too much to say that Locke embedded the story at the core of his text, especially insofar as he presents the

---

[10] See esp. P. Haggenmacher, *Grotius et la doctrine de la guerre juste* (Paris: Presses universitaires, 1983), Pt. 1, ch. 7, esp. pp. 224–49. See also S. C. Neff, *War and the Law of Nations: A General History* (Cambridge University Press, 2005), ch. 3, esp. pp. 96–7, 103–11.

[11] H. Grotius, *The Rights of War and Peace*, 3 vols. (ed. R. Tuck) (Indianapolis: Liberty Fund, 2003), vol. I, p. 186.

[12] See M. Walzer, "War and Peace in the Jewish Tradition," in T. Nardin (ed.), *The Ethics of War and Peace: Religious and Secular Perspectives* (Princeton University Press, 1998).

warfare it illustrates as the template for conflict as such, in the origins and even the possible end of the social contract.

The core of Locke's reading of Jephtha is a theory of the sort of epistemic uncertainty that the perception of norms does not abate; for there is still the problem of their interpretation and conflict – a situation the normative contention of the Israelites and Ammonites perfectly illustrates. A sample invocation of Jephtha in the *Second Treatise* (§ 21) shows Locke appealing to Jephtha for his ostensible insight into epistemic uncertainty. Jephtha's problem, Locke clearly states, is that there was no "superior Jurisdiction on Earth, to determine the right between *Jephtha and the Ammonites.*" His problem was not a lack of arguments but the difficulty of verifying them. In a more philosophical register, he sought a way to move from subjective conviction of right to objective confirmation of it. "[W]e see," Locke continues, "he was forced to appeal to *Heaven. The Lord the Judge* (says he) *be Judge this day between the Children of* Israel *and the children of* Ammon, *Judg.* 11. 27. and then Prosecuting, and relying on his *appeal*, he leads out his Army to Battle."

For Grotius already, as an exemplum of hoary traditions, Jephtha is supposed to illustrate that norms, not their absence, govern warfare. But Locke takes this reading far further, introducing a powerful fallibilist note in Jephtha's thinking. Grotius's "light of nature" is there, but it is not strong enough. The problem that Locke underlines – implicit in the original story if there at all – is that the contending arguments for just and unjust cause under general norms is an *epistemic* problem as much as it is a *political* one. More accurately, it is because resolving the just cause in a dispute is an epistemic problem that it is a political one: the difficulty of knowing how asserted norms apply is the root condition of politics. And perhaps Locke also has in mind, beyond real epistemic uncertainty about how to apply general norms in a particular case, that each actor knows he is both liable to simple interpretive error and to bias on the grounds of self-interest: fallibility and partiality. In Locke's picture, war (or violence disrupting society from within) is never an objectively warranted act. It is only, at best, subjectively warranted: and war itself is then a kind of the search for God's confirmation of the justice of one's cause, in the absence of any other kind.

For Locke, then, Jephtha wants to subsume his personal conduct under general norms, but the trouble is that it is very hard for him to know that he is properly doing so, especially when the other side claims to be doing the same thing. Another way to put this point is to say that Locke anachronistically imputes to the story the modern sense of "judging" as an intellectual activity – God's deliberation concerning the validity of contending norms deployed in good faith. True, it suits Locke to register his awareness in these passages that the office of *judge* that Jephtha holds, and that gives its name to the book of the Bible (Judges) in which his story figures, is a title of leadership and rule (see esp. § 109; compare *First Treatise*, § 163). But this fact suggests that his central and prevalent deployment of Jephtha, which cuts across this historical admission to present judging as a deliberative activity determining the validity of contending norms deployed in good faith, was quite intentional. This is why, overall, Hobbes and Locke pose the problem of a lack of a common authority so differently: for Hobbes, it is the absence of general norms, where for Locke, it is the difficulty of knowing how they fall out when in contention, one that God remedies.

Locke selected the story of Jephtha, in other words, because he believed it illustrated precisely the situation he thought could come to prevail in the state of nature, and accounts for the centrality of "appealing to heaven" to his whole political doctrine. Of course, the moralized nature of warfare does not mean wars of death and destruction are avoidable. But for Locke, the Jephtha story further illustrates that the warfare one might have to choose in the alternative to political compact is never without moral constraint, since the resolution of the appeal to God's decision – not of the war, but of the justice of one's cause – will always come. When there is no judge on earth, and no way of creating one, there is always one in heaven, watching over the battle. And that means there are just and unjust wars, even if there are times when only God can tell which is which.

*

Now, there is a powerful alternative – indeed opposite – interpretation of such passages. According to Leo Strauss, Locke's sly invocation of Jephtha, as of biblical authority generally, was in the service of relativism not moralism. Locke "quotes more than once Jephtha's saying 'the Lord the Judge be Judge,'" Strauss observes in *Natural Right in History*. "The statement of Jephtha takes the place in Locke's doctrine of Paul's statement 'Let every soul be subject to the higher powers,' which he hardly, if ever, quotes."[13] For Strauss, Locke's extravagant biblical references are part of a massive ruse to break with the authority of natural right – Greek, Jewish, and Christian – in the name of modern relativism. It is no

[13] L. Strauss, *Natural Right and History* (University of Chicago Press, 1953), pp. 214–15. In the Straussian tradition, see also R. Cox, *Locke on War and Peace* (Oxford: Clarendon Press, 1960); L. Ward, "Locke on the Moral Basis of International Relations," *American Journal of Political Science* 50, no. 3 (July 2006), pp. 691–705; and Ward, *Locke and Modern Life* (Cambridge University Press, 2010), esp. ch. 7.

accident, according to the Straussian, that Locke says little if anything at all about what norms do as a matter of fact govern conflict, even within the details of the Jephtha story, let alone in general. If he begins his chapter on conquest by dividing his reasoning into cases of just and unjust incursion, as if it were obvious deciding which were which, or even what principles distinguished them, he does not spell out his assumptions. For the Straussian, Locke's willingness to countenance violent struggle for perceived right without any real constraint besides the postponed and probably non-existent divine judgment Locke holds out is really just a recipe for selfishness on demand – no real constraint at all.

Two features of Locke's argumentation lend some credence to this interpretation. One is that he insisted on the perpetual availability of the appeal to heaven, even after the formation of organized society, because there were no circumstances in which even a human judge could provide God's objectivity. In the continuation of the example of Jephtha from the *Second Treatise*, § 21, Locke clearly shows that a sort of decisional regress can function to make the validity of the "appeal to heaven" exclusive:

And therefore in such Controversies, where the question is put, *who shall be Judge*? It cannot be meant, who shall decide the Controversie; every one knows what *Jephtha* here tells us, that the *Lord the Judge*, shall judge. Where there is no Judge on Earth, the *Appeal* lies to God in Heaven. That Question then cannot mean, who shall judge? whether another hath put himself in a State of War with me, and whether I may as *Jephtha* did, appeal to Heaven in it? Of that I myself can only be Judge in my own Conscience, as I will answer it at the great Day, to the Supream Judge of all Men. (§ 21)

One response to the lack of a judge in a substantive controversy – in the international realm or any other – is to ask for a judge of the very different questions of whether and when the controversy is irresolvable. Who has the better argument is one thing; when it is legitimate to break off that normative contention through argument and move to some other sort of resolution (for example, arms) is another. That latter question, Locke insists, is completely and equally up to each side to answer. Similarly, in a new version of the regress in a later section on the right of revolution, not just resolving a conflict between a revolutionary and the existing government, but knowing exactly when it is legitimate to become a revolutionary in the first place, is in the end entirely one's own conscientious choice, checked only by heaven's validation: "[God] alone, 'tis true, is Judge of the Right. But *every Man* is *Judge* for himself, as in all other Cases, so in this, whether another hath put himself into a State of War with him, and whether he should appeal to heaven." The upshot is that asking "Who shall judge?" at a moment of irreconcilable invocations of norms is in fact a *warrant for violent action*.[14]

Further, it should be acknowledged that Locke's Protestantism led him to individualize and postpone God's judgment to the moment of the pearly gates, so that in the end it is a far cry from the apparent biblical model he cited, in which Jephtha seems to expect the battle itself to resolve the normative contention. This deferral is even clearer in the Jephtha passage in the chapter on conquest (which I will examine shortly); because Locke is also prepared to allow infinitely renewable appeals to heaven in cases of historical loss, it is not clear how the law of nature judged by God has any real meaning – so far as this world is concerned. There can never be decisive proof that I am in the wrong, which allows me to pursue my cause stubbornly. Locke's very postponement of judgment adds force to the Straussian contention that, from the perspective of its secular outcomes, operating under moral constraint doesn't seem to differ that much from getting out of that constraint. If I nevertheless disagree with this reading, it is for two main reasons, one textual and one historical.

As the text illustrates, Locke clearly understands the Jephtha story to be about a gap between subjective conviction in the justice of one's cause and objective uncertainty about it. Though it surely leads to violence, the appeal to heaven is explicitly presented not as a straightforward objective warrant for violent action but as a search for some validation for a mere subjective conviction that one's cause is just. And contrary to Strauss, the difficulty of the move to objectivity seems very real, not simply a device through which to smuggle subjectivism into political theory. In the international order, not to mention all legal systems, situations arise all the time in which colorable claims can be offered by two contending parties and one's pursuit of justice needs to be ratified by a common judge (it is one point of judicial systems to provide such a thing). Locke's case is thus a formal one, illustrating the problem of normative contention *whatever the norms involved* – and from this perspective what looks like an unaccountable neglect of substantive theory is actually in the service of a formal point. As noted above, Locke could have chosen countless instances of biblical (or other) warfare if his

[14] This is so even if one wants, like Julian Franklin, to read the theoretical acquisition of the *Second Treatise* as the lodging of constituent authority in the people; for, as § 242 makes clear, normative contention over whether the prince has betrayed his trust is likely to be another *casus belli*: "But if the prince, or whoever they be in the administration, decline that way of determination [namely, by the people], the appeal then lies no where but to heaven; force between either persons, who have no known superior on earth, or which permits no appeal to a judge on earth, being properly a state of war." *Cf.* J. H. Franklin, *John Locke and the Theory of Sovereignty* (Cambridge University Press, 1978).

agenda were to imply that men have no real access to norms and God must decide: the exceptional case of Jephtha is one in which the problem is not that the norms are absent, but that they are there.

Then there are details of Locke's doctrine of the appeal to heaven that seem hard to explain if unrestrained license were its goal. Locke clearly sees appealing to heaven, as Jephtha did, as an option of last resort, which is constrained in many ways, and to be avoided as extremely hazardous business – hazardous morally first of all. When he mentions Jephtha in his consideration of the right of conquest, Locke first responds to the objection that the possibility of appeals to heaven would cause "endless trouble" with the bravado reply that it would create "no more [trouble] than justice does" (§ 176). But not only do such appeals have to be treated as last resort (§ 20). Locke also clarifies that "he that appeals to heaven must be sure he has right on his side ... as he will answer at a tribunal that cannot be deceived, and will be sure to retribute to every one according to the mischiefs he hath created to his fellow subjects; that is, any part of mankind" (§ 176). For Locke, you must really believe you are in the right, because the grief suffered by "any part of mankind" due to your premature or mistaken choice of the extreme solution is to be counted against you. The war does take place, because sometimes it is the only bridge from subjective conviction to objective validity. But there seems little reason for Locke to enter these warnings, especially about the extraordinarily vast scope of harm to be considered in cases of error, unless he sincerely believed that appeals to heaven were a terrible business foreclosed except when justice required them.

Classic Locke

A historical companion to these textual considerations is that it seems much more plausible and interesting to see Locke not as a closet relativist but rather as a true believer who, paradoxically enough, depended on his trust in God's ultimate judgment to introduce consent as the basis of government. Put differently, Locke still needed the assumption of God's eventual vindication of sides in potentially bloody conflict in order to claim the risky autonomy of human self-government, not simply as a foundational matter, as in Hobbes, but as an ongoing feature of human political community. If so, and very remarkably, ongoing popular consent emerged in Locke in connection with a religious prophylaxis against its potentially anarchic implications.

*

This reading of Locke as a theorist of epistemic uncertainty about the objective validity of subjectively asserted norms in contention (whether in the state of nature or the international sphere) has obvious implications for the contemporary bearing of his theory. To the extent he was already on the road – through his invocations of his biblical hero! – from the sacred to the secular, perhaps it is possible to take his theory further, and provide a fully worldly equivalent of the objectivity he assumed only God could supply.

After all, for bounded territories Locke imagines the rise of a political society to avoid the "anarchical society" of the state of nature, which is to be fled not because it lacks norms, but because the difficulty of their interpretation and enforcement still makes it a scene of considerable insecurity. Its "inconveniences," Locke puts it, "necessarily follow from every Man's being Judge in his own Case" (§ 90). "To avoid this State of War (wherein there is no appeal but to Heaven, and wherein every the least difference is apt to end, where there is no Authority to decide between the Contenders) is one great *reason of Mens putting themselves into Society*, and quitting the State of Nature: for where there is an Authority, a Power on Earth, from which relief can be had by *appeal*, there the continuance of the State of War is excluded, and the Controversie is decided by that Power." If exit from the state of nature is possible within the territorial state, why not from a still excessively anarchical international society? Why, in other words, not create at the international level precisely the sort of "superior Jurisdiction on Earth" that Jephtha had to seek in heaven? (§ 21).

Tempting as this option sounds, it seems to me that Locke would reject it, at least as a bid to supplant God's ability wholly with the objective confirmation provided by some secular agency. Leaving aside his account of the federative power, perhaps Locke might have argued that an imperfect authority in the international realm would be preferable to none. But would he have gone further? True, Locke could not have imagined the modern and especially post-World War II attempt to enact the sort of global system of peace and security in which the United Nations Security Council might play a leading role. The framers of the United Nations, as Chapters VI–VII of its charter clearly indicate, favored peace rather than justice as the organization's purpose – the pacific not moral resolution of disputes. But this fact has not foreclosed the emergence and proliferation of a large body of human rights norms that now inform global peacemaking, along with the legal guidance which the International Court of Justice was always intended to provide.[15] As such, perhaps it might one day serve as the God whom Locke saw as the sole recourse for order and justice abroad, just as he imagined the state providing it at home.

[15] Compare my *The Last Utopia: Human Rights in History* (Cambridge, MA: The Belknap Press of Harvard University Press, 2010), for a skeptical interpretation of the UN's role in the recent prominence of such norms.

On second thought, however, it seems dubious that Locke provides authority for much more than the provisional attempt to erect such suprastate agencies of normative validation, for the very same reason that he found the prince's office at home provisional, as a common judge making appeals to heaven a rarity but not an impossibility. On the one hand, Locke remained wary of any attempt to overstate the definitive authority of the secular solution even in the domestic case of the state. The risk of injustice even in local matters – which comes out most vividly in his brief for revolutionaries and insurgents who maintain their rights to resist injustice for as long as they like – reserved the appeal to heaven for all men and for all time. However fearful an option it may have been, Locke considered even the state as at best a useful attempt to achieve "superior jurisdiction," which unlike God could and did often fail to provide the very objective confirmation of subjective convictions in contest it was set up to achieve. On the other hand, no institution could foreclose the problem of decisional regress – on the possibility of which both at home and abroad Locke clearly insisted. While he hypothesized a "Power on Earth, from which relief can be had by *appeal*," ultimately whether such power reaches the just result is a matter of conscience, and does not foreclose the appeal to heaven except provisionally. No secular institution could ever, Locke clearly states, absolutely keep me from posing the question: Who shall judge?

This may simply mean that Locke becomes less and less useful for secular purposes, to the extent he is taken as much to establish a lasting and insuperable gap between subjective conviction and objective validity, as to desire to bridge it definitively. If only God can properly provide the sort of objective validation that could foreclose the appeal to heaven, one might conclude, then Locke's theory is simply inappropriate in a world in which the differences between better and worse secular alternatives are more salient than those between them and God's perfect justice. Today people still seek grounds for knowing when their wars are just or unjust, but – presumably for the better – few now permit themselves to trust that there is some nonhuman judge to check their best guess or adamant conviction about when to fight. They make do with the secular alone in crafting doctrines of war and peace; if so, the memory of God's rule that still persisted in Locke must now give way entirely to his argument that if there is a need for a common judge to settle our disputes, people must find a way to provide it themselves – in the international realm on the model of Locke's internal state.

Yet that is the point. Just as it is important to see how modern Locke was, it is fully as crucial to acknowledge that his belief in God's sole ability to provide confirmation above and beyond human distortion of the purchase of moral norms left him irredeemably premodern. Those today who seek a secular equivalent of God's judgment can therefore not easily count Locke as one of their predecessors. It was, in short, not simply a failure of the imagination that hampered Locke in the development of a theory of international law and institutions that would certify factual or normative assertions. And while he did clearly hope for post-conflict arbitration of the justice of claims advanced for intervention, he gave no sign of assuming humanity could provide it – even provisionally, in the apparently chaotic realm of the international order in which no move away from the state of nature was possible.

For all its obsolescence, however, Locke's approach might have a valuable critical function insofar as the perfection of God's justice does provide a helpful reminder that no human institutions may ever fully confirm subjective convictions to everyone's – or anyone's – satisfaction. Human institutions may provide an expedient or even the best available resolution to human conflict, but few will agree that they unfailingly provide a just or moral one.

For a vivid and counterintuitive case of the continuing relevance of Locke's argument that a subjective conviction of justice should make extreme measures available, consider the example of the American invasion of Iraq in 2003. After Security Council Resolution 1441, unanimously adopted to give Saddam Hussein a last chance to disarm, United States Secretary of State Colin Powell gave his much-remarked presentation suggesting that Iraq's continued possession of "weapons of mass destruction" violated the resolution. Thereafter, the United States government and its allies proposed another resolution formalizing this finding – but could not win enough votes for it to be passed. In conflict with Iraq, the United States and its coalition attempted an appeal to the Security Council, which failed to find in its favor. But the Security Council did not prove to be the court of last resort – for the invasion occurred anyway.

The United States, one might say, believed Iraq had put itself in a "state of war" against the American people (or the world as a whole), and Washington thus chose to appeal to heaven once it exhausted its existing appeals – an option Locke might have held out, given his insistence that no one can ever foreclose the position that the worldly search for justice is imperfect and fighting under God's judgeship alone must always be possible, when push comes to shove. One might well consider international institutions and law a good enough mechanism to provide confidence in stipulated facts or normative rules that should prospectively govern conflict. But the United States in effect posed the question to the nations of "old Europe" that opposed its invasion: Who shall judge? And while much rhetoric was aimed at the United States in its rush to war, doubtful observers did not appeal to heaven themselves to the point of opposing the venture by taking up arms – whatever that would have meant. Crucially, they apparently possessed no viable secular means to convincingly prove that the Security Council had been right in opposing the invasion until years later, when widespread consensus crystallized around the belief that the American facts had been wrong.

★

True, one might take these very events as decisive rationale for building an international system that forbids appeals outside its boundaries. But Locke's surprising inference from epistemic uncertainty to the eternally preserved right to appeal to heaven favors anyone who resorts to it, and foreclosing it only makes sense to the extent one believes that today's world is anywhere close to silencing the "noise of war" in which interventions, even ones based on claims of right, often err or are even conquest by another name. Locke's "*Aggressor[s]*" who "*never* come to *have a right over the Conquered*" have not been rare in the last century, even if the rosiest portrait of the pacifying and moralizing effects of the evolution of the international community were proved accurate. If the noise of unjust war remains deafening, the appeal to heaven is there not just for imperialists and other strident evildoers but also for insurgents and anyone who seeks justice amidst the cacophany. Insurgency against unjust conquest not liberal internationalism is perhaps in this sense the Lockean contribution that remains most morally salient today – however seldom explored theoretically.

Debates still rage about the (incontestably quite significant) extent to which the projects of European colonialism informed Locke's political theory.[16] As noted above, Locke did not systematically distinguish conquest and other forms of intervention, and had no theory of humanitarian intervention in particular. The energy in the discussion of his colonialism really turns around his chapter on property rather than his chapter on conquest; and the former in fact offers a rather full-bodied account of what we now call *jus post bellum*. (Indeed, Locke's theory of *jus post bellum* is undoubtedly the only – and therefore quite exceptional – place in the *Second Treatise* in which actual substantive norms of conduct are presented.)[17] All the same, what is perhaps most interesting from the

---

[16] For two invaluable starting points, see D. Armitage, "John Locke, Carolina, and the *Two Treatises of Government*," *Political Theory* 32, vol. 5 (October 2004), 602–27; and D. Armitage, "John Locke, Theorist of Empire?," in S. Muthu (ed.), *Empire and Political Thought* (Cambridge University Press, 2012).

[17] I object simply to inferring from these exceptional passages what Doyle calls "a powerful moral Liberal foundation for the precepts of contemporary international law," as if

standpoint of the present day is not that Locke provides continuing resources for a doctrine of intervention but that Locke did not hesitate to justify *insurgency* against unjust intervention – and indeed in the very terms this chapter has outlined, as if its votaries were also emblematic successors to Jephtha in their pursuit of justice under conditions of uncertainty.

Jephtha arises explicitly again in Locke's discussion of the right of insurgency against unlawful conquest. In the relevant passage, Locke holds out a kind of perpetual right of renewal of one's cause, whether within a legal framework or through extra-legal violence if necessary. And once again, the model is Jephtha's appeal to heaven:

[P]erhaps Justice is denied [in conquest] ... If God has taken away all means of seeking remedy, there is nothing left but patience. But my Son, when able, may seek the Relief of the Law, which I am denied: He or his Son may renew his *Appeal*, till he recover his Right. But the Conquered, or his Children, have no Court, no Arbitrator on Earth to appeal to. Then they may *appeal*, as *Jephtha* did, to *Heaven*, and repeat their *Appeal*, till they have recovered the native Right of their Ancestors ... If it be objected, this would cause endless trouble; I answer, No more than Justice does, where she lies open to all that appeal to her. (§§ 176–7)

Of course, one cannot fail to note a rather delicious irony about this invocation. After all, the situation that Locke describes is rather more like the situation of the *Ammonites*, dispossessed people who believe they have a continuing claim to the land, than that of Jephtha's Israelites. And indeed, Locke even refuses to follow a part of the Jephtha story in which he is specifically interested, the colloquy, filtering out that Jephtha himself felt that even just claims expire through the passage of time. For Locke, their renewability seems to be perpetual. All the same, these local breaks with the Bible do not alter the fact that, in this crucial moment, Locke still found its core principle of the right to appeal in a moment of subjective conviction of just cause available, given God's continuing superintendence, and his necessary confirmation of that conviction.

Locke's invocation of Jephtha in favor of insurgents is surely less well-known than his defense of the right of revolution in the *Second Treatise*.[18]

Locke's statements about property in conquest somehow made up for his silence about all other norms. Doyle, *Ways of War and Peace*, p. 221. On the neglected theory of *jus post bellum* in Locke's thought, see also now P. Kalmanovitz, "Justice in Post-war Reconstruction: Theories from Vitoria to Vattel" (Ph.D. diss., Columbia University, 2010) and Kalmanovitz, "Sharing Burdens after War: A Lockean Approach," *Journal of Political Philosophy* 19, no. 2 (June 2011), 209–28.

[18] "*Who shall be Judge*," Locke asks at the tail-end of the text in the famous section, "whether the Prince or Legislative act contrary to their Trust?" To the best-known

Yet Locke's free extension of the right of appeal to heaven to insurgents, one that he found in or at least justified by way of the Jephtha story, arguably ended up being one of the most historically influential dimensions of his text. The earliest stop, clearly, was the American scene, where indeed Locke's quixotic celebration of his favorite biblical icon remained very much part of this legacy at least for a while. Much later, the United States would become the target of accusations of unjust imperial intervention and occupation in its own right. But until recently, the most salient historical legacy of its postcolonial founding may have been the principle of sovereign equality, including that won by insurgents against onetime imperial masters and later against interventionist interference. The United States may have appealed to the Lockean right of revolution to justify its secession, but for outsiders around the world who tried to copy its success, it stood for postcolonial sovereignty won through insurgency.

In the summer of 1775, after hostilities had broken out between the American colonists and the British Empire, Locke was directly cited by Israel Putnam's Connecticut army as the key theorist of insurgency. Ironically, the Americans were not much like Jephtha's Israelites, defending their homeland against foreign incursion. But neither were they, unlike the Ammonites, an indigenous population that had preserved the sense of the legitimacy of their cause over generations under foreign thumb, renewing it again and again. Rather, they were a secessionist faction of a project of settler colonialism, a faction which owed its own sense of unity not least to bloody Indian war that had been so intense for a generation, and indeed was continuing at the same time. The Native Americans, in other words, might have recognized themselves in the biblical characters far more easily. But the Americans found Locke's defense of the *ultima ratio* for insurgent warfare there for them to claim anyway. According to an anonymous account of the Continental Army, the day came that summer to unfurl a new battle flag. "When General Putnam gave the Signal, the whole Army shouted their loud Amen by three Cheers, immediately upon which a Cannon was fired from the Fort, and the Standard lately sent to

---

part of his answer ("To this I reply, *The People shall be the Judge*") he adds: "But farther, this Question, (*Who shall be Judge?*) cannot mean, that there is no Judge at all. For where there is no Judicature on Earth, to decide Controversies amongst Men, *God* in Heaven is *Judge* ... [One can] appeal to the Supream Judge, as *Jephtha* did" (§§ 240–1). Just as in the prepolitical state of war, and "international affairs," in intrapolitical contention, Jephtha's appeal to heaven is available, even necessary, when no other recourse is possible.

General Putnam was exhibited[,] flourishing in the Air, bearing ... this Motto, APPEAL TO HEAVEN."[19]

The next year, the American Declaration of Independence "appeal[ed] to the Supreme Judge of the world for the rectitude of our intentions," once again citing the divine guarantee of just cause in the absence of human confirmation and for the sake of violence. On the model of Jephtha, Locke's appeal authorized self-government generally, and revolution in its name. In the longer term, however, the claim is also a crucial ideological source of anticolonial revolt, including against illegitimate intervention. The difficulty of bridging the gap towards the objective validity of normative conviction – and the high risk of error for those who have attempted to do so – may mean that the rights of insurgents have not just been historically influential, given a long history of intervention, but remain rather pertinent today and for the foreseeable future. Indeed, from a Lockean standpoint, present-day Afghans or Iraqis could themselves legitimately "appeal to heaven" and resort to insurgency in the face of a perceived unjust intervention and foreign occupation of their lands. It is precisely because the further secularization of political thought has not solved the problem of objective validity for which Locke saw God as the essential guarantor that no theory of military intervention can afford to ignore the critical function of his appeal to heaven – which always leaves room for claims of justice that existing institutions, and interventions with the best of intentions, will fail to meet.

---

[19] Cited in T. H. Breen, "An Appeal to Heaven: The Language of Rights on the Eve of American Independence," in R. K. Ramazani and R. Fatton (eds.), *The Future of Liberal Democracy: Thomas Jefferson and the Contemporary World* (New York: Palgrave Macmillan, 2004), 66–7. See also now Breen, *American Insurgents, American Patriots: The Revolution of the People* (New York: Hill and Wang, 2010), esp. ch. 9, and, on Indian war, P. Silver, *Our Savage Neighbors: How Indian War Transformed Early America* (New York: W.W. Norton, 2009).

6   Intervention and sovereign equality: legacies of Vattel

Jennifer Pitts

How might Emerich de Vattel (1714–67), a key source of the misleadingly termed "Westphalian" model of sovereignty that has proven so authoritative as a conception of the international realm, aid contemporary reflection about the moral and political dilemmas of humanitarian intervention? Vattel's *Droit des Gens* of 1758 arguably inaugurated the terms in which we continue to carry on debates about intervention: those of a system of legally equal and independent sovereign states that warrant protection from outside intervention in order to develop autonomously, but that also bear toward one another, and each other's citizens, robust duties of humanity and assistance.[1] A reconsideration of Vattel's views on sovereignty and intervention may help us to see both the severe limitations of the Vattelian model of the international system, as well as some resources his thought offers for confronting the dilemmas around military intervention and human rights protection that that model entails today.

Contemporary debates about humanitarian intervention have inherited a particular version of Vattel's foundational tension between the values of political autonomy and universal concern. These debates have tended to revolve around the idea that the United Nations Charter enshrines two sets of principles – the "territorial integrity and political independence" of states, and human rights – one of which must be violated by third-party states when states abuse their own populations.[2]

---

[1] See S. Krasner, "Rethinking the Sovereign State Model," *Review of International Studies* (2001), 17–42. Some have argued that the "inconsistencies" in Vattel's thought have been a key source of its appeal; for instance, see S. Beaulac, "Emer de Vattel and the Externalization of Sovereignty," *Journal of the History of International Law* 5 (2003), 237–92 at 290. Unless otherwise noted, I cite the following edition of Vattel: *The Law of Nations* (trans. C. G. Fenwick) (Washington, DC: Carnegie Institution, 1916), by book and section number.

[2] See UN Charter, arts 2(1), 2(4), 2(7) on nonintervention and arts 1(3), 55, and 56; F. K. Abiew, *The Evolution of the Doctrine of Humanitarian Intervention* (The Hague: Kluwer, 1999), ch. 2; D. Armstrong et al., *International Law and International Relations* (Cambridge University Press, 2007), pp. 131–6; N. J. Wheeler, *Saving Strangers: Humanitarian Intervention in International Relations* (Oxford University Press, 2000), p. 1.

Still too obliquely though increasingly acknowledged is the fact that intervention debates largely concern powerful "first-world" states intervening in "third-world" states in a constrained and subordinated position within an asymmetrical global order.[3] Debates around humanitarian intervention often occupy the perspective of those powerful states that regard themselves as liberal and democratic, asking what "we" liberal democrats should do about problems *out there*. Such discussions have often ignored the longstanding manipulation, domination, and intervention by those powerful states that contribute to the violence that then is said to necessitate intervention. Treatments of intervention, relatedly, have had a myopic "temporal focus": they center on the moment of crisis, when vulnerable people are at risk of slaughter and when the only alternatives appear to be immediate military intervention, with all the attendant violence and instability that intervention can unleash, or an intolerable inaction while the innocent are killed.[4] The longer temporal frame of the conditions that precipitated the violence is generally neglected in arguments for military intervention. This is true not just of arguments over what to do in a particular situation, but also in broader and more philosophical discussions.[5] It is echoed in such popular refrains as "never again," which tends to suggest that never again will outsiders stand by as genocide or mass violence occurs: not that powerful states and global civil society more generally will commit themselves to stop producing, and to overcoming, the broader conditions such as extreme poverty, a surfeit of weapons, and ecological crises that help to generate civil conflict, tyranny, and genocide.[6]

Such criticisms have, however, become increasingly central to policy debates about the Responsibility to Protect (often abbreviated as RtoP or R2P), which in UN circles is coming to replace humanitarian intervention as the rubric under which to discuss outside intervention to prevent

[3] See John Rawls's *Law of Peoples* (Harvard, 1999); D. K. Chatterjee and D. E. Scheid, "Introduction," in Chatterjee and Scheid (eds.), *Ethics and Foreign Intervention* (Cambridge University Press, 2003), p. 4 (citing "malfunctioning states" and "old ethnic and nationalistic animosities"); and the essay by Michael Blake in that volume (asking whether liberals should tolerate illiberalism), for some examples. Fernando Tesón's definition of permissible humanitarian intervention characteristically includes the caveat that force be deployed "in principle by a liberal government or alliance"; "The Liberal Case for Humanitarian Intervention," in J. L. Holzgrefe and R. O. Keohane (eds.) *Humanitarian Intervention: Ethical, Legal and Political Dilemmas* (Cambridge University Press, 2003), p. 94.

[4] A. Orford, *Reading Humanitarian Intervention: Human Rights and the Use of Force in International Law* (Cambridge University Press, 2003), p. 18.

[5] See, e.g., the essays in Chatterjee and Scheid, *Ethics and Foreign Intervention*.

[6] E.g., S. R. Grillot, "Small Arms, Sovereign States and Human Rights," in N. Shawki and M. Cox (eds.), *Negotiating Sovereignty and Human Rights: Actors and Issues in Contemporary Human Rights Politics* (Aldershot: Ashgate, 2009), pp. 215–45.

egregious human rights abuses, and which, unlike the older rubric, "situat[es] armed intervention within a broader continuum of measures that the international community might take" in response to atrocities.[7] Many representatives of developing states have expressed wariness toward the official formulations of the Responsibility to Protect, which is framed as a responsibility in the first instance by sovereign states toward their subjects (some take this to mean that the principle renders sovereignty "conditional"), and secondarily a responsibility by outsiders to provide development assistance and to intervene forcibly if the state in question fails in its own duties. During UN General Assembly debates in 2009, delegates cited not simply the potential for the principle's abuse by major powers to justify aggression but also concern that the official formulation of R2P, like earlier arguments for humanitarian intervention, occludes the structural causes and "hegemonic domination … by western imperial Powers" that, as the Venezuelan delegate argued, are the "decisive factors" causing conflict.[8] European and US representatives for the most part simply celebrated the increasing institutionalization of R2P and stressed that, as the Austrian delegate put it, "the sovereignty of States implies important responsibilities," the abdication of which invites outside intervention.[9]

Much of the literature on intervention, like the position of the European delegates, has shared a set of assumptions that still demand to be reconsidered. Most important is the assumption that a military intervention constitutes a rupture in a status quo of independence and nonintervention.[10] This is based on the related view that the so-called Westphalian, but more accurately the Vattelian, model of equal and independent sovereign

---

[7] See A. Bellamy, "The Responsibility to Protect – Five Years On," *Ethics and International Affairs* 24, no. 2 (2010), 143–69 at 143, and *Responsibility to Protect: the Global Effort to End Mass Atrocities* (Cambridge: Polity, 2009); G. Evans, *The Responsibility to Protect: Ending Mass Atrocity Crimes Once and for All* (Washington, DC: Brookings Institution Press, 2008); C. G. Badescu, "The Responsibility to Protect: Embracing Sovereignty and Human Rights," in Shawki and Cox (eds.), *Negotiating Sovereignty and Human Rights*, pp. 81–98.

[8] E.g., see the resolution proposed by the Group of 77 developing states and passed by the General Assembly (as resolution 63/304) during the meeting of July 23, 2009, A/63/PV.97, as well as the subsequent discussion, available at www.responsibilitytoprotect.org/index.php/document-archive/united-nations. Quoted phrases from remarks by Valero Briceño of Venezuela at A/63/PV/99, p. 3.

[9] A/63/PV.99, p. 1.

[10] See, e.g., M. Walzer, "The Moral Standing of States: A Response to Four Critics," *Philosophy and Public Affairs* 9, no. 3 (1980), 209–29; or N. Wheeler, who writes that after the foundation of the UN and the adoption of the 1948 Genocide Convention and the Universal Declaration of Human Rights, for "the first time in the history of modern international society, the domestic conduct of governments was now exposed to scrutiny" by outsiders, in Wheeler, *Saving Strangers*, p. 1.

states is an adequate image of the international system, or that it was true from 1648 until the system began to crumble under the pressures of late twentieth-century global transformations.[11] While debates about intervention continue to rely heavily on this image, historians have greatly criticized it in the last decade, insisting on the mythic nature of the conventional narrative in international relations and law, in which the Westphalia treaties constituted a watershed between an older hierarchical and imperial order and the modern order of equal states holding unconditional sovereignty free of any notion of responsibilities.[12] Sovereign authority has, arguably, been understood since its early articulations in the sixteenth century as entailing responsibilities on the part of states to secure their populations' safety.[13] This is not at all to deny the significance of the Vattelian conception of sovereignty as complete external independence, and as entailing a rule of nonintervention, for it has been extraordinarily influential in structuring political actors' and thinkers' understanding of the world.[14] But if we understand the system of equal and independent states as an eighteenth-century theoretical model, or aspiration, rather than as a treaty-based legal order that governed European and later world politics from 1648 until its collapse under the forces of late-modern globalization, we may avoid holding

---

[11] See, for instance, Daniel Philpott's claim that the "modern international system ... took full shape at the peace of Westphalia in 1648 [and] then spread, rapidly expanding across the globe when the colonial empire collapsed after World War II," and "has only now begun to crack": *Revolutions in Sovereignty* (Princeton University Press, 2001), 4. Philip Allott writes that the "Vattelian mind-world is withering away under the impact of the new international social reality": *The Health of Nations: Society and Law Beyond the State* (Cambridge University Press, 2002), p. 62.

[12] A. Osiander, "Sovereignty, International Relations, and the Westphalian Myth," *International Organization*, 55, vol. 2 (April 2001), 251–87; S. Beaulac, *The Power of Language in the Making of International Law* (Leiden: Martinus Nijhoff, 2004); B. Teschke, *The Myth of 1648: Class, Geopolitics, and the Making of Modern International Relations* (London: Verso, 2003); B. Simms, "'A false Principle in the Law of Nations': State Sovereignty, [German] Liberty, and Intervention in the Age of Westphalia and Burke," in B. Simms and D. J. B. Trim (eds.), *Humanitarian Intervention – a History* (Cambridge University Press, 2011). Compare S. Krasner, *Sovereignty: Organized Hypocrisy* (Princeton University Press, 1999) and Krasner, "Rethinking the Sovereign State Model," in M. Cox, T. Dunne, and K. Booth (eds.), *Empires, Systems and States. Great Transformations in International Politics* (Cambridge University Press, 2001), pp. 17–42.

[13] See L. Glanville, "The Antecedents of Sovereignty as Responsibility," in *European Journal of International Relations* 17, no. 2 (2010), 233–55.

[14] For the argument that Vattel was the first to insist on the equivalence of sovereignty and complete external independence, see Beaulac, "Vattel and the Externalization of Sovereignty"; on the central importance of this conception of independent statehood in the late eighteenth century and the "contagion of sovereignty" unleashed by the American colonists in 1776, see D. Armitage, *The Declaration of Independence: A Global History* (Cambridge, MA: Harvard University Press, 2007).

ourselves hostage to a partial vision of what it might require (military nonintervention even in the face of massive human rights violations) and also recapture more of the critical potential of Vattel's paired values of political autonomy and universal concern, for true respect for all peoples' political autonomy would require dramatic alterations in the political, military, and economic policies of dominant states.[15]

As the recent histories show, the Westphalia treaties – the 1648 treaties of Osnabrück and Münster – did not constitute a radical break, in which the intricate and multilayered sovereignties of the middle ages were replaced by a new legal entity, the equal and independent sovereign state with the right to be free from all interference by others. The Westphalia treaties neither intended to establish a new international system of equal and independent sovereign states, nor did they have such an effect.[16] Rather than entrenching a new principle of nonintervention in religious matters, in some ways the treaties constituted a retreat from the principle *cuius regio, eius religio* that had been established by the 1555 Treaty of Augsburg. By enshrining protections for religious minorities in both Catholic and Protestant states, the Westphalia treaties arguably circumscribed the existing powers of German rulers over religious practice in their realms.[17] Brendan Simms calls the Westphalian treaties "nothing less than a charter for intervention: by fixing the internal confessional balance within German principalities, they provided a lever for interference throughout the late seventeenth and eighteenth centuries."[18] And Richard Tuck's chapter in this volume argues that the seventeenth century was the scene of the most "extensive debate" on humanitarian intervention before the twentieth century.[19]

---

[15] My reading of Vattel is in sympathy with that of Andrew Hurrell, "Vattel: Pluralism and its limits," in I. Clark and I. B. Neumann (eds.), *Classical Theories of International Relations* (New York: St. Martin's, 1996), pp. 233–55. Hurrell argues that the so-called pluralist reading of Vattel that stresses his "state libertarianism" neglects Vattel's "broader moral purpose and the weight given in his work to the norms of the necessary natural law" (p. 234).

[16] Compare Krasner, who accepts the Westphalian model as a useful description of aspects of the international system but argues that it had "virtually nothing" to do with the Westphalian treaties; instead, he argues, the norm of nonintervention was first "explicitly articulated" by Wolff and Vattel (*Sovereignty*, pp. 20–1).

[17] Beaulac, *The Power of Language*, p. 85. As Beaulac argues, the key purposes of the Westphalia treaties had to do with "the practice of religion and the settlement of territories, not [with] the creation of distinct separate polities independent from any higher power" (p. 90).

[18] Simms, "'A false principle'," p. 2. See also D. Trim's discussion in ch. 1 of this volume, esp. pp. 38–41.

[19] On demolishing the 1648 myth, also see D. Armitage, "The Fifty Years' Rift: Intellectual History and International Relations," *Modern Intellectual History*, 1(1) (2004), 97–109, where he describes one of the "reigning origin-myths" of international relations:

Moreover, the European states in question were throughout the modern period global empires, and the law of nations that they developed was inflected by imperial concerns in ways little recognized in standard accounts of international law. Indeed, the early theorists most commonly associated with the Westphalian myth, above all Grotius, developed their accounts of the law of nations largely in response to imperial concerns, and these theories reflect the far more complicated imperial realities of partial and divided sovereignty that are ignored by the Westphalian model. As Tuck has shown, Grotius's account of state autonomy produced a strikingly interventionist and imperialist theory. Grotius had argued that if a ruler "manifestly" injured his subjects, other states had a right to intervene on their behalf, and he defended a right of punishment against rulers that committed "grievous Violations of the Law of Nature or Nations," including cannibalism and "inhuman[ity] to their Parents."[20] As Edward Keene has argued, Grotius did not establish a unified principle of inviolable sovereignty but rather elaborated the bases for divided and partial sovereignty, particularly in the case of Asian states with which the European powers were increasingly entangled in the course of commercial and imperial expansion.[21]

The version of the Westphalian myth that has been most influential in recent decades has it that decolonization in the 1950s and 1960s constituted another radical break in the history of sovereignty, in which the formerly colonized states, once excluded from the international community of equal and independent states, finally achieved full membership. Their sovereignty, their right to self-determination, was recognized in the UN Charter and the key human rights documents. This moment has been conventionally seen as the full fruition of the Westphalian model, in which state sovereignty that had been enjoyed only within Europe was extended equally to all. But in the conventional narrative, this moment

---

"derived from counter-revolutionary historicism, locates the foundation of the modern states-system in the Peace of Westphalia" and Edward Keene, who writes that "there is nothing new about the notion that the sovereignty of states should be compromised by a higher structure of international organization that facilitates the promotion of economic progress, good government, and individuals' rights": *Beyond the Anarchical Society: Grotius, Colonialism and Order in World Politics* (Cambridge University Press, 2002), p. 148.

[20] *De jure belli ac pacis*, II.20.40 and II.25.8 (Carnegie Endowment translation). See R. Tuck, *The Rights of War and Peace* (Oxford, 1999), esp. pp. 89–94 and 113–20; and R. Tuck, "Grotius, Hobbes and Pufendorf on Humanitarian Intervention," this volume. Wilhelm Grewe argued that Grotius had in mind specifically religious interventions, since these are the examples he gives (the persecution of Christians in antiquity and wars fought on their behalf by the Roman emperor Constantine and his successors: *The Epochs of International Law* (Berlin and New York: de Gruyter, 2000).

[21] Keene, *Beyond the Anarchical Society*.

soon inaugurated a new problem: the tension between the UN Charter principles of human rights and noninterference in the independence of states. Robert Jackson's *Quasi-States*, to cite one influential example, argues that although newly decolonized states acquired full *de jure* sovereignty, they lacked in fact the capacities of sovereign states, and it was the resulting tension between law and fact that caused their instability and their tendencies to tyranny and human rights violations: they simply did not have the empirical capacities that entities entrusted with such legal powers would need to avoid abuses. In Jackson's view, an overly permissive or inclusive international law has enabled and abetted the violence endemic to postcolonial states.[22]

In the decades following decolonization, many liberals in powerful states, distraught at widespread human rights abuses in postcolonial states, concluded that sovereignty could not enjoy the sacrosanct status it had hitherto apparently enjoyed, but instead must be circumscribed in the interests of human rights. While this debate is generally couched in universalist terms – sovereignty *as such* must be limited in the new global order – what is centrally, if often tacitly, at issue is the supposed sovereignty of third-world states, and the right to intervene by the liberal powers of the global north and by the international institutions these states dominate. Authors such as Jackson suggest that it was a mistake to grant full legal sovereignty to states that lack the necessary capacities to use it for the good of their citizens.[23] Far rarer is the recognition that such states never enjoyed full legal sovereignty, and that the world's powerful states, and the international law and institutions they sponsor and dominate, bear a portion of the responsibility for the authoritarianism, the disorder, and weakened state capacity that liberal democrats deplore. Some of the most pressing ethical issues surrounding humanitarian military intervention revolve around these still under-discussed issues of the asymmetries at the heart of intervention debates, and the intertwined histories of European imperialism and international law that form the historical context of those asymmetries.

---

[22] R. Jackson, *Quasi-states: sovereignty, international relations, and the Third World* (Cambridge University Press, 1990).

[23] "The adoption of negative sovereignty precluded other conceivable arrangements some of which might have been more appropriate to the circumstances ... Independence was not the innovative moment it might have been if novel territorial statuses suited to the special circumstances and needs of ex-colonial states and aimed at increasing the prosperity of their populations had been fashioned. The moment was lost and the one-dimensional negative sovereignty game was established instead" (Jackson, *Quasi-States*, p. 199). Jackson mentions condominia and "more intrusive forms of international trusteeship" (p. 202) as examples of the sort of limited-sovereignty arrangements that might well have been preferable for some postcolonial populations.

The notion that decolonization represented a legal watershed, in which empires were abolished and new states abruptly came into all the rights of sovereignty, was questioned from the start by lawyers and leaders from the new states. It has come under renewed scrutiny in the last decade by legal scholars such as Antony Anghie and Nathaniel Berman. As Anghie showed in his powerful 2005 book *Imperialism, Sovereignty, and the Making of International Law*, the sovereignty that was granted to the new postcolonial states was markedly circumscribed in international law. Not only, as Marxist observers had long argued, did imperial relations continue unabated in economic terms, with first-world states still extracting resources and exploiting the vulnerability and cheap labor of the developing world, but the new states also lacked key legal powers traditionally granted to sovereign states, such as the power to revise contracts unilaterally through legislative action. As conditions for decolonization, the departing colonial powers imposed such handicaps on the new states and retained, through corporations based in the first world and the international laws that governed their conduct, vast power over the resources and economies of the new states. These profoundly vitiated the ostensible *de jure* equality of the new states in ways not recognized in standard narratives that stress the sovereign equality that proceeded from decolonization and is said to have universalized the status of sovereign equality that originated in Europe. When the non-aligned nations tried to renegotiate the global order at the UN in 1974, they were blocked by the Great Powers.[24]

Although the principle of sovereign equality for much of the twentieth century served as the foundational principle of international relations and "attained almost an ontological position in the structure of the international legal system," ensuring, for instance, procedural equality for microstates and Great Powers in the International Court of Justice, it is important to stress that the system has been pervaded not simply by inequalities of power and wealth but also of legal status.[25] It is needless

---

[24] I am grateful to Jim Tully for stressing this point.

[25] B. Kingsbury, "Sovereignty and Inequality," in A. Hurrell and N. Woods (eds.), *Inequality, Globalization, and World Politics* (Oxford University Press, 1999), pp. 66–94 at 66. Also see, e.g., the 1970 Declaration on Principles of International Law, quoted in M. N. Shaw, *International Law* (Cambridge University Press, 2008), pp. 192–6; and, for an account of the principle's history, P. Kooijmans, *The Doctrine of the Legal Equality of States* (Leiden, 1964). For the argument that the international legal order based on "sovereign equality" has persistently, if in varying guises, also included legalized inequalities of status (hegemony and outlawry), see G. Simpson, *Great Powers and Outlaw States: Unequal Sovereigns in the International Legal Order* (Cambridge University Press, 2004) and R. A. Klein, *Sovereign Equality among States: The History of an Idea* (University of Toronto Press, 1974).

to elaborate here the myriad other ways in which the US and European powers kept a firm hand in the governance and economies of the new states – by fomenting coups, through covert and overt military aid, through the global arms trade. But the reality of constant military and nonmilitary intervention, alongside often severe legal disabilities, make a mockery of the idea that any given instance of humanitarian intervention represents a disruption of a status quo of nonintervention and sovereign equality, one that uniquely forces us to confront a contradiction between political independence and human rights.

Vattelian legacies

I have suggested that we owe our key concepts and dilemmas in thinking about humanitarian intervention to Vattel, whose *Droit des Gens* of 1758 was from the moment of its publication a vastly influential work of jurisprudence. It was cited as a major source on international law during the American Revolution, British debates on the French Revolution, the Napoleonic Wars, and the Congress of Vienna, and remained canonical through the nineteenth century.[26] As we have seen, one of his signal contributions was to "externalize sovereignty," that is, to associate sovereignty, a term that had been introduced to European political thought by Bodin's *Six Livres de la République* of 1576, with independence from external authority, and to define sovereign states as "free and independent of each other." Vattel's conception of sovereignty was his legal and political elaboration of what we might see as one of his two foundational norms: the right and duty of nations, as moral persons, to "preserve and perfect [their] existence" (1.14, 1.21) (the other being universal duties of mutual assistance among human beings). I would argue that the ambiguities and vacillations in Vattel's account of intervention, which may be said to have anticipated and perhaps engendered the difficulties in our own debates, stem precisely from his choice to elaborate the norm of communal self-direction in terms of absolute sovereign equality and independence.

That Vattel's conception of sovereign equality and independence was an aspiration rather than a plausible description of his world is clear from his own circumstances, for he was born in the principality of Neuchâtel,

---

[26] See C. G. Fenwick, "The Authority of Vattel," Part I, *American Political Science Review* 7 (1913), p. 395; E. Jouannet, *Emer de Vattel et l'émergence doctrinale du droit international classique* (Paris: Pedone, 1998), pp. 14–15; F. S. Ruddy, "The Acceptance of Vattel," in C. H. Alexandrowicz (ed.) *Grotian Society Papers 1972* (The Hague: Martinus Nijhoff, 1972).

at once a Swiss citizen and a subject of the Prussian king, in the twilight
of the Holy Roman Empire. While he described his birthplace as "un
pays, dont la liberté est l'ame, le trésor & la loi fondamentale," its
complex legal status epitomized the dependence of many states on outside powers and the heterogeneity of states that characterized post-
Westphalian Europe, though Vattel himself would argue in the *Droit des
Gens* that Neuchâtel was a perfectly free and independent sovereign
state.[27] Unable to secure a diplomatic post under Frederick the Great,
Vattel found employment with the state of Saxony, serving as its minister
plenipotentiary in Bern from 1749 until 1758, during which time he
wrote his *Droit des Gens*. After Frederick invaded Saxony in 1756, launching the Seven Years War, Vattel also published, anonymously, several
books of essays about that "bloody war which currently troubles all
Europe."[28]

Vattel had studied civil and natural law under Jean-Jacques Burlama-
qui, and he had made a deep study of the thought of Leibniz and
Christian Wolff, whose *Jus Gentium Methodo Scientifica Pertractatum* of
1749 was the most immediate source and interlocutor of Vattel's own
treatise.[29] Despite Vattel's rather misleading representation of himself as
in large measure simply repackaging Wolff's theory for popular con-
sumption (among other moves, substituting for Wolff's Latin the French
that had become Europe's diplomatic lingua franca), the differences
between their practical conclusions are often substantial.[30] Vattel
endorsed forms of aggression that Wolff had explicitly rejected, such as
war to disable a threatening state, and the containment and expropriation
of nomadic peoples (1.207–9). Indeed, Richard Tuck, in his powerful
revisionist history of international political thought, *The Rights of War and
Peace*, situates the two thinkers in two opposing camps: Vattel among the
Protestants and humanists including Grotius, Gentili, and Locke who
defended a belligerent and interventionist position built up around a
notion of the autonomous individual, and Wolff in a more pacific

[27] Vattel, *Droit des Gens* (London [Neûchatel], 1758), preface xlv; quoted in Beaulac,
"Externalization of Sovereignty," 242. Vattel 1.9. For background see E. Béguelin,
"En souvenir de Vattel," in *Recueil de travaux* (Neuchâtel: Attinger, 1929); A. de
Lapradelle, "Emer de Vattel," in J. B. Scott (ed.), *The Classics of International Law –
Vattel*, vol. I (Washington, DC: Carnegie Institution of Washington, 1916); and
B. Kapossy and R. Whatmore, "Introduction," in Vattel, *The Law of Nations* (eds.
Kapossy and Whatmore) (Indianapolis: Liberty Fund, 2008), pp. ix–xx.
[28] See Beaulac, "Externalization of Sovereignty," pp. 244–5.
[29] See W. Drechsler, "Christian Wolff (1679–1754): A Biographical Essay," *European
Journal of Law and Economics*, 4 (1997), 111–28.
[30] See Vattel, *Droit des Gens*, preface 7a. Also see Tuck, *Rights of War and Peace*, pp. 191–6.
Vattel justified his divergences from Wolff in his *Questions de droit naturel* (1762).

tradition, defended above all by Pufendorf, that posited a thick moral order and a sociable state of nature and was critical of intervention and imperialism.[31]

And yet, with all their differences, Wolff and Vattel shared a foundational, organizing dilemma: they posited robust sovereign states with rights to decide questions of internal constitution independent from outside interference, while insisting that in a world of such states all human beings continue to bear strong obligations toward one another – not simply perfect duties of justice and non-injury, but also positive (and imperfect) duties of assistance.[32] Both rejected Grotius's approval of the use of force to punish and correct violations of the law of nature, or to "civilize" or otherwise improve people against their will even as they insisted on those duties of assistance.[33] The pages that follow sketch the two authors' key claims with respect to this dilemma of strong external sovereignty alongside robust mutual obligation, ultimately to suggest that while we have inherited Vattel's version of the dilemma (respect for absolute sovereignty versus protection of human rights), a fresh look at his underlying normative commitments – to both spaces of political autonomy and universal duties of humanity – might help us past the agonizingly stark choice between irreconcilable values that questions of intervention seem to pose.

Wolff, following Pufendorf's understanding of the state of nature as sociable, offered the thicker conception of the international community with his construct of the *civitas maxima*, often translated as world state

---

[31] Tuck's reading of the tradition challenges (though not explicitly) Hedley Bull's long-dominant reading of Grotius as having a "solidarist" conception of international order, as well as a historiography beginning in the eighteenth century that stressed the similarities between Pufendorf and Grotius (Tuck, *Rights of War and Peace*, pp. 12, 142 and *passim*). For the more standard reading of Grotius as a proponent of a thick and moralized conception of international society, see Bull, "The Grotian Conception of International Society," (1966), rept. in K. Alderson and A. Hurrell (eds.) *Hedley Bull on International Society* (New York: St. Martin's Press, 2000), 95–124; and, for debate about this reading, *Hugo Grotius and International Relations* (eds. H. Bull, B. Kingsbury, and A. Roberts) (Oxford University Press, 1990).

[32] Christian Wolff, *Jus Gentium Methodo Scientifica Pertractatum* (trans. J. H. Drake) (Oxford: Clarendon Press, 1934), §§ 21, pp. 35–7, 174–80 (Carnegie Endowment for International Peace edition); Vattel, 1.12–25 and 1.31. Also see Whelan, "Vattel's Doctrine of the State," *History of Political Thought* 9 (1988), 59–90.

[33] Vattel chastised the "ambitious European States which attacked the American Nations and subjected them to their avaricious rule in order, as they said, to civilize them" (2.7); and he believed that missionaries with their "obtrusive zeal" posed a grave threat to "the peace of all Nations" (2.61). Also see Wolff § 168. Despite his suspicion toward European motives, Vattel did note that states should contribute not just to one another's preservation but to their advancement, so that "if an uncivilized State should desire to improve its condition and should apply to a civilized State for teachers to instruct it, the latter ought not to refuse them" (2.6).

but perhaps better rendered as the broadest commonwealth or republic, encompassing a series of smaller associations.[34] Like organs in the body, "individual men do not cease to be members of that great society which is made up of the whole human race, because several have formed together a particular society" (§ 7). Vattel too invoked the law of nature and the idea of nature's intentions for humanity to theorize a society of humanity with rigorous duties of assistance, including, as in Wolff, duties to aid others "to advance their own perfection and that of their condition" (Introduction, §§ 11–12).[35] Vattel followed Wolff in arguing for the universality of the law of nations and in regarding the duties of humanity as duties to human beings as such (2.15). He likewise followed Wolff in denying that differences of religion or level of civilization justify different rules of international conduct,[36] and in denying that shared religion gives a state special license to intervene on behalf of others. Duties to others, both argued, are based exclusively on humanity, and

---

[34] See N. Greenwood Onuf, *The Republican Legacy in International Thought* (Cambridge University Press, 1998), pp. 58–84, both on conventional accounts of this concept and on the nuances of meaning of *civitas* (which he translates as republic, not state) and *maxima* (as largest possible, not supreme). On natural sociability in Pufendorf, see I. Hont, *Jealousy of Trade* (Harvard University Press, 2005), pp. 159–84, and Tuck, *Rights of War and Peace*, pp. 140–65. Hochstrasser argues that Wolff's *civitas maxima* "reflected an older world view where the Holy Roman empire remained a living part of political debate" and that it was "simply not plausible, even as an abstract model" in Vattel's era; Hochstrasser, *Natural Law Theories in the Early Enlightenment* (Cambridge University Press, 2000), p. 179. Nevertheless, we should note the enduring appeal throughout the eighteenth century of the idea of a European federation or European republic composed of independent member states. Indeed, Vattel's own understanding of the Swiss Confederation, in which the member states were "truly sovereign and independent" (*Law of Nations*, 1.52) shares precisely the structure of Wolff's *civitas maxima*.

[35] Vattel, *The Law of Nations or the Principles of Natural Law Applied to the Conduct and to the Affairs of Nations and of Sovereigns* (trans. C. G. Fenwick) (Washington, DC: Carnegie Institution of Washington, 1916); first published as *Le Droit des Gens, ou principes de la loi naturelle, appliqués à la conduite et aux affaires des nations et des souverains*, 1758; I cite Fenwick's translation by book and section number. Also see Vattel, *Law of Nations*, Book 2 § 3 (2.3): "Since, then, one nation, in its way, owes to another nation every duty that one man owes to another man, we may confidently lay down this general principle: – one state owes to another state whatever it owes to itself, so far as that other stands in real need of its assistance, and the former can grant it without neglecting the duties it owes to itself. Such is the eternal and immutable law of nature." On similarities between Wolff and Vattel, see S. Zurbuchen, "Vattel's Law of Nations and Just War Theory," *History of European Ideas*, 35 (2009), 408–17. Also see G. Cavallar, *The Rights of Strangers: theories of international hospitality, the global community, and political justice since Vitoria* (Aldershot: Ashgate, 2002).

[36] Wolff was more absolute in his rejection of differential treatment toward "uncivilized" nations: Vattel argued that while no state has the right to attempt the improvement or civilizing of another people against its will, or to expropriate it entirely, savages may be confined within narrower territorial boundaries (1.207–9).

they both unequivocally forbade religious intervention of the convention-ally "pre-Westphalian" kind.

Both thinkers, then, emphasized both the existence of an international society and the persistence of moral duties among all human beings, but they also denied that these generated broad rights or duties of interven-tion. Against Grotius, they argued that except in the most extreme cases of oppression, intervention was presumptuous and unjust, and a tempta-tion to the abuse of power. Wolff was particularly skeptical about religious justifications for military action, since "there is no nation which does not consider its own religion to be the true one" (§ 259). Moreover, he insisted that a nation's duties are completely independent of its religious identity.[37] Wolff made no exceptions for interventions by individual states to protect the rights of humanity or to stop the oppression or severe mistreatment of other states' subjects: "To interfere in the government of another, in whatever way indeed that may be done, is opposed to the natural liberty of nations, by virtue of which one is altogether independent of the will of other nations in its action."[38] Wolff rejected intervention by individual states, though not from the concern (for instance, of contem-porary multilateralists) that individual states' interventions are unavoid-ably partial and self-interested or incur insurmountable epistemic problems related to the determination of whether a "just cause" actually exists.[39] Rather he held, on contractarian grounds, that collective inter-vention by the *civitas maxima* alone was legitimate, since all states, which he regarded as "individual free persons living in a state of nature" (§ 2), could be thought of as having joined this larger state and committed themselves to abide by its laws (also see § 13). He insisted that the laws that all states had in principle agreed to could be understood rationally, through a consideration of what is needed to promote the common good.

Wolff maintained, then, that it is plausible to think of the international community as a *civitas maxima,* with stringent duties of assistance to one's fellow human beings, while also holding that "sovereignty, as it

---

[37] Vattel similarly claimed – as a completely settled matter in his day – that "the law of nature alone regulates the treaties of nations ... different people treat with each other in quality of men, and not under the character of Christians or Mohammedans" (2.162), but he also noted that shared religious identity can strengthen the bonds between states (2.15).

[38] And: "the decision does not rest with foreign nations as to matters arising between subjects and ruler of any state, inasmuch as they ought not to intrude themselves in the affairs of others"; Wolff § 1011. Also see § 258 banning the use of force though permitting outside "intercession" on behalf of victims. Tuck, *Rights of War and Peace,* p. 190.

[39] Wolff was taken by his editor of 1917, Otfried Nippold, to have prophetically anticipated the League of Nations, a "realization" of his *civitas maxima.*

exists in a people or originally in a nation, is absolute."[40] He does not seem to have been troubled by any tension between his thick understanding of international society and its duties, and his strong conception of state sovereignty, though he offered both the thicker conception of international society and the more absolute commitment to sovereignty and nonintervention.[41] But he recognized that many readers would find this argument peculiar, and indeed Vattel's most significant departure from Wolff was precisely his rejection of this global contract as an unhelpful fiction.[42] In rejecting it, Vattel gave up too on Wolff's faith in collective intervention, and he remained more skeptical than Wolff about states' or individuals' ability to judge the actions of other states as right or wrong.

In Vattel's far more influential version of the dilemma of sovereignty and mutual concern, states do not participate in any "natural society [other] than that which nature has set up among men in general," and they remain entirely independent of any external authority.[43] He denied the parallel Wolff had drawn between each *civitas*, formed by individuals ceding some rights to the body, and a universal "civil society among Nations" (Preface, 9a). If Wolff's *civitas maxima* was patterned on the Holy Roman Empire, Vattel scorned that model, attributing the Empire's longstanding practice of regulating religion in member states to "prejudice, ignorance, and superstition" (2.58). As equal and independent sovereign bodies, states, in Vattel's theory, do not have the right to judge other states' conduct or claims about what is necessary for their security: "it does not belong to Nations to set themselves up as judges over one another."[44] Nor may they force foreign sovereigns to change their practices of rule, administration, taxation, or "severity" toward subjects.

---

[40] Wolff, § 255. But "Some sovereignty over individual nations belongs to nations as a whole" (§ 15); this is a "democratic" or popular government of the whole ("*status quidam popularis*") that cannot be handed over to or exercised by any particular nations (§ 19). Onuf has written that "Wolff never described nations as sovereign in the context of their mutual relations" (76), but this seems to me in contradiction to Wolff's statement at § 255.

[41] Richard Tuck has argued that Wolff's anti-interventionist position was consistent with his denunciation of European imperialism, just as the more interventionist theorists, notably Grotius, had also asserted broad grounds for imperial conquest (see Tuck, *Rights of War and Peace*, pp. 187–91).

[42] Wolff, §§ 13–14; Vattel, Preface, 9a. Wolff insisted on the truth of his argument as a matter of reason, not fact, acknowledging that his argument for collective intervention "will seem paradoxical to those who do not discern the connexion of truths and who judge laws from facts."

[43] *Law of Nations*, Preface 9a.

[44] 2.70 and 2.49; also see Introduction § 21, and, at 2.49: "It clearly follows from the liberty and independence of Nations that each has the right to govern itself as it thinks proper, and that no one of them has the least right to interfere in the government of another. Of all the rights possessed by a Nation that of sovereignty is doubtless the most important."

Somewhat paradoxically, however, given the greater finality of his notion of state sovereignty, Vattel also offered a far more robust set of justifications for (unilateral) intervention than Wolff, even though he presented these grounds for intervention as limited exceptions in a generally noninterventionist theory. It was in stating his principle of sovereignty that Vattel used the term *intervene* with a meaning similar to more recent usage, writing that "all such matters [of constitutional form] are of purely national concern, and no foreign power has any right to intervene [*intervenir*] otherwise than by its good offices, unless it be requested to do so or be led to do so by special reasons. To intermeddle [*s'en mêler*] in the domestic affairs of another Nation or to undertake to constrain its councils is to do it an injury."[45]

Vattel's substantial exceptions to his principle of nonintervention have seemed to some to leave it in tatters, and indeed in late eighteenth-century debates he was cited as often in support of bids for intervention as against them.[46] He accepted foreign military intervention on behalf of tyrannized subjects who appeal for assistance and to aid subjects actually in revolt against tyranny (2.56); and in a civil war when one has been unable to bring about peace between the parties (3.295–6). On aiding tyrannized subjects, Vattel writes that if a prince, "by violating the fundamental laws, gives his subjects a lawful cause for resisting him; if, by his insupportable tyranny, he brings on a national revolt against him, any foreign power may rightfully give assistance to an oppressed people who ask for

---

Likewise, "No foreign state may inquire into the manner in which a sovereign rules, nor set itself up as judge of his conduct" (2.55).

[45] 1.37; also see Trim, Ch. 1 in this volume, pp. 23–5 and esp. Winfield, "Intervention in International Law," *British Year Book of International Law* 3 (1922–23), 132–8 for a discussion of the history of the term *intervention*, citing this passage.

[46] His work was soon drawn upon during the French Revolution as justification for war by both revolutionaries who sought to export the revolution and their opponents who sought grounds for a war waged by European monarchs against the revolution. Edmund Burke appended twelve pages of excerpts from Vattel to his *Remarks on the Policy of the Allies* (1793). Jennifer Welsh argues that in quoting selectively, Burke misrepresented Vattel's position; in contrast, Richard Tuck's far more interventionist reading of Vattel is not unlike Burke's. See Welsh, *Edmund Burke and International Relations* (London: St. Martin's Press, 1995), ch. 5 and Tuck, *Rights of War and Peace*, pp. 191–6. Burke's French translator wrote to him citing an (unidentified) treatise on the law of nations and the right of assistance, arguing that "In cases where the oppression is so great that the oppressed cannot even implore assistance, unequivocal public notoriety is enough to require intervention of a foreign power" (from Pierre-Gaëton Dupont, May 21, 1791, *Correspondence of Edmund Burke*, VI.261, my translation).

On Burke's appropriations of Vattel, also see D. Armitage, "Burke and Reason of State," *Journal of the History of Ideas* 61, no. 4 (2000), 617–34; and I. Hampsher-Monk, "Edmund Burke's Changing Justification for Intervention," *The Historical Journal* 48, no. 1 (2005), 65–100.

its aid."[47] He includes a provision for religious intervention so extreme that it becomes simply tyranny, though without spelling out conditions.[48]

A just revolt may develop into a full-blown civil war, but Vattel also treats intervention in a civil war as conceptually distinct from aid to tyrannized subjects, and indeed as conceptually akin to ordinary foreign wars. If political bonds in a state rupture so completely that the two parties become, in effect, separate nations, then they are "independent of all foreign authority, [and] no one has the right to judge them. Either may be in the right, and those who assist the one or the other may think they are upholding the just cause" (2.56; also see 3.296). Vattel's two key justifications for intervention, then, are extreme (if largely unspecified) forms of tyranny, and such utter dissolution of the national community that the belligerents become like independent states, that is, attain the privilege of states not to be judged by others. In the former cases, Vattel sidesteps the issue that judgments of what counts as intolerable tyranny will invariably be controversial, even though his larger system is premised precisely on the effort to avoid the sorts of controversial moral and political judgments that he believed made Grotius's provisions for punitive war dangerous and destabilizing. For if in some important respects Vattel can, as Richard Tuck suggests, be placed in the humanist and Grotian tradition, developed by Locke, that favored balance-of-power arguments and was receptive to justifications of colonization on the grounds that nomads were not using their land properly, he also rejected key features of this strand of thought, above all its approval of punitive wars. Vattel was also alert to the imperialist ends to which arguments for punitive war had been put, the "pretexts" they could furnish for "ambitious men," (2.7) as when the Spanish "set themselves up as judges of the Inca Atahualpa" for offenses (such as polygamy and cruelty to his subjects) "for which he was not at all accountable to them" (2.56). Vattel, then, was deeply critical of civilizing interventions and of the presumptions of outsiders to interfere in the efforts of nations to direct their

---

[47] 2.56. As an illustration he cites the events of 1688, when "The English justly complained of James II" and "obtained the help of the United Provinces." Contemporary theories of intervention often include the idea of consent, as in Fernando Tesón's provision that intervention be "welcomed by the victims" ("Liberal Case," p. 94) though the great difficulties of securing express consent from people in the dire circumstances that precipitate interventions remain, despite technologies of mass communication.

[48] "When a form of religion is being oppressed in any country, foreign Nations professing that form may intercede for their brethren; but that is the extent to which they can lawfully go, unless the persecution is carried to an intolerable degree, when it becomes a case of evident tyranny, against which all Nations may give help to a vulnerable people" (2.62).

common life together, even as he upheld obligations of universal concern. The ambiguities of Vattel's account of intervention anticipate, I have argued, our own dilemmas around intervention. From the norm that groups of people should have autonomy to pursue the ends of civil society as they together understand them (1.14), Vattel produced a model of absolute sovereign equality and independence, with the attendant norm of nonintervention holding except in the most extreme cases even in the face of a ruler's tyranny over his subjects. If his model was aspirational rather than descriptive in his day, it is, arguably, dangerously misleading today in its failure to convey the depth of states' mutual influence and dependence in a globalized economy and a thick, variegated, and asymmetrical international legal order. Rather than seeking to entrench what remains of sovereign independence, or to recapture a putatively lost world of absolutely independent sovereign states, we would do better to attempt to conceive alternative elaborations, some perhaps already partly realized, of Vattel's foundational norms of universal human concern and the protection of spaces within which groups of people may pursue their "perfection" together.

Conclusion

Contemporary debates around humanitarian intervention struggle – just as, we have seen, Vattel himself did in slightly different language – with the competing principles of human rights, versus respecting sovereignty as a means of protecting the autonomy and self-determination of peoples. It is worth asking what is masked by the Vattelian model of the international realm, for it arguably obscures the asymmetries of interference that contribute so powerfully to the crises that are then seen to demand intervention.[49] The contemporary global order, legal, as well as political and economic, that is, actively contributes to the dynamics that keep postcolonial states from developing and becoming equal, self-governing members of international society. Powerful members of the international community have imposed great constraints on the self-determination of third-world peoples, by facilitating their penetration by global capital, and using international institutions like the World Bank and the IMF to make their economic and constitutional arrangements amenable to

[49] My argument here is in sympathy with Iris Marion Young's efforts to question the "too stark and dichotomous" terms of debate, in which "either sovereignty is absolute or it can be overridden; either human-rights violations legitimate the use of military force or they do not" ("Violence against power," in Chatterjee and Scheid (eds.), *Ethics and Foreign Intervention*, p. 252).

foreign investment (e.g. through structural adjustment and the "good governance" movement).[50] Those dynamics in turn create failed states in need of "humanitarian" intervention.[51] A discourse of intervention centered on the "preservation" of states' sovereign equality, and concerned about the infringement of this sovereignty only at the moment of military intervention in response to humanitarian crisis, cannot adequately address this broader context.

Although I have emphasized the contribution of the Vattelian model of sovereignty to this phenomenon, Vattel may also offer a salutary corrective to the neoliberal orthodoxy that often accompanies a picture of formal state sovereignty in contemporary international law. As Isaac Nakhimovsky has recently argued, Vattel's preoccupations with political economy, and his participation in debates about luxury versus agriculture as a means to prosperity, left an important mark on his theory of the law of nations.[52] Vattel held that each state had an obligation in conscience – according to the necessary law of nature – to be truly guided by its own welfare and self-perfection. He believed that nations' true interests were largely in harmony, so that self-interest and justice generally coincided,[53] and he saw commerce and trade as valuable tools of international relations. But he assumed no normative obligation to allow foreign commerce if a state deems particular commercial ties not in its best interests: like questions of war and alliance, this is for each country to decide.[54] He believed in particular that less powerful states have the

---

[50] See A. Anghie, *Imperialism, Sovereignty and the Making of International Law* (Cambridge University Press, 2004); S. Marks, *The Riddle of All Constitutions* (Oxford University Press, 2000); and Orford, *Reading Humanitarian Intervention*. For a recent, cautious and graduated defense of liberal paternalism, see S. Recchia, "Just and Unjust Postwar Reconstruction: How much external interference can be justified?," *Ethics and International Affairs* 23, no. 2 (2009), 165–87.

[51] See, e.g., N. Woods, "Order, Globalization, and Inequality in World Politics," in A. Hurrell and N. Woods (eds.) *Inequality, Globalization, and World Politics* (Oxford University Press, 1999), pp. 8–35; and T. Pogge (ed.), *Freedom from Poverty as a Human Right* (Oxford University Press, 2007), esp. A. Sengupta's "Poverty Eradication and Human Rights," pp. 323–44. For debate over whether the existing global order has indeed harmed the poor, see T. Pogge, *World Poverty and Human Rights* (Oxford: Polity, 2002); M. Risse, "How does the Global Order Harm the Poor?" in *Philosophy and Public Affairs*, 33, no. 4 (2005), 349–76, and the symposium on Pogge's book in *Ethics and International Affairs* 19, no. 1 (2005).

[52] I. Nakhimovsky, "Vattel's Theory of the International Order: Commerce and the balance of power in the *Law of Nations*," *History of European Ideas* 33 (2007), 157–73.

[53] Nations should exercise some generosity and self-restraint in making such judgments: "a Nation should regulate its conduct on every occasion with due regard to the needs of others, and should overlook a small expenditure, or an inconvenience that may be put up with, for the sake of the great benefits that will accrue to others" (1.131).

[54] *Law of Nations* 1.88–96. "Since it depends on the willingness of each nation to trade or not to trade with another, and to regulate the manner in which it wishes to trade, a right

right to use these tools to protect themselves from domination by the most powerful. Weaker states could and should, he thought, use preferential (and prejudicial) trade agreements and monopolies as means of checking the power of the strongest states, states that, even if they seemed pacific in their intent, were gaining so much power as to be threatening.[55] These commercial arrangements, while arguably coercive (in that they are imposed on other, albeit stronger, states against their will) and potentially destructive, could represent a means of maintaining the balance of power far less violent than pre-emptive war aimed at preventing the emergence of regional or global hegemony.

Vattel was, in effect, an early advocate of "infant industry protection," decades before Alexander Hamilton or Friedrich List. His conception of international commerce offers one critical response to the crusading ideology of globalization that insists on "liberalization" of developing economies. If such arguments had been seen more widely as part of the legacy of Vattel's work, we might have a richer conception of international relations than we have with the partial appropriation that gives us the image of sovereignty without adequate critical tools with which to interrogate it.

The power of the Vattelian conceptual model to shape our interpretation of global politics is striking. Even Stephen Krasner, who has sought in a series of works to expose the inadequacies of the traditional "Westphalian/Vattelian" model of sovereignty, and who recognizes that it is "frequently violated in practice," still writes, in the conventional mode, that "Left to their own devices, collapsed and badly governed states will not fix themselves because they have limited administrative capacity." He proposes that "To secure decent domestic governance in failed, failing, and occupied states, new institutional forms are needed that compromise Westphalian/Vattelian sovereignty for an indefinite period."[56] My claim has been that it is always misleading to speak of

over commerce is evidently a right to be exercised at will *(jus merae facultatis)*" (1.96). He calls high import duties on French wines and low ones on Portuguese, for the purposes of maintaining balance of trade, perfectly just. Similarly, the Chinese were not unjust in prohibiting foreigners: "The policy was of benefit to the Nation and did not violate the rights of anyone, nor even the duties of humanity, which allow us, where rights conflict, to prefer ourselves to others" (2.94).

[55] *Law of Nations* 1.93; also see Nakhimovsky, "Vattel's Theory," p. 165.

[56] Krasner, *Power, States, and Sovereignty Revisited* (New York: Routledge, 2009), p. 233; also see J. D. Fearon and D. D. Laitin, "Neotrusteeship and the Problem of Weak States," *International Security* 28, no. 4 (2004), 5–43; and R. O. Keohane, "Political Authority after Intervention: Gradations in Sovereignty," in Holzgrefe and Keohane (eds.), *Humanitarian Intervention*. Niall Ferguson and others have called more provocatively for a return to empire: "for *some* countries some form of imperial

such states as being left to their own devices. Their politics, economies, and militaries are already bound up with global structures of asymmetric power in such a way that neither substantively nor formally, in international law, can the states of the global south ever be said to have enjoyed equality or independence. Rather than arguing for forms of shared sovereignty, *de facto* trusteeships, or protectorates within what is assumed to be a generally Vattelian framework, we would do better to acknowledge that the international system continues to be predicated on structures of governance (whether through the Security Council, the IMF, or the WTO), and patterns of power (especially in the operations of global capital) that render the Vattelian model blinding and counterproductive.

While the issue of whether state failure in places like Somalia or Sierra Leone results more from international or domestic structures remains one of ongoing debate, such a question may be irresolvable and beside the point, since, as Thomas Pogge has put it, the "national causal factors we most like to highlight – tyranny, corruption, coups d'état, civil wars – are encouraged and sustained by central aspects of the present global economic order."[57] The argument here does not rest on a claim that international structures are *primary*; nor does it rule out the possibility that, given the dire conditions such collusions between global and local forces have brought about, military intervention by outsiders may indeed, at moments of crisis, be indispensable. It is meant, rather, to urge a consideration of the ways in which the normative ideal of a space for political autonomy is infringed all the time by the global structure and the actions of powerful states, and not only, or even most significantly, when "sovereignty" is most spectacularly violated by military intervention.

Vattel's model of the sovereign state, in which relations between rulers and their people can generally be considered an internal matter, is one

---

governance, meaning a partial or complete suspension of their national sovereignty, might be better than full independence, not just for a few months or years but for decades"; *Colossus: The Price of America's Empire* (New York: Penguin, 2004), p. 170; also M. Ignatieff, *Empire Lite: Nation building in Bosnia, Kosovo, and Afghanistan* (London: Vintage, 2003).

[57] Pogge, *World Poverty*, pp. 115–16. Alex Gourevitch has made a thoughtful argument that the Rwandan genocide, far from being the result of a failure to intervene, was enabled and indeed "sustained [and] radicalized" by a "mixture of well-intentioned, ignorant, and downright duplicitous and insidious forms of [foreign] intervention"; "Hutu's Willing Executioners? Revisiting the ethnic interpretation of the Rwandan Civil War," *Lenin's Tomb*, posted Thursday August 13, 2009; http://leninology.blogspot.com/2009/08/hutus-willing-executioners.html; Orford similarly challenges the standard representation of the international community's relationship to the Rwandan genocide as one of absence; *Reading Humanitarian Intervention*, pp. 82–105.

that J. S. Mill influentially took up a century later, when he drew the distinction between "a purely native government," against which outsiders should never intervene, and one of "foreigners, [including] every government which maintains itself by foreign support," against which they may.[58] This model continues to inform debates over intervention, as in Michael Walzer's argument for a presumption of "fit" between a community and its government, a presumption that he claims is "simply the respect that foreigners owe to a historic community and its internal life."[59] The model is problematic in my view not only, as Walzer's critics have often argued on human rights grounds, because relations between tyrannical governments and their people *should* be a matter of broader concern and responsibility. Rather, it is problematic because oppressive governments are able to exercise the power they do, not in isolation from the international community, but thanks to it. No government today can be considered "purely native," in Mill's terms. Oppressive governments owe their power in part to a destructive combination of longstanding infringements on sovereignty of the kinds already mentioned *and* attributions of sovereignty by the international community, as in so-called "odious debts," or what Pogge has called dictators' resource and borrowing privileges.[60]

The Vattelian model of sovereignty retains its power in part for the same reasons that made the *Droit des Gens* so immediately influential when it was published: its ability to steer a course between what Martti Koskenniemi has called apology and utopia.[61] That is, Vattel's theory hews close enough to actual state practice to seem a useful schema of the real world, and it presents at the same time a normative vision we can use to evaluate and criticize that world: one of an always elusive balance between the moral values of autonomy and interconnection. It seeks at

---

[58] Mill, "A Few Words on Nonintervention," in *Collected Works of John Stuart Mill*, 21.122.

[59] See Walzer's still widely read "The Moral Standing of States," p. 212. Walzer holds that states thus "can be presumptively legitimate in international society and actually illegitimate at home": foreigners are bound to act "as if" they are legitimate until the population makes clear that it sees the government as illegitimate (pp. 214–16). Walzer's more recent essays on humanitarian intervention have been more permissive, though he has long pointed out that the most successful interventions have been "acts of war by neighboring states" (India in East Pakistan/Bangladesh, Vietnam in Cambodia, Tanzania in Uganda) that do not raise concerns about imperialism; "The argument about humanitarian intervention," in *Thinking Politically: Essays in political theory* (New Haven: Yale University Press, 2007), p. 240.

[60] See O. Lienau, "Who is the Sovereign in Sovereign debt?: Reinterpreting a rule-of-law framework from the early twentieth century," *Yale Journal of International Law* 33 (2008), 63–111; and Pogge, *World Poverty and Human Rights*, pp. 112–16 and 162–7.

[61] M. Koskenniemi, *From Apology to Utopia: the Structure of International Legal Argument* (Cambridge University Press, 2005 [1989]).

once to grant communities the space and the liberty to work out a common life together, free from interference by those not committed to that common life; and to preserve bonds of moral connection and obligation across all of humanity. But there are ways other than Vattelian sovereignty to pursue this combination. Iris Young offers one in her attempt to reconceive self-determination not as sovereignty, but in terms of nondomination and relational autonomy.[62] Her approach requires, and invites, a more thoroughgoing critique of global power relations and institutions of governance than do either efforts to protect weak states against imperialist interventions by enhancing their sovereignty, or arguments for strengthening intervention's place in international law. As we seek means to combat the atrocities, human rights violations, and sheer misery rife in the contemporary global order, we would do well to stop taking our bearings from Vattel's conception of sovereignty, though we may still find compelling and instructive the moral aspirations for both self-determination and moral connection that underlay it.

[62] See *Global Challenges* (London: Polity, 2007), pp. 148–51 and 159–86; she glosses relational autonomy as the idea that "the agency and capabilities of any individual or group is relationally constituted."

7   David Hume and Adam Smith on international ethics and humanitarian intervention

Edwin van de Haar

David Hume (1711–76) and Adam Smith (1723–90) wrote on a wide range of issues but are nowadays mainly known as a moral philosopher and a political economist, respectively. Their views on international relations have been under-analyzed and frequently misinterpreted, including their position regarding military intervention.[1]

Like other Enlightenment thinkers, Hume and Smith aimed to understand human nature. They wanted to find out what motivates and drives human behavior. They believed that politics and international affairs were important processes to take into account, as politics is all about human action. People, in their view, are crucially influenced and guided by ideas, the leaders of states included. In most areas of domestic and international political decision-making, norms and values are indeed central. Therefore, the academic study of international relations is in important ways concerned with ethical questions.[2]

Moral and social theory were indeed cornerstones of the work of Hume and Smith, and of the Scottish Enlightenment in general. Both men held strong views on what is good and bad in society. They publicly took sides in all kinds of contemporary debates, not least those on war, peace, defense, the balance of power, international law, empire, and the role of the state in (world) politics. Questions about intervention in other countries were often implicit and sometimes explicit in these discussions. Of course moral issues are highly relevant to any debate about (humanitarian) military intervention, such as the question of whether there is a

I would like to thank Stefano Recchia, Jennifer Welsh, Nadia Urbinati, the anonymous CUP reviewers and Robert Jackson for their comments on earlier versions of this chapter.
[1] For an overview see E. Van de Haar, *Classical Liberalism and International Relations Theory. Hume, Smith, Mises, and Hayek* (New York and Basingstoke: Palgrave Macmillan, 2009), pp. 41–74; E. Van de Haar, "David Hume and International Political Theory: A Reappraisal," *Review of International Studies* 34, no. 2 (2008); E. Van de Haar, "The Liberal Divide over Trade, War and Peace," *International Relations* 24, no. 2 (2010).
[2] R. H. Jackson, *The Global Covenant. Human Conduct in a World of States* (Oxford University Press, 2000), pp. 130–55.

right or perhaps even a duty to intervene. This might be seen as one of the perennial questions in international relations, which in some form or another has been debated throughout the past four or more centuries. Such questions may change in form, and undoubtedly the particular circumstances differ throughout the ages, but in their core they are alike.[3] We need to acknowledge that the term "international relations" did not exist until coined by Bentham in the 1780s, and that there are big differences between the current world and the Enlightenment world, which was dominated by a small number of mostly European imperial countries. Yet seen from the perspective of the decision-makers, now or then, this does not change the basic logic, the related ethical aspects, or the importance for national security and prosperity of questions of military intervention, war, or foreign conquest.

Hume and Smith did not separate their philosophical views from their contemporary political positions. The latter followed from the former. Political events were often presented as natural consequences of the way in which human nature influenced human action. Therefore, any meaningful analysis of their political views has to go hand in hand with a look at the main related elements of their moral philosophy. Moral philosophy and its practical applications were intertwined for Hume and Smith. For example, Hume's six-volume *The History of England* served such a larger goal. It was both a "regular" historical work and an analysis of the influence of human nature on practical events. Therefore the relation between human nature and military intervention is of central importance to this chapter.

The analysis begins with a close look at those aspects of their general moral theory that are crucial for our understanding of their views on (humanitarian) military intervention. This is followed by a more specific discussion of their thinking on international politics and international ethics, which proceeds in two steps. Their general views on international politics first need to be introduced as an application of their moral philosophy. This is the foundation for answering the second question, about their views on the particular issue of humanitarian intervention. Apart from drawing the main lines of argument together, the conclusion will also discuss important lessons to be learned from Hume's and Smith's reasoning for current thinking about military intervention. As a general rule, they teach us that nonintervention should be the norm, although rare exceptions are inevitable.

[3] For a discussion see B. Jahn, "Classical Theory and International Relations in Context," in B. Jahn (ed.) *Classical Theory in International Relations* (Cambridge University Press, 2006), pp. 1–24.

Moral theory and international relations

Human nature was the main issue in Smith's *Theory of Moral Sentiments*, Hume's *Treatise on Human Nature* as well as his enquiries concerning *Human Understanding* and *The Principles of Morals*.[4] Hume and Smith had a realistic view on human nature, in the sense that they took man as he was and not how he should become. They saw within individuals a perpetual interaction between the passions and reason. Passions were the most important drivers of human conduct; reason could not be relied on to secure peaceful relations between people, either in domestic society or in world affairs. The important role of the passions implied that people would always quarrel, fight, make mistakes and choose short-term sub-optimal gains rather than the larger long-term interests. This also meant that the human condition was destined to remain full of conflict.[5] According to Hume, societal order was therefore constantly under threat. It was the originating motive to establish a government, whose main task it was to administer justice. "Human nature is the given, government the response."[6] Yet for Hume and Smith, order was not the only goal of all politics. Order was an important condition for their overall goal: to enlarge individual freedom, or as Smith called it, to establish a "system of natural liberty." It was clear that individual liberty could only be achieved by people cooperating and living together. Hume and Smith underlined that in solitude, nobody would be able to flourish. Human beings were social by nature.

This poses the question of how close the bonds are between people and what the fundamental driving force is behind these inter-human bonds, both domestically and internationally. Stronger bonds and feelings between people living in different parts of the world would make calls

---

[4] D. Hume, *A Treatise of Human Nature* (eds. D. F. Norton and M. J. Norton) (Oxford University Press, 2000); D. Hume, *An Enquiry Concerning Human Understanding* (ed. T. L. Beauchamp) (Oxford University Press, 1999); D. Hume, *An Enquiry Concerning the Principles of Morals* (ed. T. L. Beauchamp) (Oxford University Press, 1998); A. Smith, *The Theory of Moral Sentiments* (eds D. D. Raphael and A. L. Macfie) (Indianapolis: Liberty Fund, 1982).

The following abbreviations are used in this chapter:

For the work of David Hume: E=Essays, EHU=Enquiry Concerning Human Understanding, EPM=Enquiry Concerning the Principles of Morals, H(n)=The History of England (by volume), L(n)=Letters of David Hume (by number), THN=Treatise of Human Nature.

For Adam Smith's works: C=Correspondence; LJA=Lectures on Jurisprudence (version A, 1762–1763), LJB=Lectures on Jurisprudence (version B, 1766), TMS=Theory of Moral Sentiments, WN=The Wealth of Nations.

[5] TMS, 9–41; THN, 266; EPM, "Editor's Introduction," pp. 10–17.

[6] Christopher J. Berry, *Human Nature* (Basingstoke: Macmillan, 1986), p. 96

for humanitarian intervention more urgent. As indicated above, Hume and Smith employed one overarching moral theory to understand the world, from relations between two individuals to international relations. In this specific case, two elements of their moral theory are of crucial importance: their ideas about sympathy and justice. The first determined the strength of the bonds between people, the second was meant to judge whether these bonds between people and societies were ethically just.

For Smith, sympathy was a core feature of human nature. It explained in important ways why people interacted and how strong their bonds were. He defined sympathy as the natural inclination of humans for "fellow-feeling with any passion whatsoever."[7] This "fellow-feeling" was the product of the imagination, in particular the capacity to put oneself in the place of another person. This process of imagination would also lead to a judgment on "the propriety" of certain behavior and to different feelings of compassion, such as love, benevolence, pride, pity, humility, sorrow, but also hatred. Smith extended the function of the imagination in his moral philosophy, by using it to construct a theoretical device called "the impartial spectator." One had to imagine this impartial spectator, as if one was continually accompanied by a person who acted as a judge of one's actions.[8] In this way, the impartial spectator functioned as a check on people's behavior and could thus stimulate feelings of sympathy towards others. Degrees of sympathy depended on the evaluation of the other person's actions, which in turn determined how we interacted with that person.[9] Hume was largely in line with Smith, by regarding sympathy as a "principle of communication" which told people about the inclinations and sentiments of others, no matter how different these were from their own.[10] Both Scots regarded sympathy as a central mechanism for the regulation and evaluation of inter-human emotions and relations. Hume distinguished between particular and general forms of sympathy, or benevolence as he also called it. The first was a specific feeling towards particular persons, and the second the more general feeling of a shared humanity. The latter was restricted to sensitivity and responsiveness to the emotions and interests of others. It could not be a

---

[7] TMS, 10.

[8] D. D. Raphael, *The Impartial Spectator. Adam Smith's Moral Philosophy* (Oxford: Clarendon Press, 2007), pp. 12–20.

[9] L. Turco, "Moral Sense and the Foundations of Morals," in A. Broadie (ed.), *The Cambridge Companion to the Scottish Enlightenment* (Cambridge University Press, 2003), pp. 141–50.

[10] THN, 206.

motive for action.[11] It only "produces a cool preference of what is useful and serviceable to mankind, above what is pernicious and dangerous."[12]

This meant that there was no natural "brotherhood of men," let alone a natural set of duties or rights between people living in different parts of the globe. Hume and Smith asserted that only close personal bonds resulted in (particular) sympathy. Fellow feeling could not be stretched indefinitely, there were geographical and national limits to it. The ties between smaller social units were stronger and also the most important to the individual. It was natural for humans to put family, friends and the nation first, normally also in that particular order.[13] People had the strongest feelings for those near to them. Smith gave the example of a devastating earthquake striking China. No doubt people (in Europe) would be shocked to learn about such a natural disaster. They would find it terrible for the victims, but they would also quickly continue with their own lives. Humans were always far more concerned by smaller events which directly affected them.[14] In a similar vein, Hume claimed it was impossible to develop a real passion for a foreign country since there was a lack of an immediate cause for these passions.[15] Smith felt that a man was always displaced in a foreign country, no matter how polite and human the local people were.[16] Hume expressed this succinctly in the context of a discussion of the origins of natural virtues and vices:

We sympathize more with persons contiguous to us than with persons remote from us; with our acquaintances, than with strangers; with our countrymen than with foreigners. But notwithstanding this variation in our sympathy, we give the same approbation to the same moral qualities in China as in England.[17]

The natural limits to sympathy indicate that human conduct was not normally driven by concern with the well-being of humanity as a whole. Hume and Smith did not think that sympathy lost all meaning at the border, but it did transform into a much weaker phenomenon, which was hardly ever a motive for human behavior. Smith distinguished between "love of our own country" and "love for mankind." Both sentiments existed independent of each other. Countries were loved for their own sake, not as part of "the great society of mankind." Even assuming there was such a society, it would be best served by individuals who directed their love towards a

[11] J. Taylor, "Hume's Later Moral Philosophy," in D. F. Norton and J. Taylor (eds.), *The Cambridge Companion to Hume*, 2nd edn. (Cambridge University Press, 2009), pp. 318–23.
[12] EPM, 147.   [13] TMS, "Introduction," 10.
[14] C. Smith, *Adam Smith's Political Philosophy. The Invisible Hand and Spontaneous Order* (London and New York: Routledge, 2006), p. 38.
[15] THN, 218.   [16] C, 108.   [17] THN, 371.

particular portion of it: their own country, which was the most abstract entity people had an emotional attachment to beyond their immediate kin, extended family, clan, city or region. In this particular instance it worked just like a market system as it also produced positive external effects by demanding from people to take care of their well-known self-interest. Only this kind of human action was within the sphere of man's abilities, understanding, and in line with the natural system of human affections. Universal benevolence and practical good offices could seldom be stretched across the nation's borders. The administration of the great universal system, the protection of happiness of all rational and sensible beings, was solely the business of God. For humans, the duty was to mind the happiness of their relatives, friends and country.[18]

Hume and Smith acknowledged that people could temporarily be touched by the misery of others, even when they lived far away. Yet they did not see any natural inclination in human nature, or a moral obligation to translate these incidental feelings of sympathy into political action beyond the nation state. Put briefly for the specific purposes of this chapter: there could never be a moral *duty* to intervene militarily on behalf of foreigners, as there was no clear moral ground for such a demand.

It is harder to determine whether they saw a *right* to intervention. A proper answer requires one to take Smith's and Hume's views on (international) justice into account. Both argued that justice was the glue that kept societies together. On the question of domestic justice, Hume and Smith differed from their contemporaries by regarding justice as both an innate personal virtue and the result of social relations external to individuals. It was about maintaining rather inflexible rules aimed at correcting injustices. Justice was about restraint, it was a negative virtue requiring people not to hurt others. Smith declared that "we often fulfill all the rules of justice by sitting still and doing nothing."[19] Hume pointed out that ideas of justice developed spontaneously, on a case-by-case basis. Within particular societies, these ideas developed over time into common sentiments about the legitimate rules to protect life and property and about the punishment of individuals who broke these rules. This enabled cooperation between large numbers of people, thus making society possible.[20] Obviously this process had no equivalent at the international level.

[18] TMS, 229, 235–7.
[19] C. J. Berry, *Social Theory of the Scottish Enlightenment* (Edinburgh University Press, 1997), pp. 131–2.
[20] K. Haakonssen, "Natural Jurisprudence and the Theory of Justice," in A. Broadie (ed.), *The Cambridge Companion to the Scottish Enlightenment* (Cambridge University Press, 2003).

Hume referred to the rules of justice as the laws of nature. These were duties of rulers and ruled alike, comprising the stability of possession, its transfer by consent and the performance of promises.[21] He underlined that the laws of nature had the same advantages in domestic politics and international relations. The basic interests of men did not change in the international realm. Without respect for property rights, war would be the norm. Where property was not transferred in agreement, there could be no commerce and if promises were not kept, there could be no alliances. The specific relations between countries were to be regulated by the laws of nations, which were additions to these (general) laws of nature. The most important rules were diplomatic immunity or "the sacredness of the persons" of ambassadors, the principle that war had to be formally declared, the prohibition of the use of poisoned arms and the obligation to treat prisoners of war humanely.[22]

Yet Hume posited a major difference between the two realms. In international relations, the natural obligation to justice was not as strong as in a domestic situation. The intercourse between countries was in itself less advantageous than the intercourse among individuals in domestic society. Hume thought that without the latter, people were not able to subsist, while (in his time) it was possible to have a good life without being engaged in international relations. Another difference that is crucial for the current discussion was that in international affairs, moral obligations were less stringent: "there is a system of morals calculated for princes, much more free than that which ought to govern private persons." Princes could not discard all rules of justice, ignore treaties, or disregard public duties and obligations. However, he pointed out, "the morality of the princes has the same extent, yet it has not the same force as that of private persons, and may lawfully be transgressed from a more trivial motive." It is important to note that Hume neither saw nor attempted to develop any fixed rules for such cases: "the practice of the world goes farther in teaching us the degrees of our duty, than the most subtle philosophy, which was ever yet invented."[23]

Smith, too, recognized a difference in the force of the rules of justice between domestic and international politics.[24] He acknowledged the need for rules and (diplomatic) practices at the international level, because without "security from injuries" from abroad, the life and property of individuals

---

[21] THN, 363.

[22] IR theorists might note these three laws of nature are very close to Hedley Bull's three goals of international society. From an English School perspective Hume and Smith are indeed Grotian pluralists, just like Bull. See Van de Haar, *Classical Liberalism and International Relations Theory*, pp. 41–74.

[23] EPM, 99; THN, 362–4.   [24] LJA, 6–7; LJB, 399.

was not secured. In comparison to Hume, he was more critical of international law. He defined the laws of war and peace as "the different regulations that subsist betwixt different independent states, with respect both to the mutual intercourse betwixt them in time of peace and what privileges may be granted them, and to the effects of the success in war and what is permitted as lawful in the time that war is waged betwixt different nations."

The moral theory of Smith and Hume points to a limited application of both sympathy and justice in international affairs. In general, they believed that emotional ties and sympathy between people could stretch beyond national borders. But international sympathy did not have the same strength. The international level also differed substantially from national politics, because principles of justice did not have the same force internationally. This meant that there was neither a duty to military intervention for humanitarian reasons, nor a right or entitlement to intervention that could be called upon by an oppressed people.

Nevertheless, Hume's and Smith's limited application of sympathy and justice does not rule out intervention completely. They were far too subtle and moderate in their thinking to justify such strong conclusions. Whether they thought that rulers had a right to militarily intervene on behalf of others requires further analysis – notably of their political views. This will be done in two steps. First, their general views on international politics will be discussed. This will be followed by a more specific analysis of their ideas about different kinds of foreign (military) action.

International politics

It follows from Smith's and Hume's moral theory and their view on human nature that they did not see much possibility for a peaceful cosmopolitan order. Their thinking was fully in line with the "tough minded approach to problems of war and peace of Scottish predecessors like Francis Hutcheson and Gershom Carmichael," and more generally with the bellicose attitudes of eighteenth-century English and Scottish elites, at least compared to their counterparts on the Continent.[25] While both men were influenced by Stoic thought (especially Smith), they rejected Stoic cosmopolitanism, which for example for the Romans had been a legitimization for foreign intervention.[26] Hume and Smith saw international

[25] R. Tuck, *The Rights of War and Peace. Political Thought and the International Order from Grotius to Kant* (Oxford University Press, 1999), p. 183; M. Howard, *The Invention of Peace and the Reinvention of War* (London: Profile Books, 2002), p. 21.

[26] E. C. Mossner, *The Life of David Hume* (Oxford: Clarendon Press, 1980), pp. 52, 64–5; TMS, "Introduction," p. 10; Tuck, *Rights of War and Peace*, pp. 34–47.

affairs in large measure as the interplay of different countries and their leaders.[27] Yet unlike mainstream political realists, their yardstick to judge the outcomes at the level of world politics was not gain in national power, but instead the protection or expansion of natural liberty.

Before elaborating on this point, it is perhaps useful to realize that Hume and Smith differed substantially from the mainstream liberal view in the academic study of international relations, where a liberal tradition is generally crafted around the writings of thinkers such as Kant, Bentham, Cobden, Mill and Wilson. Put very briefly, the main characteristics of this "standard" liberal view are a cosmopolitan outlook in world politics and an optimistic belief in the peace-enhancing effects of international institutions, free trade and interdependence among nations. Liberals are traditionally portrayed as standing at the opposite extreme from realists, who emphasize the permanent nature of international competition and conflict, war, and the balance of power. By contrast, the standard argument goes, liberalism calls for the peaceful settlement of disputes between states, often through international law, arbitrage and international courts. Political and military leaders will also be kept in check if the public wields more influence on foreign policy, because the people are seen to be inherently peaceful.[28]

Cosmopolitan views of this kind make a fairly good fit with calls for humanitarian military intervention. The ideas of Smith and Hume differ substantially from those views. International law, they thought, could be useful to an extent, but like the underlying moral principle of justice, it could never have the same strength as domestic law. On this issue, Hume and Smith were influenced by Grotius, whom they openly praised.[29] Smith concluded the *Theory of Moral Sentiments* with the observation that Grotius was the first to systematically describe the principles of the law of nations. Thus *The Rights of War and Peace* was "the most complete work

---

[27] LJA, 7; EPM, 99; THN, 362–4; TMS, 154, 228.
[28] See for example T. Dunne, "Liberalism," in J. Baylis and S. Smith (eds.), *The Globalization of World Politics. An Introduction to International Relations* (Oxford University Press, 2005); S. Burchill, "Liberalism," in S. Burchill, et al. (eds.), *Theories of International Relations* (Houndmills and New York: Palgrave, 2005); M. W. Zacher and R. A. Matthew, "Liberal International Theory: Common Threads, Divergent Strands," in C. W. Kegley, Jr. (ed.), *Controversies in International Relations Theory. Realism and the Neoliberal Challenge* (New York: St. Martin's Press, 1995); M. W. Doyle, "Liberalism and World Politics," *American Political Science Review* 80, no. 4 (1986); M. W. Doyle, *Ways of War and Peace. Realism, Liberalism and Socialism* (New York and London: W.W. Norton & Company, 1997); R. H. Jackson and G. Sørensen, *Introduction to International Relations. Theories and Approaches* (Oxford University Press, 2003); D. Panke and T. Risse, "Liberalism," in Tim Dunne, M. Kurki and S. Smith (eds.), *International Relations Theories. Discipline and Diversity* (Oxford University Press, 2007).
[29] LJB, 545–7; TMS, 341–2; THN, 262–364.

that has thus far been written on that subject."[30] Quoting the Dutchman, Smith asserted that there were hardly occasions when a rule was agreed with the common consent of all nations and was then observed at all times.[31] The laws of nations, as international law was called in those days, were "often very little more than mere pretension and profession." Justice was hardly ever observed in war. International negotiation, truth, and fair dealing were regularly disregarded and treaties violated. Worse, such violations were hardly ever punished. Instead the "ambassador who dupes the minister of a foreign nation is admired and applauded, even when only small interests are involved. This often derives from 'the noble love of our own country'."[32] Smith further protested that the laws of nations failed to defend the most obvious rule of international justice, namely, that only the belligerent party receives punishment. In ancient times, all the people were involved in the decision to wage a war, and therefore it was just that they all suffered in war. In contrast, most contemporary wars were fought on account of the decisions and actions of kings and sovereigns, who often engaged in imprudent, unjust wars and foolish peace treaties.[33] Consequently, innocent people suffered in place of the really guilty, by having their land and houses seized, or by getting killed.[34] This was clearly unjust and Smith therefore disagreed with his teacher Hutcheson, who thought that all people were indirectly accountable, through their support for their government.[35]

Crucially, Smith and Hume believed that international rules of justice, while often disregarded, were not altogether useless, because they still helped to achieve some basic kind of order. Statesmen understood that they could only be legitimately disregarded in emergencies. In the words of Hume:

all politicians will allow and most philosophers, that reasons of state may in *particular emergencies* dispense with the rules of justice, and invalidate any treaty or alliance, where the strict observance of it would be prejudicial, in a considerable degree, to either of the contracted parties.[36]

Both men also believed that the concept of justice was helpful for assessing the legitimacy of a war, and indeed they clearly belong in the just war tradition.[37] Smith believed that no war should be waged without moral justification. War needed "the same proper foundation as a law suit before a court of justice." Infringements of just war principles, such as

---

[30] TMS, 341–2.   [31] LJB, 545.   [32] TMS, 154, 228.   [33] LJB, 407; LJA, 326.
[34] TMS, 155; LJA, 200.   [35] LJB, 547–8.   [36] EPM, 100; emphasis added.
[37] K. Haakonssen, "Introduction. The Coherence of Smith's Thought," in K. Haakonssen (ed.), *The Cambridge Companion to Adam Smith* (Cambridge University Press, 2006), pp. 13–14; F. G. Whelan, *Hume and Machiavelli. Political Realism and Liberal Thought* (Lanham: Lexington Books, 2004), p. 211.

the violation of property rights or the killing or unjustified imprisonment of one's subjects by another state, were never morally acceptable. In such cases it was the duty of a government to protect its citizens, including by resorting to war. Other just grounds for war were the continuous failure or refusal to repay debts, or violations of contractual terms in different ways. "Every offence of the sovereign of one country against the sovereign of another, or of the sovereign against the subject, or the subject of one country against the subject of another, without giving reasonable satisfaction, may be the cause of a war." This allows some room for foreign military intervention, also because Smith explicitly viewed retaliation and preventive action as justified in clear cases of conspiracy, or when territories were threatened.[38]

Hume was in full agreement with most of these points and added a number of criteria to assess the legitimacy of wars.[39] Commenting on the possible war of the British against Spain and France over the Falkland Islands in early 1771, Hume emphasized the importance of prudence, in particular through an analysis of the reasonableness and sensibility of war. He asserted that wars often commence between two nations, but they soon drag in their neighbors. Therefore prudent leaders did not lightly risk a war, and any war for frivolous causes was wrong.[40] "The rage and violence of public war ... is a suspension of justice among the warring parties." Hume regretted that leaders set the rules of justice aside in war situations. Nations in war often violated the principles of justice. Instead, the laws of war prevailed, where any enemy action, however bloody and pernicious, had to be countered in a similar way. In these situations, Hume thought, considerations about justice and moral standards often vanished.[41] Hume never actually endorsed such a "realist" disregard of international justice, and he called on leaders of states to respect the main goals and boundaries set by international law, even when, like Smith, he simultaneously recognized that norms in international relations could never be as strict and far-reaching as they were in a domestic political society. These looser and less-detailed or far-reaching demands of justice had to be regarded nevertheless.

So was there ever a right for political leaders to militarily intervene in situations where the natural rights of foreigners were breached? Hume and

---

[38] LJB, 545–7.

[39] D. Hume, *Essays. Moral, Political, and Literary* (ed. E. F. Miller) (Indianapolis: Liberty Fund, 1987), p. 337.

[40] D. Hume, *The Letters of David Hume, in Two Volumes* (ed. J. Y. T. Greig) (Oxford: Clarendon Press, 1932), 453; D. Hume, *New Letters of David Hume* (R. Klibansky and E. C. Mossner eds.) (Oxford: Clarendon Press, 1954), p. 127.

[41] EPM, 86.

Smith never addressed this issue directly, and an answer cannot be found
in their adherence to natural rights – despite the fact that these were
cornerstones of their political and moral thought.[42] Their support of
Grotius gives a better indication of their thinking, as Grotius is sometimes
seen as the source of a modern doctrine of humanitarian intervention.[43]

Grotius's concerns for the maintenance of international order and the
respect for sovereignty largely made him a noninterventionist, yet there was
one exception: he allowed, but never required, other countries to intervene
if a tyrant committed atrocities against his subjects.[44] This right was meant
to punish the particular ruler rather than to protect the people, thus strictly
speaking it is erroneous to distill an image of Grotius as a great theorist of
humanitarian intervention.[45] In his view, states were the exclusive subjects
of international law, citizens operated in a wholly different sphere.[46]

Hume and Smith followed Grotius in regarding "corrective justice"
and not "distributive justice" as the main glue of international society.
In international relations the right to punishment was a main principle of
justice. This allowed states rights to war and territorial appropriation to
punish gross violations of the laws of nature, yet without an obligation
to international assistance or redistribution.[47] While Hume and Smith
did not openly embrace the Grotian principle of intervention, this line of
reasoning fits well with their moral theory, and their views on just war
and international relations. They firmly believed in a difference between
domestic and international justice, as they pointed to the international
arena as a place of fundamental and perpetual normative disagreement.
It was impossible to agree on or implement moral norms governing the
whole globe, or even only in Europe for that matter, beyond a very basic
set of rules.[48] International order in a world of states without ultimate

[42] Van de Haar, *Classical Liberalism and International Relations Theory*, 25–8;
K. Haakonssen, *Natural Law and Moral Philosophy. From Grotius to the Scottish
Enlightenment* (Cambridge University Press, 1996), pp. 117–20, 30–5.
[43] S. Chesterman, *Just War or Just Peace? Humanitarian Intervention and International Law*
(Oxford University Press, 2001), p. 9; J. L. Holzgrefe, "The Humanitarian Intervention
Debate," in J. L. Holzgrefe and R. O. Keohane (eds.), *Humanitarian Intervention. Ethical,
Legal, and Political Dilemmas* (Cambridge University Press, 2003), p. 26.
[44] R. J. Vincent, "Grotius, Human Rights, and Intervention," in H. Bull, B. Kingsbury, and
A. Roberts (eds.), *Hugo Grotius and International Relations* (Oxford: Clarendon Press,
1990); T. Nardin, "The Moral Basis for Humanitarian Intervention," in A. F. Lang (ed.),
Just Intervention (Washington, DC: Georgetown University Press, 2003), pp. 15–16.
[45] R. Jeffery, *Hugo Grotius in International Thought* (New York and Basingstoke: Palgrave
Macmillan, 2006), pp. 40–3, 108, 30–8.
[46] K. Nabulsi, *Traditions of War: Occupation, Resistance, and the Law* (Oxford University
Press, 2005), pp. 128–76.
[47] Tuck, *Rights of War and Peace*, pp. 78–108.
[48] J. Boyle, "Natural Law and International Ethics," in T. Nardin and D. R. Mapel (eds.),
Traditions of International Ethics (Cambridge University Press, 1992); also Holzgrefe,

arbiter depended on an interplay of power and rules.[49] International law with more binding force depended on a moral consensus. In its absence, international order was never a given, but instead the result of a temporary, fragile equilibrium. Hence to the degree that they might have justified humanitarian intervention, they would have clearly seen it as the exception, always driven by mixed motives and – in a Grotian fashion – ultimately aimed at punishing the oppressive ruler, rather than protecting the innocent.

This interpretation is further supported by Hume's and Smith's views on state sovereignty and the balance of power. They thought that international order was mainly maintained through a power balance among nations, the main international actors. Depending on historical circumstances, several nations or countries (Hume and Smith were not consistent in their use of the terms) developed out of the communities that humans were naturally bound to form in order to survive. The nation was a source of emotions for all individuals. Hume and Smith believed no one was indifferent to their country, and national feelings were strong motivational forces for individual conduct. For example, they underlined that it was virtuous to fight and die for one's country.[50] As highlighted above, the nation was seen as the outer layer of any meaningful form of sympathy. Within a country, people felt they were related to each other in one form or another; but beyond the border this strong emotion evaporated into a more rational awareness of a mutually shared humanity. This sometimes led to short-term outbursts of general sympathy or benevolence when something terrible happened to these other peoples, but not to claims for political action. National interests would normally prevail over considerations of justice.

Accordingly, it was only natural that both men saw the principle of national sovereignty as a main ingredient of international order. It underpinned Smith's *The Wealth of Nations*.[51] Hume asserted that "there is nothing more favorable to the rise of politeness and learning, than a number of neighboring and independent states, connected together by commerce and policy."[52] Smith thought that international

---

"The Humanitarian Intervention Debate," in Holzgrefe and Keohane (eds.), *Humanitarian Intervention*, pp. 25–8.

[49] Whelan, *Hume and Machiavelli*, pp. 224–5; LJB, 545.

[50] THN, 79, 183–200; TMS, 154, 227–37.

[51] See also A. W. Walter, "Adam Smith and the Liberal Tradition in International Relations," in I. Clark and I. B. Neumann (eds.), *Classical Theories of International Relations* (Basingstoke: Macmillan, 1996).

[52] E, 119.

relations were dominated by considerations of interest and needs, rather than by the laws of justice, which was also Hume's bottom line.[53]

Their praise for the balance of power as an ordering mechanism in world politics fits well with this approach. Hume saw the balance as a benevolent secret in politics for both states and their citizens.[54] While fragile and at times unpredictable, the balance of power prevented many violent revolutions and unwarranted foreign conquests.[55] When the balance of power functioned well, powerful empires would be hindered from abusing their positions, which made the increase of individual freedom possible.[56] Smith did not write as extensively on the balance, a number of historical references excepted, but he also considered it an important instrument for peace and international stability.[57]

One of the biggest fallacies in international relations theory about Hume and especially Smith, is the Scots' association with the thesis that foreign trade promotes peace. This misconception has been fostered by leading scholars such as Michael Doyle, Bruce Russett, Andrew Moravscik, John Oneal and others.[58] Surely, both thinkers strongly endorsed free trade, and they opposed mercantilism and most other forms of economic protectionism. They identified a strong relation between commerce, welfare and an advanced culture; but mostly over-looked in international relations theory is that at the same time, they emphasized the relation between commerce, conflict and war.[59] Trade added to the many possible causes of war; peace depended on wise policies, not on trade.[60] While Smith famously asserted that commerce

---

[53] K. Haakonssen, *The Science of a Legislator. The Natural Jurisprudence of David Hume and Adam Smith* (Cambridge University Press, 1981), p. 146; Whelan, *Hume and Machiavelli*, p. 200.

[54] E, 93, 323–41.

[55] D. Hume, *The History of England. From the Invasion of Julius Caesar to the Revolution in 1688. In Six Volumes* (ed. W. B. Todd) (Indianapolis: Liberty Fund, 1983), vol. I, p. 296.

[56] E, 337.

[57] LJB, 552–3; TMS, 230–1; Haakonssen, *Science of a Legislator*, p. 179.

[58] For example M. A. Doyle, *Ways of War and Peace: Realism, Liberalism and Socialism* (New York: W.W. Norton, 1997), pp. 230–41; J. R. Oneal and B. Russett, "The Classical Liberals Were Right: Democracy, Interdependence, and Conflict 1950–1985," *International Studies Quarterly* 41, no. 2 (1997), 267–94; A. Moravscik, "Liberal International Relations Theory: A Scientific Assessment," in C. Elman and M. F. Elman (eds.), *Progress in International Relations Theory: Appraising the Field* (Cambridge, MA: MIT Press, 2003), pp. 159–204. For more detail see Van de Haar, *Liberal Divide*.

[59] See for example E, 255, 262–73; A. Smith, *An Inquiry Into the Nature and Causes of the Wealth of Nations* (eds. R. H. Campbell and A. S. Skinner) (Indianapolis: Liberty Fund, 1982), pp. 457–9, 493.

[60] R. A. Manzer, "The Promise of Peace? Hume and Smith on the Effects of Commerce on War and Peace," *Hume Studies* XXII, no. 2 (1996); D. A. Irwin, *Against the Tide. An Intellectual History of Free Trade* (Princeton University Press, 1996), p. 76; I. Hont, *Jealousy*

ought to be a source of friendship, he put far more emphasis on his equally famous maxim that "defense is more important than opulence."[61] This underlined his understanding of the important role of power in international politics. Hume was on the same line and observed that the public good in foreign politics would often depend on accidents, chances and the "caprices of a few persons."[62]

Free trade was good for a number of reasons, but could never be a source of lasting peaceful relations among states. There could never be such a peace, due to the strong attachment of the individual to the nation, the inevitability of conflict in the anarchic international society of states, and the idea that international justice was far more difficult to attain than domestic justice. Of course, this did not mean there would be perpetual war. Basic international order could be achieved and maintained through careful maneuvering by prudent leaders, but it would never be secure.[63]

Hume and Smith recognized the complex interplay of power, coincidence, norms and principles in international affairs. They understood that there could not be one permanent answer for all international issues. This is in line with the findings of the previous section about the limited applicability of sympathy and justice in international affairs. International order was needed, because without it individual liberty would perish. Under the anarchic conditions of a world of sovereign states, order mostly depends on the balance of power. International law and the principles of just war would be helpful, but ultimately secondary sources of order. Given human nature, considerations of justice would rarely be guiding principles in international politics. Military interventions – even when motivated by benign intentions – could upset the fragile international balance, would infringe on the right to sovereignty, and open the door to counterinterventions. Thus, it seems unlikely that Hume and Smith would have supported a general right to military intervention for humanitarian reasons.

Intervention and empire

Thus far the analysis has mainly indicated that Hume and Smith by-and-large rejected a general right of humanitarian military intervention. Still, they certainly did not exclude the possibility of humanitarian

---

of Trade. *International Competition and the Nation-State in Historical Perspective* (Cambridge, MA and London: The Belknap Press of Harvard University Press, 2005), pp. 6, 383.
[61] WN, 463–5, 493–6.   [62] E, 255.   [63] Van de Haar, *Liberal Divide*.

intervention on specific occasions. This can partially be inferred from their endorsement of Grotius's writings on these matters, as suggested above. Ultimately, however, this had less to do with their moral thought than with their views on statecraft and international politics. The previous section has shown that Hume and Smith thought that leaders of states needed ample room for maneuver in international affairs, because in the international arena moral obligations and demands do not have the same force as domestically, as there is only a limited consensus about international moral and legal rules. Conducting international affairs so as to ensure the nation's prosperity and survival comprised a most significant part of the duties of political leaders.

Prudence on the part of political leaders was crucial in this respect.[64] Without it, they would only be like an "insidious and crafty animal, vulgarly called a statesman or politician, whose councils are directed to the momentary fluctuations of affairs."[65] Instead, Smith's ideal politician, the "man of public spirit," was both prudent and virtuous. He was a legislator governed by general principles, hoping to do the right thing. Principally, this meant that he kept social order.[66] He was "the best head joined by the best heart," as opposed to the "man of system," who sought to govern society as a chess player moving the pieces on the board.[67] Hume agreed with this, which shows for example in his description of the qualities of the first leaders, or founders, in a society.[68] Prudent leaders were those who helped to maintain social order – a main Humean concern.[69]

Most likely, both Scots would thus have allowed prudent political leaders a fairly large responsibility to decide on the merits of particular questions of military intervention for humanitarian purposes. It would depend on the circumstances and could just as likely be motivated by a desire to play a part in an international coalition whose continuation was deemed crucial to maintain the balance of power. Hence interventions driven by purely humanitarian motives would be rare, if not altogether non-existent. Furthermore, as indicated in the previous section, a prime concern of both Hume and Smith in world politics was the principle of sovereignty. Hence all forms of intervention would need to be exceptions, as they would clearly violate the sovereignty of other countries. Hume and Smith were concerned about the negative unforeseen consequences of

---

[64] Haakonssen, *Science of a Legislator*, p. 146.   [65] WN, 468.

[66] See C. L. Griswold, *Adam Smith and the Virtues of Enlightenment* (Cambridge University Press, 1999), pp. 203–7; D. Winch, *Adam Smith's Politics. An Essay in Historiographic Revision* (Cambridge University Press, 1978), p. 172.

[67] TMS, 216.   [68] E, 39.

[69] R. Hardin, *David Hume: Moral and Political Theorist* (Oxford University Press, 2007), pp. 105–33.

170   *Edwin van de Haar*

military action, not least because these were potential threats to individual liberty, on both sides. War and intervention could easily disturb the perpetually fragile international order. Presumably, the two Scots would also have closely scrutinized the likely post-bellum situation: any military initiative that would not have increased the natural liberty of the people in the target society would have been hard to justify on humanitarian grounds – although it could still have been justified on other grounds, such as self-defense or upholding the balance of power.[70]

Perhaps this becomes clearer when considering Hume's and Smith's position regarding one of the most important international issues of their time, British imperialism. Given their power-oriented views on international affairs, one would perhaps expect the two thinkers to have been either indifferent towards or even supportive of empire. Yet while they did not outright call to abolish every form of empire, they continually pointed at the many negative sides of imperialism, which stands in contrast to the attitudes of some of the most prominent nineteenth-century liberals, many of whom endorsed imperialism. Pitts therefore identifies a "liberal turn to empire" in the nineteenth century.[71]

As Whelan makes clear in his comparison of the thoughts of Hume and Machiavelli, the Scot, unlike the Florentine, did not endorse conquest and empire-building for reasons of state, military glory or increased national welfare. Hume only accepted a right to conquest when there was a rightful claim based on a just war principle. Conquest for conquest's sake – for example, to increase national power – he rejected.[72] Colonies were hardly of economic importance. For example, the conquest of the West Indies led to an increase in available precious metal, but Hume noted that this had only resulted in inflation. He did see some positive effects of imperialism, most notably the advancement of knowledge, the arts and the industries, for both the imperial power and the target society.[73] This was coupled with increased levels of commerce between colonies and the motherland, and there were also a few social benefits, particularly that lower-class men got a chance to raise a fortune, while the increasingly wealthy upper classes had less reason to repress the common people.[74] But overall, these were insufficient reasons to support imperial adventures. Hume thought free trade was a much better way to increase welfare; and it would be beneficial to all people.

---

[70] See J. Mayall, "Intervention in International Society: Theory and Practice in Contemporary Perspective," in B. A. Roberson (ed.), *International Society and the Development of International Relations Theory* (London and New York: Continuum, 2002).

[71] J. Pitts, *A Turn to Empire. The Rise of Imperial Liberalism in Britain and France* (Princeton and Oxford: Princeton University Press, 2005), pp. 1–2.

[72] Whelan, *Hume and Machiavelli*, pp. 209–17.   [73] H, V 39.   [74] H, III 80–1.

Smith strongly opposed the oppression and (economic) exploitation related to imperialism. It went against his ideas of natural liberty and justice. Imperialism was unjust and harmful to both colonizers and colonized.[75] The establishment of colonies was not needed nor could it be expected "to raise utility."[76] He was broad-minded in his analysis of unfamiliar societies and did not assume that Western society was naturally superior to other societies, nor that Western countries had some historical role in advancing or educating other people.[77] Again, all these elements clearly point in the direction of Hume and Smith endorsing nonintervention as a strong prima facie norm in international affairs.

Both Scots agreed that the American colonies should be allowed to govern themselves, which was the most pressing topical issue in this respect. Hume considered their independence both inevitable and desirable.[78] In 1775 he called himself "an American in my principles." The British should not attempt to rule the Americas from such a distance.[79] Great economic or "geopolitical" losses were not to be expected, apart from some minor negative influences on navigation and general commerce. The only serious detriment was the possible damage to the reputation and authority of the English government, but this would be inevitable, since a war against the Americans could not be won.[80] Smith emphasized the role of freedom in the American experience. The main reason behind the prospering of the colonies was the inability of their "mother countries" to govern them strictly. They grew rich due to the abundance of good and cheap land, combined with numerous freedoms; the opening of a new and inexhaustible market to all commodities; new divisions of labor; higher productivity; and new sets of exchanges, improvements in arts and sciences.[81] The lack of free trade between the colonies and the British subjects was detrimental to the general welfare of Britain, and was one of the worst violations of the sacred rights of mankind.[82]

In short, for Hume and Smith, imperialism was detrimental to freedom, prosperity and progress in both colonizing and colonized countries.

---

[75] L. Billet, "Justice, Liberty and Economy," in F. R. Glahe (ed.), *Adam Smith and the Wealth of Nations. 1776–1976 Bicentennial Essays* (Boulder, CO: Colorado Associated University Press, 1978), pp. 103–7; Haakonssen, *Science of a Legislator*, p. 147.

[76] WN, 558.

[77] Pitts, *Turn to Empire*, pp. 25–8.

[78] J. B. Stewart, *Opinion and Reform in Hume's Political Philosophy* (Princeton University Press, 1992), p. 308; S. R. Letwin, *The Pursuit of Certainty. David Hume, Jeremy Bentham, John Stuart Mill, Beatrice Webb* (Indianapolis: Liberty Fund, 1998), p. 116.

[79] L, 510.   [80] L, 514, 511, 512.   [81] WN, 448–9, 567, 570, 572, 589–90.

[82] J. Rae, *Life of Adam Smith* (London and New York: Macmillan & Co, 1895), p. 384. WN, 581–2.

There is no reason to assume they would have thought more positively of
the longer-term effects of military intervention for humanitarian purposes. Therefore, the extent of humanitarian military intervention that
they would have approved would have been only a very limited form of
intervention, aimed for instance at the immediate termination of a genocide. Their negative views on imperialism suggest that they would have
disapproved of protracted international intervention and trusteeship
aimed at "nation-building."

Hume, and particularly Smith, explained historical progress as a process by which societies went through stages of development. This is now
known as "conjectural history."[83] The main idea was that while human
nature was universal, different circumstances explained the multitude
of global living situations. For Smith, these were categorized in four
stages according to the dominance of different means of economic production: hunting, shepherding, agriculture, and manufacturing and
commerce. Commercial society as found in countries such as England,
Switzerland and Holland stood at the top of the order.[84] Countries at the
more refined economic stages were also more advanced in other fields,
such as the arts. It is important to note that Hume and Smith assumed
it was possible for all nations to advance to higher stages. Progress was
possible for all peoples and it was natural for humans to strive for
the improvement of their living conditions.[85] Thus conjectural history
was both universal and progressive, with human nature as the main
driving force.[86]

This means that they thought it possible for all people to advance to a
higher stage of development, but at the same time impossible to acceler-
ate this process, for example through outside intervention. Thus, in
contrast for example to many of their French counterparts, the Scots
did not think that the right application of reason could ensure human
progress.[87] This view also extended to the use of reason from abroad.
Intervention with the aim of bringing about a fundamental change in the
targeted society would not lead to any positive results. As Smith wrote,
"the different situations of different ages and countries are apt ... to give
different characters to the generality of those who live in them." In all

[83] See for example J. G. A. Pocock, "Adam Smith and History," in K. Haakonssen (ed.)
The Cambridge Companion to Adam Smith (Cambridge University Press, 2006),
pp. 270–87.
[84] LJA, 14–29.
[85] D. L. Blaney and N. Inayatullah, "The Savage Smith and the Temporal Walls of
Capitalism," in B. Jahn (ed.), *Classical Theory in International Relations* (Cambridge
University Press, 2006), pp. 134–45.
[86] Berry, *Social Theory of the Scottish Enlightenment*, pp. 61–71.   [87] *Ibid.*, p. 7.

societies there were general and natural rules and practices of propriety, just as there were plain principles of right and wrong in every country, which all help to keep society together.[88] At most, foreigners might foster change in backward societies by influencing the prevailing ideas in a non-coercive manner; this was another positive role of free trade and other forms of international exchange. Hume and Smith saw no need for Europeans to civilize others. They were confident that other societies would be able to develop themselves, and the two Scots never argued that military intervention could play a positive role in this process.

Conclusion

British international relations scholar Martin Wight wrote that "adherents of every political belief will regard intervention as justified under certain circumstances."[89] The foregoing analysis of the thought of Hume and Smith supports this view, albeit to a limited extent. The emphasis in their thought about international relations was more on preserving order than on achieving justice for all; more on feelings of adherence to the nation than on cosmopolitanism; and more on the importance of sovereignty for individual liberty than on obligations and rights following from a shared humanity.

Still, while Hume and Smith never openly endorsed military intervention, it seems likely that they would have allowed, in rare cases, prudent political leaders to decide to intervene militarily for humanitarian purposes. These leaders would then be obliged to explain, in no uncertain terms, how such intervention would promote the natural liberty of the people on whose behalf the action ostensibly takes place.

Hume and Smith were not cosmopolitan thinkers. They distinguished natural limits to sympathy and justice in the international realm. Meaningful feelings of attachment and obligation were restricted to compatriots. Out of a shared humanity, sympathy and imagination, foreigners could be the object of short-term empathy, but that was hardly ever a ground for political action. This underlines the importance of their view on human nature for their ideas about international politics and military intervention. International politics was mainly about keeping order, not about the universal protection of natural rights. Anarchy and war were the largest threats to natural liberty; therefore caution and restraint needed to be the norm in this normatively pluralist

---

[88] TMS, 204, 208–9.
[89] M. Wight, *Power Politics* (ed. H. Bull and C. Holbraad) (London: Leicester University Press for the Royal Institute of International Affairs, 1995), p. 191.

environment. Every society had to go through four developmental stages at its own pace and under its own circumstances. Outside intervention might often be counterproductive. Positive outside influence should be exerted primarily through cultural and commercial exchange. Hume and Smith were more aware of the importance and pervasiveness of power politics than is commonly realized by modern scholars of international relations; yet they did not endorse war for "frivolous" purposes. War, they thought, is sometimes necessary for keeping the balance of power, or to protect other fundamental interests, but it has to be conducted in line with the principles of just war.

Their ideas, as discussed in this chapter, offer meaningful lessons for today. The most important one is that restraint in military intervention is always desirable, not least because international disorder remains perhaps the main threat to human dignity, liberty and prosperity. The world is still no cosmopolitan society. There has been an increase in the number of international treaties since the days of Hume and Smith; yet most of these rules continue to be frequently disregarded in international politics. World politics is not only an arena of different interests; the underlying moral views, too, continue to fundamentally differ – as suggested, for instance, by the current difficulties of reaching a shared international agreement on criteria for justified intervention.

The role of human nature is all too often overlooked by contemporary theorists of international relations. Most people lack strong emotional ties with people outside their own society, although everybody has the capacity to imagine the feelings of others and act with sympathy when something terrible happens, for example the Asian tsunami in 2004 or other natural disasters. As Smith described more than 200 years ago, for most people these are only short-term feelings, nowadays at least partially induced by the force of media coverage. Only in rare instances do these emotional outbursts provide a sufficient motivation for governments to intervene (militarily) abroad. A consequence of this is the inevitable selectivity of humanitarian intervention: some people may get help from abroad, while others won't, even though the latter may face worse circumstances. This is regrettable, but in an imperfect world, inhabited by imperfect people, it is perhaps also inevitable. In international relations, different normative principles and political interests need to be balanced, which makes a straightforward or clear case for intervention unlikely to emerge. Beyond the occasional intervention, which may be justified, the benefits of nonintervention often outweigh the costs of attempting a universal protection of even a limited set of rights.

Hume and Smith pointed out that international stability is a treasure. Without it, natural liberty and individual flourishing will be distant goals for most people. Decisions about foreign military action may be motivated by the best intentions, but unforeseen consequences should be taken into account, such as a potential disturbance of the balance of power, the costs in lives and in monetary terms, and the possibility of spreading the conflict to neighboring countries. The Scots believed that prudent leaders should always keep these issues in mind. We should be wise enough not to forget them, either.

8   Sovereignty, morality, and history: the problematic legitimization of force in Rousseau, Kant, and Hegel

Pierre Hassner

Like many of the classical thinkers discussed in this volume, we are still concerned with the problem of legitimacy, and hence of the state's monopoly on the legitimate use of violence. We are also struggling with the same moral dilemmas between the imperatives of peace and justice, or between the avoidance of inflicting death or suffering upon human beings and the duty to assist the victims of crime and injustice. Finally, we are still occasionally faced with the argument that some regimes are backward or barbaric, and their disappearance is indispensable in the name of progress and civilization.

Sovereignty, morality and historical progress can be viewed as three competing criteria for the use of force. All three are present in the thought of Jean-Jacques Rousseau, Immanuel Kant, and Georg Wilhelm Friedrich Hegel, although with differing emphases which hold the key to their mutual dialogue. I would like to suggest that this dialogue, while ultimately inconclusive, constitutes as good a guide as any to current conceptual and practical dilemmas related to military intervention.

I am primarily a student of international relations rather than a political philosopher or historian, in particular of the political and moral dimensions of the use of force, with a special attention to the problem of military intervention. My education in philosophy and my earlier work have been concerned with Kant and Hegel.[1] More recently, I have also written about Rousseau's international thought.[2] In thinking about current debates about intervention, I have often been indirectly reminded of these authors' respective discussions of the use of force, which I believe are still useful today.

---

[1] See my chapters on these two authors in L. Strauss and J. Cropsey, *History of Political Philosophy*, 3rd edn. (University of Chicago Press, 1987), pp. 581–621 and 732–60.

[2] See my "Rousseau and the Theory and Practice of International Relations," in C. Orwin and N. Tarcov (eds.), *The Legacy of Rousseau* (University of Chicago Press, 1997), ch. 10, pp. 200–19.

The chapter proceeds as follows: I first briefly show how the three authors under consideration were profoundly influenced by each other's writings in their thinking about human freedom, the use of force, and international relations: Kant was deeply influenced by Rousseau, and Hegel, in turn, was influenced by the former two; and this, I argue, warrants a comparative analysis of the three thinkers' arguments. The central part of the chapter examines each author's arguments about the legitimacy of war in more detail, highlighting some inherent tensions and contradictions. I conclude with a few general remarks about the continuing relevance of reading and re-reading those classical authors for thinking about war and intervention today.

Three thinkers engaged in a dialogue

Rousseau is the prophet of both individual conscience and the unity of a community based on equality and freedom as defined by the general will. Such a community must be able to defend itself and to safeguard its identity, by using force if necessary, but it must also be free of the greed, vanity, ambition, and spirit of competition which characterize modern man. History is a story of corruption and division, which can only be overcome either by a return to the simplicity and unity of natural man, or by the creation of small and isolated republics which recover, at the level of the community, the unity and freedom of which man has been deprived by history.

Kant agrees with Rousseau on the role of moral conscience, and the ideal of a republic based on reciprocity and on the obedience to a general law based on autonomy or self-legislation. He reformulates the Rousseauian notion in a more abstract and universalistic fashion, but he still considers Rousseau as "the Newton of the moral world," and praises him for having taught him the value of man and the imperative of defending his dignity and his rights.[3] Kant also agrees with Rousseau that civilization has developed through vices, inequality and war. But, through a dialectical reversal of Rousseau's thinking which will also be found in Hegel (Kant speaks of "the cunning of nature," while Hegel uses the term "cunning of reason"), all those morally reprehensible developments follow a secret plan leading to progress towards a universal order based on mutual recognition and peace.[4]

[3] Quoted in H. S. Reiss, "Introduction," in Reiss (ed.), *Kant's Political Writings* (Cambridge University Press, 1999), p. 4.
[4] I. Kant, "Idea for a Universal History with a Cosmopolitan Purpose," in Reiss (ed.), *Kant's Political Writings*, pp. 41–54.

Finally, Hegel acknowledges the value of Rousseau's and Kant's insights on conscience, autonomy and universality, but he considers them only as partial moments in the development of the *World Spirit*, which coincides with world history. In order to be effective, for Hegel, the Rousseauian conscience and Kantian universalistic morality must find a concrete expression and, by the same token, a limitation, in the customs and habits of nations (*Sittlichkeit*), the structure of states, and the actions of statesmen and warriors. "The moral vision of history," represented by Kant, if seen as an absolute and taken in isolation, leads to suicide out of the search for purity or to terror.[5] Conversely, while for Hegel, like for Kant, the historical mission of war tends to wither away once the whole planet has been "civilized," for Hegel war continues to fulfil a moral function: namely, that of counteracting the selfish preoccupation with material goods which dominates modern society, by reviving the sense of risk, sacrifice and, above all, of community among citizens of the state.[6]

In short, then, Rousseau, Kant, and Hegel agree that war has played and is likely to continue to play a profound role in shaping history. But for Rousseau, this role is a negative one, like the role of historical evolution more generally, which it has contributed to shaping. While martial virtues are indispensable for distinguishing the patriot or the citizen from the "bourgeois," war itself remains a horrible butchery and is legitimate only when practiced in self-defense by a people in arms. For Kant, the historical role of war is positive, but at the same time, war is absolutely forbidden by the moral law: "Moral practical reason within us pronounces the following irresistible veto: there shall be no war."[7] This duality between the positive character of war as an instrument of the "cunning of nature" and its totally unacceptable character from the point of view of the moral subject (the dirty work being transferred to a providential mechanism) creates a permanent tension in Kant's philosophy.

For Hegel, the tension between history and morality is practically non-existent. The ultimate criterion is the historical one. Furthermore, war fulfils as a moral function in itself, even for the civilized state. However, another tension appears in Hegel's thought: in a prosaic, rational world dominated by the economy, war has few opportunities to manifest itself. The only meaningful wars being fought are those against peripheral

---

[5] G. W. F. Hegel, *Philosophy of Right* (trans. T. M. Knox) (Oxford: Clarendon Press, 1942), §§ 135–210.

[6] Hegel, *Philosophy of Right*, § 324, pp. 209–10.

[7] Kant, "The Metaphysics of Morals," in Reiss (ed.), *Kant's Political Writings*, p. 174.

nations which have not yet reached the stage of the civilized, rational state. Here the problem is that, by definition, these adversaries are a declining species and that, on the other hand, the increasingly impersonal character of war makes it less apt to encourage individual heroism. In short, then, for Hegel wars will continue to occur, but both their historical and their moral justification become increasingly problematic.

Helpful questions and enlightening contradictions – but few definitive answers

I have adopted the broader term of "force" as a title for this chapter, and have started by outlining the positions of the three authors on war rather than intervention, because it seems to me that none of them has a doctrine of intervention proper – if we keep the implication suggested by the medical and legal analogies, i.e. intervention as the use of force limited in time and prompted not by a rivalry between states, but instead as an act of choice prompted at least in part by the desire to stop some kind of evil (physical or moral) and/or to protect an endangered population – often in the name of a higher authority.

All three authors raise the question of the relation between particular or national interests and perspectives on the one hand and universal or cosmopolitan ones, on the other. They are all concerned with the problem of war and its legitimacy, but neither of them recognizes a world authority or a "civitas maxima" in whose name military intervention could be ordered or justified. All three have in common a contempt for the attempt to give war a juridical character, and for the Grotius-Pufendorf-Vattel tradition of international law. Rousseau calls Grotius "a child, and what is worse, a child of bad faith."[8] Kant calls Grotius and Pufendorf "sorry comforters."[9] For both Rousseau and Kant, international law is a contradiction in terms, unless it leads states to abandoning war and submitting to an impartial authority. Hegel declares that international law is no real law, because there is no praetor and no constraint;[10] that legal or moral criticism of the behavior of great men betrays a valet's mentality;[11] and that the only real professor of international law is Napoleon.[12] And yet all three, at one point or

[8] J.-J. Rousseau, *Emile*, Book 5 (trans. A. Bloom) (New York: Basic Books, 1979).

[9] Kant, "Perpetual Peace," in Reiss (ed.), *Kant's Political Writings*, p. 103.

[10] Hegel, *Philosophy of Right*, § 333, p. 213.

[11] Hegel, *Phenomenology of Spirit* (trans. A. V. Midler) (Oxford University Press, 1977), ch. VI, § 665, p. 404.

[12] Hegel, "Letter to Niethammer," dated August 29, 1807, in *Hegel: The Letters* (trans. C. Butler and C. Seiler) (Bloomington, IN: Indiana University Press, 1984).

another, via the problem of the right or wrong use of force, do touch on the problem of intervention, if only in passing, and offer some provisional rules which are not devoid of ambiguity and contradictions. But these ambiguities and contradictions, I would like to suggest, are more enlightening than any complete and coherent doctrine.

Rousseau: patriotic unity and cohesion vs. cosmopolitan solidarity

Rousseau's position (or positions) can be presented in the form of a series of oppositions. The first and probably most fundamental one is between natural man and social man. The latter has lost the unity and peace of the former. The bourgeois is marked by a division of the soul, a tyranny of "amour-propre," and a lack of identity which, for Rousseau, is the supreme evil. Unity can be recovered either in the asocial form of the "lonely wanderer," or in the political form of the citizen who is "de-natured" by his participation in the general will of a community. This is the theme of his major political work, *The Social Contract*.

But what community? This is the issue which is arguably most relevant to the problem of military intervention, and where Rousseau's answer seems to be perhaps most changing and certainly most complex. There are at least three possibilities: 1) modern states, led by kings and princes; 2) small national republics, more or less on the model of the Greek *polis*; and 3) the world community of mankind.

Rousseau is very negative on the first category: the princes lack legitimacy and are driven only by love of gain and conquest, and their subjects are not real citizens. The state of war, in this case, is "a relation between states, not between men" (from which Rousseau draws a few provisional principles for the law of war, like immunity of non-combatants).[13] One solution in the case of these states would be that proposed by the Abbé de Saint Pierre: a European federation, which Rousseau sees as attractive but unrealistic, particularly because it could be achieved only by force.[14] Nevertheless, *The Social Contract* was supposed to end with a section on federations, which Rousseau never completed.

[13] Rousseau, "The State of War," in S. Hoffmann and D. P. Fidler (eds.), *Rousseau on International Relations* (Oxford: Clarendon Press, 1991), pp. 33–47.
[14] Rousseau, "Abstract and Judgement of Saint Pierre's Project for Perpetual Peace," in Hoffmann and Fidler (eds.), *Rousseau on International Relations*, pp. 52–100.

The two positive alternatives are the patriotic and the cosmopolitan one. Here, Rousseau's position begins by appearing shockingly contradictory from one text to the other. In Book 4 of *Emile*, he writes:

To prevent pity from degenerating into weakness it must be generalized and extended to the whole of mankind. For the sake of reason, for the sake of love of ourselves, we must have pity for our species still more than for our neighbour ... The less the object of our care is immediately involved with us, the less the illusion of particular interest is to be feared, the more one generalizes this interest, the more it becomes equitable and the love of mankind is nothing other than the love of justice.[15]

In Book 1 of the same work, by contrast, one finds the same praise of patriotism and critique of cosmopolitanism encountered in the *Discourse on Political Economy* or the *Government of Poland*:

Every particular society, when it is narrow and unified, is estranged from the all-encompassing society. Every patriot is harsh to foreigners. They are only men. They are nothing in his eyes. This is a drawback, inevitable but not compelling. The essential thing is to be good for the people with whom one lives. Abroad, the Spartan was ambitious, avaricious, iniquitous. But disinterestedness, equity, and concord reigned within his walls. Distrust those cosmopolitans who go to great lengths in their books to discover duties they do not deign to fulfil around them. A philosopher loves the Tartars so as to be spared having to love his neighbours.[16]

In the *Second Discourse*, Rousseau's view of cosmopolitans is more favorable, but he presents them as transcending politics, which is dominated by the fact that diverse societies remain in the state of nature.

Natural compassion is losing from society to society almost all the force it had from man to man and is no longer present anywhere except in a few cosmopolitan great souls who overcome the imaginary barriers which separate the peoples and who, following the example of the Sovereign being who created them, include the whole human race in their care.[17]

The kind of intervention that these "Great Souls" might envision seems to be more akin to that of "Doctors without Borders" (*Médecins Sans Frontières*) than to that of military expeditions.

When advising the Poles and the Corsicans, Rousseau definitely recommends a priority for unity, cohesion and independence, and, to that effect, an emphasis on uniqueness and, as much as possible, aloofness in order to avoid the corrupting effects of commerce and of foreign influences and the dangers of getting involved in alliances with untrustworthy

---

[15] Rousseau, *Emile*, Book 4, p. 239.   [16] Rousseau, *Emile*, Book 1, p. 39.
[17] Rousseau, *Discourse on the Origin of Inequality* (trans. D. Cress) (Indianapolis, IN: Hackett Publishing, 1992), p. 57.

foreign powers. It is preferable to be overrun and divided while keeping one's identity, than to risk losing it by becoming too big or by depending upon others. A confederation of small republics, capable of defense but not of offense, is the only acceptable external tie. According to some commentators, this is the solution he would have proposed in the last part of *The Social Contract*. But the fact is that he left it unwritten and may well have had doubts about it because it would have risked endangering the sense of identity and citizenship of the small republics. The burden of his thought seems to have been that all citizenship is local (he tells the Poles: "A Frenchman, an Englishman, a Spaniard, a Russian, are practically the same man: each leaves school already fully prepared for licence, that is to say for slavery. A Pole ought not to be a man of any sort; he ought to be a Pole"[18]); that there is no such thing as a "general society of mankind," and that cosmopolitanism is the privilege of individual thinkers, artists or world benefactors. This does not seem to leave much place for humanitarian intervention or the protection of Great Powers.

What appears, then, is another paradoxical tension in Rousseau's thought: his attitude towards war and the use of force. He hates war, finding it both criminal and not interesting (he wonders why Thucydides spends so much time on such a boring subject).[19] He thinks that by its very possibility, it creates a "mixed state" through which citizens lose the security for which they sacrificed their individual liberty. But on the other hand, he hates the bourgeois, and admires Sparta and Plutarch's heroes. He would suppress permanent armies in favor of republican citizen armies, or "nations in arms," which would seem to invalidate his distinction between state and people. He is in favor of what today has been called by the Peace Movement "defensive defense" – i.e., a military posture capable of defending a country's territory, but without the ability to retaliate or, even less, attack anybody. Very much on the model of Swiss neutrality, he wants Poles and Corsicans to have a "warlike spirit ('martial') without ambition."[20] That may be an impossible ideal short of isolation, but it seems at any rate to exclude not only ambitions of conquest and domination, but also the ambition of saving oppressed peoples or making the world safe for democracy.

This, I think, is the most likely conclusion we can reach. However, there are two objections or at least interrogations, which need to be briefly dealt with. First, in his presentation of Saint Pierre's project,

[18] Rousseau, "Considerations on the Government of Poland," in Hoffmann and Fidler (eds.), *Rousseau on International Relations*, p. 172.
[19] Rousseau, *Emile*, Book 4, p. 239.
[20] Rousseau, "Considerations on the Government of Poland," p. 176.

Rousseau mentions (without indicating any disapproval) that force should be used by all participants to the pact against any one of them who should attempt to withdraw from it.[21] More importantly, in his critical commentary, he states that the project itself would be excellent, but that it will never be adopted by the voluntary agreement of all. If a similar plan ever had a good chance of being adopted, that was through the political (and, presumably, military), strategy of Henry IV. In the future, it might again be brought about by another Henry IV, or by revolution, since small republican states would be devoid of the ambitions and rivalries of princes and kings. Rousseau concludes, however, by wondering whether that revolution might not in the end do more harm than the situation it would overthrow.[22] One cannot entirely exclude that those last remarks are intended to protect Rousseau against a suspicion of conspiracy, all the more so since elsewhere, he predicts that Europe is entering an era of revolutions.

The second observation is more important and plausible, but it concerns less the explicit or conscious intentions of Rousseau than the consequences of his work. Anybody who reads the passage in the *Fragments on War* where he chides the philosopher who is satisfied with the political institutions of his polity and does not care about war and oppression all around ("Barbarous philosopher! Come and read us your book on the field of battle!"),[23] or the final paragraph of the *Discourse on Inequality* ("It is obviously contrary to the law of nature, how ever it may be defined, for a child to command an old man, for an imbecile to lead a wise man, and for a handful of people to gorge themselves on superfluities while the starving multitude lacks necessities"),[24] or the first sentence of the first chapter of *The Social Contract* ("Man is born free but everywhere he is in chains"[25]) is bound to feel called to fight for peace and justice wherever he or she can. The wars of the French Revolution were not advocated in advance by Rousseau, but his thoughts and his words carried enough dynamite to stir up revolutions and interventions.

Nobody can legitimately decide which side would ultimately have won the struggle in Rousseau's soul between his abhorrence of wars of aggression and oppression on the one hand and, on the other, his pessimism about their elimination and his suspicion of self-appointed liberators and of their motives. All we can safely say is that he foresaw a

---

[21] *Rousseau on International Relations*, p. 78.
[22] *Ibid.*, p. 100.   [23] *Ibid.*, p. 147.
[24] Rousseau, "Discourse on the Origins of Inequality," in R. Masters (ed.), *The First and Second Discourses* (New York: St Martin's Press, 1964), p. 71.
[25] Rousseau, "The Social Contract," in *On the Social Contract* (Indianapolis, IN: Hackett Publishing, 1992), Book I, ch. 1.

time of revolutions against the social and international order of his time, but that he would have maintained his preference for small republics and his staunch opposition to wars of conquest. He would also quite certainly have been horrified by the current process of globalization which, for him, would have signified the triumph of greed, competition, and "amour-propre," and the loss of individual and collective identity and authenticity.

Kant: categorically opposed to intervention and regime change – or was he?

As we shall see, many of the problems and (at least apparent) contradictions we have found in Rousseau are present in Kant with a vengeance. They are complicated by the character of Kant's political philosophy, which is more a *philosophy of right* based on a *philosophy of morality* and confirmed or "guaranteed" by a *philosophy of history*.

The relation between the three dimensions ought not, according to Kant, be problematic since the decisive one is morality, which is a priori and universal: "There can be no conflict between politics, as an applied branch of right, and morality, as theoretical branch of right (i.e. between theory and practice)".[26] And yet, particularly concerning international affairs, grey zones and ambiguities abound and so do variations between Kant's formulations and, probably, opinions.

I shall not go into a detailed exposition of Kant's thought, since this is done very competently by Andrew Hurrell in this volume. I shall only indicate briefly the problem posed by the general framework and point to the rather ambiguous passages of Kant's works which relate directly to the question of military intervention.

The basic Kantian opposition between the world of freedom and the world of necessity, between a priori or transcendental universality and the empirical dimension, between the moral law and the passions, etc. all have a bearing upon the problem of military intervention. The most directly relevant is that between morality and the natural or historical world: according to Kant, all states should be republican and ruled by law; but morality, based upon the universality of practical reason and the categorical imperative, admits no exception to the prohibition of war. Or does it? Kant's answer is not always the same. Another classical opposition, which is not specifically Kantian, but in his conception assumes a

---

[26] Kant, "Appendix to Perpetual Peace," in Reiss (ed.), *Kant's Political Writings*, p. 116. See also Kant, "On the Common saying: this may be true in theory, but it does not apply in practice," in *Kant's Political Writings*, pp. 61–92.

moral character as well as a legal one, is that between the state of nature and the civil state.

All these distinctions converge towards the opposition between war and peace. Peace is not only preferable to war, it is an absolute moral and legal imperative and the ultimate goal of law, of politics, and even of that mysterious force, which he usually calls "nature" and sometimes "providence," and which we are used, since Hegel, to calling "history." In the conclusion of his *Metaphysical Elements of the Theory of Right*, the irresistible veto of moral-practical reason is developed as follows:

> *There shall be no war*, either between individual human beings in the state of nature, or between separate states which, although internally law-governed, still live in a lawless condition in their external relationships with one another. For war is not the way in which anyone should pursue his rights ... The task of establishing a universal and lasting peace is not just a part of the theory of right within the limits of pure reason but its entire ultimate purpose.[27]

The road towards this goal, however, is full of paradoxes. First, Kant is at least as critical as Rousseau of the immorality of war and commerce; of luxury and competition; of the development of selfish and antagonistic passions which accompany the progress of culture. But, contrary to Rousseau, he thinks they were indispensable not only for the unification of the planet, hence for the creation of a "cosmopolitan situation," but also for man's education and hence could favor a moral conversion which alone could bring about genuine peace:

> Nature should be thanked for fostering social incompatibility, envious competitive vanity, and insatiable desires for possession or even power. Without these desires, all man's excellent capacities would not have been allowed to develop. For the very conflict of individual inclinations, which is the source of all evil, gives reason a free hand to master them all.[28]

The question is raised, then, of what human beings and states should do in Kant's time and beyond. Has the stark opposition between the absolute condemnation by morality of war, greed, and vanity, on the one side, and their historical necessity or utility, on the other, run its course? Is there a prospect of making history and morality converge?

This seems to be the case for war, which becomes so costly and suicidal that, Kant predicts, mankind will have to abandon it more and more. Commerce and, in general, economic and cultural interdependence, are favorable to peace and to human rights:

---

[27] Kant, "The Metaphysics of Morals," in *Kant's Political Writings*, p. 174.
[28] Kant, "Idea for a Universal History with a Cosmopolitan Purpose," in *Kant's Political Writings*, p. 45.

The effects which an upheaval in any state produces upon all the others in our continent, where all are so closely linked by trade, are so perceptible that these other states are forced by their own insecurity to offer themselves as arbiters, albeit without legal authority, so that they indirectly prepare the way for a great political body in the future without equivalent in the past.[29]

Elsewhere he goes even further: "The peoples of the earth have thus entered in varying degrees into a universal community, and it has developed to the point where a violation of rights in one part of the world is felt everywhere."[30] But this emphatically does not mean a right of military intervention to put an end to these violations: "The concept of international rights becomes meaningless if it is interpreted as a right to go to war."[31] Again, commerce and diplomatic mediation are the saving forces:

For the spirit of commerce sooner or later takes hold of every people, and it cannot exist side by side with war. Thus states find themselves compelled to promote the noble cause of peace, though not exactly from motives of morality. And whenever in the world there is a threat of war breaking out, they will try to prevent it by mediation, just as if they had entered into a permanent league for this purpose.[32]

Therefore, the actual mechanism of human inclinations "will be now working for peace," although one cannot be certain of its success; and one can be sure that at best it will only pave the way for the real transformation produced by morality. But the status of this intermediary period and its consequences for what is permissible or not concerning the use of force remain ambiguous.

This is all the more so since a similar problem appears, concerning the basic opposition between the state of nature and the civil or constitutional state (understood as a situation in which human beings find themselves). The state of peace is not natural; the natural state – the state of nature – is a state of war. "Thus the state of peace must be formally instituted, for a suspension of hostilities is not in itself a guarantee of peace. And unless one neighbor gives a guarantee to the other at his request (which can happen only in a lawful state) the latter may treat him as an enemy."[33]

This central, fundamental and sharp distinction is never abandoned by Kant. But it becomes more and more fuzzy and problematic as one advances from the relation between individuals to the relation between

---

[29] *Ibid.*, p. 51.
[30] Kant, "Perpetual Peace," in Reiss (ed.), *Kant's Political Writings*, p. 107.
[31] *Ibid.*, p. 105.   [32] Kant, "Idea for a Universal History," p. 49.
[33] Kant, "Perpetual Peace," p. 98.

states and also, it must be said, as Kant advances from his earlier to his later works.

It is, in principle, an unconditional duty for states as for individuals to enter a lawful state which, as we have seen, is also a state of peace. For Kant, in the *Idea for a Universal History with a Cosmopolitan Purpose* (1784), this means "a system of united power, hence a cosmopolitan system of general political security," which is the fulfilment of the secret plan of nature.[34] But in *Perpetual Peace* (1795), while this goal is reaffirmed as logical and desirable, it is also affirmed as unrealistic: existing states will not accept the establishing of a global Federal State (*Bundesstaat*), nor even a looser confederation (*Staatenbund*). What remains is an alliance of republican states which renounce war between them and hope that their example will spread more and more.[35] In the *Metaphysics of Morals* (1797) the hope becomes even less assured: perhaps perpetual peace is an *Unding* – something which will never be real; but the fact that one cannot demonstrate that it is impossible is enough to oblige us to work towards that goal.[36]

Once more, then, the question arises: what are the obligations of states besides trying to build, if not a federation, at least the alliance for peace indicated in the second definitive article of *Perpetual Peace*? *Stricto sensu*, states are in the state of nature, a state in which notions of right and justice are meaningless. However, like Rousseau (but even more surprisingly, since Kant adopts the language of legal and moral imperatives), he proceeds, after pouring contempt on Grotius and the whole school of the laws of war, to formulate a similar doctrine, under the guise of the six "preliminary articles" to the perpetual peace treaty. He calls them "prohibitive laws." Several of them allow for some latitude regarding the circumstances of their application: no acquisition of an independently existing state; gradual abolition of standing armies; no national debt contracted in connection with the external affairs of the state. But three are of the "strictest" kind, and the abuses they prohibit should be abolished immediately. According to the first, "No conclusion of peace shall be considered valid as such, if it was made with a secret reservation of the material for a future war."[37] The second is of particular concern to us: "No state shall forcibly interfere in the constitution and government of another state."[38] Hence it prohibits any war for regime change, or "out of a sense of scandal or offense which a state arouses in the subjects of another state." The last, sixth preliminary article, states: "No state at war

---

[34] Kant, "Idea for a Universal History," p. 49.   [35] Kant, "Perpetual Peace," p. 105.
[36] Kant, "Metaphysics of Morals," pp. 173–4.
[37] Kant, "Perpetual Peace," p. 93.   [38] *Ibid.*, p. 96.

with another shall permit such acts of hostility as would make mutual confidence impossible during a future time of peace." Examples which Kant mentions are the use of assassins, breach of agreements, and the instigation of treason within the enemy state. The most striking for us is that "neither party can be declared an unjust enemy," and that a "war of punishment" is inconceivable.[39]

In this respect, the *Doctrine of Right* (first part of the *Metaphysics of Morals*, published only a year after *Perpetual Peace*), offers at least two important surprises.[40] It applies to the existing situation, i.e. to states being in the state of nature, and it is very close to a classical analysis of the international world, making much more allowance for war and its logical consequences. There, Kant admits not only the existence of a right to self-defense for states, provided that they use only "honorable strata-gems," as opposed to dishonorable ones.[41] (One would like to know which stratagems are honorable for an author who, in the same year, maintains against Benjamin Constant that lying is forbidden even under extreme circumstances.) Going further, he also affirms a right to what would be called today "anticipatory self-defense," i.e. preventive war, which is in conformity with his constant affirmation that in the state of nature any other state may constitute a threat.

However, much more surprising is the statement which seems to imply that states may be forced by others to adhere to the pact which will establish peace, in direct contradiction to what was previously stated in *Perpetual Peace*: "International right," Kant affirms, "is thus concerned partly ... with the right of states to compel each other to abandon their warlike condition and to create a constitution which will establish an unending peace."[42] Most surprising of all is the appearance, in paragraph 60, of the notion of an "unjust enemy," which *Perpetual Peace* had rejected as a contradiction in terms, as long as the state of nature persists. "It must mean," says Kant, "someone whose publicly expressed will, whether expressed in word or in deed, displays a maxim which would make peace among nations impossible and would lead to a perpetual state of nature if it were made into a general rule. Under this heading would come violations of public contracts, which can be assumed to affect the interests of all nations."[43]

---

[39] *Ibid.* On Kant as a noninterventionist, see also A. Hurrell's chapter in this volume, esp. pp. 198–201.

[40] See S. Shell, *Kant and the Limits of Autonomy* (Cambridge, MA: Harvard University Press, 2009), pp. 212–47.

[41] Shell, *Kant and the Limits of Autonomy*, p. 243.

[42] Kant, "Metaphysics of Morals," p. 165.   [43] Kant, "Metaphysics of Morals," p. 170.

Here, for the first and, to my knowledge, only time in Kant's writings, we have an explicit endorsement of military intervention against a foreign state that is inherently threatening and cannot be trusted – what one would call to-day a "rogue" or "outlaw" state.[44] Intervention and "regime change" are justified by the Kantian notion that just behavior in international relations is defined by whether it facilitates the advent of the "supreme good," i.e. cosmopolitan peace. This could, somewhat unjustly, be seen as not so distant from the Hegelian-Marxist doctrine according to which morality and legitimacy are defined by their conformity with the direction of history.

However, it appears proper to ask a basic question, upon which the distinction between the state of nature and the state of law is ultimately based: "Quis judicabit?" – who is to judge? Much as I hate to side with Carl Schmitt against Kant, one can only agree with the author of *The Nomos of the Earth* that an objective or legal operationalization of Kant's definition is impossible, as long as states find themselves in the state of nature, i.e. have not submitted to an institutionalized common authority.[45] And I have to sympathize with Schmitt's malicious question: between the armies of the French Revolution (of which Kant was a supporter to the point of changing the hour of his daily walk in order to get the news about the battle of Valmy), and their adversaries, whose maxims were, in the long run, incompatible with peace?

This brings us to the last surprise: that provided, another two years later, by Kant's work, the *Contest of Faculties*. Here the sympathy, close to enthusiasm, brought forth by the French Revolution in disinterested spectators across the world is interpreted as giving a powerful sign of the moral dispositions of the human species; and this, without being yet moral itself, justifies "philosophic chiliasm" in Kant's view, i.e. the hope for moral progress leading to peace.

Of course, Kant remained hostile to revolution and to war as such. He was careful to point out that he referred to the sympathy of onlookers rather than to the deeds of the revolutionaries, some of which (like the execution of Louis XVI) he seems to have strongly disapproved of. He admits that the revolution may fail, that "it may be so filled with misery and atrocities that no right-thinking man would ever decide to make the same experiment again at such a price." But, he continues, "I maintain

---

[44] For a similar justification of war against "outlaw" states from a contemporary liberal standpoint, see J. Rawls, *The Law of Peoples* (Cambridge, MA: Harvard University Press, 1999), pp. 80–1, 90–3.

[45] C. Schmitt, *The Nomos of the Earth in The International Law of the Jus Publicum Europaeum* (New York: Telos Press, 2001), Part II, ch. 2, section G: "Kant's unjust enemy."

that this revolution has aroused in the hearts and desires of all spectators who are not themselves caught up in it a sympathy which borders itself on enthusiasm."[46] And he shows that this sympathy is well founded morally and can be the basis for historical optimism:

> The moral cause which is at work here is composed of two elements: Firstly there is the right of every people to give itself a civil constitution of the kind that it sees fit, without interference from other powers. And, secondly, once it is accepted that the only intrinsically rightful and morally good constitution which a people can have is by its very nature disposed to avoid wars of aggression (i.e., that the only possible constitution is a republican one, at least in its conception), there is the *aim*, which is also a duty, of submitting to those conditions, by which war, the source of all evil and moral corruption, can be prevented.[47]

Can this not be seen as a way of defending the wars of the French Revolution, by interpreting them as defensive, and prompted by the attempt of outside powers to prevent the French people from adopting the only good constitution? In short, then, it might be concluded that Kant, that principled opponent of intervention and revolutionary change, ended up defending (if somewhat hesitantly), both an actually-occurring revolution, as well as forcible regime change in the presence of "rogue" states, portraying them as means to progress along the path to the lawful state of Perpetual Peace.

Hegel: war and intervention as civilizing instruments of the World Spirit

I shall be much briefer with Hegel, for while he may be even more ambiguous or mysterious as to the ultimate meaning of his system, on the theme of military intervention he is free of the hesitations and contradictions of Rousseau and Kant. His enthusiasm for Napoleon (the "soul of the world" he had seen passing under his windows at Jena) matched that of Kant for the French Revolution.[48] Unlike Kant, however, he did not have to face the dilemma between morality and history or between the state of nature and the state of law. He most categorically affirmed the primacy of history, which is the development of the Spirit.

---

[46] Kant, "The Contest of the Faculties," in Reiss (ed.), *Kant's Political Writings*, p. 182.

[47] "An occurrence in our own time which proves the moral tendency of the human race," quoted in Kant, "The Contest of the Faculties," in Reiss (ed.), *Kant's Political Writings*, pp. 182–3.

[48] Hegel's precise words are: "I saw Napoleon, the soul of the world, riding through the town on a reconnaissance. It is indeed a wonderful sensation to see, concentrated in a point, sitting on a horse, an individual who overruns the world and masters it." Quoted in "Letter to Niethammer," October 13, 1806.

This development takes place, in particular, through the actions of the Caesars and the Napoleons of this world.

Those great men may break all existing moral and legal rules, and nevertheless their actions lead to a higher reconciliation, because they have been the instruments of history, and ultimately "World History is the World Tribunal."[49] Hegel rebuffs traditional moralistic or legalistic critics of those leaders by quoting several times the French proverb: "No man is a hero for his valet," but adding: "this is not because the hero is not a hero but because the valet is a valet."[50] He further insists that "the wounds of the spirit leave no scars."[51]

Hegel underlines that this work of the great men is done, in a sense, without their knowledge. They think they follow their passions and their interests; yet in fact, they are but the tools of the "cunning of reason," of the *Grand Plan of the Spirit* in search of itself.[52] They don't do interventions, they do conquests and heroic deeds: it is the Spirit who intervenes through them. "The special interest of passion is thus inseparable from the active development of a general principle."[53] On the other hand, in some passages Hegel says the great men are aware, in a half-conscious manner, that they embody their time and have a mission.[54]

This emphasis on greatness and special rights becomes even clearer if one realizes that, as much as those great men, the actors of history are, in each epoch, the particular peoples, or nations, whose time has come because they embody a universal principle. That gives them a special right to be dominant internationally at a particular time, as passionate tools of the World Spirit. "But in contrast with this absolute right of being the vehicle of this present stage in the world mind's development, the minds of the other nations are without rights."[55]

This superior, privileged status sometimes seems to apply not only to the particular nation which represents the World Spirit at a given time, but to *any* more developed state against *any* less developed one:

---

[49] Hegel, *Philosophy of Right*, § 341.
[50] Hegel, *Phenomenology of the Spirit* (trans. A.V. Miller) (Oxford University Press, 1977), § 665, p. 404.
[51] Hegel, *Phenomenology of the Spirit*, § 669, p. 407.
[52] Hegel, *Philosophy of History* (trans. J. Sibree) (New York: Dover Publications, 1956), p. 34.
[53] Hegel, *Philosophy of History*, p. 32.
[54] "Such individuals had no consciousness of the general idea they were unfolding, on the contrary they were practical, political men. But at the same time they were thinking men, who had an insight into the requirements of the time – what was ripe for development." Quoted in *Ibid.*, p. 30.
[55] Hegel, *Philosophy of Right*, § 347.

The same consideration justifies civilized nations in regarding and treating as barbarians those who lag behind them in institutions which are the essential elements of the state. Thus a pastoral people may treat hunters as barbarians and both of these are barbarians from the point of view of agriculturists etc. The civilized nation is conscious that the rights of barbarians are unequal to its own and treats their autonomy only as a formality.[56]

The World Spirit always has the last word; and "because the relation of states to one another has sovereignty as its principle, they are so far in a condition of nature one to the other."[57] Nevertheless, among civilized, constitutional states – by which Hegel essentially meant the developed European nations, plus North America – there are bonds and barriers which, though fragile in the absence of a common authority, still limit the use of force: they are the balance of power, various legal commitments, and economic interdependence. Like Rousseau and Kant, Hegel thinks that Europe in some respects has become one republic where war is impossible. He quotes approvingly Napoleon's dictum: *Cette vieille Europe m'ennuie* ("this old Europe bores me").[58]

Of course, Hegel thinks that wars will still occur, but they have for the most part lost their historical function – except with less developed states, as a means to colonize them and transform them into rational states (for instance, between North and South America). War is necessary for the moral health of a people; but "real wars need also another justification," and in fact, their historical mission is to contribute to the universality of the fully developed state. When one day this mission is fully accomplished, the movement from heroic personal or national individualities to prosaic rationality will also be complete and no further great deeds worthy of being celebrated by epics will occur.[59] However, even though history has ended at a conceptual level with the completion of Hegel's all-embracing system, the "really existing" rational developed state outlined in his *Philosophy of Right* is still plagued by the contradiction between wealth and poverty, which compels it to seek expansion abroad.[60]

Even before, however, great deeds and military victories are not enough – since local resistance to foreign rule, and a people's own preferences and dispositions, might practically make it very difficult to "civilize" it according to some general principle. Forcible regime change and civilizing trusteeship, then, might be desirable in the abstract, but very difficult to implement for even the most powerful nations. The

---

[56] *Ibid.*, § 351.   [57] Hegel, *Philosophy of Right*, § 333.
[58] Hegel, *Philosophy of History*, p. 90.
[59] G. W. F. Hegel, *Aesthetics*, III, "System of Individual Acts" in *The Philosophy of Hegel* (New York: Random House, 1963).
[60] Hegel, *Philosophy of Right*, § 245–8.

example of Hegel's hero, Napoleon, carries perhaps the most important lesson for our purposes:

> Napoleon, with the vast might of his character, turned his attention to foreign relations, subjected all Europe, and diffused his liberal institutions in every quarter. Greater victories were never gained, expeditions displaying greater genius were never conducted, but never was the powerlessness of victory exhibited in a clearer light than then. The disposition of the peoples (*Gesinnung*), i.e. their religious disposition and that of their nationality, ultimately precipitated this colossus.[61]

Lessons for our time

The last quote from Hegel above might provide a quick and affirmative answer to the obvious question: how relevant are the classical thinkers examined in this chapter to the problems of the twentieth and twenty-first centuries? However, the importance of Rousseau, Kant, and Hegel for our own time goes much beyond any immediate policy relevance that their arguments may appear to have in view of current events.

As we have seen, Rousseau was deeply troubled by human suffering abroad and by the international condition of anarchy. However, his central concern is identity, which at the political level can be found only in a small, austere, democratic and patriotic community that jealously guards its unity, its originality, and its independence – and hence its sovereignty – in a world dominated by competition, conquest and commerce.

Kant's thought is marked by another contradiction: that between, on the one side, the categorical imperative of a universalistic morality, which forbids war and is distrustful of the passions; and on the other side, a vision of history according to which it is precisely war, greed and the passions which, by unifying the world, lead to peace. His plan for perpetual peace rests on a precarious combination between the republican constitution of states, international organization (in the form of an alliance of peaceful republics), and a cosmopolitan law protecting the freedom of movement and commercial exchange of all individuals.[62]

Hegel, while recognizing the value of sovereignty and morality, claimed to integrate (and by the same token overcome) them both through the primacy of the World Spirit, which is nothing but another name for the direction of history. The World Spirit works in particular through war, conquest, and empires – but also through the development of the modern economy and civil society. One might see most of the

---

[61] Hegel, *Philosophy of History*, p. 451.
[62] For a discussion, see M. W. Doyle, "Kant, Liberal Legacies, and Foreign Affairs," *Philosophy & Public Affairs* 12, no. 3 (1983), 205–35.

twentieth century as a confirmation of this vision, especially if one accepts the view of his most brilliant and controversial commentator, Alexandre Kojève, according to whom the two revolutionary doctrines which dominated the period were a left-wing Hegelianism (communism) and a right-wing one (fascism).[63] But, of course, both were lacking (to put it mildly) what for Hegel was the goal of the World Spirit and the center of the rational state, namely freedom. After the horrors of two world wars and two totalitarian revolutions and regimes, has the clock not turned or returned to the dialogue between Rousseau and Kant, leaving the Hegelian synthesis behind? In a sense, identity politics and sovereignty on the one hand, and cosmopolitanism and human rights in a globalized world, on the other, have recently moved to the forefront of the world scene.

Rousseau is of course the forerunner, and to a considerable extent the inspirer, of most radical and post-modernist movements – whether in favor of self-centered development, of cultural identity, of "defensive defense" (meaning a defensive posture centered on popular resistance and the inability to inflict harm), of environmentalism, and of slogans like "small is beautiful." But experience also shows how difficult it is to be both revolutionary and pacifist and, for small communities, to escape the influence of the Great Powers or of the world economy without becoming repressive.

Kant is in many regards the inspirer of Wilsonianism, of the League of Nations, the United Nations, and international organizations in general and, just as much, of the fight for human rights and the "responsibility to protect," which was solemnly proclaimed by the UN General Assembly in 2005.[64] But in his case, too, experience suggests that there are serious moral and practical problems involved. When Reinhold Niebuhr – anticipating the modern realist critique of liberal Wilsonianism – draws an opposition between "moral man and immoral society" and then warns against the dangers of dividing the world into "children of light and children of darkness," he shows that moralism can lead to immorality and fanaticism.[65] Kant's own hesitations about the use of force against "unjust enemies" seem justified by various experiences of our time.

---

[63] See A. Kojève, *Introduction to the Reading of Hegel* (ed. A. Bloom, trans. H. Nichols) (Ithaca, NY: Cornell University Press, 1980).

[64] See M. W. Doyle, "International Ethics and the Responsibility to Protect," *International Studies Review* 13, no. 1 (2011), 72–84.

[65] See R. Niebuhr, *Moral Man and Immoral Society* (New York: Scribner, 1932), and R. Niebuhr, *The Children of Light and the Children of Darkness* (New York: Scribner, 1944). For a discussion, see also S. Recchia, "Restraining Imperial Hubris: The Ethical Bases of Realist International Relations Theory," *Constellations* 14, no. 4 (2007), 531–56.

Of course, Hegel is second to none in his critique of the "moral vision of the world." He justifies war and military intervention in the name of the "Manifest destiny," or civilizing mission, of empires which, consciously or not, are bearers of a universal message. But then again, recent experiences at "nation-building" and "regime-change," or "democracy enforcement," in alien cultures seem to confirm the difficulty, confessed by Hegel and experienced by Napoleon, of overcoming the resistance of nationality and religion, even with the intervention of the World Spirit. In short, then, these three classical thinkers are still very much with us today, in the institutions, practices, and arguments that shape modern international relations. The questions they raised and some of the answers they provided, while hardly conclusive and marked by sometimes serious contradictions, can also help us better understand what is at stake, at least ethically speaking, in contemporary interventions.

9   Revisiting Kant and intervention

Andrew Hurrell

This volume seeks to re-examine the arguments of a range of modern European political thinkers on the use of force and intervention and to relate the thinker's arguments to contemporary world affairs. In the case of Immanuel Kant this is a particularly daunting task, partly because of the amount of recent research and partly because of the extent to which his name, his own arguments, and an even wider range of allegedly "Kantian" positions have been used to characterize the post-Cold War period. His name has been invoked constantly, and "Kantian" has become a defining attribute of a vast range of post-Cold War political, moral and legal writings.[1]

That Kant's name should be invoked in this way is in itself no great surprise. The 1990s were, after all, marked by a clear sense of the liberal ascendancy; a clear assumption that the US and its allies had the right and power to decide what the "liberal global order" was all about; and a clear belief that the Western order worked and that it had the answers. What is of greater importance for this chapter is the way in which interpretations of Kant's writing have shifted. The balance between the varying, and often contradictory, aspects of his writing shifted in part through an attempt to re-frame and extend the internal logic of his arguments and in part as a reflection of the changing external context. Hence it became common to suggest that, whatever the limits of his own position, his thought can, and should, be legitimately developed

I would like to thank Jennifer Welsh, Stefano Recchia, Gianluigi Palombella and Sergio Dellavalle for their helpful comments on an earlier version of this chapter. And particular thanks go to Tobias Berger for his excellent research assistance.

[1] By my own doubtless incomplete count, and discounting all of the work on democratic and "Kantian peace theory," a post-1990 bibliography in English quickly runs to well over fifty items. In German, the post-1990 period has seen nearly forty pieces just on Kant's writing on international relations, again leaving aside democratic peace theory. And both journal articles and monographic work has spread geographically – at least within those countries whose languages I am able to read. For a recent analysis of Kant's political philosophy see A. Ripstein, *Force and Freedom: Kant's Legal and Political Philosophy* (Cambridge, MA: Harvard University Press, 2009).

and extended within the allegedly new and transformed realities of the post-Cold War international system.

One dimension of this reinterpretation has involved laying far more emphasis on the transnational cosmopolitan and constitutionalist side of this thought, and downplaying his often harsh and pessimistic view of inter-state relations. The other dimension has stressed the implications for a "Kantian" view of international relations of the coming into existence in the post-Cold War world of a powerful core of liberal states. On this reading, Kant's views on international relations in general, and his attitude towards intervention in particular, should be legitimately re-framed within the context of the successful global order that the United States sought to construct within its own camp during the Cold War and then to globalize in the post-Cold War period. In part, this was seen to follow from the influence of democratic peace theory and the arguments for liberal or democratic intervention that were often extrapolated from the theory. But in part it reflected the broader logic and implications that were seen to flow from the simple existence of a powerful core of liberal democratic states.

The first reinterpretation and extension has been particularly common within the German-speaking world; the second within the United States. Indeed the contrast between German constitutionalist and cosmopolitan readings of Kant, and US readings that stress democratic peace and the role of powerful liberal states, provides a nice example of how national contexts are crucial in shaping theoretical (re)interpretations.[2]

This chapter is organized in three sections. In the first section I will sketch rather briefly the arguments that suggest a restrictionist reading of Kant, both in specific relation to his position on nonintervention, but also to his sober and cautious views on international relations more generally. I will next consider the two sets of arguments for a more expansive reading of Kant that have dominated so much of the recent literature. Section two explores what one might call a transnational cosmopolitan and constitu-tionalist reading, and highlights some of the issues and problems that this raises. Section three then examines those views of Kant that underscore the legal, political and moral importance of the coming into existence in the contemporary world of a powerful and homogeneous core of liberal states. Both of these views have been heavily shaped, sometimes explicitly, more often only implicitly, by a particular view of contemporary world affairs and a particular interpretation of the direction of historical change. And they have fed directly into a range of recent "Kantian" arguments concerning intervention.

[2] See D. Castiglione and I. Hampsher-Monk (eds.), *The History of Political Thought in National Context* (Cambridge University Press, 2011).

Kant as a noninterventionist

Kant is best known as a moral philosopher whose work is rationalist and systematic in form, and broad and universalist in scope. But he became ever more deeply concerned with politics; with the ways in which inner moral freedom might be reconciled with external political freedom; and with what he saw as the close relationship between individual morality, the correct internal constitution of the state, and international peace. The development of his thought took place against the dramatic developments of his time (especially the French Revolution) and within the context of a growing body of European thought on international law and relations. Although it is true for Kant that traditional international law can only be provisionally or conditionally valid until the state of nature has been abandoned and a lawful constitution established, one of the striking features of Kant's writing, both in *Perpetual Peace* and more generally, is the degree of attention that he gives to established ideas of international law and to those whom he famously describes as "sorry comforters" – Grotius, Pufendorf and Vattel. Kant's views on nonintervention provide an important measure of this attention and of his abiding concern with the specific problem of inter-state order. Kant explicitly upholds the principle of nonintervention in the fifth preliminary article in *Perpetual Peace*: "5. No state shall forcibly interfere in the constitution and government of another state." The only exception that he was prepared to allow was when internal discord had led to the state breaking up into two parts, "each of which set itself up as a separate state and claimed authority over the whole."[3]

The caution against using coercion even for good purposes is clear. In *The Metaphysics of Morals*, for example, Kant accepts (speaking of colonialism) that "there are plausible enough arguments for the use of violence on the grounds that it is in the best interests of the world as a whole."[4] "For on the one hand, it may bring culture to uncivilized peoples ... and on the other, it may help us to purge our country of depraved characters ..." But he is steadfast in rejecting such arguments:

But all these supposedly good intentions cannot wash away the stain of injustice from the means which are used to implement them. Yet one might object that the whole world would perhaps still be in a lawless condition if men had had any such

---

[3] I. Kant, "Perpetual Peace: A Philosophical Sketch," [henceforth: PP], in H. Reiss (ed.), *Kant. Political Writings*, expanded edn. (Cambridge University Press, 1991), p. 96. All page references are to this edition.

[4] Kant, "The Metaphysics of Morals," [henceforth: MM], in Reiss (ed.), *Kant. Political Writings*, p. 173.

compunction about using violence when they first created a law-governed state. But this can as little annul the above condition of right as can the plea of political revolutionaries that the people are entitled to reform constitutions by force if they have become corrupt, and to act completely unjustly for once and all, in order to put justice on a more secure basis and ensure that it flourishes in the future.[5]

What we see here are the close links between Kant's opposition to revolutionary change domestically and his opposition to liberal or humanitarian intervention internationally. More telling still is his attack on both the use of force and on confederations that seek to reform the internal structure of other states: "Although war is not so incurably evil as that tomb, a universal autocracy (*or even as a confederacy which exists to hasten the weakening of a despotism in any single state*), yet . . . war creates more evil than it destroys."[6]

The strongest textual basis for the opposite position, namely a more robust defense of intervention and of the coercive enforcement, comes in Section 60 of *The Metaphysics of Morals*:

The rights of a state against an unjust enemy are unlimited in quantity or degree, although they do have limits in relation to quality. In other words, while the threatened state may not employ every means to assert its own rights, it may employ any intrinsically permissible means to whatever degree its own strength allows. But what can the expression "an unjust enemy" mean in relation to the concepts of international right, which requires that every state should act as judge of its own cause just as it would in a state of nature? It must mean someone whose publicly expressed will, whether expressed in word or deed, displays a maxim which would make peace among nations impossible and would lead to a perpetual state of nature if it were made into a general rule.[7]

This seems to imply both a clear evaluative standard (policies and professed policy objectives that would endanger international peace) as well as a capacity to judge right and wrong in the light of that standard. It has been used (by Carl Schmitt and others) to see Kant as justifying a much more confrontational relationship between the liberal state and its "unjust enemies."

However the limits are clear. Force can only be justified in terms of clear threats. As Franceschet points out: "Force against non-liberal states cannot be justified simply if they pose what Kant calls a passive injury to others (due to their mere independence in the state of nature) . . . As this passage indicates, it is only states that pose a clear active injury to others

---

[5] MM, p. 173.
[6] Kant, "Religion within the Limits of Reason," in C. Friedrich (ed.), *The Philosophy of Kant* (New York: Modern Library, 1949), p. 381 (my emphasis).
[7] MM, p. 170.

that can be lawfully coerced."[8] Moreover, one reason why Kant devoted time and space to discussing existing international law is related to his belief that the achievement of a more satisfactory "law governed external relationship" was a long-term goal that could only be reached gradually and with much difficulty. In the meantime, Kant appears to see some merit in existing international law that draws its force from common interest and reciprocity. This is clear from the Sixth Preliminary Article in *Perpetual Peace*:

6. "No state at war with another shall permit such acts of hostility as would make mutual confidence impossible during a future time of peace. Such acts would include the employment of assassins (*percussores*) or poisoners (*venefici*), breach of agreements, the instigation of treason (*perduellio*) within the enemy state, etc."

These are dishonorable stratagems. For it must still remain possible, even in wartime, to have some sort of trust in the attitude of the enemy, otherwise peace could not be concluded and the hostilities would turn into a war of extermination (bellum internecinium).[9]

This article represents, for Kant, a law "of the strictest sort" that could be implemented immediately (i.e. in a continuing state of anarchy) and that would be "valid irrespective of differing circumstances."[10]

But the importance of nonintervention is more than just of temporary or contingent relevance. On the contrary, it is striking that Kant does not deny moral or juridical status to particular kinds of states and does not support a view of international law or morality which would entrench differential rules between the world of republican states and the rest – two sets of rules for a divided world. As Mertens notes, "It is very remarkable that Kant formulates the prohibition of intervention in the preliminary articles, which can only mean that this prohibition has a universal validity in the following sense: it protects all states against intervention, not only the republican ones."[11] The reason, as Cavallar notes, has to do with the claim that international right demands the mutual recognition of autonomy. "Allowing some states (the good ones) to intervene in others (the bad ones) violates the universal concept of

---

[8] A. Franceschet, "'One powerful and enlightened nation:' Kant and the quest for the global rule of law," in B. Jahn (ed.), *Classical Theories of International Relations* (Cambridge University Press, 2006), p. 87.

[9] PP, p. 96.

[10] As he says in *Perpetual Peace*: "All of the articles listed above, when regarded objectively or in relation to the intentions of those in power, are *prohibitive laws* (*leges prohibitivae*). Yet some of them are of the *strictest* sort (*leges strictae*), being valid irrespective of differing circumstances, and they require that the abuses they prohibit should be abolished *immediately* (nos. 1, 5, and 6)." PP, p. 97.

[11] T. Mertens, "Cosmopolitanism and Citizenship: Kant Against Habermas," *European Journal of Philosophy* 4, no. 3 (1996), p. 331.

justice ... International right must be based on the mutual recognition of all states as autonomous, or juridical, persons. It requires recognizing the autonomy of all states."[12] As Kant puts it in *Perpetual Peace*:

Yet while natural right allows us to say of men living in a lawless condition that they ought to abandon it, the right of nations does not allow us to say the same of states. For as states, they already have a lawful [rightful] internal constitution, and have thus outgrown the coercive right of others to subject them to a wider legal constitution in accordance with their conception of right.[13]

He refers here to a "rightful [*rechtliche*] internal constitution," as distinct from one that is just or lawful [*rechtmäßig*].[14] The limited pacific federation that he discusses in *Perpetual Peace* and *The Metaphysics of Morals* is therefore designed to underwrite international law in such a way as to protect the autonomy and independence of states. Unlike individuals giving up their lawless freedom in the state of nature, the danger for states is that they would lose their internal lawful condition and become part of a despotic universal monarchy.[15]

The restrictionist and limited reading of Kant is not based solely on this strong justification of autonomy, but also on a broader view of international life that takes the inter-state anarchy seriously as a problem in its own right. Military intervention is problematic on consequentialist grounds, because it will intensify the dangers of inter-state anarchy. Although Kant is less explicit than Rousseau in depicting the constraints of the security dilemma, he nevertheless argues that war is a fundamental and intrinsic characteristic of the international anarchy that exists between states.[16] He also sees any prospect of reform and progress as long-term and gradual. Kant is quite consistent in arguing that "a perfect solution is impossible," and speaks in *Perpetual Peace* of an "infinite process of gradual approximation."[17]

Transnational cosmopolitanism

This cautious picture of international life and this restrictionist view of intervention are clearly rooted in the world of inter-state conflict and of an international law built around the independence and

---

[12] G. Cavallar, "Kantian Perspectives on Democratic Peace: Alternatives to Doyle," *Review of International Studies* 27, no. 2 (2001), p. 241.
[13] PP, p. 104.
[14] Cavallar, "Kantian Perspectives," p. 242.
[15] Mertens, "Cosmopolitanism and Citizenship," p. 341.
[16] On the Hobbesian aspect of Kant, see R. Tuck, *The Rights of War and Peace. Political Thought and International Order from Grotius to Kant* (Oxford University Press, 1999), pp. 219–25.
[17] PP, p. 130.

sovereignty of states. By contrast, for many commentators, Kant's modernity and relevance rests precisely on his far-sighted intuition into the driving forces of change and even transformation, above all the increased destructiveness of war, the growing importance of trade and commerce, and the role of publicity and public reason. The consequence is that human beings have been forced to live "unavoidably side by side" in new and morally significant ways. There are three common analytical moves which lay primary emphasis on this side of the story. They rest partly on particular readings of Kant but they also depend on the view that the changed circumstances of contemporary world affairs justify re-reading or expanding Kant's original arguments.

The first common move is to stress the "inconsistencies" and "ambiguities" of Kant's arguments, above all in relation to his views on federation. As is well known, Kant's position on a limited federation as expressed in *Perpetual Peace* was by no means his only statement on the matter. There is a deep and unresolved tension across his writings.[18] In the first place, there is no single Kantian solution to the international problem. Kant's writing on the subject is characterized by a tentative and exploratory approach and he is keenly aware that all solutions involve trade-offs and costs. Furthermore, it is clear that Kant is not solely concerned with the kind of limited pacific federation in which law is not backed by stronger forms of coercive political institutions. In *Perpetual Peace* and *The Metaphysics of Morals* Kant does indeed reject both world government and a federation with the power to enforce the proscription of war. Yet in both *The Idea for a Universal History* and *Theory and Practice*, Kant's political universalism is much stronger, and he embraces both the idea of some kind of universal political system and a federation with the power to enforce the law. Kant was at times drawn to the view that self-enforcement might not be adequate, and that a more developed federation might have to form a part of a working system of peace. This would of course still be a "state system," but the existence of centralized power, the ability to determine and enforce the law and the corresponding limit on state sovereignty would represent a major structural reform of that system. International law would no longer derive from pragmatic consideration of common interest between independent sovereignties but rather from

---

[18] See A. Hurrell, "Kant and the Kantian Paradigm in International Relations," *Review of International Studies* 16 (1990), esp. pp. 191–4. For a recent detailed treatment that reinforces this general picture, see P. Kleingeld, "Kant's Changing Cosmopolitanism," in A. Oksenberg Rorty and J. Schmidt (eds.), *Kant's Idea for a Universal History with a Cosmopolitan Aim* (Cambridge University Press, 2009), pp. 171–86.

the "united power and the law-governed decisions of a united will," as he puts it in *The Idea for Universal History.*[19]

Wilfried Hinsch provides one example of how recent interpreters have dealt with Kant's inconsistencies, and sought to extend Kant's arguments.[20] Hinsch provides two readings of Kant and the relationship between a federation of states and the use of force. On the one hand, Hinsch argues that the realization of the rule of law through the Kantian federation of states (*Völkerbund*) does not exclude the possibility of implementing law through international courts with the use of force. Indeed, the very conception of peace as law seems to demand the possibility of enforcing the law. Only courts and the possibility of the legitimate use of force (*Zwangsbefugnisse*) can facilitate a situation in which everybody's rights can be guaranteed. Furthermore, any state can demand from another state that it should leave the state of nature and enter a legal order and this can be read as implying the possibility of using force to underpin this demand. On the other hand, Hinsch recognizes that Kant was convinced that states could not accept a higher-level legal-normative authority. Thus, the *Völkerbund* is based on the principle of voluntarism and allows for a permanent possibility of exit for any member state.

From these two possible readings of Kant, Hinsch concludes that Kant's conceptualization of peace as law should be appreciated independently of Kant's ambiguous position on the relationship between the use of force and international law. He argues that, for his own analysis of humanitarian intervention, he will interpret the Kantian idea of a peace-securing *Völkerbund* in a way that does not allow for global legislation through a world-republic, but explicitly demands international courts to command the use of force for the implementation of their verdicts. Hinsch recognizes the very clear Kantian difficulties involved in attempts to justify humanitarian intervention on a case-by-case basis in terms of "moral exceptionalism," accepting the existing restrictionist character of international law but arguing that it has to be overridden in cases in which human rights are violated in particularly extreme forms. As with many commentators, he can only argue that the Kantian idea of law through peace will necessitate a reform of the UN Charter and a strengthening of the UN in order to harmonize the morally necessary

[19] Kant, "Idea for a Universal History with a Cosmopolitan Purpose" [henceforth: UH], in Reiss (ed.), *Kant. Political Writings*, p. 47. (In the original: "von einer vereinigten Macht und von der Entscheidung nach Gesetzen des vereinigten Willens").

[20] W. Hinsch, "Kant, die humanitäre Intervention und der moralische Exzeptionalismus," in V. Gerhardt (ed.), *Kant im Streit der Fakultäten* (Berlin: Walter de Gruyter, 2005).

with the peace-securing legal order in face of gross human rights violations. But note: whilst this brings morality and law closer together, it says nothing whatsoever about the relationship of law and politics. As I will discuss in the Conclusion, one of the most serious challenges to Kant comes from those who stress the centrality of politics and of a political morality that takes this centrality as its point of departure.

The second move is to justify resolving the inconsistencies in Kant's views on international relations by reference to his underlying moral purposes and to the fundamental links that he sees between human freedom and peace. This involves downplaying Kant's emphasis on the sphere of international right in favor of the idea of cosmopolitan law based on the rights of the world citizen and a secure constitutionalist framework. Habermas provides one of the clearest and widely cited examples of such a move.[21] He begins by quoting Kant from the *Contest of Faculties*.

All forms of state are based on the idea of a constitution which is compatible with the natural rights of man, so that those who obey the law should also act as a united body of legislators. And if we accordingly think of the commonwealth in terms of concepts of pure reason, it may be called a Platonic ideal (*respublica noumenon*), which is not an empty figment of the imagination, but the eternal norm for all civil constitutions whatsoever, and a means of ending all war. A civil society organized in conformity with it and governed by laws of freedom is an example representing it in the world of experience (*respublica phaenomenon*), and it can only be achieved by a laborious process, after innumerable wars and conflicts. But its constitution, once it has been attained as a whole, is the best qualified to keep out war, the destroyer of everything good.[22]

Habermas highlights the "contradictory character" of Kant's construction, especially the relationship of classical international law to cosmopolitan law and the unresolved tension within his idea of a federation.

Because Kant believed that the barriers of national sovereignty were insurmountable, he conceived of the cosmopolitan community as a federation of states, not of world citizens. This assumption proved inconsistent, insofar as Kant derived every legal order, including that within the state, from a more original law, which gives rights to every person "qua human being." Every individual has the right to equal freedom under universal laws (since "everyone decides for everyone and each decides for himself"). This founding of law in human rights designates individuals as the bearers of rights, and gives to all

[21] J. Habermas, "Kant's Idea of Perpetual Peace, with the Benefit of Two Hundred Years' Hindsight," in J. Bohman and M. Lutz-Bachmann (eds.), *Perpetual Peace: Essays on Kant's Cosmopolitan Ideal* (Cambridge, MA: MIT Press, 1997), pp. 113–53.

[22] Kant, "The Contest of Faculties," [henceforth: CF], in Reiss (ed.), *Kant. Political Writings*, p. 187.

modern legal orders an inviolable individualistic character. If Kant holds that this guarantee of freedom – "that which human beings ought to do in accordance with the laws of freedom" – is precisely the essential purpose of perpetual peace, "indeed for all three variants of public law, civil, international and cosmopolitan law" *then he ought not to allow the autonomy of citizens to be mediated through the sovereignty of their states.*[23]

In addition, Habermas argues that we need to move beyond Kant's individualized understandings of subjectivity and reason, instead placing the individual subject within an integrated, inter-subjective framework, and shifting from a monologic to dialogic or deliberative understanding of reason and rationality. It is this move that provides the foundation for Habermas's own thinking on international law, including the transfer to a supranational level of the competences necessary for two purposes: the safeguarding of peace and global security and the protection of fundamental human rights.[24] This move has also helped to stimulate thinking on both "constitutionalism beyond the state" and the possibility of a plural but interlinked system of global public law.[25] And it is this move that, for its adherents, provides a potential solution to the inconsistencies and contradictions in Kant's thought discussed in the previous section. These can only be overcome by moving beyond a monadic idea of subjectivity and by recognizing the need for a post-unitary paradigm that brings the domestic, international and cosmopolitan together in an integrated but plural legal order.

Much recent interpretation, then, has shifted directly towards the level of cosmopolitan right and to the various ways in which the "transitional status" of existing international law can be overcome. Hence Kleingeld follows Habermas in arguing that cosmopolitan right could be better justified through the basic human right to freedom.[26] But her core concern is to argue that Kant's cosmopolitanism has an explicitly political dimension in its discussion of cosmopolitan law/right (*Weltbürgerrecht*) – although neither the justification for nor the institutional implications of *Weltbürgerrecht* are sufficiently developed in Kant's work itself. She defines

---

[23] Habermas, "Two Hundred Years' Hindsight," p. 128 (my emphasis). See also Mertens, "Cosmopolitanism and Citizenship," p. 338.

[24] J. Habermas, "Eine politische Verfassung für die pluralistische Weltgesellschaft?" *Kritische Justiz* 222 (2005). For Habermas's view of the Kosovo intervention as being morally justified, see J. Habermas, "Bestialität und Humanität: Ein Krieg an der Grenze zwischen Recht und Moral," *Die Zeit* 18 (1999).

[25] See, for example, A. von Bogdandy and S. Dellavalle, "Universalism Renewed: Habermas' Theory of International Order in the Light of Competing Paradigms," *German Law Journal* 10, no. 1 (2009), 5–30.

[26] P. Kleingeld, "Kants Politischer Kosmopolitanismus," *Jahrbuch für Recht und Ethik* (1997), pp. 333–48.

political cosmopolitanism (following Thomas Pogge) as a position which is "committed to a concrete political ideal of global order under which all persons have equivalent legal rights and duties, that is, are fellow citizens of a universal republic."[27] For Kleingeld the decisive criterion of political cosmopolitanism is the notion of a global order constituted by individual human beings, rather than citizens of states.

The focus therefore shifts firmly to the level of cosmopolitan right. Although Kant strictly rejects the possibility of a world state, the argument is that he moves beyond his moral cosmopolitanism in his discussion of cosmopolitan law (*Weltbürgerrecht*) as a third sphere of public law; and that cosmopolitan law is distinct from international law and can be implemented (at least partially) without installing a world state. Of course, all analysis here has to deal with the limits of Kant's position on this question. Cosmopolitan law is distinct from international law, in the sense that it addresses human beings directly as citizens of the world (*Erdbürger*) and not only citizens of particular states. At the core of Kant's understanding of cosmopolitan law is the notion of hospitality. As Kant states: "*hospitality* means the right of a stranger not to be treated with hostility when he arrives on someone else's territory."[28] This right, however, is a right of resort, not a right to be guest, and in *The Metaphysics of Morals* Kant argues that "world citizens [have] the right to attempt to enter into a community with everyone else and to visit all regions of the earth with this intention."[29]

But, however limited in scope, the really crucial point from this perspective is that both the domain of cosmopolitan right and the specific demands of cosmopolitan law recognize individual human beings as legal subjects. Hence, in *Perpetual Peace* Kant argues that a person can only be turned away "if this can be done without causing his death." Whether or not Kant recognized them, such a position has profound and radical implications. Of course, this still leaves us with the problem of enforcement. Here again the "inconsistencies" in his position need to be ironed out. Thus, for Kleingeld, the negative position on the enforcement of cosmopolitan law is inconsistent and needs to be abandoned if cosmopolitan law is to be taken seriously as public law (*öffentliches Recht*). And, as the enforcement of cosmopolitan law is compatible with Kantian principles, we need to move beyond Kant in order to define the mechanisms through which it could be implemented.

Before moving on, I would stress again just how much the level of the international has disappeared in all this, in favor of transnational legal

---

[27] *Ibid.*, p. 335.   [28] PP, p. 105.   [29] MM, p. 172.

and moral cosmopolitanism. And it is precisely this sense that meshed so closely with the Zeitgeist of the post-Cold War era. Was it not obvious that globalization was rendering obsolete the old Westphalian world of Great Power rivalries, balance of power politics and an old-fashioned international law built around state sovereignty and strict rules of non-intervention? Was it not equally obvious that non-state actors, transnationalism and global civil society were becoming ever more important?

This leads directly to the third move, namely to historicize Kant's non-interventionist arguments. On one side, this means relating his arguments to the specific circumstances of his period. On the other, it involves explaining how his arguments have to be adapted to the very different circumstances of today's world. So Hinsch of course quotes the clear statement on nonintervention: "No state shall forcibly interfere in the constitution and government of another state." But he goes on to argue that Kant is not thinking about genocide and mass violations, but about republican France that is threatened by intervention by Austria and Prussia in August 1791. In the case of cosmopolitan law, Kleingeld recognizes that the right to hospitality is limited by national sovereignty but argues that this limitation is directed against European colonialism and in specific support of the isolationist policies of China and Japan.

Again it is Habermas who provides a particularly clear view of how we can reinterpret Kant's view of historical progress and find justification for this reinterpretation in the changed character of contemporary world politics. Hence Habermas is insistent that we must bear in mind the nature of war in Kant's own time. "Kant is thinking here of spatially limited wars between individual states or alliances, not of world wars. He is thinking of wars conducted between ministers and states, but not of anything like civil wars."[30] In addition, and more crucially, although Kant's own drivers of change (the peaceful nature of republics, the pacific character of trade, and the role of publicity) have often been countered by historical developments, they have an abiding importance that often emerges out of their very contradictions.

On the other, they refer to historical trends that betray a peculiar dialectical quality. These very same trends reveal that the premises on which Kant based his theory reflect the conditions he perceived at the close of the 18th century that no longer hold. Yet these trends would seem to support the claim that a conception of cosmopolitan law that was properly reformulated in contemporary terms might well find support in a constellation of forces that meets it halfway.[31]

[30] Habermas, "Two Hundred Years' Hindsight," p. 115.
[31] Ibid., pp. 119–20.

This claim is clearly formulated here in cautious terms – a constellation of forces that meets it halfway. This no doubt reflects not just the difficulty of evaluating contemporary developments but also the complexities involved in relating regulative principles derived from universal reason to any set of concrete historical forces or circumstances. Nevertheless, both Habermas and many other neo-Kantians have found little trouble in identifying a whole range of changes in the character of international law and society that reflect this move from traditional international law to a cosmopolitan law built around the rights of the world citizen. In the 1990s, global order was widely understood through the lens of liberal internationalism or liberal solidarism. Bumpy as it might be, the road seemed to be leading away from Westphalia – with an expanded role for formal and informal multilateral institutions; a huge increase in the scope, density and intrusiveness of rules and norms made at the international level but affecting how domestic societies are organized; the ever-greater involvement of new actors in global governance; the moves towards the coercive enforcement of global rules; and fundamental changes in political, legal and moral understandings of state sovereignty and of the relationship between the state, the citizen and the international community.

The difficulty, however, is that this was always a one-sided view of the post-Cold War era. And here we might certainly note the depressingly long list of factors that seem to point towards a "return of Westphalia" – either in terms of the decentralized power-political order emphasized by neo-realism or of a limited form of international society dominated by the twin problems of managing power and mediating value conflict, as emphasized by pluralist writers within the English School. These include: the re-valorization of national security and a renewed preoccupation with war-fighting and counter-insurgency; the continued or renewed power of nationalism, no longer potentially containable politically or analytically in a box marked "ethnic conflict" but manifest in the identity politics and foreign policy actions of the major states in the system; the renewed importance of nuclear weapons to the structure of regional security complexes, and in the construction of Great Power hierarchies and the distribution of seats at top tables; and finally the renewed centrality of the balance of power as both a motivation for state policy (as with US policies in Asia) and as an element in the foreign policy of all second-tier states.

Economic globalization has also fed back into the structures and dynamics of a Westphalian state system rather than pointing towards its transcendence. The state as an economic actor has proved resilient in seeking to control economic flows and to police borders; and in seeking to exploit and develop state-based and mercantilist modes of managing economic problems, especially in relation to resource competition and energy geopolitics. Successful liberal globalization has had a vital impact on the distribution of inter-state political power. If the debate over power shifts in the 1990s concentrated on the shift of power from states to firms and non-state actors, the "power shift" of the past decade has focused on rising and emerging powers, on state-directed economic activity, and on the mismatch between existing global economic governance arrangements and the distribution of power amongst those with the actual power of effective economic decision. The importance of the global financial crisis is not solely related to its severely negative economic effects. Rather, its importance lies in the challenge that it represents to the idea of a stable Western-led global order and in the reinforcement that it is giving to the forces and factors outlined above, especially economic nationalism.

It is, of course, possible to see these developments simply as international relations returning once more to its "Westphalian norm" – the return of history and the end of dreams, as Robert Kagan would have it.[32] But it is more accurate and more helpful to face up to the complex, hybrid and contested character of international society – a society that faces a range of classical Westphalian challenges (especially to do with power transition and the rise of new powers) but one that faces these challenges in a context marked by strong post-Westphalian characteristics (both in terms of the material conditions of globalization and the changed character of legitimacy).

Whilst the gap between morality and law might have been closed within a transnational cosmopolitan and constitutionalist reading of international legal developments, the relationship of law to power remains extremely problematic. The tensions come partly from unequal power and the much-discussed relationship between US hegemony and the institutional legal order. After all, the implementation of Kantian values in the post-Cold War period has had a profoundly paradoxical character because of its dependence on powerful states for effective action, whether through economic sanctions or military intervention. The world beyond the state has depended on powerful states which, as with all states, are likely to act in accordance with their own power and interests and their own particular interpretations of global values. But tensions also come, and are likely to come increasingly, from the return of a more open global order, especially one in which previously

---

[32] R. Kagan, *The Return of History and the End of Dreams* (New York: Atlantic Books, 2008).

marginalized powers now move center-stage. Some such powers (China most obviously) may well be classified as belonging outside the liberal fold. Others (such as India and Brazil), for all their political and social problems, are large and consolidated democracies and have a legitimate claim to be part of the twenty-first century debates on the meaning and nature of democratic rule domestically and on the idea of what a liberal order should, or could, be all about globally. At a minimum, the forces and factors pointing back to Westphalia might suggest that Kant was not so wrong in insisting on the importance of the international as a sphere of politics in which progress faced severe obstacles and in which historical change was likely to be slow and beset by many contradictions. Even a "realistic utopia" needs to give sufficient regard to the ongoing problems of power-political ordering. International life is not just a domain in which we have to pay attention to the constraints of non-ideal theory; it remains a zone of the radically non-ideal.

Kant and the liberal zone

If the transnational cosmopolitan and constitutionalist reading of Kant has dominated one side of recent analysis, another trend has been to focus on Kant's analysis of the specific characteristics of republican states and of the impact of the emergence in the contemporary world of a powerful core of liberal states. Clearly a very great deal of this work has drawn on the hugely influential work of Michael Doyle and feeds directly into the academic industry that democratic peace theory has become. These claims have been much discussed.[33] Here I can only make a few brief points in order to highlight some of the difficulties of placing too great an emphasis on the power of the liberal zone.

The first point concerns the composition of the liberal core and the issue of whether, in Kantian terms, a progressive federation should be limited to particular kinds of states. On a textual level it has always been difficult to read Kant as suggesting that his federation should be limited to a particular kind of state. "Free" in the second definitive article refers to independent and autonomous states. It is true that certain passages do point in a more limited direction, most famously:

---

[33] See, for example, J. Macmillan, "A Kantian Protest against the Peculiar Discourse of Liberal State Peace," *Millennium* 24 (1995), 549–62; B. Jahn, "Classical Smoke, Classical Mirror: Kant and Mill in liberal international relations theory," and Franceschet, "One Powerful and Enlightened Nation," both in B. Jahn (ed.), *Classical Theories of International Relations*.

The idea of federalism, extending gradually to encompass all states and thus leading to perpetual peace, is practical and has objective reality. For if by good fortune one powerful and enlightened nation can form a republic (which is by its nature inclined to seek perpetual peace), this will provide a focal point for federal association among other states. These will join up with the first one, thus securing the freedom of each state in accordance with the idea of international right, and the whole will gradually spread further and further by a series of alliances of this kind.[34]

But many other passages – and the general insistence on the importance of traditional international law discussed earlier – suggest that the federation must be inclusive.

Whatever Kant's own doubts, the idea that global order should be built around the particular rights and responsibilities of a league of democratic states has become a topic of renewed political and analytical concern, at least in the United States. But the problems with such a view are many and serious. It is far from clear that a league of liberal states would actually be able to generate higher levels of agreement on contentious issues than, for example, bodies such as the UN Security Council – witness the range and depth of disagreement amongst democracies over a range of issues from the invasion of Iraq to climate change. Such a league, moreover, is likely to encourage polarization and a situation in which the democratic states see problems in Manichean fashion in terms of democracy and the nefarious actions of non-democrats, whilst outsiders see the league as an alliance or grouping that is naturally threatening to them – a problem of which both Rousseau and Kant were clearly aware. But, in his critique of Rawls, Henry Shue captures the most important difficulty and one that speaks directly to Kant's concerns. Shue is insistent that the rules of international society cannot be solely a matter for democratic states to decide upon amongst themselves. In particular he has criticized Rawls for focusing his Law of Peoples around the foreign policy of a particular kind of states, and for failing to provide sufficient guidance as to the rules that might shape relations with non-aggressive repressive states, especially those that do not accept Western liberal notions of reasonable pluralism.[35]

If the "public" at the international level consists of the states that are not at war with each other, it may be better for the "public" to be as nearly global as possible ... Irrespective of whether it would count as Rawlsian international public reason, we need to find or make a basis for a normative consensus about international conduct amongst more of those who disagree about the principles of domestic conduct.[36]

---

[34] PP, p. 104.
[35] H. Shue, "Rawls and the Outlaws," *Politics, Philosophy and Economics*, 1 (2002), 307–22.
[36] *Ibid.*, p. 318.

A second dimension of the liberal zone view of Kant stresses the degree
to which powerful liberal states have a right and duty to take the lead
in the promotion of Kantian values, including through military intervention. Here it seems very clear that there is very little support within
Kant's writings for any form of liberal vigilantism. The "powerful and
enlightened nation" is to be a focal point for change, not an engine
of coercive intervention and crusading.[37] In part, support here comes
from the very clear statements on nonintervention referred to in the
first section. But, more generally, Kant is very much aware of the
dangers of power and interest corrupting moral purpose. As he puts
it in Appendix 1 to *Perpetual Peace*, "On the disagreement between
morals and politics in relation to perpetual peace: 'And I can indeed
imagine a *moral politician*, i.e. someone who conceives of the principles
of political expediency in such a way that they can coexist with
morality, but I cannot imagine a *political moralist*, i.e. one who fashions
his morality to suit his own advantage as a statesman'."[38] Or again:
"It must likewise be demonstrated that all evil which stands in the
way of perpetual peace results from the fact that the political moralist
starts out from the very point at which the moral politician rightly stops;
he thus makes his principles subordinate to his end (i.e. puts the cart
before the horse), thereby defeating his own purpose of reconciling
politics with morality."[39]

Although Kant's own position against liberal crusading is clear, we
still need to ask whether other elements of his thought have not fed
into liberal justifications for such policies. It is certainly the case that
there is a strongly anti-colonial thrust to Kant.[40] And yet, as David
Harvey and Michel Foucault have both noted, there is a troubling
disconnect between the much-celebrated universality and generality of
Kant's ethics and the "awkward and intractable particularities of his
anthropology and geography," with their prejudicial statements on race,
gender and nation and with their anthropologically grounded views of
the historical plurality and separateness of nations.[41] In these writings
Kant is concerned with the issue of how universal reason can be linked

---

[37] For two contrary readings that have played an important influence in recent US
debates on humanitarian intervention, see F. Téson, "Kantian International Liberalism,"
in Mapel and Nardin (eds.), *International Society: Diverse Ethical Perspectives*; and
A. Applbaum, "Forcing a People to be Free," *Philosophy and Public Affairs*, 35, no. 4
(2007), 359–400.

[38] PP, p. 118.   [39] PP, p. 121.

[40] See, in particular, S. Muthu, *Enlightenment against Empire* (Princeton University Press,
2003), ch. 5.

[41] D. Harvey, *Cosmopolitanism and the Geographies of Freedom* (New York: Columbia
University Press, 2009), esp. ch. 1: "Kant's Anthropology and Geography," p. 35.

to local truths and historical rootedness and with the "conditions of possibility" for the progressive "organization of the citizens of the earth within and toward the species as a system which is united by cosmopolitical bonds."[42] But it has been the very difficulty of specifying the links between a cosmopolitan ethic and its geographical and anthropological foundations that has created a wide space which successive generations of liberals were all too happy to fill with hierarchical and exclusionist conceptions of humanity and with paternalist and interventionist policies.

Truer to Kant's own views is the claim that, once established, a core of liberal states would have less need to think in terms of direct and coercive intervention. This view stresses the Kantian idea of the gradual but progressive diffusion of liberal values, partly as a result of liberal economics and increased economic interdependence, partly as a liberal legal order comes to sustain the autonomy of a global civil society and the role of publicity, and partly as a result of the successful example set by the multifaceted liberal capitalist system of states. Unlike traditional power, the power of the liberal zone encourages not balancing and opposition, but enmeshment, emulation and socialization – the EU in microcosm, the Greater West in macrocosm. This systemic Kantianism is extremely important and has been relatively neglected, certainly relative to the volume of work on democratic peace theory.[43] It certainly captures one very important dimension of the post-Cold War global system even if it paints too black and white a picture.

A third, and strongly Kantian, reason for caution in relation to the liberal zone concerns the links between the international and the domestic – the second image reversed, as modern International Relations would express it. Following Rousseau, Kant believes that the state of war between states constitutes a twofold obstacle to the achievement of moral progress through law. In the first place, war itself is incompatible with any conception of morality. It is "the source of all evils and moral corruption," and Kant never tires of denouncing the evils of the state of war: "We regard this as barbarism, coarseness and brutish debasement of humanity."[44] Secondly, the need to solve the problem of war, or at least to explore possible solutions, is so central because

---

[42] Quoted in Harvey, *Cosmpolitanism*, p. 23. Original I. Kant, *Schriften zur Anthropologie, Geschichtsphilosophie, Politik, und Pädagogok* (Frankfurt: Suhrkampf, 1977), p. 690.

[43] For an exception see W. L. Huntley, "Kant's Third Image: Systemic Sources of the Liberal Peace," *International Studies Quarterly* 40, no. 1 (1996), 45–76.

[44] CF, p. 183; PP, p. 103.

of Kant's belief in the inseparable connection between domestic and international society. "The problem of solving a perfect civil constitution is subordinate to the problem of a law-governed external relationship with other states, and cannot be solved unless the latter is also solved."[45] Perpetual peace therefore becomes the "supreme political good."[46]

In the post-Cold War world it became rather easy to assume that human rights and democracy were matters for "us" to export to "them." And yet, the quality of democracy in apparently consolidated developed states has once more become an issue for discussion and so has the willingness of such states to uphold the human rights norms that they proclaim to be of such universal significance. As Benhabib notes, "Modern democracies act in the name of universal principles which are then circumscribed within a particular civic community."[47] The question is how these two are linked. There is much to be said for a Kantian view that sees the sustained consolidation of democracy within the particular civic community as being linked to, if not dependent on, its willingness to respect the judgments of other nations and the effective institutionalization of universal principles at the level of international and cosmopolitan right. As long as international anarchy continues, the consolidation of full and sustained political liberty domestically, even in developed, prosperous liberal states, remains under threat – including of course from the temptation to violate human rights in the name of national security. This link was well understood by the Founding Fathers but forgotten or displaced by the temptations of empire and by moral self-righteousness. As Golove and Hulsebosch note in relation to Madison, "Reflecting the Common Sense epistemology characteristic of so much contemporary constitutionalist thought, he [Madison] insisted that no nation was so enlightened that it could ignore the impartial judgments of other states and still expect to govern itself wisely and effectively."[48]

---

[45] Kant, UH, p. 47.
[46] MM, p. 175.
[47] S. Benhabib, *The Rights of Others. Aliens, Residents and Citizens* (Cambridge University Press, 2004), p. 44.
[48] D. Golove and D. Hulsebosch, "A Civilized Nation: The Early American Constitution, the Law of Nations, and the Pursuit of International Recognition," *NYU Law Review* 85, no. 4 (2010), p. 987. As Madison put it: "An attention to the judgement of other nations is important to every government for two reasons: the one is, that, independently of the merits of any particular plan or measure, it is desirable, on various accounts, that it should appear to other nations as the offspring of a wise and honourable policy; the second is that in doubtful cases, particularly where the national councils may be warped by some strong passion or momentary interest, the presumed or known opinion of the

It is crucially important to remember, then, that Kant was never solely a "second-image theorist." As I have suggested, he stressed not only inside-out links at the domestic level, i.e. why republican states behave differently; but also outward-in links, i.e. why continued international anarchy threatens political right domestically and why respect for international law reinforces good government at home. War for Kant is the result of factors and forces working at all three levels: human nature; the character of states domestically; and the constraints of the international anarchy.

And this leads to my final, Kantian, doubt concerning the dangers of giving too much emphasis to the centrality, power and importance of the liberal zone. There is a powerful foundational sense in which Kantian ethics are built on the need to find agreement precisely amongst those who do not share common values or an agreed way of thinking about the world. Let me quote here from Jeremy Waldron:

> For Kant, the idea of conflict in the state of nature is the idea of a war raised under competing and hostile banners of justice and right. He says that people "can never be secure against acts of violence from one another, since each will have his own right to do what seems right and good to him, independently of the opinion of others." Now the fact that you and I have different views about rights and justice is not a matter of concern if our interests do not converge on the same space for action, or the same objects or land or resources. But if we are, in Kant's words, "unavoidably side by side" with one another (whatever the historical reasons for our current proximity), we have no choice but to attempt to come to terms with one another in some sort of common framework of law ... In both liberal – particularly Rawlsian – and also in recent communitarian and Walzerian political philosophy, there has been a tendency to insist that a well-ordered society should be thought of as something constructed among those who *share* certain fundamental understandings which are constitutive of justice ... By contrast, the great virtue of Kant's work, it seems to me, is that he begins from the *opposite assumption*. He assumes that we are always likely to find ourselves alongside others who disagree with us about justice.[49]

In contrast to Kant, then, a great deal of recent liberal normative theory has appeared as a debate amongst people who have already agreed about many of the most central principles of justice, or whose life worlds are deeply connected and convergent. Equally, liberal interest-driven accounts of the problems of global governance have all too often disguised or evaded the deep conflict over values, underlying purposes

impartial world may be the best guide that can be followed." Federalist No. 63 (Madison), in *The Federalist Papers* (Oxford University Press, 2008), p. 309.

[49] J. Waldron, "What is Cosmopolitan?" *Journal of Political Philosophy* 8, no. 2 (2000), pp. 240–1.

and ways of seeing the world. One of the consequences of the emergence of new powers and of new forms of political and social mobilization and of the broader "provincializing" of the Western liberal order is to create a far greater heterogeneity of interests and values and a far greater capacity for effective contestation.

Conclusion

As is well known, Kant held a particularly clear view of the relationship between politics and morality. He is absolutely clear that morality should trump politics.

And although politics in itself is a difficult art, no art is required to combine it with morality. For as soon as the two come into conflict, morality can cut through the knot that politics cannot untie. The rights of man must be held sacred, however great a sacrifice the ruling power may have to make. There can be no half-measures here; it is no use devising hybrid solutions such as a pragmatically conditioned right halfway between right and utility. For all politics must bend the knee before right.[50]

This view of the priority of an abstracted, idealized morality has had an immense influence over contemporary political theory, and certainly over the many Kantian-inspired theorists who have become ever more concerned with questions of international relations, global justice, and war and intervention. It has, for example, contributed directly to the increased moralization of war, as with the view that the laws of war as developed by successive generations of "sorry comforters" need to be re-thought and that it is morally unacceptable for combatants fighting a justified war to have the same rights as those fighting on the unjustified and unjustifiable side.[51] The very abstraction of Kant's position has even been attractive to those critical thinkers who are deeply skeptical about any neo-Kantian grounding of moral claims but who nonetheless see Kant as a "placeholder for the languages of goodness, and justice, solidarity and responsibility" as against the rampant instrumentalism and managerialism of contemporary international law.[52]

It is, however, simply mistaken to suggest that "no art is required" to combine politics with morality. Nor is it correct to suggest that morality (or law) can ever be a substitute for politics and for political judgment.

---

[50] PP, p. 125.

[51] See, for example, J. McMahan, *Killing in War* (Oxford University Press, 2011).

[52] M. Koskenniemi, "Miserable Comforters: International Relations as New Natural Law," *European Journal of International Relations* 15 (2009), p. 415.

Indeed it is the perennial and perennially messy dilemmas and difficulties of intervention that have, time and again, brought to the fore a very different view of political morality. On this account, political morality should accept that there will be a recurring (but not absolute) need to give priority to order over justice; that the appropriate standards of evaluation will arise from within the political world itself rather than coming from an external legal or moral standpoint; and that politics is all too often characterized by ineliminable conflict rather than reasoned consensus. It is a view that doubts whether the maxims of law and morality can ever wholly displace the centrality of political decisions and political judgment. It is no coincidence that the sense of liberalism finding itself in far harder times at the global level is fostering a revival of this tradition of thinking.[53] Kant is clearly right to underscore the extent to which intervention brings with it many dangers in terms of power corrupting moral purpose. Military force is problematic for Kant because it does involve many choices that are deontologically unacceptable. But it should hardly come as a surprise that those who have wrestled with the dilemmas of intervention have found severe limits in the Kantian view that all politics must bend the knee before right.

The importance of Kant's writings on intervention stems from their unresolved tensions. There can be little doubt that the restrictionist, cautious position concerning intervention that I laid out in the first section faces many difficulties. But so, too, do the attempts to shift Kant in either of the directions that I sketched in the following two sections – either towards a transnational cosmopolitan constitutionalism or towards a greater emphasis on the progressive potential of a homogenous grouping of liberal states. Kant's achievement in the history of thought about international relations rests on his attempt to come to terms with both the deep-rootedness and benefits of statism on the one hand and the increasing moral and practical demands of cosmopolitanism on the other; from his recognition that the conventional separation of domestic political and moral theory from what happens "beyond the state" is both practically and logically untenable; and from his awareness that change and progress should not be viewed as a

---

[53] This form of "middle ground ethics" has long characterized English School writing – and underpinned many pluralist critiques of Kant. See, for example, M. Cochran, "Charting the Ethics of the English School: What 'Good' is there in a Middle-Ground Ethics?," *International Studies Quarterly*, 53 (2009), 203–25; and A. Hurrell, *On Global Order* (Oxford University Press, 2007), ch. 1. On the recent emergence of so-called new political realism in political theory see, for example, W. Galston, "Realism in Political Theory," *European Journal of Political Theory* 9, no. 4 (2010), 385–411.

stark choice between the continuation of the state of war in which the logic of the security dilemma is endlessly reproduced on the one hand and the complete transcendence of the state system and its replacement by some form of universal political organization on the other. It is precisely these unresolved tensions that speak directly to the complex, hybrid and mixed character of the contemporary global order – one in which a re-emerging Great Power political order coexists with increasingly embedded normative commitments and increasingly dense and complex governance beyond the state.

10 Edmund Burke and intervention: empire and neighborhood

Jennifer M. Welsh

Introduction

For some scholars, any analysis of Edmund Burke as a "theorist" of intervention – or indeed of international relations – risks distorting and magnifying aspects of his thought through a contemporary and contrived lens. I suggest here, however, that Burke's views on international affairs should not be seen as an incidental by-product of his participation as a politician in the events of his day; rather, they occupy a central place in his writings and speeches. In fact, as C. B. Macpherson has noted, "no one was more aware than Burke that national policies needed to be framed in light of the international situation."[1] Moreover, four of the most important issues that Burke addressed in his political career were largely international ones (even if they were not explicitly framed this way): trade policy vis-à-vis Ireland; the treatment of the American colonies; British imperial activity in India; and the impact of the French Revolution.

This chapter concentrates on Burke's writings and speeches with respect to two topics that remain of great interest to scholars and policymakers: empire and intervention. In particular, it examines his views on the conditions under which the shield of sovereignty can be pierced – with military force, if necessary. In the context of commenting on Ireland, America, India, and the French Revolution, Burke sets out a conception of international society that strives for diversity within unity – or what Jennifer Pitts calls "peculiar universalism"[2] – and that subjects sovereign states to (at best) scrutiny and (at worst) intervention from others. Just as Burke viewed absolute and unrestrained freedom as the "greatest of all possible evils" and a threat to social order,[3] so he refused

---

[1] C. B. Macpherson, *Burke* (Oxford University Press, 1980), p. 73.

[2] J. Pitts, *A Turn to Empire: The Rise of Imperial Liberalism in Britain and France* (Princeton University Press, 2005), ch. 3.

[3] *Reflections on the Revolution in France*, in P. Langford (ed.), *The Writings and Speeches of Edmund Burke* (Oxford University Press, 1981), VIII, p. 291. Henceforth, WS.

to assume the absolute autonomy of states, and the accompanying principle of nonintervention, in international society.

As I argue below, Burke viewed European states not as isolated enclaves, but as partners in a larger interdependent society called the Commonwealth of Europe, where "local" as opposed to international law applied. Similarly, he bundled Britain, America, and Ireland into a common imperial society underpinned by a common political and cultural core, but characterized by respect for local traditions and an aversion to heavy-handed central control. India – while outside the innermost circle of Burke's community and therefore not subject to the full suite of laws that underpinned European international society – was nonetheless to be approached with respect and informed by a morality that knew no geographical boundaries.

Prudence and tradition

It is helpful to begin by elaborating on Burke's broader approach to politics – one that champions both prudence and tradition. A consistent theme in his writings and speeches is a rejection of the application of abstract principles to political life, whether domestic or international, given the tendency of such principles to give rise to radical and destructive ideologies. Recognizing that humanity is imperfect, Burke advises states-men to accept solutions based on "compromise and barter,"[4] rather than to push for a perfect realization of the ideal. For him, prudence is the "first of Virtues" and the standard against which all others should be judged.[5]

Burke's advocacy of prudence, however, should not be confused with a preference for expediency. Moral goals and principles retain a prominent place in his thinking. In Burke's formulation, prudence is the quality that allows statesmen to bridge the worlds of morality and politics, and to reconcile notions of "right" with concrete and variable circumstances.[6] In other words, he is committed to a *moral* prudence, which requires a tolerance for ambiguity and a search for balance. The best kind of states-man, he writes, is one "who has the greatest number and variety of considerations in one view before him, and can take them in with the best possible consideration of the middle results of all."[7] Burke's championing

---

[4] "Speech on Conciliation with America," in *The Works of the Right Honourable Edmund Burke* (London: Henry G. Bohn, 1854–89), I, p. 200. Henceforth *Works*.

[5] *The Correspondence of the Right Honourable Edmund Burke* (ed. T. Copeland et al.) (Cambridge University Press, 1958–78), VI, p. 48. Henceforth *Corr.*

[6] For a further discussion of prudence in Burke and other classical thinkers, see A. R. Coll, "Prudence and Foreign Policy," in M. Cromartie (ed.), *Might and Right After the Cold War: Can Foreign Policy Be Moral?* (Washington, DC: Ethics and Public Policy Center, 1993), pp. 3–28.

[7] Cited in C. P. Courtney, *Montesquieu and Burke* (Oxford: Basil Blackwell, 1963), p. 156.

of balance, which is consistent with many conservatives' aesthetic preference for "harmonious proportion,"[8] is clearly reflected in his continual
support for the mixed British Constitution. Its careful balancing of monarchical, aristocratic, and popular principles of government, he writes,
"is like our Island, which uses and restrains its subject Sea; in vain the
waves roar. In that Constitution I know ... both that I am free, and that
I am not free dangerously to myself or to others."[9]

In this quest for balance, or the *via media*, Burke leans heavily
upon history and tradition. It is this facet of his thinking that inspired
subsequent scholars and politicians to describe and categorize Burke as a
"conservative," even though he remained a member of the Whig Party
for much of his time as Member of Parliament (until he broke ranks with
Charles Fox over the French Revolution in 1791). Burke idealizes the
British Constitution as a testament to the "wisdom of the ages,"[10] and
therefore not to be tinkered with carelessly. Much of his parliamentary
career was dominated by efforts to prevent any one of the three aspects of
government (the king, the aristocracy, and the people) from disrupting
the delicate constitutional balance that his forefathers had created, and
by warnings against the Enlightenment faith in the application of reason
to advance the human condition. Just as title to property comes from
long use rather than a formal deed, so government is bound by longstanding practices rather than abstract principles. As he famously wrote
in his *Reflections on the Revolution in France*:

We know that *we* have made no discoveries; and we think That no discoveries are
to be made, in morality; nor many in the great principles of government, nor in
the ideas of liberty, which were understood long before we were born, altogether
as well as they will be after the grave has heaped its mould upon our
presumption.[11]

For the sake of balance and stability, Burke believes current
arrangements – whether within Britain or its larger empire – should be
venerated and accepted as legitimate.

Empire

Another key component of Burke's approach to international affairs and
intervention is his particular understanding and assessment of Britain's
imperial policy. Many prominent European political thinkers in the late

---

[8] M. Auerbach, *The Conservative Illusion* (New York: Columbia University Press, 1959).
   For Burke's writings on aesthetics, see "A Philosophical Enquiry into the Origins of Our
   Ideas of the Sublime and the Beautiful," in *Works*, I, pp. 22–74.
[9] *Works*, X, p. 104.   [10] *Reflections*, WS, VIII, p. 83.   [11] *Reflections*, WS, VIII, p. 137.

eighteenth century – including Diderot, Herder, and Kant – launched an attack on imperialism and challenged the right of European powers to colonize or civilize the rest of the world. As Sankar Muthu has demonstrated, this Enlightenment anti-imperialism was underpinned by three philosophical positions: that all human beings are inherently moral and worthy of respect; that humanity is constitutively cultural and embedded in a social context; and that "whole peoples" cannot be compared and judged using a common cultural standard. But these Enlightenment figures also put forth a set of political arguments against imperialism that emphasized the inherent cruelty and brutality of imperial rule and the potential for the practice of imperialism to corrupt and bankrupt the imperialists.[12]

While Burke relied on some of the same philosophical foundations and shared the concern for the corrupting potential of imperialism, he engaged in a more muted attack on European imperial rule. As with his view on the origins of British government, he drew a "sacred veil" over the beginnings of the British Empire and focused more on the prudent exercise of power within it. Rather than challenging the legitimacy of empire itself, as Diderot, Kant, and Herder had done, Burke was more of a critical advocate,[13] questioning "the spirit of domination, oppression, and exclusion that often characterized British imperial conduct."[14] In short, the problem was with the behavior of a few, rather than with the fundamental structure of imperialism. His goal was to make the management of Britain's empire compatible with the norms of natural law, the culture and spirit of colonial peoples, and the principles of the mixed British Constitution.

It was the latter concern that motivated much of Burke's critique of the British East India Company and Warren Hastings, the Governor of Bengal. The latter's propagation of corruption, Burke believed, constituted a challenge to both international and domestic justice. He feared that ocean expanses would not defend British institutions from the contagious effects of arbitrary power being exerted by Hastings in Bengal. "If we are not able to contrive some method of governing India *well*, which will not of necessity become the means of governing Great Britain *ill*," he warned, "a ground is laid for their eternal separation."[15]

By asserting that a different kind of morality operated in India, Hastings was suggesting that the servants of the British Empire could ignore the precepts of moderation that had been enshrined in the

---

[12] S. Muthu, *Enlightenment Against Empire* (Princeton University Press, 2003).
[13] I am grateful to one of the anonymous reviewers for suggesting this term.
[14] Pitts, *A Turn to Empire*, p. 60.   [15] "Speech on Fox's India Bill," WS, V, p. 383.

British Constitution. Moreover, as Burke told his fellow parliamentarians, Hastings was denying the existence of both the law of nations and law of nature, "fundamental axioms on which every form of society was built."[16] Even though Burke had no intention of giving the peoples of India an interest in the British Constitution, he insisted that the *practice* of imperialism had to be based on sound principles, rather than coercion. The first step, he argued on the first day of the Hastings impeachment trial, was to "enlarge the circle of justice to the necessities of the Empire we have obtained."[17] Only in this way would the confluence of British and Indian cultures preserve the traditions and values of the weaker party and improve the material wealth of *both*. In sum, Britain's imperial conduct had to reflect the highest standards of the metropolis, respect the periphery as an equal member of common humanity, and contribute to the periphery's improvement. "It was our duty," he wrote, "in order to make some sort of compensation for the mischiefs inseparable from a foreign and commercial superiority, to keep a balance of justice and proportion in the several powers that were subordinate to us."[18]

In the case of India, Burke was dealing with a part of the Empire that was culturally and religiously distinct, and comprised of vulnerable and "stateless" people.[19] While the Indians possessed an established religion, property conventions, and an ancient legal system – all of which Burke viewed worthy of respect and veneration – these institutions did not share the same English "roots" as those in America and Ireland. Thus, with respect to India, relations between the metropolis and periphery had to be regulated less by positive law and more by the loose but "immutable" ties of common justice. The Irish and American colonies, which were populated by Englishmen, had a different status in imperial society and were extended the benefits of the British Constitution. In his *Speech on Conciliation with America*, he reminds his colleagues in Parliament that Americans are devoted not merely to liberty, "but to a Liberty according to English ideas, and on English principles."[20] To deny their freedom through heavy-handed taxation – or even the use of force – would be to deny English freedom as well.

---

[16] "Speech on Rohilla War Charge," WS, VI, p. 109.
[17] "Speech on Opening of Impeachment," WS, VI, p. 279.
[18] "Policy of Making Conquests for the Mahometans," WS, V, pp. 113–14.
[19] Pitts, *A Turn to Empire*, p. 61.
[20] "Speech on Conciliation with America," in D. P. Fidler and J. M. Welsh (eds.), *Empire and Community: Edmund Burke's Writings and Speeches on International Relations* (Boulder, CO: Westview Press, 1999), p. 124.

It was perhaps because of these closer connections that Burke was even more concerned about the exercise of arbitrary power vis-à-vis Ireland and America. While he acknowledged the theoretical assumption that Britain had "boundless" powers within imperial society, he rejected any attempt to implement that premise in practice. As a result, whenever British imperial policy demanded submission rather than fostered community, Burke was sympathetic toward the grievances of the colonists. More broadly, as Pitts has argued, Burke was concerned that Britain's self-image would become too exclusive and insular if it could not accommodate "marginal" populations such as Irish Catholics, or could not subject its imperial practices to the rule of law. A British nationality that could incorporate Irish Catholics (by granting them religious freedom and extending political rights) "would be a transformed Britishness."[21]

Burke's position on Irish policy was nestled in a larger framework of imperial policy: toleration of the colony's traditions and culture (through opposition to the anti-Catholic laws); recognition of empire as a unity of purpose and interest, rather than religious homogeneity; the importance of maintaining imperial free trade; and the effect of imperial activity on the British Constitution and British liberties. It was this last theme that dominated Burke's writings and speeches on America. Through war and imperial expansion in the New World, English politicians had strayed from one of the foundational principles of the British constitution: no taxation without representation. Though Burke conceded that the British Parliament had an "imperial character," superintending and guiding the legislatures of the colonies, it was "never to intrude into the place of the others, while they are equal to the common ends of their institution."[22]

Once the rumblings of revolution began to be heard in the American colonies, Burke's line of argument shifted and intensified. Only concessions to America, he argued, could restore the confidence of the periphery in the metropolis. Moreover, he stood firmly against the use of force as a means for keeping the empire intact, asserting that the effects of coercion were fleeting, uncertain, and counterproductive. A "nation is not governed," he famously wrote, "which is perpetually to be conquered."[23] To reinforce the folly of resorting to force as an instrument of rule, he provided an analysis of the "temper and character" of the Americans, who had developed a "fierce spirit of Liberty." [24] Burke sensed the power of this spirit – which he maintained was also the defining feature of

---

[21] Pitts, *A Turn to Empire*, p. 86.   [22] "Speech on American Taxation," WS, II, 460.
[23] "Speech on Conciliation with America," in Fidler and Welsh (eds.), *Writings and Speeches*, p. 123.
[24] *Ibid.*, p. 124.

Englishmen – and warned against desperate and coercive efforts to break it. In the end, while he viewed the British Empire as a historical fact, to be preserved and managed justly, it could not be kept unaltered at all costs. A change in the imperial relationship was a "necessary Evil."[25] Britain would gain more "from the affection of America, though under a separate establishment," he reasoned, "than from her perfect submission to the Crown and Parliament, accompanied by her terror, disgust, and abhorrence."[26]

Intervention

Burke's reluctance to use force arbitrarily in the context of imperial society should not be read as a blanket rejection of war as a tool of statecraft. "Wars, however it may be lamented," he wrote, "are inevitable in every state of human nature; they may be deferred, but they cannot be wholly avoided."[27] But while he admits to the reality of war in resolving fundamental conflicts among nation-states, he maintains that its causes and effects should be tempered through legal and moral regulation:

As to war, if it be the means of wrong and violence, it is the sole means of justice amongst nations. Nothing can banish it from the world ... But it is one of the greatest objects of human wisdom to mitigate those evils which we are unable to remove.[28]

In *A Vindication of Natural Society* (1756), Burke satirically renounces the Realist account of the state of war offered by thinkers such as Rousseau and Bolingbroke,[29] and calls for an alternative to the seemingly inevitable logic of *raison d'état*. For Burke, this alternative is the law of nations, that "great ligament of mankind,"[30] which set forth certain limited and defined rights of war "recognized by civilized states, and practiced in enlightened Europe."[31] Following other philosophers and jurists of his day, he distinguished between just and unjust wars, and acknowledged the constraints imposed by *jus in bello*. Consequently, during the conflict between Britain and Holland over the island of St. Eustatius in 1781,

---

[25] *Ibid.*, p. 132.
[26] "Letter to the Sheriffs of Bristol," in Fidler and Welsh (eds.), *Writings and Speeches*, p. 165.
[27] *Annual Register*, 15 (1772), p. 3.
[28] "First Letter on a Regicide Peace," WS, IX, p. 248.
[29] "A Vindication of Natural Society," *Works*, I, pp. 3–21. For Rousseau's depiction of the state of war, see S. Hoffmann and D. Fidler (eds.), *Rousseau and International Relations* (Oxford University Press, 1991), p. 44.
[30] "First Letter on a Regicide Peace," WS, IX, p. 240.
[31] *The Parliamentary History of England* (ed. W. Cobbett), Vol. XXII, pp. 228–9. Henceforth *PH*.

Burke condemned Britain's violation of neutrality and confiscation of property as "contrary to the law of nations."[32] He also invoked *jus in bello* principles in Britain's war with America, warning against the use of mercenaries and calling on his government to use a proportionate level of force.[33]

As suggested in the passage above, Burke's law of nations did not apply universally, but only to those countries which actively participated in Europe's common civilization. Following thinkers such as Grotius, he acknowledged an outer circle of mankind governed by broad principles of natural law (which, as noted earlier, encompassed India), and an inner circle of European international society governed by the law of nations – or what he sometimes referred to as the "public law of Europe."[34] Those territories that stood outside the core of European civilization, such as the Ottoman Empire, could not benefit from the rights and privileges of those within, as Burke's reaction to the Ochakov Crisis of 1791 revealed. In this case, Burke employed civilizational categories to argue against Prime Minister William Pitt's plan to assist the Turks in their military campaign against the Russians:

He had never before heard it held forth, that the Turkish empire was ever considered as any part of the balance of power in Europe ... They despised and condemned all Christian princes, as infidels, and only wished to subdue and exterminate them and their people ... I am not for favouring such barbarians and oppressing Christians, to the detriment of civilization and hindrance of human refinement.[35]

For Burke, though the Ottoman Empire was part of the European diplomatic *system*, and could be used by states as part of their alliances, it was definitely outside the realm of European international *society* and the law of nations.

As we see in his later crusade against the French Revolution, Burke was also prepared to stretch the maxims of the law of nations, articulated in the works of eminent international lawyers such as Emerich de Vattel, to justify action against "barbarians" within Europe. In contrast to Pitt's government, which maintained a neutral and noninterventionist posture toward events transpiring in France, Burke interpreted the

---

[32] *Ibid.*, p. 228.
[33] "Letter to the Sheriffs of Bristol," in Fidler and Welsh, *Writings and Speeches*, pp. 153–4, 157. Burke was particularly critical of the British tactic of using Germans and native Indians as mercenaries.
[34] For more discussion of these circles of civilization, see M. Wight, "Theory of Mankind," in G. Wight and B. Porter (eds.) *International Theory: The Three Traditions* (Leicester University Press, 1991), p. 73.
[35] *PH*, Vol. XXIX, pp. 76–8.

revolution as a profound threat to the foundations of order in Europe through its challenge to religion, property, and dynastic legitimacy.[36] It was the very essence of revolutionary regime – with its radically egalitarian and anti-dynastic beliefs – rather than its capacity to wage traditional war against its neighbors, which for Burke constituted the most significant challenge to the security of European states. In his view, sovereign frontiers could offer no protection against the "armed doctrine" of the Jacobins, which could reach the minds and hearts of human beings wherever they resided.[37] In response, Burke advocated extraordinary means – Holy War – to counteract the plague that had befallen Europe. The traditional language of diplomacy and the "mode of civilized War"[38] regrettably had to be suspended to counteract the unique threat posed by the French Revolutionaries. "This evil in the heart of Europe must be extirpated from that center," he warns, "or no part of the circumference can be free from the mischief which radiates from it."[39]

The Commonwealth of Europe

One way of understanding the seeming paradox between Burke's critique of Bolingbroke and his support for Holy War against revolutionary France is to more closely examine his concept of the Commonwealth of Europe. Following his contemporary Vattel, Burke observes the existence of a European international society, sustained by institutions such as the balance of power and regulated by international law. The Vattelian vision, inspired by Grotius, set up a rough analogy between individuals and states – the latter having the same rights of noninterference. In Vattel's words: "Une Nation est donc maîtresse de ses actions . . . tant qu'elles n'est liée que d'une obligation *interne*. Si elle abuse de sa liberté, elle pèche; mais les autres doivent le souffrir, n'aïant aucun droit de lui commander."[40]

For Burke, however, the strict analogy between the equality and autonomy of individuals and the equality and autonomy of states is

---

[36] For a discussion of how Burke's concern for European stability and liberty arose prior to the French Revolution, in relation to the 1772 partition of Poland and revolution in Sweden, see B. Simms, "'A False principle in the Law of Nations'. State sovereignty, [German] liberty, and intervention in the Age of Westphalia and Burke," in B. Simms and D. Trim (eds.), *Humanitarian Intervention*.

[37] "First Letter on a Regicide Peace," WS, IX, p. 199.

[38] "Letter to a Member of the National Assembly," WS, VIII, p. 320.

[39] "Heads for Consideration on the Present State of Affairs," WS, VIII, p. 402.

[40] E. de Vattel, *Le Droit des Gens* (Washington, DC: Carnegie Institute, 1916 [1758]), Book I, 11. "A nation is therefore mistress of her actions . . . so that she is bound only by an internal obligation. If she abuses her liberty, she sins, but others must put up with it, having no right to tell her what to do."

tempered by the "real" foundations of eighteenth-century European international society. While this society is composed of states, and therefore characterized by autonomy and decentralization, Burke believes their diverse interests are ultimately reconciled through an underlying sense of community and commitment to upholding order. In John Vincent's words: "The system worked within a society; pluralism worked because of a deeper solidarity."[41] Hence, though he acknowledges the importance of "national character," and is committed to the advancement of British national interests, he is also dedicated to preserving the longstanding traditions of Christian-European civilization.

In his *Letters on a Regicide Peace*, written near the end of his life, Burke describes Europe as "virtually one great state," marked by "some diversity of provincial customs and local establishments."[42] In particular, he accentuates the "similitude" throughout Europe of the Christian religion, Roman law heritage, Gothic custom, and the monarchical principle of government. He also highlights the role of free trade and economic interdependence in binding the members of the European Commonwealth into a common enterprise. But the strongest glue holding the Commonwealth together is common culture. Montesquieu, whom Burke greatly admired, had placed great weight on the more intangible "mores" or "manners" at work in societies. Burke follows in his footsteps, claiming that the "antient [*sic*] system of opinion and sentiment" at work in the Commonwealth of Europe is what accounts for Europe's preponderance and distinguishes it from other civilizations.[43] Such manners, which grew out of the feudal traditions of nobility and chivalry, "softened, blended, and harmonized the colours of the whole," and provided a deeper foundation for all other laws and institutions. Pivotal in perpetuating this common set of manners is the similar structure of education that exists for all Europeans. As a result of this common experience, "no citizen of Europe could be altogether an exile in any part of it ... When a man travelled or resided for health, pleasure, business or necessity, from his country, he never felt himself quite abroad."[44]

---

[41] R. J. Vincent, "Edmund Burke and the theory of international relations," *Review of International Studies*, 10 (1984), p. 211.

[42] "First Letter on a Regicide Peace," WS, IX, p. 248.

[43] *Ibid.*, pp. 242–3. As noted in the above discussion of the law of nations, an integral part of the definition of the Commonwealth of Europe is Burke's attempt to distinguish it from the non-European societies in Asia, the New World, and the Ottoman Empire. For a further elaboration of this use of the external "Other" in defining Europe's identity, see I. B. Neumann and J. M. Welsh, "'The Other' in European self-definition: An addendum to the literature on international society," *Review of International Studies*, 17 (1990), pp. 327–48.

[44] "First Letter on a Regicide Peace," WS, IX, pp. 242–3.

To summarize, though there is no formal treaty or compact uniting the members of the Commonwealth of Europe, there is a deep affection arising from their historical experience of coexistence. This emphasis on habit and sentiment is crucial to understanding Burke's approach to international order and his hostile reaction to the French Revolution. Although Burke permits some diversity within the Commonwealth of Europe, he cannot tolerate heterogeneity in the fundamental principles that underlie European international society. In other words, he holds the preservation of a common culture to be a prerequisite, and not merely an enabler, of international stability.

For Burke, this homogeneity has a crucial reinforcing effect on the maintenance of order among and within the members of international society.[45] The political and social orders of European states are integrally linked and rely on each other for survival: "I consider the conservation in England of the antient [sic] order of things, as necessary to preserve order every where [sic] else, and ... the general conservation of order in other countries, as reciprocally necessary to preserve the same state of things in those Islands."[46] Thus, Burke goes beyond the concern of many counter-revolutionaries in fearing the destabilizing effect of transnational revolutionary ideologies; he also engages in a reverse kind of logic, by emphasizing the connection between international and domestic legitimacy. For him, there is an important interrelationship between a homogeneous and stable international society and the preservation of a domestic status quo. This substantive view of international legitimacy had resonance well beyond Burke's lifetime – most notably in the efforts of Metternich to resurrect a conservative international order at the Congress of Vienna.

Justifying intervention and counter-revolution

The implications of Burke's understanding of the Commonwealth of Europe lead directly to support for interventionism. In the face of a challenge to the status quo in any part of the Commonwealth, his strong commitment to preserving homogeneity – and by extension – the mixed British Constitution – quickly overrode the rules and procedures for mutual recognition that were espoused by international lawyers such as Vattel.

Seen in this way, Burke's emphasis on preserving the homogeneity of Europe's political orders was not purely instrumental to his anti-revolutionary campaign; it was a foundational aspect of his thinking on

---

[45] For a further discussion of this aspect of Burke's theory, see J. M. Welsh, *Edmund Burke and International Relations* (Basingstoke: Macmillan, 1995).
[46] "Third Letter on a Regicide Peace," WS, IX, p. 327.

international affairs. Nonetheless, while Burke came early to the view
that military action against Jacobinism was the only option to safeguard
the stability of Europe and security of Britain, there was initially very little
appetite within the British political class to intervene in the domestic
affairs of France. Indeed, the immediate post-Revolutionary period saw a
weakened France rather than a menacing or expansionist power, making
it more difficult to make the case for immediate action.[47] As a result, Burke
had to tread very carefully when arguing his position, and took pains to
invoke a legal foundation – an authoritative medium for eighteenth-century
political and literary argument[48] – for his policy recommendations.

In his writings and speeches, we see Burke invoking three different
arguments to justify intervention in the affairs of the French state: 1) the
right of intervention in a civil war context, where outside powers are free
to support either the "challenger" or the established government which is
under siege; 2) the pretext of preventive war, derived from his understanding of the balance of power; and 3) the Roman law principles of
vicinity and neighborhood, which give those in close proximity a right to
intervene when unwanted developments are occurring on a neighbor's
"property." As Iain Hampsher-Monk has shown, Burke emphasized the
first line of argument earlier on in the revolutionary period, when the
public debate revolved around the legal question of when and how third-
party states could legitimately intervene in the affairs of another. Given
his position as a Member of Parliament, it is not surprising that he
attempted to reconcile his ideas with the arguments of others, so as to
build a stronger coalition in favor of action. By the mid-to-late 1790s,
however, Burke's concerns about the potency of Jacobinism led him to
abandon the carefully articulated assumptions of the international legal
experts, and to project his own vision of a "European juridical community
within which intervention was a domestic, not an international, act."[49]

Burke's first and more mainstream argument relied on the right given
to outside powers to intervene in a divided nation. "In this state of
things ... by the law of nations, Great Britain, like every other power, is
free to take on any part she pleases."[50] Although Vattel explicitly articulated a right of intervention in civil war,[51] he insisted that outsiders could
only support the "just" side (which most often consisted of those who
were rebelling against an oppressive government). Burke is therefore

[47] I. Hampsher-Monk, "Edmund Burke's Changing Justification for Intervention," *The Historical Journal*, 48, no. 1 (2005), pp. 65–100.
[48] See C. Reid, *Edmund Burke and the Practice of Political Writing* (Dublin: Gill and Macmillan, 1985).
[49] Hampsher-Monk, "Burke's Changing Justification," p. 66.
[50] Burke, *Thoughts on French Affairs*, WS, VIII, p. 340.
[51] Vattel, *Le Droit des Gens*, Book II, 4, pp. 2–4.

engaged in an expansive interpretation of the law by insisting that neighboring governments can support any side they choose. Furthermore, Vattel's right of intervention was highly circumscribed: it depended upon armed conflict having broken out between the opposing forces. Thus, while Burke was shrewd in using Vattel as his legal authority for a right of intervention, he was less convincing in establishing that the conditions which triggered that right – i.e., a "divided kingdom" – actually obtained in Revolutionary France. As evidence, he contrasted the Official Royal Proclamation accepting the constitution of 1791 with the king's later declaration denouncing both the Revolution and constitution. He also pointed to the string of notable personalities that had fled France and to the half-hearted participation in National Assembly elections.[52] In the end, however, this reasoning was not sufficiently compelling to move members of Pitt's government to abandon their stance of neutrality.

Second, Burke's early promotion of intervention can be read as a creative extrapolation of the principles of the balance of power. In fact, many eighteenth-century thinkers and statesmen considered intervention to be one means of maintaining the balance, despite recognition of the merits of noninterference.[53] This hierarchical relationship between the requirement of the balance of power and the principle of nonintervention reflected the conviction that equilibrium among European states was a product of conscious and deliberate policymaking, not something spontaneously generated. In this vein, Burke insisted that maintenance of the balance demanded the "unremitting attention" of statesmen to disturbing developments in any part of Europe.[54] What was notable about his position, however, was that it was focused on bringing about domestic political change in a state, rather than militarily defeating that state and destroying its coercive capabilities.

In fact, Burke went a step further to suggest that balance of power politics might require intervention in the face of the threat of imminent attack as well as *de facto* aggression. In his mind, the Jacobin menace is not primarily military, but ideological – based on subversive and contagious principles. He therefore extends Vattel's legal analysis of the balance of power and intervention to encompass political as well as

---

[52] Burke, "Thoughts on French Affairs," WS, VIII, pp. 338–40. See also Hampsher-Monk, "Burke's Changing Justification," pp. 73–4.

[53] See M. S. Anderson, "Eighteenth Century Theories of the Balance of Power," in R. Hatton and M.S. Anderson (eds.), *Studies of Diplomatic History: Essays in Memory of David Bayne Horn* (London: Longman, 1970), pp. 183–98.

[54] *Annual Register* (1772), p. 1. As Simms notes, the connection between the defense of liberty in Europe and the maintenance of the balance of power in Europe was established in Burke's mind well before the French Revolution. See Simms, "'A false principle in the Law of Nations'."

military threats, and argues that international law can accommodate pre-emptive action in cases of "hostile intention."[55] For Burke, the "pernicious maxims" of the French Revolutionaries are as threatening as the "formidable forces" of a mobilized army.[56] Revolutionary France, "by the very condition of its existence," was already "in a state of hostility with us, and with all civilized people."[57]

Ultimately, as Hampsher-Monk observes, Vattel's writings could not deliver the rationale for the kind of counter-revolutionary campaign that Burke wanted.[58] Perhaps the biggest limitation was Vattel's premise of an irrevocably divided union, where outside powers were obliged to back the "just" side – a view that sat uneasily alongside Burke's desire to restore to France not just a monarchical system of government, but also the position of the émigré nobility and other supporting "corporate orders." This preference was consistent with Burke's more general view of the state as a corporate totality, which could not be disaggregated or identified with only one of its component parts.[59] By 1793, and the publication of his *Remarks on the Policy of the Allies*, Burke was countering the view that the "real" France was divided; rather, it was a house where criminals (read Jacobins) had temporarily taken over. "The truth is, France is out of itself – The moral France is separated from the geographical. The master of the house is expelled, and the robbers are in possession."[60] What he needed now was an argument that could justify intervention to restore the original owners, and France's pre-existing unity.

As the impact of the Revolution became more sinister and more unsettling for those in France's neighborhood, Burke felt less compelled to cloak his recommendations in the mantle of established international law, and more comfortable drawing on his own understanding of the "glue" which held European international society together. To develop further his argument that the French Revolution constituted an imminent threat to that society, Burke turned to the Roman law notions of vicinity and neighborhood – precepts of *private law* – and invoked them as justification for a counter-revolutionary crusade against Jacobinism.

---

[55] Vattel had stipulated that if there was a nation "of a restless and mischievous disposition, always ready to injure others" then others had "a right to join in order to repress, chastise, and put it ever out of its power to injure them." See *Le Droit des Gens*, Book I, p. 296. However, as Hampsher-Monk argues, it is too far a stretch to argue that Vattel was endorsing intervention to bring about a change of government. See also Ch. 2 by A. Colonomos in this volume, esp. pp. 62–4.

[56] Appendix to *Three Memorials on French Affairs Written in the Years 1791, 1792 and 1793* (London, 1797). This Appendix consists of Burke's annotations on Vattel's *Le Droit des Gens*.

[57] "First Letter on a Regicide Peace," WS, IX, p. 239.

[58] Hampsher-Monk, "Burke's Changing Justification," p. 77.   [59] *Ibid.*, pp. 82–3.

[60] See "Remarks on the Policy of the Allies," WS, VIII, p. 465.

The law of vicinity, as Burke understands it, is essentially the circumstance of connectedness: proximity and habitual intercourse automatically generate certain rights and responsibilities. He frequently highlights this phenomenon of vicinage for the members of his European commonwealth, who were joined together by factors of geography, politics, religion, and above all common manners. The partner of the law of vicinity is the law of neighborhood: the right of a neighbor to protest when he "sees a new erection, in the nature of a nuisance, set up at his door." Burke then goes on to apply this precept of private law to relations among the members of the Commonwealth of Europe, thereby trumping the claim to autonomy and nonintervention in traditional international law:

Now where there is no constituted judge, as between independent states there is not, the vicinage itself is the natural judge. It is, preventively, the assertor of its own rights: or remedially, their avenger ... This principle, which, like the rest, is as true of nations, as of individual men, has bestowed on the grand vicinage of Europe, a duty to know, and a right to prevent, any capital innovation which may amount to the reaction of a dangerous nuisance ... What in civil society is a ground of action, in politick society is a ground of war.[61]

For Burke, the "nuisance" created by the contagious principles of the French Revolution activates this right for all of France's neighbors. "The Stench of such an enormous Carcass as that of France," he declares, "is enough to poison all Europe."[62] This use of the metaphor of a neighborhood illustrates powerfully the degree to which Burke believed the Revolution had instigated a *European* civil war.

Conclusion

In sum, Burke conceived the problem of international order as involving both external and internal dimensions. He did not posit state sovereignty as an absolute or guiding value, but rather adhered to a weak and qualified idea of sovereignty, which balanced the needs of European international society as a whole against the absolute liberty of its members. As a consequence, he was prepared to override the legal doctrine of nonintervention if the more fundamental components of European order were threatened. Indeed, such doctrines – designed for inter-state relations – had less power in the context of what he saw as a civil war raging in the heart of Europe.

As a result of this perspective, Burke has been depicted by some as representative of what English School scholars call a "solidarist," as

---

[61] "First Letter on a Regicide Peace," WS, IX, p. 251.   [62] *Corr.*, VI, p. 459.

opposed to "pluralist," approach to international relations.[63] Pluralism emphasizes how states with different values and conceptions of domestic legitimacy can agree on procedural rules and institutions in order to overcome clashes of interest and engage in cooperation. Solidarism, by contrast, focuses on what lies beneath that procedural consensus – the shared political, economic, social, and cultural heritage among *peoples* – and the potential for states to act on behalf of peoples beyond their own borders. Without this deeper or more substantive consensus, solidarists argue, the efficacy of the traditional instruments of international relations (such as diplomatic conventions or treaties) will rest only on a temporary convergence of interests – a less robust basis for international order.

Burke's emphasis on solidarity and common culture has significant implications for setting the boundaries of international society. To put it another way, what does one do with the "other," which stands outside the reigning consensus? As I have argued, Burke confronted this problem in his efforts both to reform British imperial policy in India and to respond to the revolutionary challenge in France. He did not refer to the standards of the Commonwealth of Europe to condemn the practices of the East India Company. In fact, Burke regarded India as outside the area where the law of nations applied, given that his conception of positive international law was "Europe bound." But at the same time, he did not revert to the purely realist view that relations with the non-European world were to be governed by "might and no right." His critique of Hastings drew upon morality and notions of universal justice – thereby placing him, ironically, closer to the anti-imperialist thinkers of the Enlightenment. In the case of the French Revolution, the "other" was a temporary deviation: criminals had taken hold of historic France. Burke maintained that it was the responsibility, and not merely the right, of adjacent European states to restore order within their neighborhood. Once a successful counter-revolutionary campaign against the great evil of his time had been completed, Burke believed European states should retreat from France, and refrain from engaging in gratuitous destruction

---

[63] For Hedley Bull's early articulation of pluralist and solidarist conceptions of international society, see "The Grotian Conception of International Society," in H. Butterfield and M. Wight (eds.), *Diplomatic Investigations* (London: Allen & Unwin, 1966), pp. 51–74. See also A. Hurrell, "Society and Anarchy in the 1990s," in B. A. Roberson (ed.), *International Society and the Development of International Relations Theory* (London: Pinter, 1998), pp. 17–42; and N. J. Wheeler and T. Dunne, "Hedley Bull's Pluralism of the Intellect and Solidarism of the Will," *International Affairs*, 72 (1996), 91–107.

or draconian punishment of individual revolutionaries.[64] In short, once the neighborhood had been secured, and the principles of dynastic right and secure property restored, the war should cease and prudence should take hold once more.

Burke's views on empire, as with the deeper critique launched by the anti-imperialists, was largely snuffed out in the nineteenth century – a time when imperialism enjoyed widespread legitimacy and when both esteemed liberals such as Mill and authoritative lawyers such as Oppenheim drew solid lines between Europe and the "barbarian" non-European world. Nonetheless, his writings about the corrosive effects of imperial behavior continue to have resonance in twenty-first century discussions about state-building – particularly his warnings about the need to temper arbitrary power and protect the "weaker" party. So too does his "law of vicinity," as powerful nations continue to justify interference in proximate territories out of concern for the stability and well-being of the entire "neighborhood."

More broadly, Burke's conservative solidarism draws our attention to the role of culture, and cultural difference, in contemporary international politics. The debate inspired by Samuel Huntington in the early 1990s rested on an assumption that heterogeneity will inevitably produce conflict among civilizations.[65] While the empirical record doesn't fully support this view, the general question of whether or how cultural heterogeneity will affect international order remains as relevant as ever. As this chapter has shown, Burke believed that international order and justice were under-pinned by deep cultural solidarity among states and peoples. Modern-day theorists of the English School, such as Hedley Bull, have tended to agree. Though Bull observed a more pluralist international society in operation during the Cold War, he speculated that in the future, international society would need a firmer foundation, and would be determined "by the preservation and extension of a cosmopolitan culture, embracing both common ideas and common values."[66] The particular political and social order embedded in Burke's eighteenth-century Europe has little relevance for fostering that kind of global solidarity today. The closest approximation we have seen is the liberalism of the late twentieth and early twenty-first centuries, which scholars have argued has the potential to promote greater order both domestically and internationally.[67]

[64] Burke, "Remarks on the Policy of the Allies," WS, VIII, p. 490.
[65] S. Huntington, "The Clash of Civilizations?", *Foreign Affairs* 72, no. 3 (Summer, 1993), 22–49.
[66] H. Bull, *The Anarchical Society* (London: Macmillan, 1977), p. 317.
[67] M. W. Doyle, "Kant, Liberal Legacies, and Foreign Affairs," in M. E. Brown et al. (eds.), *Debating the Democratic Peace* (Cambridge, MA: MIT Press, 1996), pp. 3–57; and F. Fukuyama, *The End of History and the Last Man* (New York: Penguin, 1992).

Whether liberalism can or will have universal reach, however, remains uncertain. So too is its capacity to provide a firmer foundation for international order. Some contemporary thinkers argue that current shifts in the distribution of power mean that we are reverting to a more pluralist world, rather than seeing the advance of "liberal solidarism."[68] Using Burke's tools of analysis, we can quickly see that, despite the universal aspirations and rhetoric of liberalism, the states which make up the current liberal zone of peace do share a certain cultural similitude. Moreover, while liberal concepts such as capitalism, democracy, and the rule of law find expression outside that zone of peace, that expression is sometimes only skin-deep.[69]

Finally, attempts to entrench liberal values in international institutions have not gone uncontested, as can be seen in the continuing debate over the legitimacy of intervention on humanitarian grounds. While Western liberal states argue that the meaning of sovereignty today has been transformed, such that a failure to protect or promote human rights may result in a forfeiture of the sovereign right of nonintervention, some developing countries insist that a respect for the principles of territorial integrity and self-determination are not only of value in their own right, but also remain crucial to the preservation of international order.[70] The practice of the UN Security Council shows that it is only when attacks on individuals become so egregious – such that they either threaten international peace and security, or constitute "crimes against humanity" – that the established principle of non-intervention can be temporarily abrogated.[71] From a Burkean perspective, this continuing contestation over liberal solidarism is unsurprising. The liberal zone of peace today largely remains culturally bound, just as were Burke's own notions of imperial society and the Commonwealth of Europe.

[68] A. Hurrell, *On Global Order: Power, Values, and the Constitution of International Society* (Oxford University Press, 2007).
[69] Terms like pseudo-capitalism and illiberal democracy have been used to describe the economic and political orders in some non-Western states.
[70] See N. J. Wheeler, *Saving Strangers: Humanitarian Intervention in International Relations* (Oxford University Press, 2000); and J. M. Welsh, "Taking Consequences Seriously: Objections to Humanitarian Intervention," in J. M. Welsh (ed.) *Humanitarian Intervention and International Relations* (Oxford University Press, 2004), pp. 52–68.
[71] For more on the Security Council's record with respect to intervention on humanitarian grounds, see J. M. Welsh, "The Security Council and Humanitarian Intervention," in V. Lowe et al. (eds.) *The United Nations Security Council and War* (Oxford University Press, 2008), pp. 535–62.

11 The origins of liberal Wilsonianism: Giuseppe Mazzini on regime change and humanitarian intervention

Stefano Recchia

Anglo-American scholars of international relations have long viewed Giuseppe Mazzini (1805–72) as the archetype of the crusading *liberal interventionist* – someone who justified and indeed called for military intervention by powerful liberal states to spread freedom and democracy abroad. According to English School theorists Martin Wight and John Vincent, Mazzini was the foremost nineteenth-century advocate of "international intervention against despotic governments."[1] In the United States, Kenneth Waltz has relied on Mazzini's alleged "messianic interventionism" to buttress his broader claim that liberalism in international relations displays a crusading tendency and often "develops a hubris of its own."[2] Taking this reading to its logical extreme, one scholar has associated Mazzini's internationalism with contemporary "neoconservative" ideology and related policies of forcible regime change.[3] This chapter reviews Mazzini's international thought and concludes that the aforementioned interpretations are largely unfounded. Mazzini developed a still surprisingly topical *critique* of regime change through foreign military intervention: he was convinced that democracy had to grow internally, from a genuine domestic political struggle, and believed that self-government achieved with the help of foreign armies would not be genuine and could not be lasting.

That being said, Mazzini was certainly not a pacifist. The father of the Italian Risorgimento was first and foremost a revolutionary leader who advocated and personally helped to organize popular uprisings in Italy

I am grateful to Andrew Arato, Richard Betts, Michael Doyle, Payam Ghalehdar, Nadia Urbinati, and Jennifer Welsh for their helpful comments on previous versions of this chapter.

[1] M. Wight, *Four Seminal Thinkers in International Theory: Machiavelli, Grotius, Kant, and Mazzini* (New York: Oxford University Press, 2005), p. 107. See also R. J. Vincent, *Nonintervention and International Order* (Princeton University Press, 1974), pp. 60–1.

[2] K. Waltz, *Man, the State, and War* (New York: Columbia University Press, 1959), pp. 103, 111.

[3] M. J. Smith, "Liberalism and International Reform," in T. Nardin and D. Mapel (eds.), *Traditions of International Ethics* (Cambridge University Press, 1992), pp. 14–15.

and other European countries. He saw armed insurrection against despotic governments as a legitimate last resort, and he played a key role in the democratic uprisings of 1848–9. Mazzini's ultimate objective was a reorganization of the European political order on the basis of two principles that he saw as inextricably linked: *democracy* and *national self-determination*. The triumph of these principles, he believed, would not only vastly increase individual freedom and popular participation at the domestic level; it would also disclose the possibility of a more just and peaceful international order.

Mazzini was hardly a systematic political thinker, and his writings are not free of contradictions. Nevertheless, his tremendous influence on the subsequent development of liberal internationalism, and notably on what has come to be known as "liberal Wilsonianism," warrants a detailed (re-)examination of his thought. Until recently, Mazzini's essays on politics and international relations were scattered over dozens of out-of-print and hard-to-access publications, several of which had never been translated into English.[4] That led modern Anglo-American scholars to focus largely on a few readily available fragments of his writings, reprinted in the early twentieth century, often by militant publishers intent on inflating particular aspects of his thought.[5]

The chapter proceeds as follows. After providing some background on Mazzini's life and his impact on political events, I briefly examine his thoughts on democracy and international order – including his vision of a future European federation of democracies. The bulk of the chapter is then devoted to a detailed discussion of his arguments on violent insurrection and military intervention. Mazzini called for a "Holy Alliance of the Peoples" – a transnational alliance of Europe's revolutionary democrats – but he opposed regime change achieved with the help of foreign regular armies. He justified direct military intervention only in two narrowly defined circumstances: first, as *counter-intervention*, to re-balance the situation on the ground during a popular revolution, when troops from another foreign country have already intervened in support of the local despot; and second, as *humanitarian intervention* to stop large-scale violence against ethnic or religious minorities. Throughout the

---

[4] A single-volume English language edition of Mazzini's principal writings on politics and international relations was not published until 2009. See S. Recchia and N. Urbinati (eds.), *A Cosmopolitanism of Nations: Giuseppe Mazzini's Writings on Democracy, Nation Building, and International Relations* (Princeton University Press, 2009).

[5] For instance, Kenneth Waltz relies on a short and fragmentary selection of Mazzini's writings, edited in the 1940s by N. Gangulee, an Indian nationalist scholar based at the University of Calcutta. *Cf.* Waltz, *Man, the State, and War*, pp. 108, 110.

chapter, I seek to extrapolate from Mazzini's arguments some potentially useful lessons for thinking about intervention today.

Mazzini's life and the lasting impact of his ideas

Mazzini was born on June 22, 1805 in Genoa, a port city in northern Italy with an important republican past. His middle-class background (his father was a physician) allowed him to pursue advanced studies in law as well as literature, and by 1830 he had become a leading figure in the Italian patriotic struggle for national unification. That same year, at the age of twenty-five, Mazzini had to flee his homeland, with a death warrant on his head for subversive activism against Austria's imperial rule in northern Italy. He spent most of his remaining life in exile, first hiding in Switzerland and France, before more or less permanently relocating to England.

As early as 1831, working undercover in France, Mazzini founded the revolutionary organization *Giovine Italia* (Young Italy), aimed at promoting the patriotic ideal among Italy's educated middle classes and coordinating national insurrections. In subsequent years he attempted, not always successfully, to set up similar patriotic organizations for Germany, Greece, Spain, Russia and Poland. In 1834, while in Switzerland, he founded a new transnational revolutionary association, ambitiously called *Young Europe*, with a dozen refugees from Italy, Poland and Germany. From 1837 onwards, he spent most of his time in London, where he continued to write and publish assiduously. He also attempted to coordinate what he saw as an emergent pan-European struggle against the imperial dominion of the Habsburgs, Romanovs, and Ottomans over Italy, Central Europe, and the Balkans.[6]

By the mid-nineteenth century, Mazzini ranked among the most influential European political thinkers, along with intellectual heavyweights such as Karl Marx, John Stuart Mill, Mikhail Bakunin and Alexis de Tocqueville. The Italian revolutionary's political career reached its zenith quite abruptly in the spring of 1849. A popular uprising in Rome against the despotic rule of Pope Pius IX abolished the temporal power of the papacy, and a constituent assembly proclaimed the revolutionary Roman Republic. Mazzini, called back to Italy, was elected as a member of the republic's "triumvirate," or three-person governing council – but his popularity in revolutionary circles preordained him to become the

[6] D. Mack Smith, *Mazzini* (New Haven, CT: Yale University Press, 1994), pp. 5ff. For a detailed history of Young Italy and Young Europe, see F. Della Peruta, *Mazzini e i rivoluzionari italiani: Il partito d'azione 1830–1845* (Milan: Feltrinelli, 1974), chs. 2–3.

republic's *de facto* head of government. Under Mazzini's leadership, the citizens of Rome universally enjoyed personal and political freedoms, including press freedom, religious freedom, due process, and equality among the sexes, to an extent unequalled anywhere else at the time. But the time was not yet ripe for such radical change: Europe's conservative powers, fearing possible contagion, quickly launched a military intervention aimed at crushing the republic and reinstating the pope. In June 1849, the Roman republic succumbed to a combined onslaught of French, Austrian, and Spanish troops, and Mazzini once again had to flee Italy. Back in London, he remained an influential voice in European progressive and democratic circles until his death in 1872.[7]

Mazzini's visionary essays and pamphlets, replete with calls to action, were a source of inspiration not only for revolutionary patriots and democrats in the nineteenth century, but also for subsequent generations of progressive nationalists and anticolonial leaders, from Central and South-Eastern Europe, to Latin America, Asia, and the Arab world. There is evidence that his writings, translated into many languages, influenced notably the early Zionists, as well as Gandhi, Nehru, Nasser, and Sun Yat-sen.[8]

Furthermore, Mazzini's ideas on national self-determination and his vision of an international federation of democracies appear to have crucially shaped the world view of US President Woodrow Wilson. In 1919, while briefly in Italy, Wilson affirmed that he had closely studied Mazzini's writings and had "derived guidance from the principles which Mazzini so eloquently expressed."[9] At the time, Wilson was seeking to restructure international politics according to liberal principles, with his famous "fourteen points" and the League of Nations proposal. The American president openly acknowledged his desire to contribute to "the realization of the ideals to which his [i.e., Mazzini's] life and thought were devoted."[10] Modern liberal Wilsonianism reflects Mazzini's ideals and objectives, but also some of the tensions inherent in his thought (notably between his democratic nationalism and moral universalism), to a striking degree.

---

[7] Mack Smith, *Mazzini*, p. 75. See also Indro Montanelli, *Storia d'Italia 1831–61* (Milan: RCS Libri, 1998), pp. 77, 413–15, 444.

[8] See the essays in C. A. Bayly and E. F. Biagini (eds.), *Giuseppe Mazzini and the Globalization of Democratic Nationalism, 1830–1920* (Oxford University Press, 2008); G. Srivastava, *Mazzini and His Impact on the Indian National Movement* (Allahabad, India: Chugh Publications 1982); and Mack Smith, *Mazzini*, p. 219.

[9] W. Wilson, "Remarks about Giuseppe Mazzini" and "Further Remarks in Genoa," in A. S. Lind (ed.), *The Papers of Woodrow Wilson* (Princeton University Press, 1986), vol. 53, pp. 614–15.

[10] Wilson, "Remarks about Giuseppe Mazzini," p. 615.

A democratic conception of the nation

Present-day scholars sometimes acknowledge Mazzini as a central figure of classical liberal internationalism, and as the first "liberal nationalist."[11] But international relations scholars in particular have tended to under-estimate the deeply democratic character of his arguments on national self-determination. To begin with, Mazzini's conception of the nation is eminently political, or what we might today call "nonessentialist." He did not dismiss prepolitical factors such as language, territory, and ethnicity, but he viewed them as "just *indications* of nationality" – they might facilitate the process of political association but are insufficient by them-selves to legitimize national independence.[12]

"By NATION," he wrote as early as 1832, "we mean THE ENTIR-ETY OF CITIZENS WHO SPEAK THE SAME LANGUAGE AND ARE *ASSOCIATED, UNDER EQUAL ENJOYMENT OF CIVIL AND POLITICAL RIGHTS*."[13] Linguistic unity thus undoubtedly matters (Mazzini appears to have viewed it as a social glue); but it is the notion of a commonwealth, or voluntary association among equals under a written constitution, that is central to Mazzini's democratic conception of the nation. As some of the most recent scholarship concludes: "Mazzini did not believe in the nation as a primordial, natural phenomenon but as a social construction imagined by those who would create it; ... for him, nationalism was not an end in itself but the means to another end – a democratic republic."[14]

In short, for Mazzini the nation is a political project aimed at redefin-ing the legitimacy of sovereign power. He always saw the achievement of national independence and self-determination as accomplishments of,

[11] On Mazzini as a central figure of classical liberal internationalism, see S. Hoffmann, *World Disorders: Troubled Peace in the Post-Cold War Era* (Lanham, MD: Rowman & Littlefield, 1998), pp. 73, 125, 219; and A. Franceschet, "The Ethical Foundations of Liberal Internationalism," *International Journal* 54, no. 3 (1999), p. 472. On Mazzini as a liberal nationalist, see M. Viroli, *For Love of Country: An Essay On Patriotism and Nationalism* (Oxford University Press, 1995), pp. 148–53; M. Canovan, *Nationhood and Political Theory* (Cheltenham: Edward Elgar, 1996), pp. 6–9; and M. Freeden, *Liberal Languages* (Princeton University Press, 2005), p. 212.

[12] Mazzini, "Nationalism and Nationality," [1871] in Recchia and Urbinati (eds.) *A Cosmopolitanism of Nations*, p. 65. Unless otherwise indicated, page numbers for all of Mazzini's essays cited below are from the Recchia and Urbinati edition.

[13] Mazzini, "Manifesto of Young Italy" [1832], pp. 48–50, capitals in originals, emphasis added. Almost three decades later, Mazzini reiterated this view: "The entire Nation should legislate, either directly or indirectly. By yielding this mission into the hands of a few, you put the egoism of a single class in place of the Country, which is the Union of *all* classes." *Cf.* Mazzini, "On the Duties of Man" [1860], p. 95.

[14] D. Rowley, "Giuseppe Mazzini and the Democratic Logic of Nationalism," *Nations and Nationalism* 18, no. 1 (2012), p. 40. See also Viroli, *For Love of Country*, p. 148.

rather than alternatives to, the message of the Enlightenment and the legacy of the French Revolution: "Free *nationhood*, or universal national self-determination, is the sole guarantee against the despotic rule of a single people over several others, just as *individual liberty* is the sole guarantee against the despotic subjection of human beings."[15] Mazzini also identified a crucial pedagogical element in universal suffrage and other forms of democratic participation: they would educate people to see each other as moral and political equals, ideally transcending the borders of their own nation. Therefore, national self-determination would ultimately promote a more universalistic conception of what it means to be human. At the same time, while Mazzini emphasized popular education and civic participation as means to virtuous citizenship and moral awareness, he appears to have underestimated the importance of domestic constitutional safeguards to protect the rights of individuals and political minorities.[16] That leaves his liberalism incomplete, and has led some critics to portray him as a quasi-Jacobin.[17]

Mazzini never viewed the nation-state as the end point of historical progress. He simply thought that under the historical circumstances of his time, the nation-state provided the most fertile background for the development of democracy and the civic education of individuals. But unlike his contemporary John Stuart Mill, he did not view democracy and the nation-state as inextricably linked. Mill famously opined that "free institutions are next to impossible in a country made up of different nationalities."[18] Mazzini instead thought that *post-national democracy*, notably at the European level, was a distinct possibility for the future. Based on his reading of Italian history, he was convinced that there was nothing permanent in any given culture, language, race, or ethnicity. Different ethnicities and tribes – and thus also different nationalities – could become amalgamated over the centuries, giving rise to a new and larger political association:

---

[15] Mazzini, "Principles of International Politics" [1871], pp. 233–4. See also N. Urbinati, "'A Common Law of Nations': Giuseppe Mazzini's Democratic Nationality," *Journal of Modern Italian Studies* 1 (1996), 207–8.

[16] In one of his early writings, he claims that "the nation's power is unlimited" and then insists that "any restrictions brought to ... the deputies' ultimate choice would contradict the principle of national sovereignty." *Cf.* Mazzini, "On the Superiority of Representative Government" [1832], p. 51.

[17] See, e.g. G. Salvemini, *Mazzini* (trans. I. M. Rawson) (Stanford University Press, 1957), pp. 56–61; and B. Haddock, "State and Nation in Mazzini's Political Thought," *History of Political Thought* 20 (1999), 324–7.

[18] J. S. Mill, *On Liberty and Other Essays* (ed. J. Gray) (Oxford University Press, 1998), p. 428.

We do not believe in the timelessness of races. We do not believe in the timelessness of languages ... We do not believe in the timeless impact of any given cause on human affairs ... We believe in a sole and constant general law. Therefore we also believe in a sole and constant general objective [human freedom]; and we believe in progressive development toward this given objective, which can only be achieved by means of coming closer together – that is, through *association.*[19]

The desired end state: an international federation of democracies

It was Mazzini's conviction that the moral progress achieved through the establishment of independent and democratic nation-states would also facilitate the emergence of a more peaceful international order based on mutual trust and solidarity among peoples. In the past, he argued, for "the old despotic rulers ... peace was never more ... than a mere cessation of hostilities; their pursuit of a *balance of power* was an attempt to equalize their strength, always having future wars in mind and always mistrusting each other."[20] But he thought that in the mid-nineteenth century, these age-old dynamics of international politics were about to fundamentally change. With democracy taking hold domestically, the traditional balance of power at the international level would soon be replaced by something radically new – a cooperative system of collective security and international federation:

These states, which have remained divided, hostile, and jealous of one another so long as their national banner merely represented the narrow interests of a dynasty or caste, will gradually become more and more intimately associated *through the medium of democracy.* The nations will be sisters. Free and independent ... in the organization of their domestic affairs, they will gradually unite around a common faith, and they *will enter a common pact to regulate all matters related to their international life.*[21]

Mazzini expected that Europe's newly emerging democracies, faced with a hostile international environment still dominated by despotic regimes, would inevitably be drawn together. At first they would merely become "united in a *collective defense pact* against the possible usurpations of one or the other great Power."[22] But over time, the experience of beneficial cooperation among democracies in the context of a security-based

---

[19] Mazzini, "Humanity and Country" [1836], p. 55.
[20] Mazzini, "Nationality and Cosmopolitanism" [1847], p. 60.
[21] Mazzini, "From a Revolutionary Alliance to the United States of Europe" [1850], p. 126.
[22] Mazzini, "Principles of International Politics," p. 236.

alliance would increase their mutual trust and solidarity, thus engendering further cooperation on other issues. "Free and equal Peoples will help one another; each will be able to benefit from the resources that others possess in the pursuit of their common civilization and progress."[23]

Europe's democracies would also increasingly set up more complex federative arrangements to put their cooperation on more solid institutional foundations. "The future Europe of peoples will be united through a *new type of federation*, which will avoid both the anarchy of absolute independence and the tyrannical centralization that results from conquest."[24] Mazzini remained short on details concerning the institutional architecture of this future international federation. But he felt confident enough to predict that at the European level, the deepening bond among democracies would probably result in the establishment of a "large international democratic association" with its own parliamentary committee. Presumably one day there would also be a European Court of Arbitration to adjudicate international disputes. Mazzini's avowed longer-term goal was to move beyond the nation-state, and "to create the United States of Europe."[25]

Therefore, Mazzini in many ways prefigured the modern hypothesis of a separate "democratic peace," according to which liberal democracies do not fight against each other and are likely to establish closer associational bonds than other types of regimes.[26] Arguably, Mazzini expressed the idea less ambiguously than Immanuel Kant, with whom the hypothesis is now typically associated.[27] Enlightenment philosophers including Kant had envisioned an international covenant of peace, or pact of federation, among independent (i.e., sovereign) states, regardless of their

---

[23] Mazzini, "Nationality and Cosmopolitanism," p. 62.

[24] Mazzini, "Toward a Holy Alliance of the Peoples" [1840], p. 126, emphasis added. This situates Mazzini squarely within what Daniel Deudney calls the "republican security project" in Western thinking about international relations – although Deudney never explicitly refers to Mazzini's writings. *Cf.* D. Deudney, *Bounding Power: Republican Security Theory from the Polis to the Global Village* (Princeton University Press, 2008).

[25] On the European parliamentary committee and Court of Arbitration, see Mazzini, "On Nonintervention" [1851]; and "Toward a Holy Alliance of the Peoples;" as well as Mack Smith, *Mazzini*, p. 154. On the idea of a united Europe more generally, see Mazzini, "From a Revolutionary Alliance to the United States of Europe," p. 135. For an early sympathetic discussion of Mazzini's pan-European vision, see G. O. Griffith, *Mazzini: Prophet of Modern Europe* (London: Hodder and Stoughton, 1932).

[26] See e.g. J. R. Oneal and B. Russett, *Triangulating Peace: Democracy, Interdependence, and International Organizations* (New York: Norton, 2001); E. Mansfield, H. Milner, and P. Rosendorff, "Why Democracies Cooperate More," *International Organization* 56, no. 3 (2002), 477–513.

[27] On Kant as the forebear of modern democratic peace theory, see esp. M. Doyle's seminal essay, "Kant, Liberal Legacies, and Foreign Affairs," now reprinted in Doyle, *Liberal Peace: Selected Essays* (New York: Routledge, 2011).

domestic regime type. Kant in particular recognized that the emergence of a "powerful and enlightened" republic (which, he thought, would by its nature be inclined to seek perpetual peace) might provide a focal point for international federation; yet he specifically required in his Second Definitive Article of Perpetual Peace that *"each nation,* for the sake of its own security" (and therefore not only republics), should join the *foedus pacificum,* or international league of peace.[28] Mazzini, on the other hand, more explicitly theorized the emergence of a separate democratic peace, based on an initial alliance and gradually deepening federation among democracies.

Of course, Mazzini's arguments on peace among democracies were quite speculative and at least partially intended to buttress his revolutionary program. Nevertheless, the basic causal logic he identified comes surprisingly close to explaining the emergence of a separate democratic peace during the latter half of the twentieth century. In the aftermath of the Second World War, the Western democracies – many of them newly established – set up a defensive security alliance under US leadership, to protect their freedom and independence from what was then perceived as an inherently expansionist and despotic Soviet Union. The institutionalization of this alliance under NATO's collective defense pact, in combination with the market-regulating liberal institutions that emerged out of the Bretton Woods agreement of 1947, promoted increasingly close inter-democratic contacts and exchanges. According to the liberal narrative, this led to growing levels of trust and cooperation, which in turn reduced the security dilemma among democracies and made war among them increasingly unthinkable.[29]

The rocky transition: democratic revolution and regime change

As a revolutionary leader, Mazzini was interested less in theorizing the specific institutional architecture of a future federation of democracies,

---

[28] Immanuel Kant, "Perpetual Peace: A Philosophical Sketch" [1795], in *Kant: Political Writings* (ed. H. Reiss) (Cambridge University Press, 1991), pp. 104, 102, emphasis added. For further discussions, see G. Cavallar, "Kantian perspectives on democratic peace: alternatives to Doyle," *Review of International Studies* 27, no. 2 (2001), esp. pp. 243–6; S. Recchia, "Kant, la pace democratica, e la governance mondiale federale," in S. Maffettone and G. Pellegrino (eds.), *Etica delle relazioni internazionali* (Cosenza: Marco, 2004); J. MacMillan, "Immanuel Kant and the Democratic Peace," in B. Jahn (ed.), *Classical Theory in International Relations* (Cambridge University Press, 2006); and Ch. 9 by A. Hurrell in this volume, esp. pp. 210–11.

[29] This is broadly the story told by G. J. Ikenberry in *Liberal Leviathan: The Origins, Crisis, and Transformation of the American World Order* (Princeton University Press, 2011), esp. ch. 5.

than in elucidating the *means* by which Europe's oppressed peoples – the Italians, Hungarians, Poles, and many others – could achieve the more urgent goal of national and democratic self-determination. Mazzini was no liberal pacifist who believed in a natural "harmony of interests" among states, like his British contemporaries Richard Cobden and John Bright, or someone who followed Kant in the belief that republican peace would naturally triumph in the long run, fostered by the "asocial sociability" of human beings. Quite the opposite, Mazzini felt impatient with long-term evolutionary processes, and believed that history could be actively shaped by the human will.[30]

Nevertheless, Mazzini was not a warmonger who invariably called for violent insurrection, or who blindly invoked international military intervention to advance the cause of democracy and national self-determination. He insisted until the end of his days that democratic governance and national liberation had to be achieved primarily through *domestic* political struggles. Wherever possible, those struggles should be non-violent: Mazzini saw peaceful political propaganda, or the struggle for "hearts and minds" aimed at mobilizing the people for the national cause, as having both strategic and moral priority over any resort to revolutionary violence.[31]

Only where there was no freedom of speech and of the press and the establishment of democratic associations was entirely proscribed, force might legitimately be used in order to gain a position from where one's voice could be heard in the first place. Mazzini thought that those circumstances clearly applied to mid-nineteenth-century Italy, where any form of political dissent was silenced by the iron fist rule of Austria in the north, the Bourbon monarchy in the south, and the papal theocracy at the center. Therefore, Italian patriots should organize for partisan *guerrilla warfare*, by establishing a centralized revolutionary organization, and then launch limited military operations with the objective of raising the entire nation to protest. Guerrilla bands, Mazzini affirmed in one of his earliest essays, are the "precursors of the nation," and they should "attempt to rouse the nation into insurrection."[32] Ideally, targeted acts of

[30] Mazzini's argument is thus compatible with the recent empirical finding that while consolidated liberal democracies may have established a separate peace among themselves, transitions to democracy are often rocky and violent. See E. Mansfield and J. Snyder, *Electing to Fight: Why Emerging Democracies Go to War* (Cambridge, MA: MIT Press, 2005).
[31] Among the means for rallying public opinion, Mazzini mentions politically active associations, public meetings, and popular newspapers. *Cf.* Mazzini, "Letters on the State and Prospects of Italy" [1839], in *ibid.*, *Scritti Editi ed Inediti* (Imola, Italy: Galeati, 1909), vol. 22, p. 166. See also Salvemini, *Mazzini*, p. 70; Mack Smith, *Mazzini*, p. 51.
[32] Mazzini, "Rules for the Conduct of Guerrilla Bands" [1832], p. 111.

violence would trigger brutal governmental repression and thus "foster insurrection in large towns and cities."[33]

Over the last century, national resistance movements across the globe (from the Jewish Irgun in British-ruled Palestine, to the FLN in Algeria, the Kosovo Liberation Army, and the Iraqi Kurds) have used similar tactics, often ruthlessly, to generate mass-popular revolt and attract international support for their cause.[34] It is worth noting, however, that Mazzini always called on his followers to avoid wanton destruction, and reminded them that when resorting to violence they should proceed with as much circumspection as the circumstances allowed:

We disagree with those dreamers who preach peace at any cost, even that of dishonor, and who do not strive to make Justice the sole basis of any lasting peace. We believe war to be sacred under certain circumstances. But war must always be fought within the limits of necessity, when there is no other way to achieve the good ... No war must ever be contaminated by the spirit of vengeance, or by the brutal ferocity of a boundless egoism.[35]

More specifically, Mazzini consistently opposed acts of terrorism against civilians (although he clearly approved of guerrilla warfare against regular armies). "We do not want terror," he insisted, and then went on to "reject terror as both cowardly and immoral."[36] In the long run, any revolutionary struggle would lack legitimacy and be doomed to failure, unless broad segments of public opinion – both domestically and internationally – were willing to support it. Therefore, the motto of revolutionary guerrilla bands should be: "Respect for women, for property, for the rights of individuals, and for the crops."[37] Throughout his life, Mazzini insisted that revolutionary democrats should use violence only as a last resort, making every effort to fight "as virtuously as possible, and to conclude it [the violence] as soon as possible."[38]

Historically, Mazzini's views on political violence reflect the experience of the French Revolution and the subsequent Napoleonic wars.

---

[33] *Ibid.*, p. 112.

[34] B. Hoffman, *Inside Terrorism*, second revd. edn. (New York: Columbia University Press, 2006), chs. 2–3. On how radical nationalist and secessionist movements might deliberately provoke governmental repression, in order to trigger international intervention, see A. J. Kuperman, "Suicidal rebellions and the moral hazard of humanitarian intervention," *Ethnopolitics* 4, no. 2 (2005), 149–73.

[35] Mazzini, "Neither Pacifism nor Terror: Considerations on the Paris Commune and the French National Assembly" [1871], p. 157.

[36] Mazzini, "Against the Foreign Imposition of Domestic Institutions." See also Mack Smith, *Mazzini*, p. 9.

[37] Mazzini, "Rules for the Conduct of Guerrilla Bands," p. 111.

[38] Mazzini, "Gemiti, Fremiti e Ricapitolazione" [1871], in *ibid.*, *Scritti editi e inediti* (Imola: Galeati, 1941), vol. 92, p. 327.

The older generation of Italian patriots had fought for Napoleon's army in Spain between 1808 and 1814, where they had experienced a fierce, well-organized, and highly effective guerrilla-type resistance by the local population. In the 1820s and 1830s, it was natural for those older Italian patriots to suggest the formation of similar guerrilla bands for the fight against despotism and foreign occupation in Italy, given their homeland's rough and mountainous terrain. Mazzini quickly made those arguments his own, and he placed guerrilla warfare at the center of his own theory of national liberation.[39]

But Mazzini also viewed the Italian fight for national unification as part of a broader European struggle, aimed at the emancipation of oppressed nationalities from Poland to the Balkans. He had close links with the leaders of revolutionary movements in Central and Southeastern Europe and repeatedly called for the organization of a "Holy Alliance of the Peoples" – by which he meant a transnational association aimed at coordinating popular uprisings across the continent. The association's goal should be to fracture and undermine the alliance of Europe's conservative powers, which dated back to the Holy Alliance forged by Austria, Russia, and Prussia in 1815, and had resulted in repeated counter-revolutionary interventions on the Italian peninsula and elsewhere. Mazzini believed that a coordinated uprising of several oppressed nationalities (e.g. the Italians, Poles, Serbs, and Hungarians), would force each of Europe's multinational empires (Austria, Russia, and Ottoman Turkey) to concentrate on their own troubles, making it impossible for them to dispatch their armies abroad to support fellow despots. "What we need [is] ... a single union of all the European peoples who are striving towards the same goal ... When we will rise up simultaneously in every country where our movement is currently active, we will win. Foreign intervention [by the despots] will then become impossible."[40]

Advancing democracy and national independence through foreign intervention?

Notwithstanding Mazzini's revolutionary zeal, he never called on powerful liberal states to intervene militarily abroad in support of democracy and national liberation. His thinking on this matter has frequently been misinterpreted and is therefore worth discussing in some detail.

---

[39] F. della Peruta, "La guerra di liberazione spagnola e la teoria della guerra per bande nel Risorgimento," in *ibid.*, *L'Italia del Risorgimento: Problemi, momenti e figure* (Milan: Franco Angeli, 1997), pp. 11–29.

[40] Mazzini, "Toward a Holy Alliance of the Peoples," p. 121.

To begin with, Mazzini unambiguously condemned the foreign imposition of democracy (or other social and political arrangements) as morally
unacceptable. Such blatant international paternalism, he argued, would
violate the principle of popular sovereignty and be incompatible with
each nation's fundamental right to freely determine its own governance
structures:

> If a people were to impose their own solution to the specific social problems of
> another country, they would thereby commit an act of usurpation. It is the same
> as if an individual or a school of thought were to impose their own model on their
> brothers ... they would thereby commit an act of tyranny and violate the central
> belief of Democracy, the dogma of collective sovereignty.[41]

Therefore, supposing that the people of a country freely decided to set up
an undemocratic government for themselves, liberals and democrats
abroad might condemn the decision but should abstain from any forcible
interference: "Foreigners do not have a right to forcibly intervene against
a People that were to ... establish a tyrannical regime."[42] Each people
ought to be left free to find their own path to collective self-governance,
proceeding at their own pace and relying on their own cultural background and historical experiences. "The nation alone has the inviolable
right to *choose* its own institutions, to *correct* them and *change* them when
they no longer correspond to its needs."[43]

But Mazzini went considerably further: he claimed that even where a
despotic government is upheld by foreign imperial domination, and local
intellectuals and parts of the local public proclaim their desire for democracy and national independence, rising up in protest, direct military
intervention by foreign regular armies to aid the insurgents would
be unwarranted. Moral and political solidarity from abroad; financial
and material assistance; and even the contribution of foreign volunteer
militias – all should be welcomed. But direct intervention by foreign
regular armies was another matter. Mazzini's argument against regime
change and national liberation achieved with the help of foreign armies is
largely prudential or consequentialist in nature, derived from his reading
of history and his republican political philosophy.

---

[41] Mazzini, "Against the Foreign Imposition of Domestic Institutions," p. 140.
[42] Mazzini, "On the Duties of Man," p. 97.
[43] Mazzini, "On the Superiority of Representative Government," p. 50. Michael Walzer
has made a similar argument as to why it would be wrong for outsiders to impose liberal
democracy on a country that lacks a strong indigenous democratic tradition – even if it
could be done nonviolently. *Cf.* Walzer, "The Moral Standing of States," in C. Beitz
et al. (eds.), *International Ethics* (Princeton University Press, 1985), p. 234.

First, Mazzini was diffident of the maneuverings and intentions of
powerful states capable of intervening militarily abroad – even liberal
and democratic ones. History, he believed, teaches that governments
deciding to intervene in foreign revolutions are, at best, driven by mixed
motives, regardless of their proclaimed intentions. Consequently, many
such interventions have merely substituted new despots for old ones,
without any real benefit to the local population. Second, Mazzini's
democratic republicanism requires that each people develop its own *ethos*
of liberty, by fighting for it without the help of foreign armies and actively
participating in its sustenance and progress day after day. "Liberation"
achieved through foreign military intervention would be only a chimera –
ultimately unsustainable – and most likely resulting in either prolonged
tutelage by outside powers, or a rapid slide into anarchy and civil war as
soon as the outside troops left. Therefore, Mazzini reminded his compatriots over and over again that their revolutionary war for national
liberation and democracy *"must be exclusively Italian*, fought with our
own forces and without any foreign intervention on our own soil." Italy,
he went on, "must fight her *own* war," so that, like other nations struggling for their own freedom and independence, it will "acquire a genuine
liberty that will not be bound to any fate other than her own. Otherwise
she will be ... a satellite of France," or of other powerful states.[44]

Finally, Mazzini thought it would be important for any nation's self-
esteem that its members think of themselves as having achieved
self-government and independence largely through their own bravery
and domestic political struggle. In the absence of such a shared national
understanding, the revolutionary movement itself could end up discredited, and pockets of violent resistance might persist for generations
to come.[45] Summing up, then, Mazzini was unambiguously opposed to
regime change achieved through foreign military intervention. Oppressed
peoples struggling for democracy and national independence, he
thought, should "not look for liberty at the hands of the foreigner."[46]
We might thus speculate that, in more recent times, Mazzini would
have applauded the largely home-grown "velvet revolutions" that over-
threw Eastern Europe's despotic communist regimes in 1989, as well as
the popular uprisings of the 2011 "Arab spring." But he would probably
have opposed direct military intervention to support local insurgents in

[44] Mazzini, "For a truly national war" [1859], p. 147. See also Mazzini, "Letters on the
state and prospects of Italy" [1839], in *ibid.*, *Scritti editi e inediti*, vol. 22, p. 5.
[45] Mazzini, *Note autobiografiche* (Milan: Rizzoli, 1986), p. 127.
[46] Mazzini, "Manifesto of Young Italy," p. 36.

Iraqi Kurdistan, Kosovo, or Libya, on grounds that foreign intervention is usually harmful to self-determination in the long run.

Mazzini's arguments to some extent resemble those of his contemporary John Stuart Mill, who affirmed that "the only test possessing any real value, of a people having become fit for popular institutions, is that they, or a sufficient portion of them to prevail in the contest, are willing to brave labor and danger for their liberation ... The liberty which is bestowed on them by other hands than their own, will have nothing real, nothing permanent."[47] It is worth noting, however, that although Mill opposed military intervention to support a people struggling against "merely domestic oppressors," he was actually willing to countenance such intervention in support of national resistance movements – that is, in "the case of a [European] people struggling against a foreign yoke."[48] Mazzini stopped short of that, largely because of his skepticism about the motives of foreign interveners and his worries about the impact of foreign intervention on the patriotic movement itself.

Understanding Mazzini's strong rhetorical critique of "nonintervention"

While Mazzini opposed direct military intervention in support of regime change and national liberation, he certainly did not think that powerful liberal states should take a hands-off approach to such matters. Quite the opposite, he believed that liberals and democrats everywhere have a duty to assist their less fortunate brethren abroad. He thus repeatedly voiced strong criticism of international "nonintervention," by which he meant the traditional Anglo-American policy of isolationism and aloofness in the face of popular uprisings on the European continent. "The absolute nonintervention doctrine in politics," he wrote in 1845, "appears to me to be what indifference is in matters of Religion, namely: a disguised atheism. It represents the negation of all belief, of all general principles, of every mission of nations on behalf of Humanity."[49] Taken out of its context, this pathos-laden critique of "nonintervention" might be interpreted as supporting the view of Mazzini as a crusading interventionist.[50]

---

[47] Mill, "A Few Words on Nonintervention" [1859], in G. Himmelfarb (ed.), *Essays on Politics and Culture* (Gloucester, MA: Peter Smith, 1973), p. 381.

[48] Mill, "A Few Words," p. 383. For a discussion see also Ch. 12 by M. Doyle in this volume, pp. 267–8, 279–80.

[49] Mazzini, "Foreign Despotism to Civilize a People? Italy, Austria, and the Pope" [1845], p. 181.

[50] I am grateful to Andrew Arato for encouraging me to clarify this point.

Yet behind Mazzini's verbose rhetoric, there is a coherent argument for an activist but largely peaceful foreign policy on the part of liberal Great Powers that stops short of direct military intervention in all but the most extreme circumstances. His argument, in short, is that the most powerful liberal nations of his day – notably England and what he saw as an increasingly self-confident United States of America – ought to have "interfered" in the affairs of foreign countries, by offering their moral, diplomatic, economic, and perhaps even indirect military support (in the form of arms shipments, logistical assistance, and intelligence) to democratic movements on the European continent. Towards the end of his life, Mazzini increasingly hoped that significant help in the cause of democracy and national liberation might come from the United States. He believed that after the victory of Union forces in the American Civil War, the United States could – and indeed should – help European democrats to successfully face the huge challenges that still confronted them:

You [the United States] have become a *leading* Nation. Now you must act as such ... you must feel that to stand aloof would be a sin ... You must then help your republican brothers ... morally, and materially if needed, whenever the sacred battle is being fought and you have the ability to effectively inspire and support those who toil and bleed for truth and for justice.[51]

When writing for liberal and progressive audiences in Britain and the United States, Mazzini sought to appeal to not only their moral convictions, but also their enlightened self-interest. He therefore acknowledged that in the short run, British and American support for popular revolutions on the European continent might result in increased political turmoil; but he quickly added that in the longer run, a rapid triumph of democracy and national self-determination would clearly benefit the liberal Great Powers. Popular uprisings against despotic rule were likely to occur with increasing frequency, spurred by the accelerated pace of social and economic change. Withholding international support for those revolutions would merely prolong a bloody European conflict that the forces of democracy were bound to win no matter what: "Those who are openly hostile to our movement or give us at best lukewarm support should know that they will only prolong the crisis with all its attendant damage. The governments have tried everything from seducing the masses to scaring them – all in vain. God sides with the peoples."[52]

---

[51] Mazzini, "America as a Leading Nation in the Cause of Liberty" [1865], p. 221. See also H. R. Marraro, "Mazzini on American Intervention in European Affairs," *Journal of Modern History* 21, no. 2 (1949), 109–14.

[52] Mazzini, "Toward a Holy Alliance of the Peoples," p. 121.

Britain and the United States should therefore have strongly supported the Italians, Poles, Hungarians, and other European peoples struggling for democracy and national self-determination – but usually without direct military intervention. Mazzini was willing to justify direct military intervention only under exceptional, narrowly defined circumstances – either to offset previous counter-revolutionary interventions by despotic states, or in the face of genuine humanitarian emergencies. Even then, he believed that foreign intervention should be limited in both time and scope, so as not to distort the process of domestic self-determination.

Liberal counterintervention

Mazzini, following prevailing doctrine at the time, accepted the international use of force as a means of individual and collective self-defense. Faced with external aggression, he argued, the peace-loving nations should bond together to confront and defeat the evildoer: "Like the members of a family, the nations should support each other against aggression. They are called on to fight such Evil whenever it manifests itself."[53] But Mazzini went beyond this traditional understanding. He also justified military intervention to "defend" a people struggling for liberty, when regular troops from a foreign country have already intervened on the side of the local despot. In the face of such blatant "co-operation of despots against peoples," he affirmed, the principle of nonintervention ceases to be valid, and the world's liberal nations are justified and possibly required to intervene in turn, to re-balance the situation on the ground:

If the government of a state is despotic and if the people … resist that government, carry on a war of the press against it, and at last, in spite of police and military force, defeat it; then … the decision is final … But should the government of a neighboring despotic state, either invited by the vanquished party or fearing the contagion of liberal ideas in its own territory, invade the convulsed state and so interrupt or repeal the revolution, then the principle of Nonintervention is at an end, and all moral obligation on other states to observe it is from that moment annulled.[54]

The goal of counterintervention is to allow popular self-determination to take its course, by "mak[ing] good all prior infractions of the law of Noninterference." If the rule of nonintervention is to mean anything, Mazzini insisted, "it must mean that in every state the government must deal directly and alone with its own people."[55] Mazzini developed his

[53] Mazzini, "Principles of International Politics," p. 227.
[54] Mazzini, "On Nonintervention," p. 217.
[55] *Ibid.*, p. 216.

case for liberal counterintervention against the backdrop of Europe's political reality at the time: since the defeat of Napoleon in 1815, Europe's despotic powers (mainly Austria, Russia, and their smaller vassal states) had been openly supporting each other, including through repeated military interventions aimed at crushing popular uprisings that threatened to overturn the status quo.[56]

Thus for instance, liberal Britain should have first threatened and then if necessary launched a counterintervention on Italian soil in the spring of 1849, when France led an international military expedition to crush the revolutionary Roman republic. As Mazzini recalled with his characteristic pathos in a letter to a British friend: "Ah! If you had in England, condescended to see that the *glorious* declaration of non-interference ought to have begun by taking away the French interference in Rome! How many troubles and sacrifices you would have saved us."[57] Mazzini seems to have understood that even progressive British opinion might have viewed a general duty of counterintervention as exceedingly onerous and potentially destabilizing. He therefore sought to persuade his readers that in most instances, the credible *threat* of counterintervention by a powerful liberal state would suffice to deter despotic regimes from intervening in the first place. "It would not be necessary," he insisted, for the British "government to plunge itself into a revolutionary crusade, which no one dreams of invoking . . . It would only be necessary to tell the European despots in a firm and calm voice, so as to be heard by all: 'Stay at home now, and let not your action overpass your frontiers! . . . If you interfere for evil, we will interfere for good. Then God will judge.'"[58]

In the twentieth century, arguments for liberal counterintervention were often used during the Cold War, for example in attempts to justify US intervention in Vietnam as a "legitimate response" to previous military interference by the North Vietnamese regime.[59] Since the collapse of the Soviet Union, the competitive interventions characteristic of the

---

[56] Mazzini may also have been influenced by the arguments on counterintervention developed by Italian patriots and constitutionalists in the late eighteenth century. See M. Isabella, "Mazzini's Internationalism in Context," in Bayly and Biagini (eds.), *Giuseppe Mazzini and the Globalization of Democratic Nationalism*, p. 49.

[57] Mazzini, "Extract from a Letter to Peter Taylor" [1860], in E. F. Richards (ed.), *Mazzini's Letters to an English Family, 1855–1860* (London: John Lane, 1922), p. 236.

[58] Mazzini, "The European Question: Foreign Intervention and National Self-Determination" [1847], p. 195. A similar defense of liberal counterintervention can also be found in Mill's essay *A Few Words on Nonintervention*, published only a few years later.

[59] Michael Walzer discusses, and rejects, counterintervention as a justification for US military operations in Vietnam in his *Just and Unjust Wars* (New York: Basic Books, 1977), pp. 97–100.

Cold War have become less frequent, and arguments about counter-intervention are nowadays rarely used to justify military interference abroad. Nevertheless, Mazzini's argument on counterintervention might be interpreted as more generally justifying liberal intervention in civil wars, where the leading oppressors are openly supported by outside powers. For instance, evidence of direct military support for the Bosnian Serbs by the Yugoslav National Army during the Balkan wars in the early 1990s arguably justified limited NATO intervention on behalf of the Bosnian Muslims. Contemporary international legal scholars recognize that "international counterintervention on behalf of either party to a civil war is probably lawful, provided that it is limited to neutralizing a prior illegal intervention by another state."[60] But this limited conception of counterintervention as a balancing act, which Mazzini endorsed, offers scant guidance for policy today: if followed, it risks prolonging bloody civil wars, by preventing any of the local parties from scoring a decisive victory.[61] In cases like Bosnia (or more recently Syria), marked by large-scale ethnic cleansing and massacres of civilians, Mazzini himself would probably have justified a more decisive use of force aimed at *imposing a settlement* – albeit on a different, humanitarian rationale.

Humanitarian intervention

Mazzini's reasoning on humanitarian intervention is quite tentative, and he wrote down his thoughts on this matter fairly late in his life, mainly in the 1850s and 1860s. Sovereignty and nonintervention, in his view, are valuable as principles of international society insofar as they afford each people the necessary space to freely determine their political institutions and more generally the direction of their own society. Therefore, Mazzini appears to have envisioned humanitarian intervention as a true exception – justified only when large-scale killings of civilians empty the concept of self-determination of any meaning. That makes Mazzini's argument much more modern than the writings on humanitarian intervention of earlier natural-law thinkers like Vitoria or Pufendorf, who lacked a strong conception of national sovereignty and remained indebted to medieval notions of a universalist *Res publica Christiana*.[62]

---

[60] D. Wippman, "Change and Continuity in Legal Justifications for Military Intervention in Internal Conflict," *Columbia Human Rights Law Review* 27 (1995), 435–85.

[61] Recent scholarship suggests that when outsiders intervene in civil wars, they should decisively support one of the local factions to achieve a lasting settlement. See R. Betts, "The Delusion of Impartial Intervention," *Foreign Affairs* 73, no. 6 (1994), 20–33.

[62] See e.g. the chapters by William Bain and Richard Tuck in this volume.

For Mazzini, a twofold consideration dictates concern for large-scale violence perpetrated against civilians abroad. First, if such massive human suffering anywhere is left unanswered, it sends powerful cues to would-be oppressors and *génocidaires* in other parts of the world, making similar gruesome behavior more likely in the future. In his own words: "no people can suffer ... without their suffering affecting all other peoples, ... by setting a dangerous precedent."[63] Hence the world's liberal and democratic nations should do anything they can to prevent such precedents from being set, seeking to uphold universal moral principles – what Mazzini calls the common "Law of Humanity" – and notably the sanctity of human life. But beyond such prudential considerations, Mazzini also believed that we have a basic duty to come to the aid of those who suffer from large-scale violence abroad:

Above anything else, such suffering ... degrades our very existence, by attacking it in what we all share in common, namely *human dignity and human conscience* ... Every single one of us is responsible for his brother's safety: it is not only when we kill him, but also when we permit others to kill him, although we would have been able to defend him, that we have to fear the question with which God pursued the first violator of the solid bond of humanity.[64]

It was not so much the violation of basic human rights that concerned Mazzini – after all, the notion of individual claims and entitlements is not central to his political and moral philosophy.[65] Instead, his argument, which illustrates his profoundly solidarist conception of international society, is that *humanity itself* – our common identity as creatures endowed with a moral conscience – is harmed by evil committed against men and women anywhere. He asserts that "we are ... all brothers, held to a common duty of love and cooperation," before noting that if left unanswered, other people's "suffering breaks the divine unity – and therefore saps the foundation – of our common faith."[66] Mazzini's moral universalism and democratic solidarism were to a significant degree inspired by Christian ethics: though critical of the Catholic Church and especially of the papacy as political institutions, he remained a devout Christian throughout his life, and his theory of political association clearly reflects New-Testament ideas of Christian fellowship.[67]

---

[63] Mazzini, "The European Question," p. 196.

[64] *Ibid.*, emphasis added.

[65] See e.g. S. Mattarelli, "Duties and Rights in the Thought of Giuseppe Mazzini," *Journal of Modern Italian Studies* 13, no. 4 (2008), 480–5.

[66] Mazzini, "The European Question," pp. 196–7.

[67] Mazzini was heavily influenced by the writings of Félicité de Lamennais, a French priest and philosopher who attempted to combine political liberalism with Roman Catholicism after the French Revolution. See R. Sarti, *Mazzini: A Life for the Religion of Politics*

In short, Mazzini envisaged an international society in which liberal and democratic nations might combine as a matter of *moral duty* to bring an end to egregious acts of violence being committed within the borders of an independent state.[68] It appears that his preference was for collective, or what we might today call multilateral, humanitarian intervention: "Whenever such blatant breaches of the moral Law are committed, all the nations that recognize and accept the common goal should bond together to oppose the crime."[69] Apart from this brief reference, he never explicitly discussed the desirability of collective endorsement, but his concern about self-serving interventions by the powerful suggests that he would have been quite sympathetic to multilateral safeguards in this context.

Elsewhere, Mazzini more directly suggests what types of crimes would warrant humanitarian military intervention, and what mechanisms might drive it:

People begin to feel that … there are bonds of international duty binding all the nations of this earth together. Hence, the conviction is gaining ground that if on any spot of the world, even within the limits of an independent nation, some glaring wrong should be done … – if, for example, there should be, as there has been in our time, a massacre of Christians within the dominions of the Turks – then other nations are not absolved from all concern in the matter simply because of the large distance between them and the scene of the wrong.[70]

There is no specific discussion in Mazzini's writings of the threshold of violence that justifies humanitarian intervention, though genocide and massacres of ethnic or religious minorities would seem to qualify. We might infer from the centrality of national sovereignty and self-determination to his thought that such large-scale killings are indeed the only circumstance in which he was willing to justify humanitarian military intervention. That sets the bar fairly high, but it is in line with the reasoning of contemporary liberal internationalists like Michael Walzer or Stanley Hoffmann, who justify humanitarian intervention only to stop exceptional acts of violence that "shock the moral conscience of mankind." It also accords with the conclusions of the 2005 UN World Summit, which – referring to the "Responsibility to Protect" – justify military intervention only in the face of ongoing genocide, war crimes, ethnic cleansing, and crimes against humanity.[71]

(Westport, CT: Greenwood, 1997), pp. 59–60; and L. Pivano, *Lamennais e Mazzini* (Turin: Associazione mazziniana italiana, 1958).

[68] On this point, see also Vincent, *Nonintervention*, p. 61.

[69] Mazzini, "Principles of International Politics," p. 227.

[70] Mazzini, "On Nonintervention," p. 218.

[71] Walzer, *Just and Unjust Wars*, pp. 101, 107; S. Hoffmann, "The politics and ethics of military intervention," *Survival* 37, no. 4 (Winter 1995), 29–51; UN General Assembly,

Mazzini sensed that the issue of humanitarian intervention might become more relevant in the future, as improved means of information, communication, and transport were increasing people's awareness of events in foreign countries and their sense of belonging to a common humanity. The bond of "international duty binding all the nations of this earth together," he observed, "is perceived more widely and the likelihood of meeting [our duty] increases, as the improvement of our means of transport and communication between one land and another reduces our earth to a more manageable compass, making its inhabitants more conscious of being but one family."[72] Nevertheless, it should be noted that Mazzini's international society was essentially Christian and European. Historically, his reflections on humanitarian intervention appear to have been motivated by repeated instances of European military interference in the Ottoman Empire, ostensibly to protect local Christian populations there from religiously motivated violence. As early as 1827, Russia, Great Britain, and France had intervened in the Greek war of independence, partially justifying their actions on humanitarian grounds. In 1860, France dispatched six thousand troops to Lebanon to stop recurring acts of violence perpetrated against the local Christian Maronite population (the "massacre of Christians within the dominion of the Turks" to which Mazzini may be referring), and the intervention was endorsed by most European powers.[73]

Finally, Mazzini did not explicitly discuss the justifiable scope and duration of humanitarian military intervention. But his opposition to externally imposed regime change and trusteeship in the European context suggests that he envisioned humanitarian intervention as a limited, "surgical" form of interference: powerful liberal countries should deploy military force to stop large-scale violence against civilians abroad, but after halting the killing they should swiftly withdraw, in order to allow the local population to freely determine its own future. Of course, we know today that following humanitarian intervention in failed states and deeply divided war-torn societies (such as Kosovo or East Timor), a longer-term external presence may be necessary to maintain political stability and (re-)establish the conditions under which meaningful self-determination becomes possible. Such protracted international trusteeship raises a

---

Resolution 60/1: 2005 World Summit Outcome, UN Doc. A/RES/60/1, October 24, 2005, p. 30, §139.

[72] Mazzini, "On Nonintervention," p. 218.

[73] See M. Finnemore, *The Purpose of Intervention: Changing Beliefs About the Use of Force* (Ithaca, NY: Cornell University Press, 2003), pp. 58–62. On the 1827 intervention in Greece, see also D. Trim, "Intervention in European history," Ch. 1 in this volume, pp. 41–2.

number of difficult ethical questions of its own. Mazzini had some
important things to say about international trusteeship for the purpose
of "nation-building," although as we shall see his discussion was highly
problematic.

"Nation-building" through international trusteeship?

Somewhat surprisingly, given Mazzini's status as an icon of anti-
imperialist movements, he thought that all of the aforementioned limits
on military intervention should apply only among fully developed (i.e., in
his time, European) nations. Martin Wight probably exaggerated when
he suggested that Mazzini was "a Victorian in every sense except that he
was not a British subject";[74] and yet the Italian patriot shared with his
Victorian contemporaries a philosophy of progress that portrayed most
non-European peoples as backward, in need of being "educated" and
trained to become ready for self-government. As Mazzini wrote in a letter
to his mother in 1845: "Europe has been providentially called to conquer
the rest of the world to progressive civilization."[75] Several years later,
following the completion of Italy's national unification, he expressed the
hope that his homeland, too, would "contribute to the great civilizing
mission suggested by our times" and "invade and colonize the Tunisian
lands when the opportunity presents itself."[76]

Mazzini's paternalistic endorsement of colonialism as an instrument of
Europe's "civilizing mission" parallels Mill's idea that "Nations which
are still barbarous ... should be conquered and held in subjection by
foreigners."[77] More generally, as Jennifer Pitts has shown, nineteenth-
century liberalism rejected earlier natural rights theories produced by the
Age of Enlightenment in favor of the idea that civil and political liberties
are historically contingent and require the achievement of a certain stage
of social and moral development before they can take hold.[78]
For nineteenth-century liberals, the putatively barbarous nature of the
individual men and women living in faraway places in Asia, Africa, and
elsewhere was the underlying cause of broader social and political

[74] Wight, *Four Seminal Thinkers in International Theory*, pp. 90, 109.
[75] Mazzini, *Letters* (trans. A. De Roses Jervis) (Westport, CT: Hyperion Press, 1979), p. 98.
[76] Mazzini, "Principles of International Politics," pp. 238–9.
[77] Mill, "A Few Words on Nonintervention," p. 377. See also Mill, *On Liberty and Other Essays*, pp. 264, 454ff.
[78] J. Pitts, *A Turn to Empire: The rise of imperial liberalism in Britain and France* (Princeton University Press, 2005). On Victorian theories of empire in particular, see also D. Bell, "Empire and International Relations in Victorian Political Thought," *Historical Journal* 49, no. 1 (2006), 281–98.

backwardness. Hence, those barbarous individuals first had to be educated by benevolent colonialists to think rationally and obey general laws,
before they could aspire to collectively govern themselves.[79] For Mazzini
in particular, the goal of benign European trusteeship was to raise backward societies to a level of moral and political development where the
principle of nationality could take hold, so that meaningful self-
determination would become possible.

The nineteenth-century defense of external political tutelage as a
means to "civilize" less developed peoples will strike most contemporary
readers as untenable. We know today that the anthropological foundations of the classical liberal argument were scientifically unsound, to say
the least. Most of the societies targeted by European colonialism were
effectively self-governing on their own terms, while imperial rule was
often an obstacle to further development and progress. At the same time,
classical liberals such as Mazzini and Mill made the valid conceptual
claim that international paternalism may be justified in the face of structural impediments to self-government that make it impossible for a
people to freely determine their own future. From a contemporary point
of view, international trusteeship might still be acceptable as a
transitional measure, to assist war-torn societies like Bosnia, Somalia,
or Afghanistan overcome *political* (as opposed to racial or cultural)
impediments to collective self-government stemming from the collapse
of domestic authority structures.[80]

Conclusion

Mazzini saw himself as a political activist and pamphleteer (today, we
might say a "public intellectual"), more than as a scholar or theorist.
His overarching goal was to steer Europe's political change in a decidedly
liberal and democratic direction. Thus, he was less concerned with
analytical rigor and deductive consistency than with persuading his
readers to support his struggle. Most of the causes he championed –
national self-determination, democracy, international federation, even
humanitarian intervention – were part of progressive political discourse

[79] Finnemore, *The Purpose of Intervention*, p. 70. For a helpful discussion see also
S. Holmes, "Making Sense of Liberal Imperialism," in N. Urbinati and A. Zakaras
(eds.), *J. S. Mill's Political Thought* (Cambridge University Press, 2007), pp. 298–346.
[80] See S. Recchia, "Just and Unjust Postwar Reconstruction: How much external
interference can be justified?" *Ethics & International Affairs*, 23, no. 2 (2009), 165–87;
and R. Keohane, "Political Authority after Intervention: gradations in sovereignty," in
J. L. Holzgrefe and R. Keohane (eds.), *Humanitarian Intervention* (Cambridge University
Press, 2003).

in his time. But Mazzini developed those notions further in an original way, combining them into a powerful vision that influenced generations of progressive democrats and liberals until well into the twentieth century. It might therefore be appropriate to recognize Mazzini as the founding figure of the more activist, or *democratic Wilsonian*, branch of modern liberal internationalism. As previously noted, President Wilson himself was profoundly influenced by Mazzini's life and writings. Going even further, Samuel Moyn has recently termed Mazzini "the most globally influential heir of the French Revolution."[81]

The political reality that Mazzini was facing in mid-nineteenth century Europe in many ways resembles broader world political circumstances today. Following the Napoleonic Wars, the principles of state sovereignty and nonintervention were solemnly reaffirmed as foundations of European international society. At the same time, in the face of rapid social and economic change, people across the continent were yearning for greater personal and political freedoms; and democratic political activists hoping for outside assistance were naturally looking to Britain and the United States, the leading liberal nations of the time. Today, almost two centuries later, the principles of sovereignty and nonintervention have been solemnly enshrined in the Charter of the United Nations. But as a result of increasing global interconnectedness, and stimulated by broader social, political, and economic transformations, oppressed peoples across the globe are once again struggling for greater freedom, and they are calling on the most powerful liberal nations to assist them in their fight.

The similarities between post-Napoleonic Europe and contemporary international society – combined with Mazzini's thoroughly modern effort to square a strong belief in national sovereignty and independence with an equally deep commitment to human dignity and equality – may explain why many of his arguments appear so familiar today. Europe, for Mazzini, was a solidarist international society, within which different peoples, or nations, had special rights (to independence) and duties (of assistance) towards each other. In recent years, something close to a globalized version of Mazzini's account of international society has been developed by John Rawls, with his idea of a "Society of Peoples."[82]

[81] S. Moyn, "Giuseppe Mazzini in (and Against) the History of Human Rights," in Miaa Halme-Tuomisaari and Pamela Slotte (eds.), *History of Human Rights*, forthcoming.
[82] Rawls's peoples are "free and independent"; they "are to observe a duty of non-intervention"; and they "have a duty to assist other peoples living under unfavorable conditions." *Cf.* Rawls, *Law of Peoples* (Harvard University Press, 1999), p. 37.

Perhaps the principal lesson from Mazzini's political thought is that while liberals and democrats ought to display solidarity with peoples abroad struggling for political freedom and social betterment, they should refrain from projecting their own "thick" normative convictions on foreign societies, accepting that there might be different national paths to self-determination. Furthermore, even when "thin" universal principles appear unequivocally violated, liberals should exercise great prudence in calling for military intervention, keeping in mind that the motives of interveners are always mixed and the consequences difficult to foresee.[83] Notwithstanding Mazzini's often verbose rhetoric and revolutionary zeal, he was aware that principled morality in international relations always needs to be combined with a more prudential type of reasoning, to have a realistic chance of improving the human condition in a highly imperfect world. "The theory of international politics," he explained, "can be perfected in no other way than by dealing sincerely and thoroughly with individual cases as they successively arise."[84]

---

[83] On the distinction between "thin" universal morality and "thick" national moral traditions, see M. Walzer, *Thick and Thin: Moral Argument at Home and Abroad* (Notre Dame, IN: University of Notre Dame Press, 1994).

[84] Mazzini, "On Nonintervention," p. 218.

12   J. S. Mill on nonintervention and intervention

> There is a country in Europe ... whose foreign policy is to let other nations alone ... Any attempt it makes to exert influence over them, even by persuasion, is rather in the service of others, than itself: to mediate in the quarrels which break out between foreign states, to arrest obstinate civil wars, to reconcile belligerents, to intercede for mild treatment of the vanquished, or finally, to procure the abandonment of some national crime and scandal to humanity such as the slave trade.
>
> J. S. Mill, "A Few Words on Nonintervention" (1859/1973), p. 368.[1]

Nonintervention has been a particularly important and occasionally disturbing principle for liberal scholars who share a commitment to basic and universal human rights. Its disturbing quality is well illustrated when we compare the opening words of the quotation above – "let other nations alone" – with the lengthening list of interferences. On the one hand, liberals have provided some of the very strongest reasons to abide by a strict form of the nonintervention doctrine. It was only with the security of national borders, liberals such as Immanuel Kant and John Stuart Mill thought, that peoples could work out the capacity to govern themselves as free citizens. On the other hand, those very same principles of universal human dignity when applied in different contexts have provided justifications for overriding or disregarding the principle of nonintervention.

In explaining this dual logic I present an interpretive summary of J. S. Mill's famous argument against and for intervention, presented most clearly in his "A Few Words on Nonintervention" (1859/1973). Here, Mill illustrates what makes his "few words" both so attractive and so

I am most grateful for the research assistance of Stefanie Pleschinger and Mark Hobel, and of Kate Cronin-Furman, Axel Domeyer and David Hambrick. I thank Stefano Recchia, Melissa Schwartzberg and Jennifer Welsh for their helpful comments. This chapter draws on and revises "A Few Words on Mill, Walzer and Nonintervention," *Ethics and International Affairs* 23, no. 4 (Winter 2009), 349–69.
[1] Citations to the 1859 "Nonintervention" essay are to J. S. Mill, "A Few Words on Nonintervention," in G. Himmelfarb (ed.), *Essays on Politics and Culture* (Gloucester: Peter Smith, 1973), pp. 368–84.

alarming to us. We should be drawn to Mill's arguments because he is among the first to address the conundrums of modern intervention. The modern conscience simultaneously tries to adhere to three contradictory principles: first, the cosmopolitan, humanitarian commitment to assistance that protects basic human welfare, irrespective of international borders; second, respect for the significance of communitarian, national self-determination; and, third, accommodation to the reality of international anarchy, the absence of reliable world government, that puts a premium on the pursuit of national security. Each makes a claim that must be considered. Understanding yet rejecting ideal solutions and balancing those three considerations practically is what makes Mill's arguments so distinctive, so attractive and so disturbing.

I thus stress, more than has been conventional, the consequentialist character of the ethics of both nonintervention and intervention. It makes a difference whether we think that an intervention will do more good than harm, and some of the factors that determine the outcome are matters of strategy and institutional choice. I also engage in a one-sided debate with Mill as I explore the significance of the many historical examples he employs to support his argument. Do they actually support his conclusions? Could they, given what he knew or should have known? Given what we now think we know? My conclusion will be that, persuasive as the moral logic of his argument for liberal intervention sometimes is, the facts of the particular cases he cites actually tend to favor a bias toward nonintervention – that is, against overriding or disregarding nonintervention. That said, enough of his argument survives to warrant a firm rejection of strict noninterventionism.[2]

Principles of nonintervention and intervention have been justified in various ways. In international law, "intervention" is not any interference but, according to Lassa Oppenheim, the influential late nineteenth-century international legal scholar, it is "dictatorial interference" in the political independence and territorial integrity of a sovereign state. No single treaty has codified principles underlying this prohibition and customary international law, while condemning intervention, contains numerous but contested exceptions.[3] Relevant principles in the just war tradition have

---

[2] In a forthcoming book, provisionally titled *The Question of Intervention*, I explore the possibility that the deeper interdependence embodied in globalization both requires a stronger commitment to intervention in order to prevent or halt crimes against humanity and fosters a greater capacity in the UN to halt protracted civil wars.

[3] L. Oppenheim, *International Law* (London: Longmans, 1920) vol. I, p. 221. Art. 2(4) of the UN Charter prohibits the use of force in general, and GA Res. 2131 (XX) (1965) provides partial evidence for customary law norms when it outlines potential violations and declares the "Inadmissibility of Intervention into the Domestic Affairs of States." For the complicated legal record, see L. Damrosch et al., *International Law: Cases and Materials* (St Paul, MN: West, 2001), ch. 12.

been proposed by scholars, by politicians, and by citizens who have sought to provide good reasons why one should abide by these conventional principles of classic international law and good reasons why one should, on some occasions, breach them.[4] J. S. Mill, though far from the first, makes one of the most persuasive contributions to this ongoing debate.

Principles underlying nonintervention and intervention

John Stuart Mill developed the core of a modern understanding of human dignity, conceived of as autonomy, and its implications for political decision-making. He saw human beings as being fundamentally equal, and therefore equally capable of experiencing pleasure and pain. Our natural sympathy should thus lead us to choose acts and rules that maximize pleasure and minimize pain for the greatest number. But – an important qualification – he wanted to constrain this maximization of utility by prioritizing both the freedom to lead unrestricted lives as long as those life plans did not harm the freedom of others and the realization that not all pleasures and pains were equal. Some were higher; some lower. Some expressed human creativity; others did not. Poetry was better than "pushpin."[5]

Politically, Mill defends two ideal principles. The first is maximum equal liberty, allowing each adult to develop his or her own potentiality on the view that each individual is the best judge of what is and is not in his or her interest, so long, however, as no one interferes with the equal

---

[4] As surveys of a large literature, I have found especially valuable: J. Vincent, *Nonintervention and International Order* (Princeton University Press, 1974); C. Beitz, *Political Theory and International Relations* (Princeton University Press, 1979); S. Hoffmann, *Duties Beyond Borders* (Syracuse, NY: Syracuse University Press, 1981); A. Ellis, "Utilitarianism and International Ethics," in T. Nardin and D. Mapel (eds.), *Traditions of International Ethics* (Cambridge University Press, 1992); F. Téson, *Humanitarian Intervention: An Inquiry Into Law and Morality* (Irvington-On-Hudson, NY: Transnational Publishers, 1997); E. Mortimer, "Under What Circumstances Should the UN Intervene Militarily in a 'Domestic' Crisis," in O. Otunnu and M. Doyle (eds.), *Peacemaking and Peacekeeping for the New Century* (Lanham, MD: Rowman & Littlefield, 1998); N. Wheeler, *Saving Strangers* (Oxford University Press, 2000); S. Chesterman, *Just War or Just Peace* (Oxford University Press, 2003); D. Chatterjee and D. Scheid (eds.), *Ethics and Foreign Intervention* (Cambridge University Press, 2003); J. L. Holzgrefe and R. Keohane (eds.), *Humanitarian Intervention: Ethical, Legal and Political Dimensions* (Cambridge University Press, 2003); M. Finnemore, *The Purpose of Intervention* (Ithaca, NY: Cornell University Press, 2003); J. Welsh (ed.), *Humanitarian Intervention and International Relations* (Oxford University Press, 2004); T. Weiss, *Humanitarian Intervention* (New York: Polity, 2007); G. Bass, *Freedom's Battle* (New York: Knopf, 2008).

[5] Pushpin was a mindless game in which boys stuck pins in each other's hats and then took turns knocking them off. Good discussions of the wider aspects of Mill's ethical theory are found in A. Ryan, *J.S. Mill* (London: Routledge and Kegan Paul, 1975) and N. Capaldi, *John Stuart Mill: A Biography* (New York: Cambridge University Press, 2004), pp. 249–65.

liberty of others. When public regulation is necessary, the second, representative government, should govern. To maximize effective consent and the utility of collective decisions it would be best to give decisive weight to the preferences of the majority, as represented by knowledgeable politicians.[6]

Tyranny of the Majority [handwritten annotation]

Internationally, one might think that these principles would give rise to a commitment to an international version of the US Constitution's "Guarantee Clause" (art. 4, sec. 4) in which each state is guaranteed (i.e. required to have) a republican representative form of government, and the Fourteenth Amendment by which all states are required to provide equal protection of the laws to all persons. But Mill does not draw this implication, arguing instead that there is an important distinction between domestic and international justice.

Nonintervention

Arguments against intervention have taken the form of both direct principles and indirect, or procedural, considerations. Like many liberals, Mill dismisses without much attention some Realist arguments in favor of intervention to promote "territory or revenue" in order to enhance national power, prestige or profits. However prevalent those motives might have been in history, for Mill they lack moral significance, as, for that matter, did justifications associated with some Liberal or Socialist arguments that favored intervening to promote an "idea" or ideology.[7] War and intervention have to be justified by morally relevant reasons of self-defense or beneficence.

The most important direct consideration for the liberals was that nonintervention reflected and protected human dignity. Nonintervention could enable citizens to determine their own way of life without outside interference. If democratic rights and liberal freedoms were to mean something, they had to be worked out among those who shared them and were making them through their own participation. Kant's "Perpetual Peace" (1795) had earlier made a strong case for respecting the right of nonintervention because it afforded a polity the necessary territorial space and political independence in which free and equal citizens could work out what their own way of life would be.[8] For Mill,

---

[6] For analysis of Mill's politics, see D. Thompson, *John Stuart Mill and Representative Government* (Princeton University Press, 1976).

[7] Mill, "Nonintervention," p. 376.

[8] Kant's fifth preliminary article of *Perpetual Peace* prohibits forcible interference in "the constitution and government of another state" for to do so would violate "the right of people dependent on no other and only struggling with its internal illness." I. Kant,

intervention avowedly to help others actually undermines the authenticity of domestic struggles for liberty. First, a free government achieved by means of intervention would not be authentic or self-determining but determined by others and not one that local citizens had themselves defined through their own actions. "But the evil [of intervention]," Mill declares, "is, that if they have not sufficient love of liberty to be able to wrest it from merely domestic oppressors, the liberty which is bestowed on them by other hands than their own, will have nothing *real*."[9] (Authentic governance was more like poetry than pushpin.)[10]

John Stuart Mill provides a second powerful direct argument for nonintervention, one focusing on likely consequences, when he explains in his famous 1859 essay, "Nonintervention," that it would be a great mistake to export freedom to a foreign people that was not in a position to win it on its own. In addition to not being "real," forcibly imported freedom would have "*nothing permanent*" to it.[11] A people given freedom by a foreign intervention would not, he argues, be able to hold on to it. Connecting *permanence* to *reality*, he notes that it is only by winning and holding on to freedom through local effort that one acquires a true sense of its value. Moreover, it is only by winning the "arduous struggle"[12] for freedom that one acquires the political capacities to defend it adequately against threats of foreign invasion or of domestic suppression, whether by force or subtle manipulation. The struggle mobilizes citizens into what could become a national army and mobilizes as well a capacity and willingness to tax themselves for public purposes.

Mill is not romanticizing self-determination. Self-determining representation does not necessarily mean good government. Good government for Mill is a complex amalgam of participation and competence, popular engagement and bureaucratic direction, both sustained by education. Lacking the right conditions of popular subservience to law and popular engagement in policy, democracy and the policies adopted by democratic

"Perpetual Peace," in H. Reiss (ed.) *Kant's Political Writings* (trans. H. B. Nisbet) (Cambridge University Press, 1970). See also the chapters by P. Hassner and A. Hurrell in this volume. For further comment, see S. Muthu, *Enlightenment Against Empire* (Princeton University Press, 2003), chs. 4–5 and the concluding chapter of my *Liberal Peace* (New York: Routledge, 2011).

[9] Mill, "Nonintervention," p. 381; emphasis supplied.
[10] For an exposition of the "romantic individualist" elements and "republican moralist" in J. S. Mill's political thought, see H. S. Jones, "John Stuart Mill as Moralist," *Journal of the History of Ideas* 53, no. 2 (1992), 287–308.
[11] Mill, "Nonintervention," p. 381; emphasis supplied. Mazzini developed a strikingly similar argument around the same time. See ch. 11 by S. Recchia in this volume, esp. pp. 249–51.
[12] *Ibid.*, p. 382.

governments can be destructive. Educated elites have vital roles to play. The best that can be said for popular self-determination is that under the right conditions (see the discussion of the imperial exception below), it is better than autocratic rule, particularly foreign autocracy.[13]

If liberal government were to be introduced into a foreign society, in the knapsack (so to speak) of a conquering liberal army, the local liberals placed in power would immediately find themselves in a difficult situation. Not having been able to win political power on their own, they would have few domestic supporters and many non-liberal domestic enemies. They then would do one of three things:

Either (1) begin to rule as did previous governments, that is, by repressing their opposition and acting to "speedily put an end to all popular institutions." Indeed, "when freedom has been achieved *for* them, they have little prospect of escaping this fate."[14] The intervention would have done no good; it simply would have created another oppressive government.

Or (2) simply collapse in an ensuing civil war because the imposed government lacked the popular support to achieve and hold power on its own. Intervention, therefore, would have produced not freedom and progress, but a civil war with all its attendant violence.

Or (3) the interveners would have continually to send in foreign support. Rather than having established a free government, one that reflected the participation of the citizens of the state, the intervention would have created a puppet government, one that would reflect the wills and interests of the intervening, truly sovereign state. "No people ever was and remained free, but because it was determined to be so; because neither its rulers nor any other party in the nation could compel it to be otherwise."[15]

A third argument against intervention points to the difficulties of transparency or uncertainty. Historically, it has proven difficult to identify authentic "freedom fighters." Particular national regimes of liberty and oppression are difficult for foreigners to "unpack." They often reflect complicated historical compromises made today or long before – contracts of a Burkean sort among the dead, the living and the yet to be born. "Every civilized country," he adds, "is entitled to settle its internal affairs in its own way, and no other country ought to interfere with its discretion, because one country even with the best intentions, has no chance of properly understanding the internal affairs of another."[16]

---

[13] See Mill's *Considerations on Representative Government*, and Thompson, *John Stuart Mill and Representative Government*, esp. chs. 1 and 2.

[14] Mill, "Nonintervention," p. 382; original emphasis.   [15] *Ibid.*, p. 381.

[16] Letter to James Beal, April 19, 1865; quoted in K. Miller, "John Stuart Mill's Theory of International Relations," *Journal of the History of Ideas* 22, no. 4 (1961), 509.

Mill acknowledges that sovereignty and the legitimacy of intervention ultimately depend upon the consent of those intervened against (or as Mill says, is subject to "their own spontaneous election"[17]). If the people welcome an intervention, then, the contemporary just war theorist Michael Walzer adds in a Millian vein, "it would be odd to accuse them [the interveners] of any crime at all."[18] But we cannot make those judgments reliably in advance, either because our information is incomplete or because the case is complicated by competing reasonable claims to justice that foreigners do not have a reasonable basis to adjudicate.

Fourth, the necessarily "dirty hands" of violent means often become "dangerous hands" in international interventions.[19] International history is rife with interventions justified by high-sounding principles – ending the slave trade, or suttee, or introducing law and order and civilized behavior – turning into self-serving, imperialist "rescues" in which the intervener stays to profit and control. So Mill, referencing French sympathy for the Polish rebellion against Russia, warns that even if liberal France undertakes "for no selfish object" a war "in less than a twelve-month, the national character would again be perverted, as it was by Napoleon, – the rage for victory and conquest would again become the dominant passion in the breasts of Frenchmen."[20] Thus he requires that the intervener govern its actions according to the interests of the intervened, looking for something more than a unilateral decision, and respecting the multilateral processes of international law: these are important procedural considerations in weighing the justice of an intervention.

Indirect reasons for nonintervention, those bearing on other valued ends, have also been important constraints, including for Mill. Key among the indirect considerations are the rules of international law among sovereign civilized states that prohibit intervention. These laws, unenforceable moral norms though they be, embody the value of coordination and consensual legitimacy and help, as Mill argues, to proclaim

[17] Mill, "Nonintervention," p. 380.
[18] M. Walzer, "The Moral Standing of States," in C. Beitz et al. (ed.), *International Ethics* (Princeton University Press, 1985), p. 221, fn. 7.
[19] For discussion, see J. Welsh, "Taking Consequences Seriously: Objections to Humanitarian Intervention," in Welsh, *Humanitarian Intervention*, pp. 56–68.
[20] One wonders whether the British and other national characters are similarly subject to this. Mill, "French News Examiner," Dec. 19, 1830, p. 809, in A. Robson and J. Robson (eds.), *Collected Works*, vol. XXII, Newspaper writings (Toronto: Toronto University Press, 1986).

international equality and protect the weakest states.[21] And rules – almost any rules – have a value in themselves by helping to avoid unintended clashes with severe consequences to human life. They serve as focal points for coordination – rules of the road, such as "drive on the right." Without some rule, unsought strife would ensue. International laws, moreover, were painstakingly achieved compromises among diverse moralities. The mere process of achieving consent made them legitimate. They were agreed upon and *pacta sunt servanda*.[22]

Ideal theory and non-ideal practical reason

Given the importance Mill attaches to self-determination and nonintervention, it is not surprising that he envisages elements of an ideal world in which both would have a better prospect of being realized. Like many other nineteenth-century liberals, he thinks that progress, the spread of free governments (which to be stable would need to rest on nationality, *one* nationality), commerce, international federalism in a "universal congress of mankind" are all conducive to international harmony and peace. Less conventionally, he stresses moral education above institutions and highlights the political enfranchisement of women.[23]

Sensible of the fact that such an ideal world is remote in the extreme, he discusses the value of multilateral decision-making to better regulate the likely use of force in his 1837 essay on the "Spanish Question," which assesses British and French intervention to halt a "prolonged civil war" (addressed below). "When a struggle," he urges, "breaks out anywhere between the despotic and the democratic principles, the powers should never intervene singly; when they interfere at all, it should be jointly, as a general European police."[24] But even that stricture, he hastens to add, is an ideal standard suitable only "If it were possible, as it will be in time, that the powers of Europe should by agreement among themselves adopt a common rule for the regulations of wars of political opinion."[25] Clearly this consensus had so far proven illusory in Europe,

---

[21] See Mill, "Treaty Obligations" in *ibid.*, *Dissertations and Discussions* (London: Holt, 1875), vol. V, p. 137.

[22] "Agreements must be upheld;" see T. Nardin, *Law, Morality, and the Relations of States* (Princeton University Press, 1983), and T. Franck, *Fairness in International Law and Institutions* (Oxford: Clarendon Press, 1995).

[23] On "universal congress," see "The Spanish Question," in J. Robson (ed.), *The Collected Works of John Stuart Mill*, vol. XXXI (University of Toronto Press, 1989); on women, see *The Subjection of Women* (London, 1924) p. 115, and for his general international theory, Miller, "John Stuart Mill's Theory of International Relations."

[24] Mill, "The Spanish Question," p. 374.   [25] *Ibid.*, p. 16.

where Russia and Austria typically intervened on opposite sides from France and the United Kingdom, and so it was to prove for generations. Today, of course, Europe and the wider international community have evolved standards for non-defensive uses of force. The "Responsibility to Protect" doctrine enunciated at the 2005 UN General Assembly Summit outlines the principles of legitimate intervention against genocide, crimes against humanity, war crimes and ethnic cleansing when the Security Council so approves. Whether these principles will prove effective in practice is yet to be determined.[26]

But Mill's truly outstanding contribution to international ethics is not his systematic ideal theory – of which there is little and even less that he does not contradict. Instead, it is his practical judgments that repeatedly qualify general precepts in the name of utility and principles, neither of which can be rightly understood absent a particular case. Mill favors democracy and representation, but only for peoples who are capable of exercising such freedoms well. He favors national self-determination, but only for peoples who have truly become one nation. Even then he can recommend that some nations (Basques, Bretons, etc.) should stay part of their larger political communities for "protection," "dignity and power." Rather than "to sulk on his rocks, the half-savage relic of past times," these nationals should sublimate their nationalism in a larger unit.[27] Every general proposition is contingent, sometimes balancing competing values of human welfare and self-determination and national security, always shaped by what is possible and beneficial in the particular circumstances. And, for these reasons, despite the merits of non-intervention, Mill finds that intervention is sometimes both right and feasible.

Interventions

Liberal arguments supporting intervention fall into various camps. Some liberals – strong cosmopolitans – hold that the rights of cosmopolitan freedom are valuable everywhere for all people. Any violation of them should be resisted whenever and wherever it occurs, provided that we can do so proportionally – without causing more harm than we seek to

---

[26] I explore this issue and the considerable literature it has generated in "International Ethics and the Responsibility to Protect," *International Studies Review* 13, no. 1 (2011), 72–84.

[27] *Considerations on Representative Government*, pp. 363–4 and quoted on p. 497 of Miller, "John Stuart Mill's Theory of International Relations."

avoid.[28] But other liberals, notably J. S. Mill and, among contemporary just war theorists, Michael Walzer – often called communitarians – limit the cases that justify intervention. Mill limits them to seven. Some cases involve reasons to override the nonintervention principle; others, to disregard the principle. In the first, the principles in favor of nonintervention still hold, but other considerations seem more important. In the second, the principles do not apply to the particular case.

Exceptions that override

Mill argues that there were three good reasons to override what should be the usual prohibition against intervention. In these arguments the considerations against intervention are present, but other more important values, "considerations paramount," such as national security and humanitarian concern for suffering, as Mill says,[29] trump them. Although interventions usually do more harm than good, Mill noted three exceptions (see Table 1 below).

First, Mill noted, "We must except, of course, any case in which such assistance is a measure of legitimate self-defense."[30] Acknowledging the primacy of self-help in an anarchic international system, just war philosophers and international lawyers typically raise the difficult cases of intervention to enforce the rights of nationals or rescue them from unjust imprisonment (e.g. the 1976 rescue of the Israeli airliner at Entebbe, in our time) or pre-emptive or preventive interventions designed to remove a looming threat before an attack takes place. But Mill in the "Few Words," focuses on a less familiar case: international civil war. In an international system-wide war that is an internationalized civil war, such as that waged between Protestantism and Catholicism in the sixteenth century, or liberalism and despotism in Mill's own time, nonintervention can neglect vital transnational sources of national security. "If ... this country [Great Britain], on account of its freedom, should find itself menaced with attack by a coalition of Continental despots, it ought to consider the popular party in every nation of the Continent as its natural ally: the Liberals should be to it, what the Protestants of Europe were to

---

[28] See, for example, the influential works of D. Luban, "Just War and Human Rights," *Philosophy and Public Affairs* 9, no. 1 (Winter 1980), 160–81 and H. Arkes, *First Things: An Inquiry into the First Principles of Morals and Justice* (Princeton University Press, 1986). Both Luban and Arkes are cosmopolitans in this sense, but their conceptions of which rights are fundamental differ profoundly, the first tending toward social democratic and the second libertarian in orientation, with correspondingly large differences in judgment on interventions.

[29] Mill, "Nonintervention," p. 383.   [30] *Ibid.*, p. 382.

Table 1 *Mill's cases for intervention*

JS Mill's cases favoring intervention

	Overriding			Disregarding			
Cases	Legitimate self-defense	Post-war standing menace	Protracted civil war mediation	Self-determination secession	Counter-intervention	Humanitarian intervention	Benign imperialism
Mill's examples	16th C Protestant – Catholic Wars; 19th C "Liberals vs Despots"	Napoleon; Reconstruction in US South	Portuguese mid-century	Greek-Turkey; Belgium-Holland; Austria-Hungary 1848–9	Austria-Hungary 1848–9	"severities repugnant to humanity"	Oude/Awadh
Contemporary examples considered	Cold War Brezhnev and Reagan Doctrines	Occupations of Germany and Japan	UN peace enforcement and peacekeeping	Hungary, 1956; Kosovo; East Timor; South Ossetia	Vietnam	Cuba, 1898; India-Bangladesh 1971; Tanzania-Uganda	Chapter VII mandates in peace enforcement

273

the Government of Queen Elizabeth."[31] In the extreme case, if everyone of each ideological faction truly aligns with its fellows overseas, irrespective of collective national interests or inter-state borders, and if others are intervening in support of their faction, then not intervening in support of your own is dangerous.

This kind of logic led Sir Nicholas Throckmorton, Elizabeth I's ambassador in France, to advocate intervention in support of fellow Protestants, warning: "Now when the general design is to exterminate all nations dissenting with them in religion ... what will become of us, when the like professors with us shall be destroyed in Flanders and France."[32] It also resonates in twentieth-century Cold War logic and neatly matches the rhetoric of the Reagan Doctrine, which pledged "We must not break faith with those who are risking their lives ... on every continent from Afghanistan to Nicaragua ... to defy Soviet aggression and secure rights which have been ours since birth. Support for freedom fighters is self-defense." Reagan adds "rollback" to the original "containment" of the Truman Doctrine, and it fits the equally interventionist Brezhnev Doctrine.[33]

In practice, the early Cold War witnessed covert actions by the United States in Albania and China, and Soviet efforts to control local communist parties in Europe and elsewhere. Reagan and Brezhnev practiced their doctrines in Nicaragua and Czechoslovakia, respectively.[34] But the exceptions to Cold War interventionism were at least as important. The exceptions included the West's support for Tito's Yugoslavia and the East's support for Third World nationalists, not to speak of the effective combination of East-West détente with triangulation devised by the Nixon Administration to exploit the Chinese split from the Soviets in the 1970s.

[31] *Ibid.*, p. 382.
[32] Quoted from Lord Burghley's State Papers in W. MacCaffrey, "The Newhaven Expedition: 1562–1563," *The Historical Journal* 40, no. 1 (1997), 1–21. For an insightful and wide-ranging analysis of religious internationalism in this period, see J. Owen, "When do Ideologies Produce Alliances?" *International Studies Quarterly* 49 (2005), 73–99.
[33] Ronald Reagan, State of the Union Address, 1985. President Truman's doctrine promising to defend free peoples from external or internal aggression was presented to the joint session of Congress in justification of the assistance he proposed for Greece and Turkey in March, 1947. President Brezhnev presented his doctrine in a speech at the Fifth Congress of the Polish Worker's Party in November, 1968, following the intervention against the Czechoslovak Prague Spring. Brezhnev proclaimed: "When forces that are hostile to socialism try to turn the development of some socialist country towards capitalism, it becomes not only a problem of the country concerned, but a common problem and concern of all socialist countries."
[34] See T. Weiner, *Legacy of Ashes: The History of the CIA* (New York: Doubleday, 2007), esp. pp. 45–6, 58–61; and for a general comparison, the classic by S. Huntington and Z. Brzezinski, *Political Power: USA/USSR* (New York: Viking, 1961).

Even during the polarizing religious wars of the sixteenth and seventeenth centuries, we should recall that Queen Elizabeth learned from the disastrous 1562–3 armed expedition to "Newhaven" (today: Le Havre, in Normandy, France). In 1559, she successfully intervened to roll back the Catholic threat in Scotland. She sent troops to assist the more powerful faction of Scottish Protestant lords who were struggling against a regime sustained by French forces. When her more radical advisers pressed her to do the same in France, she reluctantly agreed to intervene in support of the French Protestant nobles in Normandy, only to see them defect to a better deal with their own monarch.[35] She learned to limit intervention to vital necessity (Scotland, and preserving the independence of the Low Countries) and to armed action only with the support of strong local allies. She also developed a policy of alternatively aligning with Spain and France and successfully played them against each other.[36] A half-century later, Cardinal Richelieu wisely aligned with the Protestant principalities that would support France against the Catholic Holy Roman Empire and Catholic Spain, which were its greatest threats. Consistent as the logic of internationalized civil war is, probing the actual examples suggest that Mill should have adopted a bias toward more proximate conceptions of "legitimate self-defense" in order to limit the interventionism invoked in Cold War-style diplomacy.

Second, following a successful defensive war against an aggressive despot, the liberal victor, rather than halting his armed forces at the restored border, can intervene to remove a "perpetual" or at least standing "menace" to peace, whether a person or a regime.[37] Mill's implicit reference was the sending of Napoleon to Elba, off the Italian coast, and then, after Waterloo after the point was proved, further away to St. Helena, far in the South Atlantic. Reconstruction in the US South could be seen to draw inspiration from these considerations. And in that case, Mill explicitly noted the need not just to remove Jefferson Davis from office, but to "break altogether the power of the slaveholding caste" so that they did not "remain masters of the State legislatures [where] they w[ould] be able effectually to nullify a great part of the result which ha[d] been so dearly bought by the blood of the Free States."[38]

---

[35] MacCaffrey, "The Newhaven Expedition," p. 19.
[36] See R. B. Wernham, *Before the Armada* (London: Cape, 1966) and G. D. Ramsey, *The Reign of Elizabeth I* (ed. C. Haigh) (London: Macmillan, 1984), who describe dual balancing, against both foreign and domestic threats. On Elizabethan interventions, see also D. Trim's discussion in Ch. 1 of this volume, pp. 28–36.
[37] Mill, "Nonintervention," p. 383.
[38] See E. Foner, *Reconstruction: America's Unfinished Revolution* (New York: Harper, 2002) for background and Mill's letter to Parke Goodwin quoted in M. St. John Packe, *The Life of JS Mill* (New York: Macmillan, 1954), p. 427.

In our time, the relevant reference is "de-Nazification" in Germany following World War Two, and the breaking up of the imperial principle, the militarist faction and the *zaibatsu* in Japan. The Allies clearly had a right to end German and Japanese aggression and drive their armies back to their borders. But could they reform Germany and Japan? And, if they could, what cost, Michael Walzer asks,[39] should the victors and vanquished pay to guarantee reliable security? When should the victors relinquish the goals of unconditional surrender and pacific reconstruction in order to spare the lives of the vanquished and the (soon to be) victors that the campaign for total conquest will cost?

Michael Walzer sharpens that modern moral conundrum, without (to my mind) fully resolving it. Should a negotiated arrangement have been struck with Nazi Germany, had it been willing to surrender to the Western Allies? The special nature of the evil of Nazism makes it apparent that this was not a deal many, including Walzer, would have wanted to be made, even to save the lives of the many noncombatant Germans and Allied soldiers lost in the invasion of the German homeland. But Walzer does not address the Millian argument directly. He, like many liberals, would have preferred a German revolution that had toppled Nazism and with which the Allies could then have made peace. But he also argues that the Nazi leaders should have been punished and, in the absence of a German revolution, occupying Germany was necessary to achieve this. But the trial would have been an act of "collective abhorrence" for their crimes, rather than an act to prevent future aggression.[40]

Walzer further argues that Japan's government should have been accommodated and that therefore Hiroshima and Nagasaki were two bombs too many, on top of the previously unjustified firebombing of Tokyo and other Japanese cities which violated *jus in bello* restrictions on bombing noncombatants. The US dropped the two atomic bombs on noncombatant targets and used the destruction of those cities to coerce the war cabinet into surrender. Unfortunately, the two bombs were barely adequate for their purpose of persuading the war cabinet, if their purpose was the surrender of Japan on terms likely to make the peace last. The victors conceded the emperor, but demanded the authority that would reconstruct Japan. It is not at

---

[39] M. Walzer, *Just and Unjust Wars* (New York: Basic Books, 1977), pp. 111–24.

[40] *Ibid.*, p. 117. See also G. Bass, "Jus Post Bellum," *Philosophy and Public Affairs* 32, no. 3 (Fall 2004), who explores the justice of these kinds of settlements, but limits his arguments to the demonstrably necessary case of post-genocide.

all clear that the war cabinet would have accepted this without the shock of the two bombs.[41]

Leaving Japan in the hands of the same militarists who had launched the conquest of Asia would, it seems to me, have been unwise. Were there other, less unjust, means of coercing the Japanese War Cabinet into a sufficiently complete surrender that would have permitted political reconstruction? Would a demonstration detonation have worked? What about a protracted naval blockade that prohibited Japan access to any goods other than food and medicine necessary for survival? Neither of these looked promising at the time (the looming competition with the Soviet Union also colored US estimations of how to end the war); but both in retrospect seem to have been worth further exploration.

The third exception, and one pertinent for today's debates on multi-lateral mediation and peacekeeping,[42] covers a "protracted civil war, in which the contending parties are so equally balanced that there is no probability of a speedy issue; or if there is, the victorious side cannot hope to keep down the vanquished but by severities repugnant to humanity, and injurious to the permanent welfare of the country."[43] Mill argues that some civil wars become so protracted and so seemingly irresolvable by local struggle that a common sense of humanity and sympathy for the suffering of the noncombatant population calls for an outside interven-tion to halt the fighting in order to see if some negotiated solution might be achieved under the aegis of foreign arms.[44] Mill here cites the at least partial success of outsiders in calling a halt to and helping settle the protracted mid-nineteenth-century Portuguese civil war and the Greek-Turkish conflict. Outsiders can call for separation or reconciliation in these circumstances.

On the one hand, two peoples contending a single territory have been forced to partition it. Greece was thus separated from

---

[41] Ian Buruma surveys the debate on the issue in "The War over the Bomb," *New York Review of Books*, September 21, 1995, 26–34. T. Hasegawa, in *Racing the Enemy: Stalin, Truman and the Surrender of Japan* (Cambridge, MA: Harvard University Press, 2005) discusses the difficulty of persuading the Japanese Cabinet to limit negotiations to the preservation of the emperor, after the atomic bombs on Hiroshima and Nagasaki had been dropped, pp. 205 ff.

[42] For a discussion of the circumstances favoring successful peacekeeping and peacebuilding in a civil war context, see M. Doyle and N. Sambanis, *Making War and Building Peace* (Princeton University Press, 2006) and the large literature we cite. For discussions of the ethical issues raised in reconstruction, see the article by S. Recchia, "Just and Unjust Postwar Reconstruction," pp. 165–88, and related articles in the special section in the Summer 2009 edition of *Ethics and International Affairs* 23, no. 2.

[43] Mill, "Nonintervention," p. 380.

[44] Here Mill appears to loosely follow an argument first developed by the eighteenth-century legal theorist Emerich de Vattel. See Ch. 6 by J. Pitts in this volume, pp. 46–7.

[handwritten margin notes: Israel / Palestinian / conflict / protracted / civil / war]

Turkey[45] and Belgium from Holland in 1830 following the forceful mediation of two liberal statesmen, one British, one French – Palmerston and Guizot.

On the other hand, two factions struggling to control and reform a single state, each in order to fulfill its own visions, have been forced to share it. Impartial mediation imposed this kind of power-sharing reconciliation – the "equitable terms of compromise" insisted upon by Mill – on the Portuguese factions. This produced two generations of peace among the contesting factions under the rules of King Pedro (1853–61) and King Luis (1861–9). H. V. Livermore, one of the leading historians of Portugal, described the political scene in the first half of the century during the reign of Queen Maria as follows:

> There were now three main currents of opinion in Portugal: absolutist, moderate and radical. Each had its constitutional and institutional preferences: the absolutists stood for no written constitution and the traditional *cortes*, summoned and not elected; the Chartist moderates for an *octroye* charter and a parliament of two houses; the Septembrist radicals for the constitution of 1822 and a *cortes* of a single chamber.[46]

Britain intervened in 1827 with a naval force, but only (so Prime Minister Canning claimed) for the sake of "nonintervention," in order to deter a right-wing intervention supported from Spain.

The intervention that Mill appears to have had in mind in "Nonintervention" took place in 1846. Portuguese politics by then had split between the last two groups of liberals, the Chartists and the Septembrists – one "moderate" and pro-monarchical, and the other "radical" and pro-constitutionalist (that of 1822). In the 1830s, Britain supported Queen Maria and her monarchist ministers. When the Septembrist constitutionalists took up arms, Palmerston (then Foreign Secretary) was cross-pressured between his ideological preference for the constitutionalists and Britain's established relationship with the monarchists. When France and Spain also agitated for intervention (on various sides), Palmerston sent Colonel Wylde as a special envoy to exercise what Palmerston called "a perspective of force" that involved pressuring them both and eventually led to a joint Anglo-Spanish armed force that cornered the recalcitrant Septembrists in Oporto. Palmerston

---

[45] Bass, *Freedom's Battle*, chs. 4–12, treats this conflict under the rubric of humanitarian concern. It fits there but also a war for secession, as noted below. Conflicts typically overlap: Great Powers forcibly mediated a protracted civil war with large casualties and promoted the secession of a new nation, Greece, from an established empire, Ottoman Turkey.

[46] H. V. Livermore, *A New History of Portugal*, 2nd edn. (Cambridge University Press, 1976), p. 274.

required the Queen to restore the constitution and civil liberties and deal with the constitutionalist rebels indulgently, and the rebels to lay down their arms.[47] It looked "ill at the commencement," Mill comments, but "it could be justified by the event . . . a really healing measure."[48]

Nonetheless, genuine stability took a few more years. Its decisive impetus was less the compromise of 1846 than the (unpredictable) reform led by the wise and industrious King Pedro who replaced his mother in 1853. During his short reign (he died of cholera in 1861), Pedro helped construct a political center that served as the foundation for more extensive administrative reforms and the launching pad for an ambitious program of road and rail construction that began the economic modernization of the countryside.[49] Still, England remained a constant presence, promoting the interests of British merchants in Portugal, bullying the Portuguese overseas when Britain's trade and colonial interests required interference and, overall, limiting the effective sovereignty of Portugal and thus undermining the self-determination that Mill (in 1859) had sought.

Exceptions that disregard

While some external considerations thus call for overriding nonintervention, there are other injustices that justify us in disregarding the prohibition against intervention. Sometimes the national self-determination that nonintervention is designed to protect is so clearly undermined by the domestic oppression and suffering that the principle of nonintervention should be disregarded. In these circumstances, the local government in effect loses its claim to rule as the representative of a singular national authenticity; there is no "self" to be determined. The reasons for nonintervention, Mill then claims, should be disregarded – they operate in "an opposite way," "the reasons themselves do not exist"[50] and intervention "does not disturb the balance of forces on which the permanent maintenance of freedom in a country depends."[51] Mill's classic essay discusses and develops three cases where an intervention serves the underlying purposes that nonintervention was designed to uphold.

The first is when too many nations contest one piece of territory. When an imperial government opposes the independence of a subordinate

---

[47] See J. Ridley, *Lord Palmerston* (London: Constable, 1970), pp. 317–20; and W. Smith, *Anglo-Portuguese Relations 1851–1861* (Lisbon: Centro de Estudios Historicos Ultramarinos, 1970), p. 16.
[48] Mill, "Nonintervention," p. 381.
[49] Livermore, *A New History of Portugal*, pp. 288–90.
[50] Mill, "Nonintervention," p. 383.   [51] *Ibid.*, p. 383.

nation or when there are two distinct peoples, one attempting to crush the other, then national self-determination cannot be a reason to shun intervention. What is missing is the "one" nation. Here foreigners can intervene to help the liberation of the oppressed people, once that people has demonstrated through its own "arduous struggle" that it truly is another nation. Then decolonization is the principle that should rule, allowing a people to form its own destiny. One model of this might be the American Revolution against Britain; another in Mill's time was the 1848–9 Hungarian rebellion against Austria.[52] Statespersons have long been hard-pressed to identify reliably when a people is truly a people, and to recognize consistently what steps are needed to prove their fitness for independence and justify foreign assistance. The many anti-colonial movements in Africa and Asia and the secession of East Timor from Indonesia and Kosovo from Serbia seem to fit well this category, but also illustrate the perplexities of just assistance.

The contemporary difficulty is identifying when multiple nationalities warrant independence. One approach is substantive. We try to discern a genuine nation by cultural, historical or democratic standards with a legitimate claim to independence.[53] One difficulty with this approach is the problem of minorities within minorities, who want to secede from the newly seceded community. Even worse is the problem of majorities within former minorities, as in Abkhazia, where at the time of secession (1993), since recognized by Russia, only 17 percent of the population was Abkhaz, while 46 percent was Georgian, 14.6 percent was Armenian and 17 percent other Slavic nationalities. (The Abkhaz are themselves divided between Christian and Muslim communities.)[54] The other approach is inter-communal proceduralism. Here a claim, any claim, to secede undergoes a series of procedural steps, beginning with self-administration that tests whether something less than full secession satisfies local demands for autonomy.[55] Unfortunately, the recent decision of the International Court of Justice on the independence of Kosovo (by not ruling on the merits of the Kosovo declaration) did not contribute toward advancing this discussion.

[52] *Ibid.*, p. 383.
[53] For good examples of this approach, see A. Buchanan, *Secession* (Boulder, CO: Westview, 1991) and D. Philpott, "In Defense of Self-Determination," *Ethics* 105, no. 2 (1995), 352–85.
[54] J. Waterbury, "Avoiding the Iron Cage of Legislated Communal Identity," in W. Danspeckgruber (ed.), *The Self-Determination of Peoples* (Boulder, CO: Lynne Rienner, 2002), p. 125.
[55] See the "Liechtenstein Draft on Self-Administration and Self-Determination" in Danspeckgruber, *Self-Determination of Peoples*.

The second instance in which the principle against intervention should be disregarded is counterintervention in a civil war. A civil war should be left to the combatants. When conflicting factions of one people are struggling to define what sort of society and government should rule, only that struggle should decide the outcomes, not foreigners. But when an external power intervenes on behalf of one of the participants in a civil war, then another foreign power can, in Mill's words, "redress the balance" – to counterintervene to balance the first intervention. This second intervention serves the purposes of self-determination, which the first intervention sought to undermine. Even if, Mill argues, the Hungarian rebellion were not clearly a national rebellion against "a foreign yoke," it was clearly the case that Russia should not have intervened to assist Austria in its suppression. If "Russia gave assistance to the wrong side, England would aid the right."[56] By doing so, Russia gave others a right to counterintervene.[57] Following Mill, Walzer has more recently delved further into the Hungarian case as an instance of legitimate counterintervention; and he then explores the Vietnam interventions of the 1960s (the North Vietnamese and US in South Vietnam), stressing the need to ensure that foreign intervention or counterintervention does not overwhelm the local struggle, the only legitimate determinant of whom should govern.[58]

Third, one can intervene for humanitarian purposes – to halt what appears to be a gross violation of the rights to survival of a population. When we see a pattern of massacres, the development of a campaign of genocide, the institutionalization of slavery – violations that are so horrendous that in the classical phrase repeated by Walzer, they "shock the conscience of mankind" – one has good ground to question whether there is any national connection between the population and the state that is so brutally oppressing it. In the "Nonintervention" essay, in discussing protracted civil wars, Mill has already raised "severities repugnant to humanity" as closely related, humanitarian reasons to forcibly mediate a civil war. And humanitarian motives do arise in the next case for intervention, against the uncivilized "barbarians." But, lacking the advantages of a twentieth-century perspective, Mill does not directly consider the case of an established, civilized government turning to

---

[56] Mill, "Nonintervention," p. 383.
[57] For a modern interpretation stressing Hungary's success in civil reform, while not succeeding in acquiring independence, see D. Kosáry, *Hungary and International Politics in 1848–1849* (trans. T. Wilkinson) (Boulder, CO: Atlantic Research and Publications, 2003).
[58] Walzer, *Just and Unjust Wars*, pp. 97–9.

massacre its own subjects, or appear to understand how barbaric the thoroughly civilized could be.[59]

For Walzer, perhaps the contemporary theorist of intervention most thoroughly inspired by Mill, humanitarian intervention is different from civil war, which also involves much suffering, for here the government is in altogether too much control. But Walzer, extrapolating from Mill, makes a good case that a disregarding logic should apply. Outsiders can intervene, but the intervener should have a morally defensible motive and share the purpose of ending the slaughter and establishing a self-determining people. Furthermore, interveners should act only as a "last resort," after exploring peaceful resolution. They should then act only when it is clear that they will save more lives than the intervention itself will almost inevitably end up costing, and even then with minimum necessary force. It makes no moral sense to rescue a village and start World War Three, or destroy a village in order to save it. Humanitarian motives have often been exploited, as Walzer shows they were in the US intervention in Cuba in 1898. But even though often abused, those motives can apply in a reasonable case, such as was the Indian invasion of East Pakistan in 1971, designed in part to save the people of what became Bangladesh from the massacre that was being inflicted upon them by their own government (in West Pakistan). Despite India's mixed motives, this was a case of legitimate humanitarian intervention. It allowed the people of East Pakistan to survive and form their own state.[60] In recent times, intervention in Rwanda in 1994 could have been justified in these terms.

Today, Mill's most controversial case of disregard would be benign colonialism. His principles of nonintervention only hold among "civilized" nations. "Uncivilized" peoples, among whom Mill dumps most of Africa and Asia in his time, are not fit for the principle of nonintervention.[61] Like "Oude" (now Awadh, in India), which he references, they suffer four debilitating infirmities – despotism, anarchy,

---

[59] Writing roughly at the same time, Giuseppe Mazzini developed a more explicit argument for humanitarian intervention in the case of large-scale violence against ethnic or religious minorities. See Ch. 11 by S. Recchia in this volume, pp. 255–59.

[60] Walzer, *Just and Unjust Wars*, pp. 101–8.

[61] Mill, however, conceives of many circumstances in which analogous forms of paternalism or benign despotism can be justified, including over children and domestically when populations are not fit for self-government. For a discussion of various forms of despotism, see N. Urbinati, "The Many Heads of the Hydra: J. S. Mill on Despotism," in N. Urbinati and A. Zakaras (eds.), *J. S. Mill's Political Thought: A Bicentennial Reassessment* (Cambridge University Press, 2007) and M. Tulnick, "Tolerant Imperialism: John Stuart Mill's Defense of British Rule in India," *Review of Politics* 68 (2006), 586–611.

amoral presentism and familism ⌐ that make them incapable of self-determination. The people are imposed upon by a "despot . . . so oppressive and extortionate as to devastate the country."[62] Despotism long endured has produced anarchy characterized by "such a state of nerveless imbecility that everyone subject to their will, who had not the means of defending himself by his own armed followers, was the prey of anybody who had a band of ruffians in his pay."[63] The people as a result deteriorate into amoral presentism in which present gratification overwhelms the future and no contracts can be relied upon. Moral duties extend no further than the family; national or civic identity is altogether absent.

No civilized government, Mill adds, can maintain a stable relationship with these uncivilized societies. ("In the first place, the rules of ordinary morality imply reciprocity. But barbarians will not reciprocate."[64] And, in the next place, these "nations have not got beyond the period during which it is likely to be for their benefit that they should be conquered and held in subjection by foreigners."[65] In these circumstances, Mill claims, the best that can happen for the population is a benign colonialism, such as he recommended during the annexation of Awadh in 1857. Normal interstate relations cannot be maintained in such an anarchic and lawless environment. The most a well-intentioned foreigner owes these peoples is paternal care and education. For like children or lunatics, they presumably can benefit from nothing else.] *Bye bye self determination*

It is important to note that Mill advocates neither exploitation nor racialist domination. Indeed, as Mark Tulnick has to my mind persuasively argued, the imperialism Mill recommends is in many respects "tolerant," neither totalitarian nor racist.[66] Instead, it is grounded in the principles of human dignity that also ground his view of just relations among "civilized" states. Significantly, Mill applies the same reasoning to once primitive northern Europeans who benefited from the imperial rule imposed by civilized Romans. Unlike the much stronger paternalism of his father James Mill and other imperial liberals, Mill's imperial education does not require conversion to Christianity, nor does it call for the adoption of English culture – only the cultivation of the ethos of the rule of law and the material sciences that are needed for economic progress. The duties of paternal care, moreover, are real, precluding oppression

---

[62] Mill, "Nonintervention," p. 377.
[63] *Ibid.*, p. 379.   [64] *Ibid.*, p. 377.   [65] *Ibid.*, p. 377.
[66] Tulnick, "Tolerant Imperialism," and S. Holmes, "Making Sense of Liberal Imperialism," in Urbinati and Zakaras (eds.), *J. S. Mill's Political Thought*, for related arguments.

and exploitation and requiring care and education designed to one day fit the colonized people for independent national existence.

Nonetheless, the argument also rests on what appear to be wildly distorted readings of the history and culture of Africa and Asia. Ancient cultures embodying deep senses of social obligation made nonsense of presentism and familism. Jennifer Pitts points out that J. S. Mill, like his father James Mill, stressed the moral and intellectual failings of the "barbarous" peoples and lumped the varieties of social structures they exhibited, from nomadic tribes to feudal and bureaucratic empires, all into one barbarism. In doing so, the Mills broke with earlier liberal traditions that posited a common rationality and varying societal and political regimes, as did Bentham and philosophers such as Adam Smith.[67] But anarchy, corruption and despotic oppression did afflict many of the peoples in these regions. Two current experts, Mukherjee and Metcalf, agree with Mill's indictment of the nawabs (rulers) of Awadh who "abandoned the attempt to govern ... and amused themselves with wine, women and poetry."[68] Sources contemporary to Mill, including the Treaty of 1837, negotiated but never ratified between Awadh and Britain, warned that if "gross and systematic oppression, anarchy and misrule" continued, the nawab's land would be seized.

More significantly, while Mill's treatment does convey Britain's responsibility for some of the misrule and consequent responsibility (in Mill's judgment) to redress it,[69] he does not seem able to parcel out the responsibilities of the shared causation he does acknowledge, including the responsibility not to contribute to the weakening that later justifies imperial rule. Awadh's condition was very much a product of the irresponsible dependent condition to which the nawabs had been reduced by the treaty of 1801. That treaty established the British protectorate, for which Awadh paid a heavy subsidy to the East India Company and guaranteed unfettered access for British merchants to Awadh's markets. The nawabs soon found themselves without local authority (usurped by the British resident), incapable of fostering native industry and responsible for 76 lacs of rupees ($3.8 million in 1856 dollars) in annual tribute to Britain. If Awadh's misrule was partly occasioned by British rule,

---

[67] See J. Pitts, *A Turn to Empire: The Rise of Imperial Liberalism in Britain and France* (Princeton University Press, 2003), ch. 5, passim. On Smith, see also Doyle, *Ways of War and Peace* (New York: Norton, 1997), ch. 7, and Ch. 7 by E. van de Haar in this volume.

[68] R. Mukerjee, *Awadh in Revolt: 1857–1858* (Delhi: Oxford University Press, 1984) quoting Metcalf, p. 33.

[69] Mill, "Nonintervention," p. 379.

Britain may have had the obligation to correct it that Mill notes, but it also had an obligation not to (partly) cause it in the first place and use the misrule as a justification for annexation.[70]

Mill thus admits that the anarchy of Awadh was partly "morally accountable" to British rule and known to be the case "by men who knew it well."[71] But what he does not mention is that he himself was the responsible official under the Court of Directors of the East India Company charged with the oversight of the Company's relations with Awadh. Indeed, Awadh was his first (beginning in 1828) and continuing assignment in the London headquarters of the East India Company.[72]

Shorn of its cultural "Orientalism," Mill's argument for trusteeship addresses one serious gap in strategies of humanitarian assistance: the devastations that cannot be readily redressed by a quick in-and-out intervention designed to liberate an oppressed people from the clutches of foreign oppression or a domestic genocide. But unilateral interveners have a special obligation to discuss how one can prevent benign trustee-ship from becoming malign imperialism, particularly when one recalls the flowery words and humanitarian intentions that accompanied the conquerors of Asia and Africa. How far is it from the Anti-Slavery Campaign and the Aborigine Rights Protection Society to King Leopold's Congo and Joseph Conrad's *Heart of Darkness?* Multilateral interveners carry less imperial burden. Their challenge, given the sorry history of the UN in Somalia, Bosnia and Rwanda, seems to be effectiveness.

Mill's contributions

John Stuart Mill has sketched out a powerful moral geography of when to and when not to intervene. Mill advanced seven circumstances that would favor overriding or disregarding nonintervention. His arguments for ethical intervention are ones that no international moralist who subscribes to principles of beneficence, self-determination and national security can neglect.

Judging from the actual historical record, Mill makes a reasonable case that nonintervention should be overridden both to prevent the recur-rence of aggressive war and to end protracted civil wars. Moreover, we

---

[70] See Karl Marx's article in the *New York Daily Tribune*, May 28, 1858, "The Annexation of Oude."

[71] Mill, "Nonintervention," p. 379.

[72] For background on Mill's career in this connection, see L. Zastoupil, *John Stuart Mill and India* (Stanford University Press, 1994), p. 87.

can add that the interdependencies of globalization seem to make these two reasons even more persuasive than they were in the nineteenth century, if only because of the wider consensus on human rights, the greater lethality of war and the ways in which the world economy fuels civil wars by providing a very large "sovereignty" premium to whoever wins.[73] But the more extensive list of examples Mill invokes each reveal more complexity than he recounts, and in each case that complexity leans against the interventionist conclusions he reaches. Internationalized civil wars tend to display less ideological consistency than would justify ideological solidarity. Reconstructive occupations raise material and moral costs that may not be worth incurring for a marginal gain in long-run security. Successful coercive mediation in protracted civil wars depends both on the local balance of forces and well-designed peacebuilding operations. National liberations, counterinterventions and humanitarian interventions also raise problems and require clearer doctrines than we now have. The case for imperial annexation is made problematic because local anarchy is rooted in ills inflicted as much as by previous informal interference as in local "barbarism." *Edmond Burke*

Insightful as Mill's lessons are, his major contributions are elsewhere. First, his method of practical reason warns policymakers that formulae cannot be abstractly applied; each conclusion applies to a case. General patterns can be inferred and drawn upon, but their ethical significance comes from their specific application to a specific case.

Last and most important is how Millian practical reason thus outlines an array of varying ethics of intervention. Modern discourse tends to assimilate all interventions to humanitarian interventions – and some then meet the threshold, and others do not. Concern for casualties is always relevant. But an exclusive concern for casualties flattens and impoverishes the variety of moral discourse that Mill outlined. As one example, we should recall that nations do not need to suffer genocide to have a claim to independence from other larger nations that rule them. The debate over Kosovo was especially distorted in this way. Typically proponents of intervention highlight Milosevic's violent repression in Kosovo, his record of much more extensive crimes against humanity in Bosnia and Croatia and the strong likelihood that he would inflict equivalent devastations in Kosovo. The critics reply that the KLA also committed atrocities and that the "West" had tolerated equally if not worse atrocities elsewhere (in Cambodia in the 1970s; in various places

New particulars cases cannot be universalized [handwritten margin note]

---

[73] This includes the ability to borrow on sovereign credit, renegotiate investment and raw material contracts and obtain foreign aid, as detailed by T. Pogge in *World Poverty and Human Rights* (Cambridge: Polity, 2002).

in Africa) and done nothing to stop them.[74] What is missing is the Kosovar (78 percent of the pre-expulsion population) demand to rule themselves as an independent nation. Without underestimating the substantive and procedural difficulties of identifying a justifiable case for supporting secession, missing the national self-determination claim, misses the essence of the case.

In short, interventionist and noninterventionist arguments should and can draw on Mill, but they will want to appreciate the distinctions he draws and then develop a more convincing set of criteria for when such interventions are likely to do more good than harm.

---

[74] For among the best of these two literatures see S. Power, *A Problem from Hell: America and the Age of Genocide* (New York: Basic Books, 2002) ch. 12 and for the other side D. Gibbs, *First Do No Harm: Humanitarian Intervention and the Destruction of Yugoslavia* (Nashville, KY: Vanderbilt University Press, 2009) ch. 7.

Select bibliography

Abiew, Francis Kofi, *The Evolution of the Doctrine of Humanitarian Intervention* (The Hague: Kluwer, 1999).

Alderson, Kai and Andrew Hurrell (eds.), *Hedley Bull on International Society* (New York: St. Martin's Press, 2000).

Anghie, Antony, *Imperialism, Sovereignty and the Making of International Law* (Cambridge University Press, 2004).

Applbaum, Arthur Isak, "Forcing a People to Be Free," *Philosophy & Public Affairs* 35, no. 4 (2007), 359–400.

Armitage, David, "Burke and Reason of State," *Journal of the History of Ideas* 61, no. 4 (2000), 617–34.

"John Locke's International Thought," in Ian Hall and Lisa Hill (eds.), *British International Thinkers from Hobbes to Namier* (Basingstoke: Palgrave Macmillan, 2009).

Bass, Gary, *Freedom's Battle: The Origins of Humanitarian Intervention* (New York: Knopf, 2008).

Beaulac, Stéphane, "Emer de Vattel and the Externalization of Sovereignty," *Journal of the History of International Law* 5 (2003), 237–92.

Beitz, Charles, *Political Theory and International Relations* (Princeton University Press, 1979).

Bell, Daniel A., "Just War and Confucianism: Implications for the Contemporary World," in D. Bell (ed.), *Confucian Political Ethics* (Princeton University Press, 2008).

Bell, Duncan, "Empire and International Relations in Victorian Political Thought," *Historical Journal* 49, no. 1 (2006), 281–98.

(ed.), *Political Thought and International Relations: Variations on a Realist Theme* (Oxford University Press, 2009).

Bellamy, Alex, "Ethics and Intervention: The 'Humanitarian Exception' and the Problem of Abuse in the Case of Iraq," *Journal of Peace Research*, 41, no. 2 (2004), 131–47.

Responsibility to Protect: the Global Effort to End Mass Atrocities (Cambridge: Polity, 2009).

Betts, Richard K., "Striking First: A History of Thankfully Lost Opportunities," *Ethics & International Affairs* 17, no. 1 (2003), 17–24.

Brown, Chris, Terry Nardin, and Nicholas Rengger (eds.), *International Relations in Political Thought* (Cambridge University Press, 2002).

Cavallar, Georg, *The Rights of Strangers: Theories of International Hospitality, The Global Community, and Political Justice since Vitoria* (Aldershot: Ashgate, 2002).

Chatterjee, Deen K. and Don E. Scheid (eds.), *Ethics and Foreign Intervention* (Cambridge University Press, 2003).

Chesterman, Simon, *Just War or Just Peace? Humanitarian Intervention and International Law* (Oxford University Press, 2001).

Clark, Ian and Iver Neuman (eds.), *Classical Theories of International Relations* (London: Palgrave, 1999).

Clinton, W. David (ed.), *The Realist Tradition and Contemporary International Relations* (Baton Rouge, LA: Louisiana State University Press, 2007).

Colonomos, Ariel, *The Gamble of War: Is it possible to justify preventive war?* (New York/London: Palgrave Macmillan, 2013).

Donnelly, Jack, "Human Rights: A New Standard of Civilization?" *International Affairs* 74, no. 1 (1998), 1–23.

Doyle, Michael W., "International Ethics and the Responsibility to Protect," *International Studies Review* 13, no. 1 (2011), 72–84.

Striking First: Preemption and Prevention in International Conflict (Princeton University Press, 2008).

Ways of War and Peace: Realism, Liberalism, and Socialism (New York: Norton, 1997).

Drechsler, Wolfgang, "Christian Wolff (1679–1754): A Biographical Essay," *European Journal of Law and Economics*, 4 (1997), 111–28.

Evans, Gareth, *The Responsibility to Protect: Ending Mass Atrocity Crimes Once and for All* (Washington, DC: Brookings Institution Press, 2008).

Fidler, David P. and Jennifer M. Welsh (eds.), *Empire and Community: Edmund Burke's Writings and Speeches on International Relations* (Boulder, CO: Westview, 1999).

Finnemore, Martha, *The Purpose of Intervention: Changing Beliefs About the Use of Force* (Ithaca, NY: Cornell University Press, 2003).

Franceschet, Antonio, "The Ethical Foundations of Liberal Internationalism," *International Journal* 54, no. 3 (1999), 463–81.

Glanville, Luke, "The Antecedents of Sovereignty as Responsibility," *European Journal of International Relations* 17, no. 2 (2010), 233–55.

Grewe, Wilhelm, *The Epochs of International Law* (Berlin and New York: de Gruyter, 2000).

Habermas, Jürgen, "Kant's Idea of Perpetual Peace, with the Benefit of Two Hundred Years' Hindsight," in James Bohman and Matthias Lutz-Bachmann (eds.), *Perpetual Peace: Essays on Kant's Cosmopolitan Ideal* (Cambridge, MA: MIT Press, 1997).

Hampsher-Monk, Iain, "Edmund Burke's Changing Justification for Intervention," *The Historical Journal* 48, no. 1 (2005), 65–100.

Hassner, Pierre, "Rousseau and the Theory and Practice of International Relations," in Clifford Orwin and Nathan Tarcov (eds.), *The Legacy of Rousseau* (The University of Chicago Press, 1997).

Havercroft, Jonathan, "Was Westphalia 'all that'? Hobbes, Bellarmine, and the norm of non-intervention," *Global Constitutionalism* 1, no. 1 (2012), 120–40.

Hoffmann, Stanley, "The Politics and Ethics of Military Intervention," *Survival* 37, no. 4 (Winter 1995), 29–51.

Hoffmann, Stanley and David P. Fidler (eds.), *Rousseau on International Relations* (Oxford: Clarendon Press, 1991).

Holzgrefe, J. L. and Robert O. Keohane (eds.), *Humanitarian Intervention: Ethical, Legal and Political Dilemmas* (Cambridge University Press, 2003).

Howard, Michael, *War and The Liberal Conscience* (New York: Columbia University Press, 2008).

Hurrell, Andrew, "Kant and the Kantian Paradigm in International Relations," *Review of International Studies* 16, no. 3 (1990), 193–205.

Ignatieff, Michael, *Empire Lite: Nation building in Bosnia, Kosovo, Afghanistan* (London: Vintage, 2003).

Jackson, Robert H., *The Global Covenant. Human Conduct in a World of States* (Oxford University Press, 2000).

Jahn, Beate (ed.), *Classical Theory in International Relations* (Cambridge University Press, 2006).

Jeffery, Renée, *Hugo Grotius in International Thought* (New York and Basingstoke: Palgrave Macmillan, 2006).

Kalmanovitz, Pablo, "Sharing Burdens after War: A Lockean Approach," *Journal of Political Philosophy* 19, no. 2 (2011), 209–28.

Keene, Edward, *Beyond the Anarchical Society: Grotius, Colonialism and Order in World Politics* (Cambridge University Press, 2002).

Kingsbury, Benedict and Benjamin Straumann, "The State of Nature and Commercial Sociability in Early Modern International Legal Thought," *Grotiana* 31 (2010), 22–43.

Kleingeld, Pauline, "Kant's Changing Cosmopolitanism," in Amelie Oksenberg Rorty and James Schmidt (eds.), *Kant's Aim for a Universal History with a Cosmopolitan Aim* (Cambridge University Press, 2009).

Koskenniemi, Marrti, *From Apology to Utopia: the structure of international legal argument* (Cambridge University Press, 2005 [1989]).

"Miserable Comforters: International Relations as New Natural Law," *European Journal of International Relations* 15 (2009), 395–422.

Krasner, Stephen, *Sovereignty: Organized Hypocrisy* (Princeton University Press, 1999).

Kratochwil, Friedrich, "Sovereignty as Dominium: Is there a Right of Humanitarian Intervention?" in Gene M. Lyons and Michael Mastanduno (eds.), *Beyond Westphalia* (Baltimore, MD: Johns Hopkins University Press, 1995).

Lang, Anthony F. (ed.), *Just Intervention* (Washington, DC: Georgetown University Press, 2003).

Luban, David, "Just War and Human Rights," *Philosophy & Public Affairs* 9 (1980), 160–81.

MacQueen, Norrie, *Humanitarian Intervention and the United Nations* (Edinburgh University Press, 2011).

Mapel, David R. and Terry Nardin (eds.), *International Society: Diverse Ethical Perspectives* (Princeton University Press, 1998).

Marshall, John, *John Locke: Resistance, Religion, and Responsibility* (Cambridge University Press, 1994).

Mayall, James, "Intervention in International Society: Theory and Practice in Contemporary Perspective," in B. A. Roberson (ed.), *International Society and the Development of International Relations Theory* (London and New York: Continuum, 2002).

McMahan, Jeff, *Killing in War* (Oxford University Press, 2009).

Meinecke, Friedrich, *Machiavellism: The Doctrine of Raison d'Etat and its Place in Modern History* (trans. D. Scott) (New Haven, CT: Yale University Press, 1957).

Miller, Kenneth, "John Stuart Mill's Theory of International Relations," *Journal of the History of Ideas* 22, no. 4 (1961), 493–514.

Moyn, Samuel, *The Last Utopia: Human Rights in History* (Cambridge, MA: The Belknap Press of Harvard University Press, 2010).

Muldoon, James, "Francisco de Vitoria and Humanitarian Intervention," *Journal of Military Ethics*, 5, no. 2 (2006), 128–43.

Muthu, Sankar, *Enlightenment Against Empire* (Princeton University Press, 2003).

Nabulsi, Karma, *Traditions of War: Occupation, Resistance, and the Law* (Oxford University Press, 2005).

Nakhimovsky, Isaac, "Vattel's Theory of the International Order: Commerce and the Balance of Power in the *Law of Nations*," *History of European Ideas* 33 (2007), 157–73.

Nardin, Terry, "The Moral Basis of Humanitarian Intervention," *Ethics and International Affairs*, 16, no. 1 (2002), 57–70.

Nardin, Terry and David R. Mapel, *Traditions of International Ethics* (Cambridge University Press, 1993).

Nardin, Terry and Melissa Williams (eds.), *Humanitarian Intervention* (New York: NYU Press, 2005).

Neff, Stephen C., *War and the Law of Nations: A General History* (Cambridge University Press, 2005).

Neumann, Iver B. and Jennifer M. Welsh, "'The Other' in European Self-Definition: An addendum to the literature on international society," *Review of International Studies*, 17 (1990), 327–48.

Orford, Anne, *Reading Humanitarian Intervention: Human Rights and the Use of Force in International Law* (Cambridge University Press, 2003).

Osiander, Andreas, "Sovereignty, International Relations, and the Westphalian Myth," *International Organization* 55, no. 2 (2001), 251–87.

Pape, Robert, "When Duty Calls: A Pragmatic Standard of Humanitarian Intervention," *International Security* 37, no. 1 (2012), 41–80.

Pattison, James, *Humanitarian Intervention and The Responsibility to Protect: Who Should Intervene?* (Oxford University Press, 2010).

Philpott, Daniel, *Revolutions in Sovereignty* (Princeton University Press, 2001).

Pitts, Jennifer, *A Turn to Empire: The Rise of Imperial Liberalism in Britain and France* (Princeton University Press, 2005).

Rawls, John, *The Law of Peoples* (Cambridge, MA: Harvard University Press, 1999).

Recchia, Stefano, "Just and Unjust Postwar Reconstruction: How much external interference can be justified?" *Ethics and International Affairs* 23, no. 2 (2009), 165–87.
  "Restraining Imperial Hubris: The Ethical Bases of Realist International Relations Theory," *Constellations* 14, no. 4 (2007), 531–56.
Recchia, Stefano and Nadia Urbinati (eds.), *A Cosmopolitanism of Nations: Giuseppe Mazzini's Writings on Democracy, Nation Building, and International Relations* (Princeton University Press, 2009).
Robinson, Paul (ed.), *Just War in Comparative Perspective* (Aldershot: Ashgate, 2003).
Rodin, David, *War and Self-Defense* (Oxford University Press, 2002).
Roeloofsen, C. G., "Some Remarks on the 'Sources' of the Grotian System of International Law," *Netherlands International Law Review* 30 (1983), 73–80.
Rogow, Arnold A., *Thomas Hobbes: Radical in the Service of Reaction* (New York: Norton, 1986).
Rowley, David G., "Giuseppe Mazzini and the Democratic Logic of Nationalism," *Nations and Nationalism* 18, no. 1 (2012), 39–56.
Schwartz, Daniel, "The Principle of the Defence of the Innocent and the Conquest of America: 'Save Those Dragged Towards Death'," *Journal of the History of International Law*, 9 (2007), 263–91.
Simms, Brendan and D. J. B. Trim (eds.), *Humanitarian Intervention: A History* (Cambridge University Press, 2011).
Simpson, Gerry, *Great Powers and Outlaw States: Unequal Sovereigns in the International Legal Order* (Cambridge University Press, 2004).
Teschke, Benno, *The Myth of 1648: Class, Geopolitics, and the Making of Modern International Relations* (London & New York: Verso, 2003).
Trachtenberg, Marc, "Preventive War and U.S. Foreign Policy," *Security Studies* 16, no.1 (2007), 1–31.
Tuck, Richard, *The Rights of War and Peace: Political Theory and the International Order from Grotius to Kant* (Oxford University Press, 1999).
Turner Johnston, James, "The Idea of Defense in Historical and Contemporary Thinking About Just War," *Journal of Religious Ethics* 36, no. 4 (2008), 543–56.
Urbinati, Nadia, "'A Common Law of Nations': Giuseppe Mazzini's Democratic Nationality," *Journal of Modern Italian Studies* 1 (1996), 197–222.
Urbinati, Nadia and Alex Zakaras (eds.), *J. S. Mill's Political Thought: A Bicentennial Reassessment* (Cambridge University Press, 2007).
Van de Haar, Edwin, *Classical Liberalism and International Relations Theory. Hume, Smith, Mises, and Hayek* (New York and Basingstoke: Palgrave Macmillan, 2009).
Vincent, R. J., "Grotius, Human Rights, and Intervention," in Hedley Bull, Benedict Kingsbury, and Adam Roberts (eds.), *Hugo Grotius and International Relations* (Oxford: Clarendon Press, 1990).
  Nonintervention and International Order (Princeton University Press, 1974).
Waldron, Jeremy, *God, Locke, and Equality: Christian Foundations in Locke's Political Thought* (Cambridge University Press, 2002).

Waltz, Kenneth, *Man, the State, and War* (New York: Columbia University Press, 1959).

Walzer, Michael, *Just and Unjust Wars: A Moral Argument With Historical Illustrations* (New York: Basic Books, 1977).

Weiss, Thomas, *Humanitarian Intervention*, 2nd edn. (Cambridge: Polity, 2013).

Welsh, Jennifer M., "Authorizing Humanitarian Intervention," in Richard Price and Mark Zacher (eds.), *The United Nations and Global Security* (London: Palgrave, 2004).

(ed.), *Humanitarian Intervention and International Relations* (Oxford University Press, 2004).

Edmund Burke and International Relations (Basingstoke: Macmillan, 1995).

Wheeler, Nicholas J., *Saving Strangers: Humanitarian Intervention in International Society* (Oxford University Press, 2000).

Wight, Martin, *Four Seminal Thinkers in International Theory: Machiavelli, Grotius, Kant, and Mazzini* (New York: Oxford University Press, 2005).

Zacher, Mark W. and Richard A. Matthew, "Liberal International Theory: Common Threads, Divergent Strands," in Charles W. Kegley (ed.), *Controversies in International Relations Theory* (New York: St. Martin's Press, 1995).

Zurbuchen, Simone, "Vattel's Law of Nations and Just War Theory," *History of European Ideas*, 35 (2009), 408–17.

Index

natural law (cont.)
  and human dominion (Aquinas) 82
  and modern human rights 93
  norms of 119–20
  war permitted in (Vitoria) 72
natural rights
  of foreigners (Grotius) 165
  Locke's 114, 121
Navarino, Battle of (1827) 43
neighboring states 90
  threats to, as just cause for war
    Bodin on 105
    early modern 26, 31
    Grotius and Vattel on 65
    Hume and Smith 164, 175
  see also vicinity
Netherlands 225
  and Belgian independence 43–44
  Dutch revolt 32, 96
  Elizabeth I and 9, 31–36, 104
  and Habsburgs 25, 31
  Spanish atrocities in 27–28
  see also Dutch republic
Neuchâtel, as sovereign state 140
Niebuhr, Reinhold 194
Nixon, Richard, and China 274
nonintervention 9, 17, 148
  exceptions that disregard (Mill) 279–85
  exceptions that over-ride (Mill) 272–79
    in protracted civil war 277–79
    removal of perpetual threat to peace
     275–77
    self defense 272–75
  Hobbes and 107–10
  indirect reasons for (Mill) 269
  Kant and 198–201, 212, 263
  Mazzini's critique of 251–53, 255
  Mill and 18, 263, 266–71
  Vattel's exceptions 146–47
  Vitoria and 89
  Wolff and 144, 145n
non-resistance, to tyranny (Bodin) 105
norms
  of human rights 1, 214
  of natural law 119–20
  in state of nature (Locke) 115
nuclear facilities, preventive destruction
  of 59
nuclear weapons 208

Ochakov Crisis (1791) 226
Oliva, Treaty of (1660) 39
oppression
  and request for intervention (Pufendorf)
   110–12

and self-determination (Mill) 279
  by tyrants 9
order
  as goal of government (Hume) 156
  maintained by prudent leaders (Smith)
   169
Osnabrück, Treaty of (1648) 136
Ottoman Empire
  Burke on 226
  and independence of Greece 41–43
  interventions 45, 258
  massacres 41

Pakistan
  Al-Qaeda in 61
  Indian invasion of East (1971) 282
Palatinate, army in Netherlands 32
Palestine, Israeli targeted killings as
  preventive war 51
Palmerston, Viscount 278
papacy, abolition of temporal power (1849)
  239
papal bulls, Inter Caetera 80
papal jurisdiction 78, 87, 89n
  in temporal affairs 80
past wrongdoing
  as justification for anticipatory attack
   (contemporary) 50, 59
  as justification for anticipatory attack
   (Suarez) 51
paternalism
  international 282n
  J.S. Mill's 283
  Mazzini's 249
  see also dominion
patriotism, Rousseau on 181
peace
  enforcement of (Kant) 188, 203
  imposition of settlements (modern) 46
  Kant's "preliminary articles" 187
  as moral imperative (Kant) 185, 187
  restoration of as purpose of just war
   (Vitoria) 72
  see also democratic peace theory
Pedro, King of Portugal 278–79
periphery
  and law of nations (Burke) 226
  respect for (Burke) 223
personal glory, not a justification for war 74
Philip II, King of Spain
  Elizabethan policy towards 33
  and Netherlands 31
  tyranny in Netherlands 33–34
Philippines, American colonization 46
Pinerolo, Treaty of (1655) 38